CAMBRIDGE STUDIES IN EARLY MODERN HISTORY

Editors

J. H. ELLIOTT   OLWEN HUFTON
H. G. KOENIGSBERGER

Turning Swiss
Cities and Empire, 1450–1550

CAMBRIDGE STUDIES IN EARLY MODERN HISTORY

Edited by Professor J. H. Elliott, The Institute for Advanced Study, Princeton; Professor Olwen Hufton, University of Reading; and Professor H. G. Koenigsberger, King's College, London

The idea of an 'early modern' period of European history from the fifteenth to the late eighteenth century is now widely accepted among historians. The purpose of the Cambridge Studies in Early Modern History is to publish monographs and studies which will illuminate the character of the period as a whole, and in particular focus attention on a dominant theme within it, the interplay of continuity and change as they are represented by the continuity of medieval ideas, political and social organization, and by the impact of new ideas, new methods and new demands on the traditional structures.

For other titles in this series, see page 301.

Turning Swiss

Cities and Empire, 1450–1550

THOMAS A. BRADY, JR.

University of Oregon
Eugene, Oregon

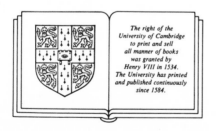

The right of the
University of Cambridge
to print and sell
all manner of books
was granted by
Henry VIII in 1534.
The University has printed
and published continuously
since 1584.

CAMBRIDGE UNIVERSITY PRESS

Cambridge
London   New York   New Rochelle
Melbourne   Sydney

Published by the Press Syndicate of the University of Cambridge
The Pitt Building, Trumpington Street, Cambridge CB2 1RP
32 East 57th Street, New York, NY 10022, USA
10 Stamford Road, Oakleigh, Melbourne 3166, Australia

First published 1985

Printed in the United States of America

Library of Congress Cataloging in Publication Data
Brady, Thomas A., Jr.
Turning Swiss.
(Cambridge studies in early modern history)
Bibliography: p.
Includes indexes.
1. Germany – History – Frederick III, 1440–1493
2. Germany – History – Maximilian I, 1493–1519.   3. Germany
– History 1517–1648.   4. Cities and towns – Germany,
Southern – History.   5. Germany, Southern – History.
I. Title.   II. Series.
DD171.B7   1985   943'.029   84–29242
ISBN 0 521 30525 X

To
Ruth and Elmer Ellis
and to
Fern and Newell Gingrich

Wer meret Schwytz?
Der herren gytz.

'But where can we draw water,'
Said Pearse to Connolly,
'When all the wells are parched away?
O plain as plain can be
There's nothing but our own red blood
Can make a right Rose Tree.'

William Butler Yeats

Contents

Contents

Preface

This volume continues an interpretation of the Reformation and Germany's political life from a social-historical point of view that began with a volume on the internal politics of a single city (*Ruling Class, Regime and Reformation at Strasbourg, 1520–1555* [Leiden, 1978]) and will conclude with a volume on the rise and fall of the Smalkaldic League. The trilogy's constant thread is the fate of the South German free cities.

There is more about ends than beginnings in this volume. It tries to bring us closer to understanding the failure in the German-speaking world of a process that elsewhere supplied a social basis both for absolutist monarchy and its downfall: the transformation of the communal burghers of the Middle Ages into the royal bourgeoisie of the early modern era. The main elements in this story, which relates how a German state did not come to be, are the extraordinary political freedom of the common people, the weakness and foreign distractions of the monarchy, the regional character of relations between king and cities, and the eruption into the political arena of an uncontrollable movement, the German Reformation.

There is no longer or sadder song in the literature about modern Germany than the lament over the weakness, cowardice, and failures of the German bourgeoisie, whose unwillingness and inability to play a specifically national role deprived the Germans, it is said, of the early and full benefits of liberalism and industrial capitalism. The blindness that most perpetuates this myth is the "national" error, which assumes that history was necessarily making a German nation of Bismarckian shape and character, only to be sidetracked and deformed by mysterious powers on the way. This is wrong. Had Emperor Charles V and the free cities not failed in their brief political marriage, had the intervention

ix

Preface

of the Common Man not disrupted the evolution of Habsburg power in South Germany, had the Protestant Reformation not completed the disruption, had Charles and his brother not neglected German problems for other issues, Bismarck's Germany might never have been born. This is not to say that the failure of national consolidation before the Reformation was a tragedy, no more – and here I agree with Heiko A. Oberman – than the Reformation itself was to be. It did mean, however, that Germany was never to experience that organic connection between its modern present and its medieval past that lent such rocklike confidence to French and English culture in the modern age.

A preface is the place to acknowledge the mountain of debts every scholar accumulates. This book was drafted in Tübingen in 1981, thanks to the German Fulbright Commission. My thanks go, too, to the directors and staffs of the Hauptstaatsarchiv Stuttgart, the Staatsarchiv Basel, the Hessisches Staatsarchiv Marburg (especially Oberarchivrat Dr. Fritz Wolff), and the municipal archives of Augsburg and Strasbourg, as well as the University of Oregon Library and the Universitätsbibliothek Tübingen.

Debts to colleagues stud this book like the calks on a logger's boot-soles. First in line are those who read and criticized all or parts of the manuscript: Heiko A. Oberman, Hans-Christoph Rublack, Peter Blickle, Roger Chickering, Kaspar von Greyerz, and James D. Tracy. Then come those who permitted me to read their unpublished work: Hans-Christoph Rublack, Ingrid Bátori, Kaspar von Greyerz, Georg Schmidt, Heinrich R. Schmidt, and Dieter Mertens.

Two more debts must be acknowledged. The first is to Enid Scofield, who typed the manuscript. The other is to my collaborator, editor, best critic, and wife, Katherine G. Brady, whose sharp eye has rescued me from many an error and whose support has been this project's bedrock.

My first book was dedicated to my parents. This one is dedicated to four other persons who have treated me as a son.

A note on usages

The capitalized form "Imperial" refers to the Holy Roman Empire and its institutions, while lower-case "imperial" means imperium in a general or a larger Habsburg sense.

"Evangelical" means all those who joined the movement against the established church in Germany during the 1520s, both those who later became Protestants and those who did not. The names "Lutheran" – except in the most obvious cases – "Reformed," and "Protestant" would be anachronistic in this study.

The abbreviation "fl." stands for the money known in German as the "rheinischer Gulden" and in English as the "rhenish florin."

Personal names of rulers are given English forms where they exist. All other persons are called by the names they were given, often in the older spellings (e.g., Jacob and Caspar, not Jakob and Kaspar). Where there was a choice, as between "Ulrich" and "Huldrych" for the Swiss reformer Zwingli, I have chosen the vernacular form (but not the modernized form, "Huldreich," for which there is no warrant).

Maximilian I began to call himself "emperor" (*Kaiser*) in 1508, though he was never crowned. I have tried to be consistent in calling him "king" until 1508 and "emperor" from then on.

Place names are given in the forms then used, so that I use Basel, Mainz, and Regensburg, not Basle, Mayence, and Ratisbon. The one exception is that the leading Alsatian towns are called by their French names, not least because these are the names used on modern maps. Other usages, such as the distinction between "Upper Rhine" and "High Rhine" and the term "Western Austria," are explained in the text and notes.

This book is founded on political and cultural geography, and the

A note on usages

reader will use the maps that precede the book's introduction with profit. Most unfamiliar usages are explained at first mention, such as the distinction between the "High Rhine" (above Lake Constance) and the "Upper Rhine" (below the lake). Much use is made of the old district names based on the word *Gau* (Middle High German: district), including the Hegau, Klettgau, Sundgau, Breisgau, Aargau, Thurgau, Allgäu, and Vinschgau. Sometimes the initial "g" in *Gau* was dropped, as in the Ortenau. These names were all current during the era in which this book is set. It may also help the reader to know that the division of provinces and regions into "upper" and "lower" parts, as Upper and Lower Swabia or Upper and Lower Alsace, is based not on map orientation but on altitude and drainage, so that in Central Europe the upper part of a province is generally south of the lower part.

Publisher's Note: The use of gender-specific language in this book reflects the speech of the age it studies.

Abbreviations and special notations

Full entries for the following titles that are abbreviated in the footnotes may be found in the bibliography.

AMS	Archives Municipales de Strasbourg
ARC	Pfeilschifter, Georg. *Acta Reformationis Catholicae.*
EA	*Amtliche Sammlung der älteren eidgenössischen Abschiede*
fol(s).	folio(s)
HStA Marburg	Hessisches Staatsarchiv Marburg
HStA Stuttgart	Hauptstaatsarchiv Stuttgart
PCSS	*Politische Correspondenz der Stadt Strassburg im Zeitalter der Reformation*
r	recto
RTA, jR	*Deutsche Reichstagsakten, jüngere Reihe*
RTA, mR	*Deutsche Reichstagsakten, mittlere Reihe*
StA	Stadtarchiv or Staatsarchiv
v	verso
WA TR	*D. Martin Luthers Werke. Tischreden*
Z	*Huldrych Zwinglis Sämtliche Werke*

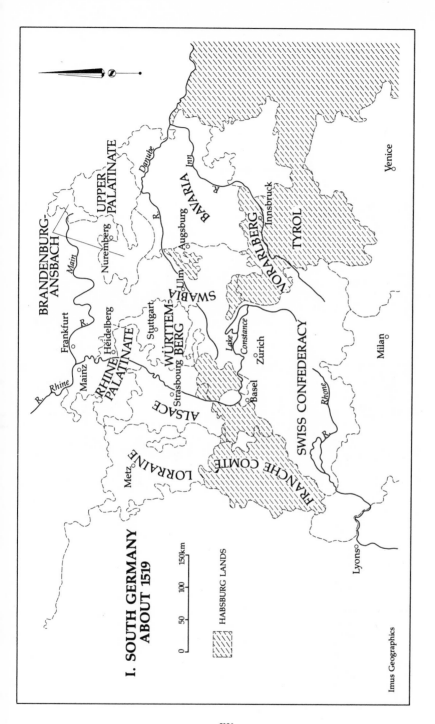

I. SOUTH GERMANY
ABOUT 1519

0   50   100   150km

HABSBURG LANDS

BRANDENBURG-
ANSBACH

UPPER PALATINATE

Danube

Nuremberg

Main

R.

R.

Frankfurt

R.

Mainz

Heidelberg

RHINE PALATINATE

Strasbourg

ALSACE

Stuttgart

WÜRTTEM-BERG

SWABIA

Ulm

Augsburg

BAVARIA

Inn

R.

VORARLBERG

Innsbruck

TYROL

Lake Constance

Zürich

Basel

SWISS CONFEDERACY

LORRAINE

Metz

FRANCHE COMTÉ

Rhine

R.

Rhône

R.

Milan

Venice

Lyons

Imus Geographics

xv

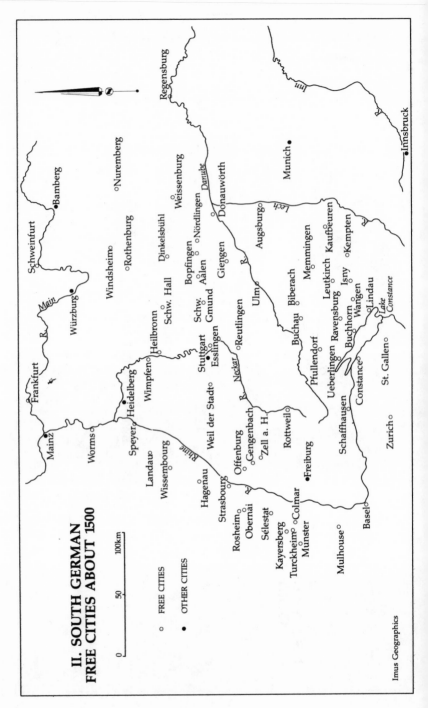

II. SOUTH GERMAN FREE CITIES ABOUT 1500

| 0 | 50 | 100km |

o FREE CITIES

● OTHER CITIES

Regensburg

Inn

Innsbruck

Bamberg

Schweinfurt

Nuremberg

Munich

Main

Würzburg

Weissenburg

Danube

Donauwörth

Windsheim

Rothenburg

Dinkelsbühl

Nördlingen

Lech

Augsburg

Frankfurt

Heilbronn

Schw. Hall

Bopfingen

Aalen

Giengen

R.

Ulm

Memmingen

Kaufßeuren

Kempten

Mainz

Heidelberg

Wimpfen

Stuttgart

Esslingen

Schw.
Gmund

Neckar R.

Reutlingen

Buchau

Biberach

Leutkirch

Isny

Wangen

Lindau

Lake
Constance

Worms

Speyer

Weil der Stadt

Pfullendorf

Ueberlingen

Ravensburg

Buchhorn

Landau

Rhine

Offenburg

Gengenbach

Zell a. H.

Rottweil

Schaffhausen

Constance

St. Gallen

Wissembourg

Hagenau

Strasbourg

Freiburg

Zurich

Rosheim

Obernai

Sélestat

Kayersberg

Turckheim

Colmar

Münster

Basel

Mulhouse

Imus Geographics

xvi

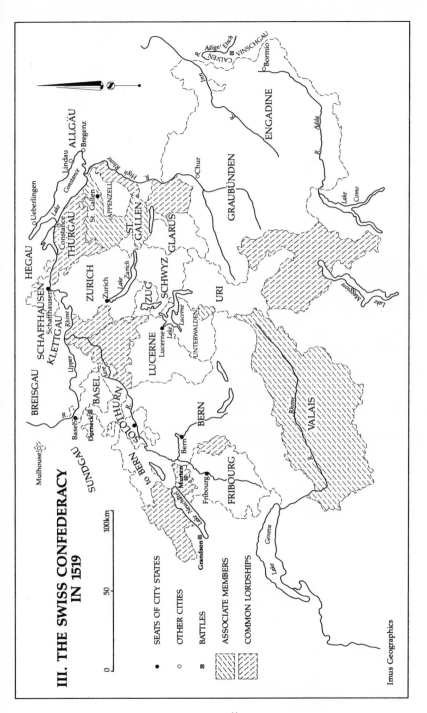

III. THE SWISS CONFEDERACY IN 1519

Imus Geographics

SEATS OF CITY STATES
OTHER CITIES
BATTLES
ASSOCIATE MEMBERS
COMMON LORDSHIPS

0   50   100km

SUNDGAU
BREISGAU
HEGAU
Mulhouse
Ueberlingen
Lindau ALLGÄU
Bregenz
Lake Constance
Constance
THURGAU
St. Gallen
APPENZELL
ST. GALLEN
SCHAFFHAUSEN
Schaffhausen
KLETTGAU
Upper Rhine
R.
BASEL
Basel
Dorneck
SOLOTHURN
to BERN
ZURICH
Zurich
Lake Zurich
Rhine
GLARUS
SCHWYZ
ZUG
Lucerne
Lake Lucerne
LUCERNE
UNTERWALDEN
URI
Aar
BERN
Bern
Murten
Neuchatel Lake
FRIBOURG
Fribourg
Grandson
Lake Geneva
Geneva
VALAIS
Rhone
R.
GRAUBÜNDEN
Chur
Hi. Rhine
ENGADINE
Inn R.
CALVEN
VINSCHGAU
R. Adige/ Etsch
Bormio
Adda R.
Lake Como
Lake Maggiore

Introduction: the setting

This book is about Germany, more specifically "South Germany," which in its broadest sense embraces the entire German-speaking world south of the Central Highlands, roughly the area whose inhabitants spoke Swabian-Alemannic, Austro-Bavarian, and Franconian forms of German. This Germany corresponded and corresponds neither to the Holy Roman Empire nor to any subsequently formed country. Today its peoples are divided among six states, which in order of population are West Germany, Italy, France, Switzerland, Austria, and Liechtenstein. Only one enduring boundary took shape within this region during the century covered by this book, the line between the Swiss Confederacy and the rest of the Holy Roman Empire, and it marked no natural, linguistic, or social division.

This book is about cities, more specifically the republics called "free cities" or "Imperial cities," which clustered so densely between the Main River basin and Lake Constance, and between the Lech River and the Vosges Mountains. Except in the Swiss Confederacy, the South German free cities never attained the full autonomy of city-states nor came to dominate fully their economic hinterlands. The lives, wants, and fates of the rural folk, both peasants and nobles, come into this story only when they impinged on urban political decisions, which they commonly did. The political relationships between self-governing cities and the vast stretches of productive land and vast numbers of productive people on the land lurk behind all the explicit assumptions and conclusions of this book.

This book is about oligarchies, more specifically the mixed rentier-merchant classes who ruled most of the South German free cities most of the time. They formed, with occasional exceptions, the "political class" of the cities, supplied most of the significant urban politicians, and confronted, before all other urban folk, the troubling connection between external forces and internal order. It goes without saying that external security and internal order were linked, and that the cities' walls proved, when tested, no stronger than the loyalty of the urban commons to their ruling betters.

This book is about politics, more specifically diplomacy and war, external security and internal order. It is also about alternate strategies for urban governments in an age when, less because of what occurred inside the cities than because of what happened without, the governments could no longer defend their own and their citizens' interests through the traditional instrument of the urban federation. Economic life, social stratification, religion, and culture, popular and high, lay and learned, are not this book's subjects, except when they furnish – as they commonly do – explanations for political events.

This book is about liberty, more specifically the social devolution of power in South Germany after the great European depression of the fourteenth and fifteenth centuries. Liberty meant both the independence of small units and the participation in political life of people whose normal social role was the performance of productive labor. This ambiguity covered, on the one hand, the localization of political power that was native to the European feudal order, but also, on the other hand, the weakening of the feudal principle of hierarchy in favor of the right of ordinary folk to be their own masters.

This book, finally, is about the German Reformation, more specifically the urban commons' intervention in high politics during the mid-1520s. It is now widely recognized that the common folk of South Germany and parts of Central Germany intervened in history dramatically and heroically during the events of 1524–6, which are variously known as "the German Peasants' War," "the revolution of the Common Man," or "the Revolution of 1525." The Evangelical movement for reform of the Church initially promoted and ultimately helped to destroy this revolutionary effort, leaving permanent scars on South German social life and on the Protestant Reformation in Germany. The intervention of the urban commons helped to drive the decisive wedge between their own ruling oligarchies and the Crown, thereby wrecking the alliance between the cities and the monarchy and leaving the free cities and the region open to new political fates.

These are the six elements of a story that unfolded during the century after about 1450. After they lost the Cities' War of 1449–53, the South German urban governments at first could establish neither a new urban league nor a lasting partnership with the Imperial monarchy. Mounting threats from the princes, either in individual actions against cities or collectively throught the Imperial Diet, drove the cities to action. They found two possible partners, each of which operated on a level greater than the local but smaller than the Imperial one. One was the Swiss Confederacy, the other the Imperial monarchy.

The Confederacy presented the urban regimes with a doubly ambiguous face, because of its mixed composition of city republics, just like the other South German ones, with free rural federations. The contemporary phrase "to turn Swiss" thus could mean, on the one hand, either to join the Confederacy or to imitate it through a new federation. On the other hand, it could mean either the full autonomy of a city-state, such as Bern or Zurich, or the self-liberation of the rural folk from their noble masters.

The Confederacy's social ambiguities, plus the relatively great distances among the cities and the power of the princes, made the Imperial monarchy a safer choice as partner. Their association developed through the Swabian League (est. 1488) and the Lower Union (reest. 1493) in partnership with the Austrian lands through a series of struggles: against Bavaria in 1492, the Confederacy in 1499, the Palatinate in 1504, and Württemberg in 1519. These clashes marked the major steps in the formation of Emperor Maximilian I's South German system of hereditary lands, federations, and clienteles, which may be seen as the chief political fruit of the brief but potent economic recovery between 1475 and 1525.

During the early years of Charles V's reign, his involvement in Italy and Spain did not prevent the urban oligarchies from forming a new and solid urban front for political action, especially in the Imperial Diet. Some signs appeared that Charles might develop his grandfather's system into a centralized dynastic state, an "Austrian way" to a German monarchy. This possibility was then blocked by the Habsburgs' foreign engagements and by the coming of the Reformation. The wreckage of

3

the partnership of cities and Crown then sealed the supremacy of the German princes.

This story bears directly on the great social crisis that engulfed Germany during the first half of the sixteenth century, which "with its politically self-defeating qualities,"[1] shaped German politics for generations to come. The lack of political unity and centralization left Germany prey to foreign interests and to some degree hindered German participation in the growth of what has been called "the European world-economy." There exists a remarkable unity of opinion on the effects of Germany's failure to achieve either a strong state or a favorable climate for early capitalism, and there is little disagreement about the critical moment:

The first years of Charles V were the moment of Goethe's phrase which, once lost, eternity will never give back. The moment for making a national middle-class Germany was lost in 1521 perhaps forever, certainly for centuries. By 1525, it was evident that the period of national awakening had passed, and there began from that moment a steady advance of absolutism and authoritarianism which continued uninterruptedly for more than 250 years.[2]

Why this opportunity was missed has been a matter for debate. The view of the Prussian school, that Charles V was simply an alien monarch, had its grain of truth in Charles's deep preoccupation with his imperial system, the demands of which prevented him from ever considering the German question from a German point of view.[3] The Habsburg imperial structure, however, permitted the continued life of the small city-republics, which a centralized national monarchy would have absorbed. It is thus misleading to speak, as some have done, of national unification as the natural political goal of the "middle class" or the "bourgeoisie."[4] In the German free cities, at least, palpable political interest attached to the security of the greater imperial system, and it outweighed the putative long-range economic gain that a smaller, more centralized state might have brought.

A further qualification to the problem of a German national state

---

[1] Wallerstein, *World-System*, 1:177.
[2] Taylor, *Course*, 162.
[3] Wallerstein, *World-System*, 1:170-9.
[4] Steinmetz, "Theses," 18.

4

around 1500 concerns the term *national*. Many writers assume that the only possibilities for a German nation were the Germany of 1871 or that Germany plus Austria, respectively the "little German" and "greater German" notions. The relations between the free cities, the Swiss, and the monarchy around 1500, however, demanded a quite different, much smaller stage.

Blink away the familiar modern map of Central Europe. Stand midway on the great wall of the High Alps and look down into the rolling landscape that stretches northward as far as the Central Highlands. To the east and northeast are the Danube's tributary basins; to the west, northwest, and north are those of the Rhine. These river valleys, which lie like interlaced fingers before you, are the chief structures of this story's stage: The Aare, the High Rhine, the Upper Rhine, the Neckar, and the Main flow into the Rhine; and the Inn, the Lech, and the Upper Danube form the Danube. In the central foreground is the "Swabian Sea," Lake Constance, then untroubled by the hard national boundaries that divide its waters today. Thousands upon thousands of tiny lines reveal the region's shifting lacework of lordships, principalities, and federations; of abbeys, priories, and bishoprics; of self-governing peasant leagues and free cities. Among them, one line seems harder than the rest: the jagged line, flanked by rows of exclaves, between those powers that belong to the Swiss Confederacy and those that do not. Why this boundary lay where it did, and why it remained there, are questions raised by this book.

The region, "South Germany" for short, possessed a unity that is more easily imagined from the sources than from the modern historical literature. Historiographically, the region belongs to five national traditions: German, Swiss, French, Austrian, and Italian. No apologies are made here for the failure to honor those parts of national historiographies that project into the deep past the political settlements of 1681, 1815, 1871, and 1918.

Another of the story's elements, liberty, is susceptible of confusion. The social devolution of power, which occurred in many parts of Europe between about 1250 and 1500,[5] ought not to be confused with the

---

[5] Blickle, *Untertanen*, 23. On medieval notions of liberty, see in general Grundmann, "Freiheit," 23–53; Arnold, "Freiheit," 1–21.

egalitarian ideal of democracy that has dogged the steps of industrial capitalism during the past two centuries. Liberty in the old sense, which began to fade during the seventeenth century,[6] appeared in the heart of the feudal order and could, and did, become lordship's bitterest foe. It could mean a monastery's immunities, a city-state's autonomy, the clergy's freedom from lay jurisdiction, the provincial estates' right to consent to taxes, or simply the rights of self-administration of a city or of rural folk. Though radically egalitarian only by contrast with dominant social patterns, nowhere did liberty in this sense flourish more radically than in the Swiss Confederacy, and there nowhere more fully than in the Forest Cantons.[7] What seems radical about this self-administration of ordinary people is the association of liberty with productive labor, a European idea that departed dramatically from Graeco-Roman culture's belief in the incompatibility of human labor with true humanity.[8] The disruptive power of the idea of liberty lay therefore not so much in its formal definition as in its extension to the commons, those free and mostly free persons who were normally ruled by their social betters and who "are now allowed to have minds and spirits."[9]

The propensity of ordinary "minds and spirits" to express themselves in religious language and symbols, which in the past has often made their aspirations grist for the mills of social pathologists rather than students of politics, no longer need do so. As a wise historian of slavery has warned, "in this secular, not to say cynical, age few tasks present greater difficulty than that of compelling the well educated to take religious matters seriously. Yet, for all except the most recent phase of the history of a minority of the world's peoples, religion has been embedded in the core of human life, material as well as spiritual."[10] This embeddedness forbids us to divorce politics from religion and forces us to recognize the dynamic union in Europe's chief religion, Christianity, of conservative and hierarchical with radical and egalitarian tendencies. Although the age of the Reformation saw a reinforcement of authority in both Church and State, it was also a time when "the authority and

---

[6] See Macpherson, *Individualism*, especially 137–59.
[7] See Carlen, *Landsgemeinde*; Peyer, *Verfassungsgeschichte*, 48–55.
[8] I rely here on Anderson, *Passages*, 19–28.
[9] Dickens, *German Nation*, 210.
[10] Genovese, *Roll, Jordan, Roll*, 161.

legitimacy of lordship had been badly shaken – when submission to an earthly lord receded in society and could therefore recede in spiritual consciousness."[11]

This story raises more questions than it answers, especially about the possible political exits from the feudal age. Some elements clearly existed in South Germany to construct large political units through a federation of small units rather than through a centralized, dynastic monarchy, Europe's commonest solution, which formed "the new political carapace of a threatened nobility."[12] Europe's other two regions of successful small units, Italy and the Netherlands, are commonly cited as examples of "failed transitions" to industrial capitalism and therefore of political failure.[13] This suggests that, had the Swiss Confederacy become a more successful model through expansion or imitation, South Germany would have lagged even further than it did behind the economic development of northwestern Europe. The nagging persistence of such themes reminds us that the story of the burghers and their governments is but one part of the greater story of the struggle of ordinary people for self-rule in South Germany. If it is also the more easily told part, this reflects not on the story but on the teller.

---

[11] Ibid., 167.
[12] Anderson, *Lineages*, 18.
[13] See Krantz and Hohenberg, *Failed Transitions*.

oo

The political dilemma of the urban
ruling classes

"In these teeming, boisterous, glorious cities," Lucien Febvre wrote of
the South German free cities around 1500, "an unparalleled prosperity
drew strength from all available sources. A bourgeoisie, too, incompar-
ably active and tough."[1] In the biggest cities – Augsburg, Nuremberg,
Strasbourg, and Ulm – lived the men who sold cannon and clocks to
the known world, who organized the mines of Tyrol and Saxony and
had their fingers in the Eastern slave trade, who bought noble estates
and titles and married their offspring into the best families of the land,
and who ruled like lords over tens of thousands of lesser folk. "These
men," Febvre mused with wonder, "were the kings of a new world
which inverted the old scale of values." And the cities, where they lived
and where they inverted the old scale of values, were "Germany's pride
– and her weakness." Here Febvre touched the inner paradox of late
medieval urban life: the coincidence of economic vigor, great wealth,
and cultural pride with political timidity and passivity. "Sprinkled among
the princes' territories," he continued his meditation,

the cities formed holes and indentations in the territories, limited their expansion and hindered them from growing strong. Could the cities themselves come
to an understanding? No. Could they form a federation? No longer. Beyond
their walls lay the countryside, where the land was ruled by a law of which
their own law was a contradiction. There, ruled by greedy lords, were the rude
and rough peasants, sometimes miserable, ready to revolt and groaning under
the yoke, at all events strangers to the city's culture ... The cities ... these

---

[1] Febvre, *Martin Luther*, 74–5, from which the other quotes in this pararaph are also taken (my
thanks to Heiko Oberman for bringing this passage to my attention).

prestigious urban cultures, these oases of culture. These cities, prisoners dedicated to isolation, watching out for the princes – and for each other.

"Weakness under the mask of prosperity," Febvre concluded, "their astonishing political weakness contrasted with so much economic power" and with the behavior of France's *bonnes villes*,

just as their citizens are far from this [French] national sensibility, from the political sense that in times of crisis brought all the fair cities of France around the king, zealous to support Louis XI against the men of the Common Weal or against the princes.

Economic vigor, cultural pride, political weakness – Febvre's judgment on the South German free cities seems just about right.

The South German free cities around 1500

> Der Veneter Macht
> der Augsburger Pracht
> der Nürnberger Witz
> der Strassburger Geschütz
> der Ulmer Geld
> regieren die Welt – sic transit gloria mundi![2]

South Germany was one European region in which the towns gained extensive rights of self-government. Much ink has been spilt on definitions of "Imperial cities," which possessed liberties chartered by the king, and "free cities," which had won their liberties from bishops or other lords, much as the Lombard and Tuscan towns had done.[3] By the later fifteenth century, however, royal documents called them indiscriminately "Imperial cities" (*Reichsstädte*), meaning the towns that could expect to be summoned to the Imperial Diet.[4] The Imperial tax

---

[2] "Venice's might, Augsburg's magnificence, Nuremberg's brains, Strasbourg's guns, and Ulm's gold rule the world – how fleeting is the world's glory!" Roth von Schreckenstein, *Patriziat*, 552 (without source); there are other versions in Franz, *Nürnberg*, 43, and Zorn, *Augsburg*, 159.
[3] G. Schmidt, *Städtetag*, 1–2, 80–6; Isenmann, "Reichsstadt," 19–31; and Moraw, "Reichsstädte," 385–424. I will call them "free cities." On their amalgamation into a single juridical category, see E. Schubert, *König*, 285–96, 332–4.
[4] E. Schubert, *König*, 334. On whether there was a Diet before Maximilian's time, see Moraw, "Versuch," 1–3 (my thanks to Peter Blickle for this reference).

9

lists (*Reichsmatrikeln*) contained, if shorn of such anachronisms as the duke of Jülich's Duisburg, the bishop of Paderborn's Brakel, and the count of Lippe's Lemgo, about sixty-nine cities.[5] They can be grouped by regions as follows:

Upper Rhine from (but not including) Basel to Frankfurt	18	(26%)
Swabia, including Lake Constance (5), Upper (13) and Lower (12)	30	(43%)
Franconia	6	(9%)
Western francophone fringe	5	(7%)
Central and northern Germany	10	(14%)
Total	69	(100%)

The lands south of a line across the Central Highlands (Hunsrück-Taunus-Vogelsberg-Rhön-Thuringian Forest) contained 78 percent of the free cities; and if the francophone cities, which rarely sent to Diets, are excluded, the southern share rises to 83 percent.

The southern-centeredness of the free cities reflected a situation that has never been accorded proper recognition: The political structure of the Holy Roman Empire was to a very great degree a South German one. The choice of sites for Imperial Diets – Nuremberg, Regensburg, Speyer, and Worms – illustrates this fact, but so does the attendance at Diets.[6] Although electors and leading lay princely dynasties from both north and south normally attended Diets or sent envoys, among the bishops the South's weight began to tell, and among the prelates it was even greater. As for the free cities, only Cologne from the North attended as many as twenty Diets during the sixteenth century, whereas seventeen

---

[5] I follow G. Schmidt, *Städtetag*, 39–46, whose treatment seems definitive; the list by Aulinger, *Bild*, 371–4, should be used only with Schmidt's corrections.

[6] Aulinger, *Bild*, 358–74, as amplified by G. Schmidt, *Städtetag*, 36–9.

southern cities did so; and only five of the thirty-five cities that attended fifteen or more Diets lay outside the South. If this pattern is coupled to the geographical pattern of Habsburg lands, alliances, and clienteles, one begins to understand why the old Imperial structure could contain a movement of southern origin, such as the Revolution of 1525, but not one of northern origin, such as Lutheranism.

Though legally equal, the southern free cities varied greatly in political weight and military might. The leading cities were Nuremberg, Augsburg, Strasbourg, Ulm, and perhaps Frankfurt am Main.[7] The next tier of middling towns (between four and eight thousand inhabitants) included Worms, Constance, Heilbronn, Reutlingen, Esslingen, and Nördlingen, and the bottom ranks ranged downward to tiny Zell am Harmersbach and Bopfingen, which, though they had all the urban trappings, were not much larger than big villages. Small, and often middling, towns appeared on the Imperial political stage only as clients of large cities or in structured groups, such as the cities of the Swabian League or the Alsatian Decapolis. Thus the Franconian towns of Windsheim, Schweinfurt, Dinkelsbühl, and Weissenburg im Nordgau swam in Nuremberg's wake; Ulm, though challenged by Constance, led the Upper Swabian cloth towns of Memmingen, Biberach an der Riss, Kempten, and Isny; and Augsburg's clientele included Donauwörth, Kaufbeuren, Wimpfen, Nördlingen, and Schwäbish Hall.[8] Strasbourg's clientele embraced not the Alsatian Decapolis, which gave their proxies to Hagenau and Colmar, but only the small Kinzig Valley towns, Offenburg, Gengenbach, and Zell am Harmersbach.[9]

In economic and social structures, if not in political weight, the free cities – and, for that matter, the territorial ones, too – were remarkably similar.[10] The cities were centers of trade and manufacturing, of borrowing and investment, of ecclesiastical and civil administration, and of communication and learned culture. The variations could be considerable, of course, as, for example, between cities closely integrated into regional market economies, such as Ueberlingen, Basel, and Strasbourg,

---

[7] Gollwitzer, "Capitaneus," 274; and see below, note 42.
[8] Isenmann, "Reichsstadt," 107.
[9] *RTA, mR,* 6:351, no. 51 (1496–7), and 745, no. 119 (1498); *RTA, jR,* 3:474.
[10] Maschke, "Deutsche Städte," 56–99, is the best synthesis; see also Blickle, *Untertanen,* 52.

and cities living from specialized manufactures, such as Augsburg, Nörd-lingen, and little Isny.[11] Such differences had profound implications for a city's social stability, because specialized export industries tended to widen the gap between rich and poor, but more balanced economies normally meant more peaceful towns.

The cities' ties to the countryside were especially close at the social pyramid's two extremes. Wealthy urbanites migrated between town and land, married rural nobles, and became landed gentlemen and vassals.[12] Merchants bought land and lent money to peasants, bought patents of nobility, and aped noble manners. "They think they have no equals and call themselves 'the Roman Empire,'" mocked one songster, "but in truth they are only peasants."[13] Another poet joined in:

> His seal is polished, very great,
> And of a formidable weight;
> His rank comes not from family,
> But India across the sea;
> Cash for the way of life he apes
> Is drawn from Negro boys, and grapes.

Honest genealogies would have, in truth, revealed parvenu merchants in many a noble family tree.

To swell the urban lower classes, the countryside furnished a steady stream of laborers, servants, and petty tradesmen to the cities. Such folk often concentrated in the suburbs, the social transition zones between walled town and hinterland. In Alsatian cities, there were even "agricultural guilds," whose masters practiced land-linked trades, such as truck gardening and wine growing.[14]

The strongest link between town and land was the urban territory.[15] Urban territorial formation in South Germany, it is true, reached Italian

---

[11] Blickle, *Untertanen*, 69–70; Eitel, *Reichsstädte*, 123–38, 159; Brady, *Ruling Class*, 96–104; idem, "Patricians," 38–45.

[12] Brady, *Ruling Class*, 127–52; Kiessling, *Bürgerliche Gesellschaft*, 197–201; idem, "Herrschaft-Markt-Landbesitz" and "Bürgerlicher Besitz."

[13] Quoted by E. Schubert, *König*, 290. The following verse is quoted by Rörig, *Medieval Town*, 126.

[14] Maschke, "Verfassung und soziale Kräfte," 296; idem, "Unterschichten," 16; and Czok, *Vorstädte*.

[15] Raiser, *Territorialpolitik*; Blickle, "Territorialpolitik"; Leiser, "Territorien"; Wunder, "Reichs-städte." For economic conflict between town and land, see in general Kirchgässner, "Verlag."

dimensions only in the Swiss Confederacy, where the Bernese city-state dwarfed in land and population the largest urban territory further northward, that of Ulm.[16] Cities expanded sometimes through conquest but more often through purchase from local nobles and princes, such as the Habsburgs for Zurich and the Hohenzollerns for Nuremberg. The process slowed perceptibly during the later fifteenth century and ground nearly to a halt by 1500,[17] leaving the small red blotches sprinkled across historical maps of South Germany, whose scattered patterns suggest what weak contenders the free cities were in the competition to control the surplus wealth produced by millions of peasants.

The slowing of external expansion coincided with the internal growth of oligarchy.[18] Though similar in phases – communal independence, guild revolts, oligarchy – the political histories of the cities differed markedly in tempo, and some guild revolts, such as at Schwäbisch Hall in 1511 and at Basel in 1521, occurred well into the sixteenth century.[19] Size had little to do with the political structure: At Nuremberg, a solid merchant-patrician class ruled; at Strasbourg and Ulm, mixed noble-merchant classes shared power with the guilds; and at Basel, the guilds took sole power. Whatever the constitution, wealth and power went together, not because only rich men were permitted to hold office but because only they could afford long careers in government. Oligarchy was both personal and institutional. On the one hand, fewer individuals held more offices, and more important offices, for longer periods of time; on the other, the rise of privy councils replaced more broadly based councils and selection procedures with cooptation and life tenures. City councils were coming to think of themselves less as servants of the commune than as "lords" who ruled over "subjects," not least because the governments strove for external recognition in a world in which authority and lordship were nearly synonymous. The growth of oligarchy also made the resolution of social conflict, especially between poor and

---

[16] Ulm's territory during the sixteenth century embraced 3 towns, 55 villages, and 22 parishes, a total of about 830 km². Schmolz, "Herrschaft," 32. Bern ruled some 60 lay and ecclesiastical lordships, plus the directly ruled territory. Walder, "Reformation," 470–1.

[17] This is based on the relevant entries in Keyser, *Deutsches Städtebuch.*

[18] Maschke, " 'Obrigkeit' im spätmittelalterlichen Speyer," 7–22; Naujoks, *Obrigkeitsgedanke*; idem, "Obrigkeit," 61–7; Brady, *Ruling Class*, 163–96; Eitel, *Reichsstädte*, 87–106.

[19] Wunder, *Bürger von Hall*, 74–6; R. Wackernagel, *Geschichte*, 3:85–6; Füglister, *Handwerksregiment*, 1–4. The best general study is by Maschke, "Verfassung und soziale Kräfte."

rich, more difficult than it had been in the more expansive age of guild revolts. Everywhere the drive for greater control appeared in sumptuary ordinances, poor laws, censorship of printing, regulation of apprentices and journeymen, and controls on the urban clergy. The need for such measures seemed more than justified by the wave of revolts that jolted the cities between 1509 and 1514.[20]

External threats also stiffened the bonds of oligarchy within. The rural nobles often held the burghers in contempt and preyed on them when they could. Their well-advertised hatred for the big trading firms easily excused banditry, especially when it was edged with real or imagined wrongs. There was Cuntz Schott, for example, who in 1499 cut the right hand off a Nuremberg senator to warn the townsmen to treat him, Schott, with more respect.[21] The worst conditions obtained in wild Franconia, grazing ground for Götz von Berlichingen (c. 1480–1562), the "marvelous young fellow" who raised banditry to a high art, and other notorious robber gentlemen.[22] In Alsace, the urban militias burned out at least thirty robbers' nests during the fifteenth century, but in the 1510s Hans Balthasar von Endingen, whose brother was a noble senator of Strasbourg, was still preying on Swabian and Lorraine merchants from his country seat.[23]

Bandit nobles preyed on merchants and travelers, but predatory princes threatened the liberties of whole cities. Some simply lost their independence, either permanently, as Mainz and Erfurt, or temporarily, as Regensburg and Worms.[24] Some princes, such as Elector Palatine Frederick the Victorious (r. 1449–76), eschewed such methods; he sent his agents on regular borrowing tours to the big Rhenish cities, whose favor he cultivated.[25] Other dynasties, however, sought to acquire the cities'

---

[20] Maschke, "Deutsche Städte," 76–7, 95 n. 206 (also in his *Städte und Menschen,* 76–7, 95 n. 206); see Endres, "Zünfte und Unterschichten," 151–70.

[21] He was the worst of the many robber nobles who plagued the Nurembergers, on whom see Reicke, *Geschichte,* 473–6, 539–50, 802–6; Strauss, *Nuremberg,* 52–4.

[22] See Ulmschneider, *Götz von Berlichingen,* 57–77, who also reviews (pp. 25–30) the subject of robber nobles.

[23] Brady, *Ruling Class,* 83, 90–1, 365 (with the wrong year of death); Klüpfel, *Urkunden,* 2:156, 187, 199, 204, 208, 218–19, 224, 228, 233. In Salch, *Dictionnaire,* I count thirty castles razed by the free cities.

[24] Maschke, "Deutsche Städte," 56–7 (also in his *Städte und Menschen,* 56–7); E. Schubert, *König,* 293–4.

[25] Cohn, *Rhine Palatinate,* 117–18; Brady, "Themes," 68.

wealth and military potential in more direct ways and conducted very long feuds, such as those between the margraves of Brandenburg-Ansbach and Nuremberg and between the princes of Württemberg and Esslingen.[26]

From within and without, therefore, dangers beset the urban oligarchies of South Germany around 1500. Within, the governments had to control social tensions – between rich and poor, master and journeyman, noble and servant, merchant and artisan, priest and parishioner – through persuasion, arbitration, police power, and, above all, the invocation of fundamental civic values. Without, the governments needed solidarity and political partners, for recent experience showed that urban solidarity alone could no longer check the great princes. The search for security proceeded after 1450 on these two fronts, aided and hampered by the proud weakness that formed the cities' chief burden.

Proud weakness: an urban paradox

> Jubileus ist uns verkündt,
> wir solten tilgen unser sünd:
> das hat der bös vernomen,
> valschen samen hat er gesät,
> . . . .
> Den steten hat er hochvart geben,
> wie si dem adel widerstreben
> und den genzlich vertreiben
> wider got, on alles recht,
> und damit gaistliches geschlecht,
> si liessens wol beleiben.
> Si bdunkt es sei nit ir geleich
> und nennen sich das römisch reich,
> nun sind si doch nur pauren:
> si stand mit ern hinder der tür,
> so die fürsten gand herfür
> die land und leut beschauren.[27]

---

[26] On the former, see Reicke, *Geschichte*, 404–35, 462–76, 492–506, 537–9; Strauss, *Nuremberg*, 51–2, 54–5. On the latter, see Borst, *Geschichte*, 171–96; Naujoks, "Reichsfreiheit," 279–302; G. Schmidt, "Reichstadt und Territorialstaat," 71–104.

[27] "The jubilee is now proclaimed, now we must confess our sins. The Evil One has heard of this

15

Turning Swiss

The united power of the South German cities, once a "third Germany"[28] alongside the king and the princes, had during the thirteenth and fourteenth centuries emerged in military leagues that swept over the land and humbled great lords. The last such league went down to total defeat in the Cities' War of 1449–53, though the dream of an urban military federation lived on for more than two hundred years – until 1671 – as a political will-o'-the-wisp.[29] The free cities were finished, at least as an independent force, in Imperial politics.

The cities' low political reputation in the modern literature, expressed in such epithets as "negative Imperial consciousness" and "sad decadence,"[30] has focused on their governments' particularism. In this view, their modest position after 1500 "was essentially due to their failure to recognize, let alone fulfill, their position and their natural duties."[31] Their strength "lay in their mutual solidarity alone. When the age of the great urban leagues was past, the great political role of the free cities was also finished." By the later fifteenth century, then, "the cities had lost both the constructive will and the goal for a common policy."[32] Against the charge that the cities' political decline reflected a lack of political will, it may be argued that there was no realistic alternative to particularism. "For from the moment when a central power was denied them, the towns were defending a lost position. They had no choice, within a world of pseudo-states dissolving into little circles, but to form a small separatist state for themselves..." a particularism that then found expression in "a corresponding economic policy."[33]

The southern free cities' particularism softened some, but not much,

---

and sowed about his base seed...He has made the cities proud, so that they strive against the nobles and try to crush them utterly against God and all that is right, while the clergy for their part look on with satisfaction. The cities believe they have no peer and call themselves 'the Roman Empire,' but in truth they are mere peasants. They guard their honor behind thick doors while the princes then take the lead and watch over land and folk alike." Liliencron, *Volkslieder*, 1:417, no. 90, stanzas 1–3.

[28] Hermann Heimpel, quoted by Isenmann, "Reichsstadt," 15. On the Cities' War, see Angermeier, *Königtum*, 404–20; E. Schubert, *König*, 285; Isenmann, "Reichsstadt," 14–16; and in general, G. Schmidt, *Städtetag*, 2–4.

[29] Bog, "Betrachtungen," 91.

[30] Bader, *Studien*, 1:57–8; Walton, "Reformation," 146.

[31] Bader, *Studien*, 1:151; the following quote is at pp. 159–60.

[32] Angermeier, *Königtum*, 406–7.

[33] Rörig, *Medieval Town*, 187; for other dissents, see Naujoks, *Obrigkeitsgedanke*, 8; and E. Schubert, *König*, 290.

during the impressive but incomplete economic recovery after 1470.[34] The next eighty years saw the accumulation of wealth on a vast scale in the larger cities. It was the age of Jacob Fugger (1459–1525), called "the Rich," who raised nearly a million gold florins to secure the Imperial throne for Charles in 1519; the age, too, of Grünewald, Dürer, and Baldung in painting, of Riemenschneider and Flötner in sculpture, and of the last great, playfully vaulted Gothic churches; the age of printing, when the German presses poured forth a river of books and pamphlets; the age of Augsburg armor, Nuremberg clocks, Strasbourg guns, Memmingen fustians, and Nördlingen loden; the age of the Frankfurt fairs and the Welsers' colonization of Venezuela. The South Germans became bankers to much of the known world[35] and especially to the infant Habsburg empire. It was brief, however, this age of wealth and glory, lasting only about eighty years, and it was pockmarked by structural dislocations that foreshadowed the long decline to come, when the South Germans were to be gradually shut out of the nascent European "world-economy."[36] The wealth of a Jacob Fugger, "an ornament of all Germany,"[37] never found a connection to a permanent and powerful political structure in Germany itself, despite the Fuggers' role in the wider Habsburg empire. This lack, this failure, is a microcosm of the wider political failure of the economic boom of 1470–1550. Nor were the boom's benefits universal; although Augsburg and Nuremberg fed from the new prosperity, other cities, such as Constance, Esslingen, Frankfurt, and Memmingen, were already sliding downward from their peaks.[38] Such qualifications soften somewhat but do not truly relieve the contrast between economic vigor and political feebleness.

Contemporary judgments about South Germany's free cities were rather more mixed than are modern ones. The Augsburg chronicler Burkard Zink (1396–1474), it is true, lamented the cities' helplessness:

---

[34] Kellenbenz, "Gewerbe und Handel 1500–1648," is comprehensive but weak on interpretation. Briefer but more penetrating is Wallerstein, *World-System*, 1:173–8; and see Miskimin, *Economy*, 24–32, 67–8.
[35] Bergier, "From the Fifteenth Century in Italy to the Sixteenth Century in Germany," 116–20.
[36] Wallerstein, *World-System*, 1:15.
[37] Sender, "Chronik," 167, lines 3-4.
[38] For Constance, see Kirchgässner, *Steuerwesen*, 183–94; for Esslingen, see Borst, *Geschichte*, 173–87; for Frankfurt am Main, see Jahns, *Frankfurt*, 25–6; and for Memmingen, see Schlenck, *Memmingen*, 19, 122–3.

Turning Swiss

"They are now divided and separated from one another... and are as helpless as sheep without a shepherd... The Roman emperor, our natural lord, has no regard for them and lets the nobles treat them as they please... Their power, their might, and their lordship, which they had had so long, are all gone."[39] Zink employed Aesop's story of the four oxen, whose solidarity magnified their strengths and made them invincible until a sly wolf turned them against one another. The free cities "were powerful, mighty, bold and confident, because they stood together in true friendship and formed firm alliances among themselves." After the Cities' War, however, they fell apart, and each went running for protection to the nearest prince.

The picture of hopeless impotence was not shared by a contemporary Italian observer, the Sienese patrician and future pope, Enea Silvio Piccolomini (1405–64). "Truly," he wrote in 1457/8,

nowhere else in the world is there such freedom as these cities enjoy. In Italy the citizens, who are called "free," in fact live like serfs – just look at Venice, Florence or Siena! – because, except for a few who rule the others, they are treated like slaves. They may not manage their own properties as they wish, nor may they say what they want; and they are crushed by taxes.

In Germany everything is pleasant and charming. No one is robbed of his property... and the authorities harm only those who harm others. Here no parties rage against one another, as they do in Italian cities. More than one hundred cities enjoy this freedom, many of which lie along the Rhine and the Danube, others on the coast, and still others inland. They are allied in leagues, and they defend themselves with their own forces against the princes' depredations.[40]

Piccolomini had his own reasons, of course, for flattering the Germans, whose aid he wanted against the Turks. Two generations later, his view was repeated, though in characteristically terser language, by his fellow Tuscan, Niccolò Machiavelli (1469–1527). Allowing for a Tacitean exaggeration of alien virtues to illuminate domestic vices, Machiavelli's remarks reflected his nostalgia for a bygone age of pristine republican freedom: "The German cities are utterly free, have small territories, and obey the Emperor when they feel like it; they do not fear him or

---

[39] Zink, "Chronik 1368–1468," 228–9, and there, too, the following quote at pp. 229–30.
[40] Piccolomini, *Germania*, 62. See Voigt, *Italienische Berichte*, 136–43.

18

any other potentate near them because they are so fortified that everybody reckons their capture as sure to be tedious and difficult."[41]
The historical perspective missing in the Italian authors was supplied by Willibald Pirckheimer (1470–1530), Machiavelli's exact contemporary, who looked over the South German political landscape from his native Nuremberg and saw the wreckage of urban liberties, relieved only occasionally by the upright posture of a major city. "Formerly," he lamented,

the free cities were great in number and power, but in these latter days most of them have fallen to the power of tyrants or through perverse regimes. Most especially they have suffered from the arrogance and greed of the bishops, this all-consuming flame, to whom the old emperors, following their princes' ruinous advice, gave over royal rights in the cities. The bishops exploited this position by setting the common people against the urban notables and driving the latter from their cities; then, of course, the stupid commons was soon suppressed, and the bishops were masters of the cities.

Although countless cities fell in this way, just as many were ruined by bad government. For the rich and powerful forced with relentless pressure the commons to revolt; and so it happened that almost everywhere the people began to rule, chiefly in the maritime cities, from Riga in the far north (where they have twenty hours' daylight!) down into North Germany – a tremendous distance!

Some South German cities alone run their own affairs correctly and justly, for which reason they are more powerful than the Lower German cities, though they have no shipping. Augsburg in particular has grown unbelievably rich through the Portuguese monopoly. Ulm has not so much private wealth as Augsburg, though it has greater public wealth and a larger territory. Then comes, if a step lower, Frankfurt am Main. Nuremberg also belongs, of course, to the big cities. These four free cities are the only ones in South Germany on this side of the Rhine of which one could say that they have real power. On the other side lies Strasbourg, whose power, though formerly greater than now, is not to be despised. Metz in Lorraine still recognizes its Imperial status and is mightier than all other free cities, except for Nuremberg.[42]

---

[41] Machiavelli, *The Prince*, chap. 10 (English: *Chief Works and Others*, trans. A. H. Gilbert, 1:43, but translating "territories" instead of "farm land"). Machiavelli called the German free cities "il nervo di quella provincia ... perché la intenzione loro principale à di mantenere la loro libertà, non di acquistare imperio." *Arte della guerra e scritti politici minori*, ed. S. Bertelli, 205, 212–13.

[42] W. Pirckheimer, *Opera politica*, 201–2. For his biography, see *Willibald Pirkheimer 1470/1970*, ed. Willibald-Pirkheimer-Kuratorium; and Spitz, *Renaissance*, 155–96.

Pirckheimer's pride in these large cities paled beside his gloomy epitaph on the urban liberties in general, lost through episcopal aggression and bad government. In contrast to Piccolomini, who praised the proper management of internal affairs, and Machiavelli, who emphasized the cities' military strength, Pirckheimer indicted bishops, oligarchs, and urban commons alike for the present misery.[43]

No writer of that age understood better than did Machiavelli the politics of urban republics. He believed that when burghers extended their rule outside their own walls, they prepared the downfall of their own liberties.

> Athens and Sparta, which once had such great
> renown in the world, fell into ruin only after they had
> conquered the powers round about them.
> But in Germany at the present day each city lives secure
> through having less than six miles round about.
> To our city [i.e., Florence] [Emperor] Henry [VII]
> in his time caused no fear with all his might when
> he had seized her territories up to the walls [in 1312];
> but now that she has extended her power to the lands
> round about and become great and vast, she dreads
> everything, not merely huge armies,
> because strength which is enough to support one body only
> is not sufficient to sustain a greater weight.[44]

Machiavelli attributed the freedom of the South German cities to their "goodness and respect for religion," their isolation from corrupting foreign (French, Spanish, and Italian) influences, and, above all, their hatred of "gentlemen."

The other reason is that those republics where a government has been kept orderly and uncorrupted do not allow any citizen of theirs to be a gentleman or live in the fashion of one, but they preserve among themselves a complete equality. To the lords and gentlemen who live in that region they are entirely

---

[43] Whereas Machiavelli saw in the German cities' small territories a mark of strength, Pirckheimer regarded Ulm's large territory as an advantage.

[44] Machiavelli, "Dell'asino d'oro," chap. 5 (English: *Chief Works and Others*, trans. A. H. Gilbert, 2:762–3).

hostile; and if by chance any come into their hands, they put them to death as the beginning of corruption and the causes of all evil.[45]

The same is true of the Swiss, who "are hostile not only to the princes, as the free cities also are, but they are likewise enemies of the gentlemen, neither of which type – prince or gentlemen – is to be found in their land."[46] These passages must not be taken in a literal, social-historical sense – there were gentlemen enough in Strasbourg, Ulm, and Augsburg[47] – but in Machiavelli's sense of the term *gentleman*. He did not mean simply a person of wealth, prestige, and breeding but one who held direct, personal (i.e., truly feudal) power over others. "To explain what this name of gentleman means," he wrote,

I say that they are called gentlemen who without working live in luxury on the returns from their landed possessions, without paying any attention either to agriculture or to any other occupation necessary for making a living. Such men as these are dangerous in every republic and in every country, but still more dangerous are they who, besides the aforesaid fortunes, command castles and have subjects who obey them.[48]

In the Italian provinces where such folk are numerous,

there never has arisen any republic or well-ordered government, because men of these types are altogether hostile to all free government.

To introduce a republic into those regions would be impossible; if a man who were their master attempted to reorganize them, he could find no other way than to set up a kingdom there.

Here Machiavelli broached the problem of the social basis of state building.

So from this discussion I draw these conclusions. He who attempts to set up a republic in a place where there are many gentlemen cannot do so unless he first wipes them all out. Where there is great equality, he who wishes to set up a kingdom or a principality cannot do so unless he draws away from that equality many of ambitious and restless spirit and makes them gentlemen in fact and

---

[45] Machiavelli, *Discorsi*, 1:55 (English: *Chief Works and Others*, trans. A. H. Gilbert, 1:308).
[46] Machiavelli, *Arte della guerra e scritti politici minori*, ed. S. Bertelli, 203–4. For what follows, see Bonadeo, "Role of the 'Grandi' " and "Role of the People."
[47] Brady, *Ruling Class*, 123–62.
[48] Machiavelli, *Discorsi*, 1:55 (English: *Chief Works and Others*, trans. A. H. Gilbert, 1:308, and the following three quotes at pp. 309–10).

not in name only, granting them castles and possessions and giving them aid with property and men, so that, standing in their midst, by their means he supports his power. They, by his means, support their ambition.

Successful republican government, therefore, requires relative social equality and the absence of men who enjoy direct mastery of others – that is, true lords.

Machiavelli's reflections can help us to understand the situation of the urban ruling classes in South Germany around 1500. The region's deep fragmentation made it susceptible to political consolidation in either, or so it appears, of Machiavelli's two directions, republican or monarchist. A republican solution would have required the elimination of the gentlemen, especially the princes, from the land and the organization of the countryside either into city-states or into rural republics that could federate with the urban ones. The former would have been an Italian solution, the latter a Swiss one. Neither was very probable, given the progress that some "gentlemen," the princes, had made in transforming feudal lordship into genuine states, together with the cities' interest in the continued *economic* subordination of the land to the city. If the "gentlemen" could not be eliminated, the situation perhaps fitted Machiavelli's second direction, monarchy. In fact, the South German free cities still lay somewhere between these two directions, pulled between the alternatives of building up security from below, from the communes, and seeking it above, from the king. The two horns of their political dilemma may thus be named *monarchism* and *communalism*.

Monarchism and ideals of order

Teutschland sol sich iez freuwen
des edlen keisers zeit:
das gūt wirt er verneuwen;
der Türk zū felde leit,
was recht ist, wirt er loben,
der edel keiser gūt,
er wirt wenden sein toben,
rechen der Christen blūt.
. . . .
Und dass auch alle strassen
in dem heiligen reich

werden sicher gelassen
von raub und mord geleich
und ein gūt regimende
in teutscher nation
durch alle reiches stende.
Lob sei gott im höchsten thron![49]

Except, perhaps, for the praise and honor of God, no value was more central to the free cities' political culture than the common good (*bonum commune, gemeiner Nutz*),[50] which enjoined through the citizens' oath the primacy of common over individual, family, clan, or craft interest. In it was rooted the common duty of government and citizenry to pursue peace, justice, unity, and the common good.[51] The 1478 codification of Nuremberg's laws expressed these values: "And as also peace, concord, and due obedience of the whole community are promoted, defended and established by a proper and equal administration of justice; therefore, to the praise of God and the salutary and blessed increase of the common weal of this honorable city and the entire commune... "[52] When, a century later, the Alsatian writer Johann Fischart (1546/7–90) outlined the magistrate's duties, the essential points had changed very little:

to legislate wholesome laws and customs; to appoint good men to the councils, the Church and the schools; to reconcile citizens who quarrel with one another; to administer justice; to protect the dutiful and the pious; to punish miscreants; to watch over the poor, widows and orphans... In short, to foster the common tranquility, security, calm, and peace.[53]

---

[49] "Rejoice, O Germany, rejoice for this noble emperor's reign! He will renew all that is good and lead us out against the Turk. He will foster what is right, this good and noble monarch. He'll turn his fury against the foe, and avenge the martyrs' blood... And now the roads and highways of our Holy Roman Empire will at last be left in peace from theft and murder both. And he will lay down a goodly rule for each and every member of our beloved German nation. Praise be to God on high!" Liliencron, *Volkslieder*, 4:5–6, no. 421, stanzas 2, 11.

[50] E. Schubert, *König*, 282–5, discusses the term's double meaning (*publicus* and *communis*). Whereas Oberman (*Werden und Wertung*, 260, 294–5, 301, 302 n. 127, 336, 351, 357–9, 361, 376–7 [English: *Masters*, 204, 210, 231, 237, 238 n. 127, 266, 276, 280–4, 294–5]) interprets the idea as a conservative one, Blickle (*Revolution von 1525*, 233–4 [English: *Revolution of 1525*, 150–61]) shows that it was capable of extreme radicalization. For the background, see Skinner, *Foundations*, 1:44–8, 58–9, 60–5, 175–80.

[51] See Rublack, "Political and Social Norms," 27.

[52] Quoted by ibid., 26 n. 8.

[53] Quoted by Abray, *People's Reformation*, 75, quoting Fischart, *Ordenliche Beschreibung* (Strasbourg, 1588), Aii^r–Aiii^v (translation hers).

23

Turning Swiss

Hegemonic values must be believed if they are to foster social discipline, and the fact that such values could, on occasion, be enforced *against* oligarchs is proof that they were believed.[54] They were an essential political glue in cities that united rough legal equality with great social inequality, where the oligarchs practiced usury, and where potentially dangerous bonds persisted between urban folk and rural subjects.[55] Even in the more broadly based guild governments, the oligarchs must have believed privately what Christoph Scheurl (1481–1542), a lawyer in patrician-ruled Nuremberg, wrote frankly: "The common folk have no power; it does not belong to their estate, since all power comes from God, and good government belongs only to those who have been endowed with special wisdom by the creator of all things and nature . . . "[56] Such men naturally looked upward to God, but also to the emperor. Although the cities were officially subject to "Emperor and Empire" *(Kaiser und Reich)*,[57] the term *Empire* referred to the Imperial estates, the Diet, and especially the princes, against whose collective pressure and individual violence the free cities most needed help. They put their trust in their own strengths and solidarity, true, but also in their sovereign.

In a sense, monarchism was a natural part of good citizenship, and even the angriest writers, such as the anonymous authors of the *Reformation of Emperor Sigmund* and the *Book of the Hundred Chapters*, and the framers of reform programs in 1525, rarely questioned the emperor's place at the head of Christian society.[58] Self-interest was a part of this monarchism, of course, feeding on royal loans and privileges, patents of nobility and arms, royal judicial favors and contracts for armor and cloth, paintings and monuments, food and drink, and cannon and crossbows. Solid ties of this sort, between the Luxemburg dynasty and Nuremberg, for example, had existed in the past; new ones sprang up between the Habsburg dynasty and Augsburg.[59]

---

[54] Brady, *Ruling Class*, 259–75.
[55] Ibid., 147–52; Blickle, *Revolution von 1525*, 165–88 (English: *Revolution of 1525*, 105–20); Rammstedt, "Stadtunruhen 1525," 244–50.
[56] Scheurl, "Epistel über die Verfassung der Reichsstadt Nürnberg (1516)," 791, lines 24–8 (English: Rublack, "Political and Social Norms," 44.
[57] E. Schubert, *König*, 254–6.
[58] H. Schmidt, *Städtechroniken*, 64, 72; Knepper, *Nationaler Gedanke*, 182–4.
[59] Stromer, *Oberdeutsche Hochfinanz 1350–1450*, esp. 436–60; Huter, "Kaiser Maximilian," 41–57.

24

Political dilemma of urban ruling classes

Monarchism also fed on cultural innovations of the age. The reception of Roman law and the rising marketability of a legal education brought into court and urban culture a body of learning whose very language conveyed the worth of monarchy.[60] Classical humanism, which seeped into the German cities during the last third of the fifteenth century, magnified this effect.[61] No German humanist yet studied deviated much from the deep conservatism displayed by the northern humanists as a group:

Virtually all the northern humanists ... spell out the more general and deeply conservative message underlying this commitment to the traditional ruling classes. Having admitted that government ought to be placed in the hands of those with the greatest virtue, and having affirmed that those with the greatest virtue happen to be the nobility and the gentry, they proceed to draw the pleasingly obvious conclusion: that in order to maintain the best-ordered form of political society, we ought not to tamper with any existing social distinctions, but ought on the contrary to preserve them as far as possible.

Arguing from antiquity to the German status quo met a special difficulty, in that the humanists could not claim for the present order descent from the Greeks, Trojans, or Romans. Tacitus's *De Germania*, their central key to early Germanic history, told only too clearly how their ancestors had been the barbarian foes of Rome.[62] Through the monarchy, however, and the doctrine of *translatio imperii*, the cantus firmus of their political song, the German humanists could draw together Roman and German history into a single story.

These humanists found little or no use for classical republicanism, of which Florentine writers had made such strikingly practical use during the previous century. One text, ascribed to Sebastian Brant (1457/8–1521) of Strasbourg, adorned one of a series of political allegories painted in the city's old city hall (destroyed in the eighteenth century):

---

[60] Anderson, *Lineages*, 24–9; Koschaker, *Europa und das römische Recht*, 178–80.
[61] There is no adequate guide to this subject. Skinner, *Foundations*, 1:chaps. 8–9, and 2:chap. 2, devotes one paragraph to German humanism (2:54); Schellhase, *Tacitus*, chaps. 2–3, is stronger on history than on political ideas; and Spitz, "Course," 371–436, ignores political ideas altogether. See Knepper, *Nationaler Gedanke*, and Zorn, "Die soziale Stellung," 35–50. The following quote is from Skinner, *Foundations*, 1:238–9.
[62] Schellhase, *Tacitus*, chaps. 2–3; Ridé, "L'image du germain," vol. 1.

25

Turning Swiss

Julius Caesar was merciful and just;
But he treated Rome as his slave
And wanted to be its sole lord,
As though Liberty no longer lived!
Fearful vengeance was his pay,
And he died of many wounds.[63]

Ulrich von Hutten (1488–1523) struck a related note in his dialogue called *Arminius*, whose title character compares his being "driven by the sacred merit of my nation's cause" to the motives of the Roman "patriots who drove out the Tarquins and assassinated Julius Caesar."[64] In Florence, to side with Caesar's assassins had become a touchstone of political republicanism, but these German texts relate hardly at all to the ideal of the ancient polis and express no genuine republicanism. The German humanists, in fact, rarely drew on the world of the ancient city-state to interpret the political forms and values of their everyday life, in the thick of which many of them – Brant of Strasbourg, Pirckheimer of Nuremberg, Conrad Peutinger (1465–1547) of Augsburg – lived and worked. We may apply to most of them what Heinrich Lutz has written of Peutinger:

The educational culture, which humanism so copiously extracted from antiquity and the Middle Ages, lacked any direct point of contact with and any historical connection to the urban life and federal politics that were the forums of most of Peutinger's activities ... For him as humanist the direct sphere of his activity in the politics of semi-autonomous city-states of South Germany and the federation of the Swabian League was free of any overt ideology; while the wider sphere of the Empire was sated with an ideology which was in all respects conservative and in some respects even restorationist.

---

[63] Brant, *Das Narrenschiff*, ed. F. Zarncke, 160. The panels adorned a chamber in the old city hall, which was razed in 1780. Oberlé, "La Pfalz," 38–55. The attribution, if correct, is puzzling, because Brant was a passionate monarchist. Knepper, *Nationaler Gedanke*, 89–106.

[64] Hutten, *Opera*, ed. E. Böcking, 4:409–18 (English: Strauss, ed., *Manifestations*, 81). Hutten was a thoroughgoing monarchist (see Press, "Ulrich von Hutten," 75, 85). Erasmus, however, who in 1511 described Julius Caesar as a bloody tyrant, was not. See Tracy, *Politics*, 27–8. For the Florentine contrast, see Baron, *Crisis*, 48–61; and Skinner, *Foundations*, 1:54–5. At least one German writer from more popular circles identified the Roman emperors with tyranny in the Florentine civic-humanist manner. The anonymous author of *An die Versammlung gemeiner Bauernschaft* wrote in 1525: "Sobaldt die Römer vom gemaynen regiment auf die kayser fielent, sobaldt fieng an all ir jamer under inen so lang, bisz sy arm aigenlewt wurdent, welcher irer gewalt darvor mechtig herschet in aller welt." Hoyer, ed., *An die Versammlung*, 101, lines 27–30.

26

This is all the more remarkable, because Peutinger's example shows how the engagement of urban culture with humanism produced the renewal of the theory of the *imperium* and Imperial patriotism ... Economic and political motives and needs always forged a strong bond between free cities and emperor, for they were common opponents of the expansionist powers of the princely oligarchy. But whereas this was rarely expressed in the practical political world, and nowhere in graspable form, a clear and powerful movement arose in the cultural consciousness of the urban bourgeoisie. The civic Imperial idea, which the *Reformation of Emperor Sigmund* still expressed in a sacral and sentimental form, was both strengthened and secularized through the humanist influence.[65]

The Germans' civic ideal clothed itself not in classical but in Christian images. The ideal of the sacral commune, the sense of common standing before God that the Protestant reformers would refurbish to such good effect, owed less to the polis than to the monastery. As Erasmus asked Paul Volz, an Alsatian abbot, in 1518, "I ask you, what else is a city but a great monastery?"[66] The chief political ideal nourished by classicism in the German free cities was monarchism, which exploited Roman imperial history in favor of the Holy Roman emperors and, more especially, the Habsburg dynasty.[67] Nowhere did this ideal develop more quickly or more strongly than in Alsace during the generation after the Burgundian Wars (1471–7). The leading voice was Jacob Wimpheling (1450–1528) of Sélestat, who loudly and longly insisted that Alsace had always been ruled by German, not French, monarchs; and Sebastian Brant strongly seconded Wimpheling's devotion to Maximilian I.[68] In the next generation, Hieronymus Gebwiler (d. 1543) of Kaysersberg continued the refrain in his *Libertas Germaniae* (1519) and his *Panegyris Carolina* (1521), a long paean to the House of Austria.[69] That this was their solution to the dilemma of the urban ruling classes is clear from Wimpheling's simul-

---

[65] H. Lutz, *Peutinger*, 134–5.

[66] Quoted by Oberman, *Werden und Wertung*, 62 n. 17.

[67] Koenigsberger, *Habsburgs and Europe*, 26–7; Yates, *Astraea*, 1–28. W. Köhler's "Die deutsche Kaiseridee am Anfang des 16. Jahrhunderts" is steeped in the national euphoria of its time (May 1933) and is not of much use. Skinner, *Foundations*, 1:213–21, explores the attraction of princes' courts for the northern humanists.

[68] On Wimpheling, see Mertens, "Maximilian I. und das Elsass," 179–87; Brady, "Themes," 65–76; Herding, "Pädagogik, Politik und Geschichte," 113–30. On Brant, see Knepper, *Nationaler Gedanke*, 68–77; and Ridé, "L'image du germain," 1:303–44.

[69] Mertens, "Reich und Elsass," 160–61, 297, 299.

taneous polemics against the chief opponents of the Habsburgs, the Swiss Confederacy. After Alsatians and Swiss had fought side by side to liberate their lands from the "Latin tyranny" of the Valois dukes of Burgundy, the humanists' praise of the emperor and the House of Austria sounded an unmistakable note of political choice.

Communalism and model neighbors

Darumb so ist zū prisen
die eidgenossenschaft:
von Berne die vil wisen,
von Soloturn mit kraft,
und was zū in da gehört
das haben si dick wol gewert;
si sind mit fromkeit wol behert,
mit trüwen recht behaft.

Von Zug, von Schwiz, von Luzern,
von Glaris feste lüt,
von Uri und von Ursern,
die habent herte hüt.
die von Underwalden
türrent's [trauen sich] wagen balde,
si machent es nit lange,
was in im herzen lit.[70]

Europe's chief exit from the feudal age moved through the dualistic prince-and-estates constitution[71] toward the absolutist monarchy of the early modern era. A second exit formed around what for Germany has been called "the main line of late medieval social development," communalism.[72] Communes, sworn associations of adult males formed to

---

[70] "Therefore let us praise the noble Swiss Confederacy: From Bern come wise folk and from Solothurn strong ones who know how to keep in hand whatever they may have. They are all pious folk and loyal to the end. From Zug they come, from Schwyz, and Lucerne, from Glarus stout, bold lads, from Uri and the Urser land, whose boys are tough as they can be; and men from Unterwalden, too, who are ready for any task. Soon enough they set about whatever is on their minds." Tobler, *Volkslieder*, 1:14.

[71] This term translates *Ständestaat*, on which see the articles collected by Rausch, *Grundlagen*, vol. 2.

[72] Blickle, *Reformation im Reich*, 156; idem, *Untertanen*, 23.

28

get, guard, and exercise rights of self-administration and government, appeared over much of Europe during the twelfth and thirteenth centuries. They developed most richly in areas of dense urbanization and weak royal authority, such as northern and central Italy, South Germany, and the Netherlands.[73] In the countryside, somewhat later, appeared rural communes:

The individuals and families who cultivated the same ground and whose houses stood close to one another in the same hamlet or village were not separate individuals and separate families, living side by side. They were neighbours, *voisins* ... linked by economic and sentimental ties and forming the small society of the "rural community" which was the ancestor of most of the communes – or communal subdivisions existing in our own day.[74]

In German-speaking lands, the late medieval agrarian crisis brought the possibility for greater autonomy to rural communes, as many seigneurs seemed content to trade direct lordship for more secure and bigger incomes, whereas royal and princely administrations were neither quick enough nor powerful enough to step in at the village level.[75] Rural communes became politically significant when they federated to exercise higher judicial and military functions, as they did in two regions on the edges of the Empire, the coastal lands along the North Sea and the Alpine regions.[76] Their potential in South Germany was greatest in Switzerland, great in the unconsolidated areas, such as Upper Swabia and the Upper Rhine, and weakest where successful prince-and-estates constitutions had been established. During the Revolution of 1525, the communal-federal principle emerged as the rebels' leading political ideal, a tremendous extension of the notion of neighborhood.[77] Its realization

[73] Planitz, *Die deutsche Stadt*; Waley, *Italian City-Republics*; Gemperle, *Städteverfassungsgeschichte*; Lestocquoy, *Aux origines de la bourgeosie*. Blickle, *Untertanen*, 51–5, 147, compares urban with rural communes, and the fat volumes of Gierke, *Das deutsche Genossenschaftsrecht*, especially vols. 1 and 2, can be searched with profit.
[74] Bloch, *French Rural History*, 167; and see Blickle, *Untertanen*, 23, on neighborhood and commune.
[75] Blickle, *Revolution von 1525*, 72–4 (English: *Revolution of 1525*, 44–7), and *Untertanen*, 28–43. See Bader, *Studien*, 2:21–62, 292–310, 367–70; Mayer, ed., *Die Anfänge der Landgemeinde*; and Steinbach, "Geschichtliche Grundlagen," 17–72, and "Ursprung und Wesen," both now in his *Collectanea Franz Steinbach*, 487–555, 559–94. For Switzerland, see Carlen, *Landsgemeinde*, 9–10.
[76] Gierke (*Genossenschaftsrecht*, 2:832) recognized the political potential of the rural commune; also see Slicher van Bath, *Boerenvrijheid*, 4, 6.
[77] Gierke, *Genossenschaftsrecht*, 1:515; Peyer, *Verfassungsgeschichte*, 21–6; Blickle, *Untertanen*, 114–15.

Turning Swiss

would have required the political emasculation of the lords of the land, a condition that had already been met only in the nearby Swiss Confederacy. Communal federations had long flourished on the northern slope of the western Alps in Uri, Schwyz, Unterwalden, Zug, and Glarus. The leagues of upland and mountain stockmen had allied with five valley city-states, Zurich, Bern, Lucerne, Fribourg, and Solothurn, and their union became a political model for surrounding peoples. Its attraction radiated into a belt of lands that stretched from the eastern and south-western borders of the modern Confederacy – the leagues of Grau-bünden, Sankt Gallen, Appenzell, and the Thurgau, plus Austrian Vorarlberg – westward through the Swabian Allgäu, Hegau, and Klett-gau, west of Lake Constance, and then across the southern Black Forest to the Upper Rhine valley from Basel downstream past Strasbourg.[78] In this belt, during the fifteenth and sixteenth centuries, "new Switzer-lands" tried to form alongside the old one. First of all was the League above the Lake, which in 1405–8 embraced the city of Sankt Gallen, Appenzell, the lands along the High Rhine (so the Rhine is called above Lake Constance), Voralberg, and parts of Tyrol; and it had a short-lived satellite, the "New League" (1405) in the Swabian Allgäu.[79] A second "new Switzerland" formed in the Graubünden, the three Rhae-tian leagues of mountain folk in the High Rhine and Upper Inn valleys, who won their independence with Swiss aid at the end of the fifteenth century.

The Swiss Confederacy reproduced itself by example, aided by the agitation of fighting men from the rural federations and money from the cities; and wherever their influence spread, noble power waned.[80] The rural cantons preferred to subvert the nobles' subjects, as the League above the Lake did in Vorarlberg, Tyrol, and the Thurgau during

---

[78] This is the zone of what Blickle calls "the corporate-federal state," as distinguished from the dualistic prince-and-estates constitution. *Untertanen*, 114–18; idem, *Revolution von 1525*, 197–223 (English: *Revolution of 1525*, 126–45); for the greater historical context, see Blickle, *Landschaften im alten Reich*. On the general conception of the Confederacy and its development, see the rich, suggestive book by Englert–Faye, *Vom Mythus zur Idee der Schweiz*.

[79] Bilgeri, *Bund ob dem See*; Blickle, "Bäuerliche Rebellionen," 215–27, 256–60.

[80] For Blickle's argument that communalism was antifeudal, see *Untertanen*, 55–60; idem, *Reformation im Reich*, 133, 156, 168. On the spread of the Confederacy, see Gasser, *Die territoriale Entwicklung*, 133–7; and Vasella, "Vom Wesen der Eidgenossenschaft," 165–83.

the Appenzell War; whereas the city-states preferred to buy rights of lordship from nobles, as Zurich did in the Toggenburg. The communal-federal idea embodied "an alternative principle to feudalism," because the commune, resting as it did on the relative equality of heads of households, formed "a threat to the feudal order" that rested on inequality and the exclusion of the common folk from political life.[81] Each of the nearly sixty rural uprisings in this great region between 1336 and 1525, plus every alliance of rural with urban communes, formed a link in the tremendous running social war that began with the Swiss victory at Morgarten in 1315 and ended with the Revolution of 1525.[82]

This movement fed a mounting wave of hatred and fear among the Austrian and other South German nobility, who dreaded the rise of "new Switzerlands" or expansions of the old one. When the Upper Swabian nobles, for example, led by the bishops of Augsburg and Constance, allied against the League above the Lake in 1407, they swore "that we, both as individuals and collectively, shall aid one another faithfully and promptly in the most effective and most direct ways, against the peasants of Appenzell and against all who support them at this time."[83] The League subverted rural subjects wherever its power spread and admitted towns to its ranks as well.[84] "They deprive the nobles against their will of their serfs," wrote a pro-Habsburg chronicler during the Appenzell War, "and they stir up the subjects to refuse taxes and dues, and they make the subjects disobedient."[85] "Peasants!" the Swabian nobles called their foes in this war, though they knew perfectly well that ranged against them were also the burghers of Sankt Gallen and the Vorarlberg towns. Against these "peasants," the nobles procured a

---

[81] Blickle, *Untertanen*, 56–7.

[82] Bierbrauer, "Bäuerliche Revolten im Alten Reich," 62–5, omitting no. 4. According to Schulze, *Bäuerlicher Widerstand*, 88, after 1525 peasants' revolts gradually shifted their target from feudal lordship to the early modern state.

[83] Quoted by Blickle, *Untertanen*, 55. The League also included 1 duke, 7 counts, and 86 knights, and it grew into the Swabian "Gesellschaft mit St. Georgenschild," one of the goals of which was to block the formation of another New League, the satellite federation of the Vorarlbergers sponsored in the Allgäu in 1405. Obenaus, *Recht und Verfassung*, 13–16.

[84] Dierauer, *Geschichte*, 1:483; Bilgeri, *Bund ob dem See*, 66; Baumann, *Geschichte des Allgäus*, 2:35. The New League's name was the "Geburschaft gemainlich in dem Algow."

[85] Quoted by Bilgeri, *Bund ob dem See*, 99; the following quotes in this paragraph are from ibid., 75, 128. The Pope John XXIII referred to below was of the Pisan line and was therefore not recognized by Rome; the same name and number could thus be adopted by the twentieth-century Roman pope.

bull of excommunication in the name of Pope John XXIII, which condemned those "who, seduced by the foe of the human race, after founding a league of communes in that region, participated in many and various
murders, lootings, robberies, and arson against laymen; and they have
aided and abetted such actions, as well as committing them with their
own hands." King Ruprecht crowned this litany with a declaration at
the Peace of Constance (April 4, 1408) that the federation of Appen-
zellers, Sankt Gallers, and "the others who are allied with them" was
"against the Holy Church, the Holy Empire, the electors, princes and
bishops, as well as the nobles, the cities and the common weal of the
land." With these words, the rulers condemned the age's great political
heresy, the belief that the Common Man might rule himself.

The Common Man[86] was a term used by the lords for those who, in
their minds, should only be subjects. The Common Man was not necessarily poor or grievously oppressed – the concept excluded beggars,
criminals, and gypsies and other marginal folk – but he had no possibility
for political life except through common action with others of his kind,
his equals. To the lords' eye, all commoners were "peasants," as the
old legal maxim affirmed: "Only a wall separates the burgher from the
peasant."

The Swiss Confederacy seemed a socially uniform union of "peasants" only to the lords' fearful and hostile eye. In fact, the Confederacy
united two quite different kinds of formations, rural leagues and city-
states, between which important differences and tensions persisted.[87]
Clashes between them punctuated the fifteenth century, for example in
the Toggenburg, where in 1439–42 the Schwyzers tried to liberate the
peasantry from Zurich, which had purchased rights of lordship over the
valley. The ensuing Old Zurich War drove the city-state for a time into
Habsburg arms.[88] After the Burgundian Wars, a plot of some Unter-

---

[86] On this concept, see Blickle, *Untertanen*, 56–7; idem, *Revolution von 1525*, 191–5 (English: *Revolution of 1525*, 122–4). I agree with his critique (p. 194 n. 30 [English: p. 220 n. 43]) of Robert H. Lutz's attempt to restrict the concept to full members of corporations. See R. Lutz, *Wer war der gemeine Mann?*, 5–15. For discussion, see Oberman, "Gospel of Social Unrest"; Press, "Herrschaft, Landschaft"; and Scott, "The Peasants' War," 957, 966. The legal maxim at the end of this paragraph is quoted by H. Planitz, *Die deutsche Stadt*, 229, as a gloss on the Saxon law: "Einen burger und einen gebuer / scheit nicht me wen ein czuhen und ein muer."

[87] Peyer, *Verfassungsgeschichte*, 21–44; Bilgeri, *Bund ob dem See*, 101–5.

[88] Dierauer, *Geschichte*, 2:41–9, 70–162; Raiser, *Territorialpolitik*, 82.

walden politicians to subvert some of Lucerne's rural subjects led to the Compact of Stans on December 22, 1481.[89] The city-states surrendered their goal of a more centralized confederation, and the rural states renounced the right to aid the subjects of others and even pledged themselves to help suppress illegal assemblies of subjects everywhere. The spirit of this compromise, a severe setback for the rural powers, was summed up by its remarkable mediator, Brother Nicholas of Flüe (1417–87), who wrote that "obedience is the greatest form of love that exists on earth or in heaven. Therefore, make sure that you obey one another."[90]

The Swiss Confederacy presented two faces to the South German free cities. The oligarchs might see in it a federation of urban oligarchies like themselves, which Zurich, Lucerne, and Bern surely were; whereas peasants might take Uri, Schwyz, and Glarus as proof that ordinary folk needed no lords. To the nobles both faces might appear ugly, though not equally so, for both challenged the division of society into a few lords and many subjects; and both benefited from the enhancement of communal values of peace, unity, and justice through Christian symbols and language. From the village commune to the Church Universal,[91] collective norms and religious values were capable of forming a great variety of combinations, from extremely conservative ideals to very radical ones.

Old Switzerland gave birth to a powerful triple marriage of communal with Christian ideas during the era of the Reformation. First, in 1524–5 the program of communal federalism swept out of Upper Swabia and the Upper Rhine into the lands further northward.[92] Secondly, the Zwinglian ideal of the city as sacral corporation moved through the southern free cities during the mid-1520s. "A Christian man is nothing

---

[89] Dierauer, *Geschichte*, 2:318–36; Feller, *Geschichte Berns*, 1:431–2; and Heusler, *Verfassungsgeschichte*, 136–42, who calls the compact "die erste eigentliche Verfassungsurkunde der Eidgenossenschaft." Peyer, *Verfassungeschichte*, 36–7, is more skeptical. See now Walder, "Bestimmungen des Stanser Verkommnisses," 80–94, and "Entstehungsgeschichte des Stanser Verkommnisses," 263–92.

[90] Quoted by Feller, *Geschichte Berns*, 1:434; and see Peyer, *Verfassungsgeschichte*, 40–1.

[91] Blickle, *Revolution von 1525*, 196–244 (English: *Revolution of 1525*, 125–54); Black, *Council and Commune*, 204–6.

[92] Blickle, *Revolution von 1525*, 197–212 (English: *Revolution of 1525*, 126–37); Scott, "The Peasants' War," 710–13. On Zwingli's political ideas, see Potter, *Zwingli*, 123 n. 1; Locher, *Zwinglische Reformation*, 167–71.

33

more than a good and loyal citizen," wrote Huldrych Zwingli (1484–
1531) of Zurich, and "the Christian city is nothing more than the Christian Church."[93] In the third wave, Swiss Anabaptism spread northward
in the wake of the lost Revolution of 1525, seeking its New Jerusalem
at Strasbourg but finding it in 1533–4 at Münster in far Westphalia.[94]
The German Protestant reformers as a group "gave the commune its
first [religious] legitimation," though they later "sacrificed their pref-
erence for an autonomous Christian commune to the state-church."[95]
Anabaptism, for its part, dribbled away into tiny rural sects. By 1550,
Old Switzerland had lost forever its role as model neighbor to the other
South Germans.

"Turning Swiss": a South German revery

Es sigend stet oder puren
klein ist der underscheid,
es teil ein wenig muren,
es ist in allen leid:
si wären selb gern heren
und sind im doch ze grob;
küng, do solt in's weren,
so meret sich din lob.
Wan es hört dinem adel
und diner herschaft zū.
Erschütt den pfawenwadel,
es wirt in noch ze frū.
Mann muss das unfich stöuben,
So belibt das essen rein;

---

[93] *Z*, 14:424, lines 19–22. Potter, *Zwingli*, 123 n. 1, cites the older literature on Zwingli's political
theology, and Locher, *Zwinglische Reformation*, 167–71, boldly stresses the corporate nature of
Zwingli's concept of liberty. So does Walton, "Reformation," 140–3, though his intemperate
attack (138–9) on Ozment's *Reformation in the Cities*, especially 120, is based on a misunderstanding of Ozment's argument.
[94] Clasen, *Anabaptism*, 1–29, whose maps of Anabaptist communities (pp. 19, 23) and figures on
conversions, spread of doctrines, and origins of leaders (p. 21) show that Anabaptism's heartland
– Switzerland, the Rhine Valley, Swabia, and Tyrol – was also the heartland of the Revolution
of 1525. See Scott, "The Peasants' War," 969, 969 n. 228; idem, "Die Bauernkriege," 289–
92.
[95] Blickle, *Reformation im Reich*, 128–9.

mit pfifen und mit töuben
Füert man die brüte hein.[96]

"Everyone wants to be free, just like the Swiss," complained a Hessian official, Ludwig von Boyneburg, early in the sixteenth century.[97] What was meant by "free like the Swiss" is suggested in a song from 1525:

> The peasants tried to learn
> Evil tricks from the Swiss
> And become their own lords, ...[98]

The idea's two elements were the commons' will to remove the lords and rule themselves and their ability to fight for their freedom. In this sense, many South German peasants were already "half-Swiss," as some were called in a poem from the time of the Burgundian Wars:

> And the rugged Black Forest
> Sent its ugly folk,
> Who are not to be despised,
> For they are half-Swiss ...[99]

The confederates, therefore, were the models of armed struggle for self-rule in South Germany, whose peoples were widely suspected of wanting to "turn Swiss."

At the outset, it bears repeating that the conception and forms of liberty then must not be confused with the modern idea that the liberty of some requires the liberty of all. The Confederacy had its "common

---

[96] "The townsmen or the peasants, there's little difference there. A wall alone divides them, too bad about them all! They'd love to be great lords, although they are too crude. O king, if you prevent it, great praise will be your pay. The task is for your nobles and for your lordship fair. The peacock's tail is waving but its time is not yet come. First the vermin must be cooked before the meal is done. Then to sounds of fife and drum the bride can be led home." Tobler, *Volkslieder*, 2:28. The peacock ("pfauenwadel") was a Habsburg symbol. *Unfich* = *Unvieh* = *Ungeziefer*, and *touben* = *blasen*.

[97] Neuhaus, "Supplikationen," 136. Boyneburg was a leading figure in the Hessian government of Landgrave William (r. 1485–1509). Gundlach, *Die hessischen Zentralbehörden*, 1:36, 101, 103, 115, 135–6, 140, 279, 293; 2:28, 108. The only study of connections between Swiss and South German ideas is by Stern, "Zusammenhang," 13–29.

[98] Liliencron, *Volklieder*, 3:448, stanza 6.

[99] Quoted by Roth von Schreckenstein, *Reichsritterschaft*, 2:89. For the belief that peasants wanted to "turn Swiss," see Feller and Bonjour, *Geschichtsschreibung*, 1:113.

custodies" (*gemeine Vogteien*), ruled by groups of the full members (*Orte*); it had city-states whose subjects were ruled by urban oligarchies;[100] and even its rural states were divided between full citizens and dependents (*Hintersassen*). The essential point remains, however, that each of these formations appeared subversive of law and order to the nobles, who believed that they alone could rightly rule. It is only from this point of view, which was the dominant one in that social order, that the threat from the Confederacy to noble lordship in South Germany, as a model to be imitated by the subjects of others and not just as a territorial rival, can correctly be estimated. The idea that confederate power fed on the destruction of lords and lordship was fact, not fantasy. So testified the words one poet put in the mouth of a nobleman:

> The Common Man can't be beaten,
> For the Swiss take no prisoners.
> Therefore, let's get out of here,
> For they are wild with anger
> And will murder and despoil
> The nobles on the spot.[101]

This was what a later French writer would call giving the nobles "the Swiss treatment." A combination of fear and class contempt lay behind the practice, common also to Maximilian and his courtiers, of lumping all Swiss under the epithet "peasants,"[102] by which they meant not just farmers but all folk who ought to be ruled by others.

The Swiss were believed to be the natural friends and even liberators of other South Germans. One Swabian count reported in 1460 about a rebellion in the Hegau, "They have received in this affair notable support, aid, and counsel from the Schaffhausers and other Swiss fellows, which helped them quite a lot; and we believe that the Swiss have allowed this all to happen."[103] Years later, another writer warned that

---

[100] Bern had no territorial estates at all. Walder, "Reformation," 474.
[101] Liliencron, *Volkslieder*, 1:433, no. 93, lines 284–8. The following quote is from Bitton, *French Nobility*, 25.
[102] Mömmsen, *Eidgenossen*, 283.
[103] Franz, ed., *Quellen*, 61, lines 23–6, also quoted by Laufs, *Der Schwäbische Kreis*, 72. The following quote is from Klüpfel, *Urkunden*, 1:325, and see 280, 294, 319, 328, 345–6, 373.

"if the Swiss invade Duke Ulrich's [of Württemberg] lands, I fear that all the peasants will join them." So powerful was the belief in this bond that in 1525 Leonhard von Eck (c. 1480–1550), Bavaria's shrewd chancellor, long suspected that the rural risings were a Swiss trick, a smoke screen for their strike to restore Ulrich in Württemberg.[104] Such fears gained powerful substance from the fact that the peasants of South Germany possessed weapons and knew how to use them.[105]

Free cities, too, could turn Swiss. Zurich, Lucerne, Bern, Solothurn, and Schaffhausen had done so before 1500; Basel, Mulhouse, and Rottweil followed them during the sixteenth century's first twenty years. For a city to turn Swiss meant, despite protestations of the Swiss chroniclers to the contrary,[106] for it to remove itself from the direct jurisdiction of emperor and Diet. This was charged by a hostile source during the Cities' War, which said of the free cities, "They want to turn Swiss [*sweytzer werden*], so that they can escape His Majesty's obedience." Similar charges were made against the Swabian League,

> the League will leave the Empire
> and place its loyalty elsewhere,
> just like the Swiss,

and against the Alsatian powers whom Maximilian corralled into the revived Lower Union in 1493. The attraction of a confederacy, old or new, for the urban ruling classes lay less in protection from Habsburg aggrandizement than in the security from predatory princes and nobles that the emperor could or would not provide. This need is suggested by a song that describes a defeat by Nuremberg of Margrave Albrecht of Brandenburg-Ansbach during the Cities' War:

> Many nobles lost their lives
> And were buried here and there

---

[104] Eck to Duke William of Bavaria, Feb. 11 and 27, 1525, in Vogt, ed., *Die bayerische Politik*, 380, 398, and see 400, 408, 411.
[105] Hoyer, *Militärwesen*, 35–45.
[106] Mommsen, *Eidgenossen*, 58–60, 73–4, 81, 85, 103; Gasser, *Die territoriale Entwicklung*, 28–9, 102, 140–1, 152–3, 155; E. Schubert, *König*, 294–6. The following two quotes are from E. Schubert, *König*, 296. See Sigrist, "Reichsreform und Schwabenkrieg," 115–18.

Turning Swiss

In Bavaria and in Franconia;
All free cities should thank
The Nurembergers for this deed.[107]

Among the urban commons as well, the idea of turning Swiss took root. Swabian chroniclers noted sympathies for the Swiss foe in the free cities during the Swabian War of 1499, and in 1519 a Bavarian lawyer wrote from Augsburg that

it is said here that some of the electors are gathered at Frankfurt to deliberate on the Imperial election and other matters. Perhaps they will elect a king and then, with Württemberg's aid, attack Nuremberg, as some folk here think. For the common folk here stupidly say that they want to turn Swiss, come what may. They see what is happening and know what is going on at Ulm – the Württemberg matter – and that the Swabian League's councillors have no common purpose. The commons make many such stupid, evil statements.[108]

The year of Maximilian's death and Charles's election, indeed, marked a high point of worries about South Germany's turning Swiss. Not without reason, for a plan really was drafted then for a general alliance of the free cities with the confederates in preparation for the reign of an absentee Spanish or French emperor.[109] Just this was feared by some powerful men, among them Cardinal Albrecht of Mainz, who mused that "if the Common Man is burdened with a general tax, we'll hear wondrous things... And the cities and other powers will join the Swiss, each doing his best to find security where he may."[110] Even more stridently came the voice of a Brabantish councillor to Charles V, Maximilian van Bergen (d. 1521), who urged the young monarch to take Württemberg from the Swabian League in 1520 with the argument that otherwise the captured duchy and the free cities would join the Confederacy, and the entire German South and West would become "one vast commune."[111] During this same time of transition, in 1519, Ulrich Arzt wrote home to Augsburg of his fear that the old prophecy would

---

[107] Liliencron, *Volkslieder*, 1:423, no. 91, stanza 19.
[108] Quoted by Jörg, *Deutschland*, 30 n. 4.
[109] StA Basel, Deutschland B 2 I, no. 23. This fragment is cited by Gollwitzer, "Capitaneus," 275–6.
[110] *RTA, jR*, 1:843–4, no. 379 (c. June 27, 1519), also quoted by Endres, "Zünfte und Unterschichten," 152 n. 3.
[111] See Chapter 4, section titled "Maximilian van Bergen and the Austrian Way."

now come true, that "when a cow stands on the bridge at Ulm and moos, she'll be heard in the middle of Switzerland."[112]

The cow was to moo not only at Ulm. In the midst of the bloody summer of 1525, a South German pamphleteer predicted that tyranny would last "until perhaps the prophecy [*prophecey*] and the old proverb will be fulfilled, that a cow will stand on top of the Schwanberg in Franconia and will bellow, and she'll be heard in the middle of Switzerland."[113] At this point, in the midst of the Revolution of 1525, the idea of South Germany becoming one vast confederacy, a new Switzerland, received its most pointed exposition from this writer, the Swabian author of *An die versamlung gemayner Pawerschafft*, which has been called

the only known evidence from peasant circles that takes up the burning question of revolutionary political goals and their military achievement.[114]

The pamphlet explicitly draws the parallel between the rise of the Swiss Confederacy and the great movement then underway in South Germany. The root of such movements lies in the greed and tyranny of the lords, as a motto on the famous title woodcut says: "Who makes Switzerland grow? The lords' greed!"[115] The entire Confederacy, the pamphlet proclaims,

grew out of the blatant tyranny of the nobles and other lords, who drove and forced the Common Man unceasingly and without scruple, against all justice, with their unchristian, tyrannical violence, motivated by their own arrogance, mischievous power, and plans. This all had to be abolished and wiped out through great wars, bloodshed, and combat, just as the Swiss chronicles and many other reliable histories and books tell.[116]

These great deeds ought to be imitated by the present movement, for

---

[112] Arzt to Conrad Peutinger, Feb. 9, 1519, quoted by H. Lutz, *Peutinger*, 147.

[113] Hoyer, ed., *An die Versammlung*, 118, lines 16–20, and the editor's comment at pp. 23–4. The Schwanberg lies near Iphofen, east of Kitzingen. The proverb was collected by Johannes Agricola in the sixteenth century, whence it came into the collection of the Brothers Grimm, *Deutsche Sagen*, no. 293 (here in the 2d ed. of Berlin, 1865, 1:336), though they incorrectly place this Schwanberg in Styria (my thanks to Siegfried Hoyer for bringing this text to my attention).

[114] Hoyer, ed., *An die Versammlung*, 44. On this pamphlet and its significance, see Buszello, *Der deutsche Bauernkrieg*, and idem, "Die Staatsvorstellung des 'gemeinen Mannes.' "

[115] Hoyer, ed., *An die Versammlung*, 87, line 15, and p. 118 lines 22–3.

[116] Ibid., 96, lines 36–97, line 8.

39

what indescribably great deeds were often performed by the poor peasants, your neighbors, the Swiss! How often one thought to arm and catch the Swiss unawares, thinking that each could take care of three Swiss, or that they be beaten by shepherds and church wardens. Most such folk were driven back, and kings, emperors, princes, and lords made themselves ridiculous, no matter how many and well armed they were. And whenever these Swiss have had to defend their land, wives, and children against arrogant violence, they mostly have won and earned great honor thereby. This has doubtless happened from the power and decree of God. How else could the Confederacy, which daily grows in strength, have arisen from only three simple peasants?[117]

Those three peasants were named "Uri," "Schwyz," and "Unterwalden." To the author of *An die versamlung gemayner Pawerschafft*, these founders of Old Switzerland stood as heroic models to those of his own day who strove to create new Switzerlands along similar communal-federal lines.

How realistic were the notions of turning Swiss? Quite realistic for the free cities closest to the Confederacy, as the admissions of Basel and other towns, plus the plans for Swiss–South German urban federations during the 1520s, show. The one great precondition, however, for a "Swissification" of South Germany was the liberation of the countryside and its peoples from seigneurial and princely power. Only then could federations form between rural and urban communes in the Swiss manner.

How would a liberation of the land have affected the cities? The urban governments were also, in their own ways, lords over their own citizenries and over the subjects of their territories, not to speak of the seigneurial powers of individual urban families. Then, too, the notion of political liberation of the land might well strike similar sparks – as the cooperation of burghers and miners with the peasants in 1525 suggests – among the urban Common Man as well. Further, even though the urban governments took little or no part in the revival and intensification of serfdom in the wake of the late medieval agrarian crisis,[118] there is some reason

---

[117] Ibid., 117, line 35, through 118, lines 1–13. On the communal-federal program in 1525, see Blickle, *Revolution von 1525*, 156, 199–200, 209 (English: *Revolution of 1525*, 103, 128–9, 134–5).

[118] Blickle, *Revolution von 1525*, 105–11, 254–6 (English: *Revolution of 1525*, 68–71, 170–1).

to believe in a "marked divergence of aims within, and between, the rural and urban populations" of South Germany.[119]

A second reason for reservations about the Swissifying potential of South Germany concerns the peculiar character of the Swiss rural powers. The Forest Cantons' peoples had developed away from mixed grazing-farming economies toward the classic pastoral economy since the thirteenth century,[120] making them ultimately as dependent on urban markets as were the farmers of the city-strewn landscapes of Upper Swabia and the Upper Rhine. The Swiss cities were small, however, and the rural federations developed politically *before* they associated with the city-states. The Swiss uplanders had the great advantages that their valleys were defensible and their economies required much less labor from the men than the farms of the lowlands did, which gave them the leisure to train for war.

Could the rural folk of the valleys and the plains have duplicated the uplanders' achievements? Probably not, for the performances of the rebel armies in 1525 suggest that their great weaknesses lay not in getting and employing weapons but in organization and strategy – political weaknesses, therefore, that indicate a level of political experience inferior to that of the Swiss.[121] Their failures contrast dramatically with Swiss performance in this age of glory, when the confederates dominated battlefields from Grandson to Novara. There were other reasons, of course, for this contrast. For one thing, the Swiss uplanders had the towns with them, not allied with the seigneurs, the princes, and the Habsburgs against them. For another, the lower valleys and plains were hardly defensible, particularly against mercenary armies, coordinated arms, superior communications, and credit. It was a question of walls. In the Alps, the mountain walls protected the Common Man; in the valleys and plains, the city walls shut him out.

By the opening decades of the sixteenth century, therefore, the pos-

---

[119] Scott, "Reformation and Peasants' War, II," 166; however, his findings might have been different had he studied a larger town over a longer period of time.
[120] Peyer, *Verfassungsgeschichte*, 226–7. Recent work on village history, especially David Sabean's seminal *Landbesitz*, which treats a farming population in Upper Swabia, emphasizes social differentiation within the villages and should make us cautious about extending conclusions in either direction across the lines between farming and pastoral peoples.
[121] Hoyer, *Militärwesen*, 180.

sibility for a Swissification of the German South was not very great. The urban governments allied with the lords and the monarchy, not the peasantry; the nobles and princes were too powerful to be crushed and driven out; and the peasants had neither the political skills nor the defensible homelands that so favored the Swiss uplanders. Confederation does not seem to have been a very convincing alternative to the centralized dynastic states, in which the coercion of the peasants was "displaced upwards towards a centralized, militarized summit – the Absolutist State. Diluted at the village level, it became concentrated at the 'national' [or 'territorial'] level."[122] For a short while, the Confederacy nonetheless continued to play the role of countermodel, a standing reminder to the lords of why they supported the king or the prince and to the subjects that lordship was not necessarily God's eternal ordinance for the world. Viewed realistically, however, the role of the Swiss rural folk in this countermodel came from their military prowess, which was not a sign of economic power but quite the opposite. Besides, to the age of overseas discoveries and empire, the beginnings of capitalistic manufacturing, and far-flung trade – when a man could sit in Augsburg and invest in the American trade – self-governing commons were a political curiosity. Soon, the role of countermodel to absolutism would pass to the United Netherlands.[123]

For all these reasons, turning Swiss proved a very limited alternative for the urban oligarchs of South Germany during the first half of the sixteenth century – an alternative, that is, to the search for safety under the Imperial eagle's wings. It was an issue faced sooner or later by most self-governing cities in Europe, and it is "not clear that the city-states resisted this form of 'domination' all that much."[124] Perhaps they did not because the alternatives all looked so bleak, although in South Germany it took an entire century after the Cities' War of 1449–53 to make the situation clear.

---

[122] Anderson, *Lineages*, 18–19.
[123] Polišenský, *Thirty Years War*, 264.
[124] Wallerstein, *World-System*, 1:173.

2

The free cities under Frederick III and Maximilian I, 1450–1500

Under Maximilian I, the South German free cities more or less became clients of the Crown. Faced with the rivalry between the House of Habsburg and the great princely houses of the South, plus the princes' collective pressure on the cities in the Imperial Diet, the free cities had to choose between old-fashioned urban federations and Habsburg patronage. They generally chose the latter, and from their choices arose two great alliances – the Swabian League (1488–1534) and the Lower Union (est. 1474, 1493) – and two dramatic South German wars – the Swabian War of 1499 and the Bavarian War of 1504.

The problem of Imperial government, 1450–1500

> Und Maria die edel kungin
> die woll unser helfern sin
> und woll den steten helfen usser not,
> wan es tut werlich not,
> dass sie einander bibestan,
> si musten anders den herren zu dienst gan,
> als es den steten gescheen ist,
> Wissenburk, Lüttich, Menz bezwungen ist
> von den herren wonsan,
> Von den sachen ich lan.
> . . . .
> Ich wunsch den steten gluck und er,
> dar zu aller selikeit,
> dass sie bliben bi ir gerechtikeit,

43

Turning Swiss

dass sie da von nit werden getrungen
und nit werden von den herren bezwungen![1]

The Holy Roman Empire's overriding political problem between about 1450 and the coming of the Reformation was the establishment of a public peace (*Landfriede*) to protect law and order.[2] This became the central issue in the efforts between 1495 and 1521 to create a dualistic or limited monarchy through such new institutions as a High Court (*Reichskammergericht*), a Governing (regency) Council (*Reichsregiment*), administrative districts called "Circles" (*Reichskreise*), and a property tax (*Gemeiner Pfennig*). The chief beneficiaries of these efforts were not the monarchy or the free cities but the great princes, who through the Imperial Diet advanced their claims to collective control of justice, law and order, and taxes in the Empire.[3]

The movement for law and order, which began in South Germany around 1466, seems at first glance to have been made to order for the free cities, who wanted "good government, the public peace, law and order and sound coinage."[4] Yet the urban governments never truly warmed to the constitutional reforms. Only twenty-four of them sent envoys to the great reform Diet at Worms in 1495, and a deep suspicion of the reforms lingered on in their city halls.[5] The oligarchies feared not law and order but law and order as defined and controlled by the princes, for the reforms proved a major step toward what Jean Bodin later described as "an aristocratic principality, in which the Emperor is only the first magnate."[6] In the Diet's two upper houses, those of the electors and the princes, sat the dynasties that had long striven to humble and subjugate the free cities.[7] The Bavarian Wittelsbachs, for example,

---

[1] "Mary, noble Queen of Heaven, who offers us your aid, help the cities in their need that they should stand together in the peril of this day. Else must they serve the princes, as cities have before; as Wissembourg, Liège, and Mainz were crushed to the lords' great delight, so far as I can see.... The cities should have luck and honor and happiness as well, that they stick to their proper rights, that they still defend those rights and outrun the princes' grasp." Hans Judensint of Speyer, in Liliencron, *Volkslieder*, 2:36, no. 132, lines 184–93, 199–203.

[2] Angermeier, *Königtum*, 503–66.

[3] Wiesflecker, *Maximilian*, 2:226.

[4] Angermeier, "Begriff und Inhalt," 181–205; F. H. Schubert, *Reichstage*, 57–87.

[5] Laufs, "Reichsstädte und Reichsreform," 185; Angermeier, *Königtum*, 421–35; Wuttke, "Wunderdeutung und Politik," 223–4.

[6] Bodin, *Six Books of the Commonwealth*, chap. 5 (trans. M. J. Tooley, 67). See F. H. Schubert, *Reichstage*, 360–82.

[7] E. Schubert, *König*, 307.

briefly ruled Regensburg and conducted a long war of nerves against Augsburg and Donauwörth. Augsburg, wrote Leonhard von Eck in 1525 to his lord, "is Your Princely Grace's enemy and fears no one more than Your Grace."[8] Their Wittelsbach cousins in the Palatinate had tried for years to bludgeon the tiny city of Wissembourg into their power.[9] Next came the Hohenzollerns, whose two lines, Swabian and Franconian, were old foes of the towns. Their family seat, the fortress of Hohenzollern, perched on a magnificent conical mountain in the upper Neckar valley, "the very best in all Swabia," as an Augsburger wrote.[10] In 1423, the allied towns laid a grim, year-long siege to this castle, took it, and razed it. The Franconian Hohenzollerns, for their part, maintained a generations-long feud, amounting almost to a family religion, with Nuremberg. To such families and to the prince bishops of the South, a series of free cities – Mainz, Erfurt, Worms, Boppard, and Regensburg – lost their liberties through persuasion, pressure, and force.[11] Both princes and cities marked these events. The Elector Palatine, for example, warned Wissembourg to mind "the example of the Bopparders and what was promised to them [i.e., by King Maximilian] but not delivered." On the other side, a Frankfurter reflected on the fall of Boppard to the Elector of Trier in 1497: "And there was much talk and wonderment among the Common Man, that the princes of the Empire could undertake such a campaign and do such violence against a free city, despite the established public peace [of 1495] and other laws, and against the emperor's edicts." Boppard's situation differed little from those of other cities that lay close to ambitious princes, such as Ulm, Reutlingen, and Esslingen to the dukes of Württemberg.

Some free cities fell to their bishops, giving credence to Willibald Pirckheimer's charge that the bishops were the cities' greatest foes.[12] In fact, the political distinction between lay and ecclesiastical princes grew less significant than formerly, as the major sees were becoming dependencies of the great families.[13] The forty-six bishops who sat in the

---

[8] Eck to Duke William of Bavaria, Feb. 8, 1525, in Jörg, *Deutschland*, 99 n. 3.
[9] Cohn, *Rhine Palatinate*, 12–13, 64, 66, 188; Gollwitzer, "Capitaneus," 252–60.
[10] Zink, "Chronik 1368–1468," 230, lines 13–14.
[11] Gollwitzer, "Capitaneus," 265–73, and the following quotes are from ibid., 265, and Ziehen, *Mittelrhein und Reich*, 2:57.
[12] See Chapter 1, section titled "Proud weakness: an urban paradox."
[13] Feine, *Bezetzung der Reichsbistümer*, 305–10; Raab, "Die oberdeutschen Hochstifte," 81–5; Dug-

Diet were commonly the cousins, uncles, nephews, and brothers of the lay princes in this great age of princely pluralists. No less than four sons of the Elector Palatine Philip (d. 1508), for example, became bishops, a record that their Bavarian cousins, the margraves of Baden, the Wettins of Saxony, and the Hohenzollerns strove with considerable success to match. This enhancement of the great dynasties' power made slimmer the probability that the Imperial Diet might act on the cities' grievances. That the princes were individually and collectively the greatest foes of urban liberties in South Germany can hardly be doubted, though it is worth remembering that until quite recently the emperors had mortgaged urban liberties to princes with great abandon.[14] Well into the reign of Frederick III (1440–93), more cities fell to royal borrowing than to princely threats and armies, and many of them never regained their independence.

In the Diet, the free cities' struggle for rights nonetheless met resistance from the great princes.[15] The cities claimed the right to sit on committees, to propose and be consulted on legislation, and to veto measures from the upper houses, rights that were finally recognized in 1648. Concentration on the struggle's legal aspects has obscured its political significance, which derived from the growing problems of Imperial finance in the later fifteenth century. New military pressure from the Ottoman Turks struck a treasury ravaged by the royal practice of mortgaging incomes and by the monarchy's failure to establish the principle of regular taxation.[16] From Frederick III's point of view, Austria was carrying the Empire on its back. The free cities, on the other hand, tended to be seen as bottomless purses, and hence pressure mounted on them to assume an ever greater share of the civil and military costs of government.

---

gan, "Church as Institution," 153–6. The number of bishops is taken from Aulinger, *Bild*, 361–2; and the Palatine example is from Cohn, *Rhine Palatinate*, 38–9.

[14] Landwehr, *Verpfändung der Reichsstädte*, 109–1; E. Schubert, *König*, 151–71. Of 107 cities in the royal domain, only 13 were never mortgaged, and of 1,112 mortgages collected by Landwehr, only 64 occurred after Frederick III's time.

[15] Isenmann, "Reichsstadt," 114–41. On the fixing of the cities' constitutional position, see idem, "Zur Frage der Reichsstandschaft," 91–110; E. Schubert, *König*, 332–4; and G. Schmidt, *Städtetag*, 247–90.

[16] F. H. Schubert, *Reichstage*, 87, argues for defense against the Ottoman Turks as the major cause of centralization. See Isemann, "Reichsfinanzen," 8, 70–3, 75. For belief in Nuremberg's inexhaustible wealth, see E. Franz, *Nürnberg*, 169–75.

During the first half of the 1470s, responding to the same fiscal and military pressures that were gradually shaping the Imperial Diet into a fixed form, the free cities constructed their own instrument of solidarity and voice for common interests, the Urban Diet.[17] At ten assemblies called to Frankfurt, Esslingen, and Speyer between 1471 and 1474, and then at fifteen more during the 1480s, envoys of the urban governments debated and formulated common policy both toward the actions, or proposed actions, of the Imperial Diet and toward the protection of individual cities from invasions of their governmental rights and liberties by princes. The true "motor" of this development were the taxes imposed to fight the expansion of Ottoman power, the pressure for which was more compelling, perhaps, further eastward than it was among the Rhenish cities, whose resistance to taxation culminated under Strasbourg's leadership at the Diet of 1481. The electors and princes, grumbled Hans von Seckingen (d. 1509) of Strasbourg, who had won his knight's spurs on the field of Nancy in 1477, fix the taxes, "while the townsmen sit outside the door like snuffling dogs."[18] Lacking the rights of consultation or veto, the urban envoys could only protest against assessments they felt were too high, especially a general property tax, which they called "eternal tribute" and "eternal dues."[19] "We fear," they complained to the Diet of Frankfurt in 1489, "that the intention is to place an eternal cost and high tax on the cities,"[20] and the first general property tax, the Common Penny of 1495, had to be abandoned – partly because of urban opposition – by 1505, bringing back the old matricular levies, called "Roman months."

The need of the cities and especially their merchants for law and order might argue for a more favorable attitude toward financial support

---

[17] A list of Urban Diets for this era is given in Appendix A. See G. Schmidt, *Städtetag*, 17–143; Isemann, "Reichsstadt," 90–1.

[18] Quoted by Isenmann, "Reichsstadt," 121. On Seckingen, see ibid., 117–18; Brady, *Ruling Class*, 59–60.

[19] Quoted by Isenmann, "Reichsfinanzen," 216. See idem, "Reichsstadt," 74 n. 192; Rowan, "Imperial Taxes and German Politics," 203–17; and G. Schmidt, *Städtetag*, 331–51.

[20] Quoted by Isenmann, "Reichsfinanzen," 135 n. 349. See ibid., 190–216; idem, "Reichsstadt," 68–82; Rowan, "Imperial Taxes and German Politics." The levy of 1489, for example, was not paid by 17 percent of the electors; 32 percent of the free cities; 80 percent of the archbishops; 68 percent of the bishops; 69 percent of the lay princes; and 77 percent of the counts, barons, and prelates. Isenmann, "Reichsstadt," 69. It is not yet clear who was favored and who not by the Common Penny, though the princes scuttled it (my thanks to Peter Blickle for pointing this out to me). See Schulze, "Reichstage und Reichssteuern," 43–58.

for the Imperial governmental reform; but the stake of the free cities in
what the reforms established was outweighed by their fear of *who* established it.[21] The fear seems to have been justified. In the Governing
Council established in 1500, for example, the cities got only two of the
twenty seats, and these were to rotate quarterly among four pair of larger
towns.[22] They received no direct voice in the appointment of justices to
the High Court, though some towns did have weight in nominations
from the Swabian and Upper Rhenish Circles.[23] From the towns' point
of view, therefore, the reformed Imperial constitution and the Diet had
become the upper nobility's instrument for collective financial pressure
on the cities, different in form and tempo from individual princes' attempts to subjugate particular towns, but in the end leading just as surely
to submission and ruin. Against such instruments, however, only political
action, solidarity, and alliances would serve, for walls and cannon were
powerless. The need for political countermeasures to this creeping threat
was the root of the alliance that formed between the urban governments
and the monarchy under Maximilian I.[24]

There are both light and shadow in the history of relations between
monarchy and cities before Maximilian's time. The free cities, many of
whom had gained their freedom *from* the kings, enjoyed relatively good
ties to King Sigmund (r. 1410–37), who, like his Luxemburg predecessors, had borrowed heavily from the urban bankers, especially the
Nurembergers.[25] Though the cities were also invited regularly to royal
assemblies and sometimes given parity with the princes in committee –
this was the age of the expensive Hussite wars – they also suffered from
Sigmund's free-spending ways and his practice of mortgaging cities with
royal abandon.[26]

---

[21] Laufs, "Reichsstädte und Reichsreform," 172; G. Schmidt, *Städtetag*, 289–97.

[22] The cities' order of rotation was: Cologne and Augsburg; Lübeck and Strasbourg; Goslar and Nuremberg; and Frankfurt and Ulm. Schmauss, ed., *Neue und vollständigere Sammlung der Reichs-Abschiede*, 2:58, para. 4. Their envoys were no more punctual than others were. Janssen, ed., *Frankfurts Reichscorrespondenz*, 2,2:665, no. 819.

[23] Smend, *Reichskammergericht*, 110–12, 265–7, 278. In the Franconian Circle, the margraves of Brandenburg and the three bishops (Bamberg, Würzburg, and Freising) claimed exclusive right to appoint justices. Hartung, *Geschichte*, 1:168–82.

[24] Wiesflecker, *Maximilian*, four volumes and a fifth promised, is now the standard work, though Ulmann, *Maximilian*, is still very useful. See now Benecke, *Maximilian I*, which is erratic but often suggestive.

[25] E. Schubert, *König*, 334; Stromer, *Oberdeutsche Hochfinanz 1350–1450*, 436–60.

[26] See Berthold, "Städte und Reichsreform," 59–111, who is properly cautious about asserting

Cities under Frederick III and Maximilian I

Frederick III's long reign, which brought the crown once more to the House of Austria, also brought the cities much trouble. One decade into his reign, the Cities' War smashed the urban leagues and sent the towns scurrying to neighboring princes for protection. Frederick inaugurated a two-pronged policy for rebuilding Habsburg power: the stubborn redemption of all titles, rights, and incomes the Crown had lost through mortgage or default; and the erection of a network of Habsburg clients in South Germany.[27] A second-rate dynasty in a sensitive region, such as the margraves of Baden on the Upper Rhine, was a prime candidate for Habsburg patronage, though the marshaling of smaller powers – counts, knights, prelates, and free cities – into the system was the work of a later time. Frederick put little reliance on the cities, and their oligarchies returned his mistrust in kind.

Maximilian's South German system, 1488–98

> Hören, ir lieben gesellen,
> und losen nüwe mer,
> ich will üch etwas erschellen,
> das kompt frömd hieher,
> als mir ist worden kund,
> wie dass küng Maximilian
> hab gemacht ein nüwen pund.[28]

Well before the princes and electors, with Maximilian's grudging cooperation, began to inaugurate the Imperial constitutional reforms, a new partnership of the king with the cities was forming in the South.[29] It took the form of two military alliances: The Lower Union, founded on the Upper Rhine in 1474, was reorganized under Habsburg patronage in 1493; and the Swabian League came into being in 1488. The biggest

---

any fixed relationship between cities and Crown, though Koller, "Die Aufgabe der Städte," 216, believes their support was vital to judicial reform. See now G. Schmidt, *Städtetag*, 247–50.

[27] Press, "Die Erblande," 47, 51–3; Krimm, *Baden und Habsburg*; Isenmann, "Reichsstadt," 19–20, 58–9.

[28] "Come, boys, come and listen to my tale, I'll tell you something new, just as it came to me from ever so far away, about our King Maximilian and the new league he has made." Liliencron, *Volkslieder*, 2:367, no. 196, stanza 1.

[29] Feine, "Territorialbildung," 285–9; Mertens, "Reich und Elsass"; Press, "Erblande," 54–5.

free cities – Strasbourg and Basel in the Lower Union; Nuremberg, Augsburg, and Ulm in the Swabian League – led the smaller ones into alliance with the king against common foes: the Bavarian Wittelsbachs during the early 1490s, their Heidelberg cousins in 1504, and the duke of Württemberg in 1519. They also supported, more or less willingly, Maximilian's war against the Swiss Confederacy in 1499.

The Lower Union, so called to distinguish it from the "Upper Union," the Swiss Confederacy, arose from the Eternal Settlement between Duke Sigmund of Tyrol and the confederates in 1474.[30] It brought together Sigmund; the bishops of Basel and Strasbourg; the free cities of Basel, Strasbourg, Colmar, and Sélestat; plus the Württemberg governor in Montbeliard and Duke René (r. 1473–1508) of Lorraine. The Lower Union was a kind of "Alsatian Switzerland." Its immediate object was to recover Sigmund's lands on both sides of the Rhine, roughly the Sundgau, Breisgau, and Klettgau, from Duke Charles the Bold (r. 1467– 77) of Burgundy, to whom he had mortgaged them in 1469.[31] In 1474, the Union allied with the Confederacy in the League of Constance, hoping that their combined might would suffice to overcome the Burgundian governor, a bluff and violent Sundgauer named Peter von Hagenbach (d. 1474).[32] Hagenbach, determined to subjugate the region's cities, forbade Strasbourg's senate to elect a new mayor (*Ammeister*). Instead, he wrote, "we will come in person to give you one, who will be neither a butcher nor a baker nor a ribbon merchant; you will have the honour of having for chief the noblest of princes, the duke of Burgundy."[33] Hagenbach threatened the Baselers that he would seize and flatten their town, just as Dinant had been crushed, and behead or scalp all the leading men there; he also was reported to have said "that he would shortly conquer many of the Swiss lordships and would soon be

---

[30] On the Lower Union, there is only Matzinger, *Zur Geschichte der niederen Vereinigung*, especially 566–73, based heavily on Basel documents, who calls it (566) "eine elsässische Eidgenossenschaft." On the Eternal Settlement, see Janeschitz-Kriegl, "Geschichte der ewigen Richtung," 150–224, 409–55; Dierauer, *Geschichte*, 2:205–17.

[31] Wiesflecker, *Maximilian*, 2:315; Vaughan, *Charles the Bold*, 84–9, 261–81.

[32] On Hagenbach, see Brauer-Gramm, *Der Landvogt Peter von Hagenbach*. Knebel, *Diarium*, 1:60, describes the joy at Basel upon the establishment of the League of Constance; see also songs in Tobler, *Volkslieder*, 2:52, 55.

[33] Quoted by Vaughan, *Valois Burgundy*, 202; there, too, the quotes in the following two sentences (203–4, 277). On Basel and Hagenbach, see Knebel, *Diarium*, 3:369–80; and R. Wackernagel, *Geschichte*, 2,1:55–62.

lord of Bern." The attack on Hagenbach was not just personal, however, nor was it merely an act of hostility against a foreign, that is, "Latin," power – Duke René was also Latin – but it was much more a strike against Duke Charles, the lord who had humbled Ghent and Mechelen and wrecked poor Liège, and whose activities "threatened the very existence of the towns and, more important, interrupted what is the life blood of any urban system, the free movement of goods and commodities." The real foe of Charles the Bold and the Burgundian power was not Louis XI of France, "it was the towns," who fought him "with a bitter and consistent hatred."[34]

The combined might of the Upper and Lower unions smashed the Burgundian power. The seizure, trial, and execution (May 9, 1474)[35] of Hagenbach by the Lower Union were followed by the Burgundian Wars, from the campaign to Héricourt in November 1474 to the Battle of Nancy on January 5, 1477. Alsatians and Swiss fought side by side in armies ranging up to twenty thousand men. To Héricourt, Strasbourg alone sent two thousand foot, 250 horse, 140 wagons, and the great gun named "Strus" (ostrich), which, "when it had its crop full of powder, laid hard eggs"; and the Bernese came more than seven thousand strong to Grandson.[36] The allies left the last Valois duke a naked corpse on the frozen field of Nancy, and though they later fell out over the division of Burgundian booty, the wars left a legacy of cooperation and comradeship between the Alemannic-speakers of the Upper Rhine and those of the Confederacy.

The Lower Union expired in 1484, and its renewal under Habsburg leadership in 1493 was made possible by Maximilian's succession to Tyrol and Western Austria in 1490 and by the founding of the Swabian League in 1488. Western Austria (the "Vorlande" or "Vorderöster-reich") stretched in a broken belt from Tyrol and Vorarlberg across Upper Swabia and the southern Black Forest into the Upper Rhine valley.[37] For half a century they had been ruled by the thriftless, quar-

---

[34] Vaughan, *Charles the Bold*, 40, 311.

[35] Ibid., 283–6; Wiesflecker, *Maximilian*, 1:105–12. The leading powers of the Lower Union had already been allied with the Swiss *before* they formed the union. Matzinger, *Zur Geschichte der niederen Vereinigung*, 567.

[36] Vaughan, *Charles the Bold*, 295, 375. The quote is from a poem by Conrad Pfettisheim.

[37] Evans, *Habsburg Monarchy*, 158–62, gives an excellent discussion of the Austrian lands. The Vorlande were the lands from Vorarlberg westward to the Sundgau in Upper Alsace, sometimes,

relsome Duke Sigmund, son of Duke Frederick "Empty Pockets," who sired forty bastards but no legitimate heir. Tyrol now became the pivot point of Habsburg Austria, because of its strategic control of the Brenner Pass to Italy, the wealth of its copper and silver mines, and its position as the bridge between the eastern and western parts of Austria.[38] The Bavarian dukes, George "the Rich" (r. 1479–1503) and Albrecht "the Wise" (r. 1465–1508) of the Landshut and Munich lines respectively, had lent large sums to Sigmund and had claims on his lands, and when Sigmund abdicated in 1490, "the hour of the Bavarians seemed to strike."[39] If they got and kept Tyrol, they would cut off Austria proper from Western Austria, Burgundy, and the Netherlands. The first stage of a new struggle for the German South had begun.

The Swabian League, which was to become the strongest Habsburg instrument in the South, formed in 1488 against Bavarian ambitions.[40] It was both a royal and a regional answer to the demands for a new quality of law and order.[41] Swabia, the lands between the Black Forest and the River Lech and between Lake Constance and the northern borders of Württemberg, had emerged from the feudal era as a kaleidoscope of political forms – free cities, abbeys, counts, knights, and even free peasants – among which the only major powers were Austria and Württemberg.[42] Two other powers, however, pressed in on the region, the Bavarian dukes from the east and the Swiss from the south. With the admission of Schaffhausen, one of two free cities admitted in 1454 (the other was Sankt Gallen), the Swiss broke over the Rhine–

---

but not always, including Tyrol. The strict contemporary term for the Vorlande plus Tyrol was "Upper Austria" (Oberösterreich), whereas the five duchies of Austria proper were called "Lower Austria" (Niederösterreich). These two names have quite different meanings in modern times: Upper and Lower Austria have their capitals at Linz and Vienna, respectively. See Metz, *Vorderösterreich*; there is also a helpful, brief discussion by Benecke, *Maximilian I*, 39–48.

[38] Press, "Die Erblande," 54.

[39] Wiesflecker, *Maximilian*, 1:249–53, with the quote at 251. See A. Kraus, "Sammlung der Kräfte," 288–90.

[40] Fundamental on the Swabian League are Bock, *Der Schwäbische Bund*; Hesslinger, *Die Anfänge*, who surveys the sources (218–19); Frey, "Das Gericht"; and Laufs, *Der Schwäbische Kreis*, who surveys the literature (58–60, 74–6, 90).

[41] What E. Schubert in his review of Hesslinger's book (*Jahrbuch für Geschichte der oberdeutschen Reichsstädte*, 17 [1971]:166–7) calls "ein Sieg des Regionalismus in der entsprechenden Umpolung von Reichsreformideen auf dem regionalen Bereich." See Bader, *Der deutsche Südwesten*, 90; Hesslinger, *Die Anfänge*, 47–51.

[42] Evans, *Habsburg Monarchy*, 160; see also Baumann, "Schwaben und Alamannen," 555–63.

Lake Constance line and threatened to continue northward, eating ever deeper into the lands of their ancient Habsburg foes. The original structure of the Swabian League comprised one house for the Swabian free cities and one for the Upper Swabian nobility, though the subsequent admission of princes gradually deformed the structure, until the constitution of 1500 created a third house – a princes' house – in the League's assembly. The contrast between the cities' weight in the League and their marginal place in the Imperial Diet could not have been more striking: one of two (after 1500, one of three) commanders (*Hauptleute*) and nine of eighteen (after 1500, seven of twenty-one) members of the ruling council (*Bundesrat*). The League's formal charge was protection of the public peace in Swabia, and though the Habsburgs used it, sometimes with success, for purely dynastic purposes, the cities pressed again and again for its renewal, despite the expenses of its meetings and campaigns.[43] The League, unlike the Imperial Diet, was responsive to urban interests, and at its peak this alliance became more or less an infant alternative government for the German South. Years later, when the Swabian League was dead (it expired in 1534), a Nuremberger confirmed this point: "In summary, the Swabian League was the proper form of the German nation, it was feared by many, and in many ways it protected and preserved the public peace and law and order."[44]

The Habsburgs never intended to restrict the Swabian League to Swabia proper. As early as during the summer of 1488, Frederick ordered the chief Alsatian powers to join, and he repeated his command until the Strasbourgeois replied in 1492 that they lay "too distant" from Swabia to join the alliance.[45] In the following year, one week before the old emperor's death on August 26, the Lower Union reconstituted itself.[46] Within five years between 1488 and 1493, therefore, most of the southern free cities had joined two leagues that had sprung up under

---

[43] Bock, *Der Schwäbische Bund*, 171. See Angermeier, *Königtum*, 435, and Frey, "Das Gericht," on the effectiveness of the League's court.
[44] Quoted by Laufs, *Der Schwäbische Kreis*, 58.
[45] AMS, AA 342, fol. 51 (Aug. 13, 1492). On July 6, 1488, Frederick III ordered the leading Alsatian powers, plus the city of Constance and the margraves of Baden, to join the Swabian League within 20 days. Strasbourg responded by striking alliances with the League's enemies. Mertens, "Reich und Elsass," 212–17.
[46] Matzinger, *Zur Geschichte der niederen Vereinigung*, 578–9; Wiesflecker, *Maximilian*, 1:404.

Turning Swiss

Habsburg leadership between the Lech and the Vosges mountains. Together with the Austrian lands, now united under one lord who was also king of the Romans, the Swabian League and the Lower Union provided the territorial and financial basis for a revitalized German monarchy. It was not hope of territorial gains that drove the free cities into Habsburg arms. Very few cities – Nuremberg in 1504 is the leading exception – expanded their holdings during the succeeding decades. Far more important was the commercial and banking boom of the larger cities, which offered to supply some of the king's boundless needs,[47] plus the hope for law and order and the protection of merchants, goods, and travelers. The Imperial Diet's rude treatment of the cities in 1489 also showed what they might expect from that quarter.[48] The urban governments' hope for a regional solution to their need for security could not be harnessed without conflict to Maximilian's obligations and plans, of course, and they found themselves sending him aid early on for far distant undertakings, in 1488–9 to the Netherlands and in 1493 to the French war.[49] Maximilian nonetheless acted vigorously at least in Swabia, when his interests and those of his clients ran together, as they did against the Bavarians.

The Swabian League cut its military teeth in 1492 on Duke Albrecht IV of Bavaria. Ever since Duke Sigmund's pro-Bavarian councillors had been purged from the Innsbruck administration in 1487, Albrecht had been intriguing with the Swiss against Maximilian.[50] He also took over the free city of Regensburg, albeit with the town council's approval, and pressed his way into the Swabian Allgäu, moves that brought Maximilian and the Upper Swabian free cities ever closer together. In April 1492, the League's army gathered on the banks of the Lech, perhaps twenty thousand strong, and made ready to invade Bavaria. Albrecht came to terms, disgorged Regensburg, and renounced his claim to Tyrol.[51] Without a pike raised or a gun fired, Bavarian expansion was halted for a generation.

---

[47] See Chapter 3, section titled "King and cities in the Habsburg system."
[48] Isenmann, "Reichsstadt," 117–18; Angermeier, *Königtum*, 421–5.
[49] Baumann, *Geschichte des Allgäus*, 2:73–6; Gothein, *Volksbewegungen*, 64–5.
[50] Hegi, *Die geächteten Räte*, 145–72. On Bavarian expansion, see Baumann, *Geschichte des Allgäus*, 2:68–70; A. Kraus, "Sammlung der Kräfte," 289–90; Layer, "Entwicklung," 989.
[51] Wiesflecker, *Maximilian*, 1:268–70. The Peace of Augsburg (May 25, 1492) ended Albrecht's designs on Tyrol, his dream of regaining the Imperial throne for his family, and the Wittelsbach–Swiss connection. Hegi, *Die geächteten Räte*, 450–1.

Complex motives lay behind the Lower Union's reconstitution. The Upper Rhenish cities' trade ran along the Rhine axis, not over the mountains to Swabia,[52] and their region lay under no immediate threat of subjugation by a great prince. Their sense of relative isolation had been perfectly expressed in 1489, when they had refused an Imperial tax their Swabian and Franconian colleagues had agreed to accept.[53] That they were nevertheless willing by 1493 to join a Habsburg-led alliance may have been due at least in part to their growing estrangement from their old Swiss comrades in arms. The creeping animosity between the northern and southern peoples of the Swabian-Alemannic language group poses a difficult historical problem, though the fact of it is easily traceable in chronicle and song.[54] Anti-Swiss feelings in Alsace and Swabia may have stemmed from resentment over the distribution of Burgundian booty, or simply from fear of the power of Swiss arms, now at the pinnacle of their glory. Whatever the reasons, the sentiments moved the free cities' governments toward the nobles of Tyrol, Western Austria, and the independent areas of Upper Swabia and the Upper Rhine, whose hatred for the Swiss is far less puzzling. Swiss power corroded noble power in two ways, corresponding to the Confederacy's dual political nature. First, the confederates aided neighboring city-states against nobles, for example, Schaffhausen against the Hegau nobles prior to 1454 and Mulhouse against the Sundgau nobility during the 1460s.[55] In both cases, aid led to permanent association. Second, the Confederacy expanded by subverting rural subjects; at least they were believed to have this goal.[56] Even after Swiss expansion northward began to slacken, during the later fifteenth century, every clash with neighboring nobles brought the threat of rural rebellion behind the frontier, and the Confederacy remained the favorite refuge for rural rebels.[57]

The Swabian League aimed to meet the Confederacy's threats through

---

[52] F.-J. Fuchs, "L'espace économique rhénan," 289–325; idem, "Les foires et le rayonnement économique," especially 260–2, 275–306; Ammann, *Wirtschaftsgeltung des Elsass*, 10–11.
[53] Janssen, *Frankfurts Reichscorrespondenz*, 2,2:531–6, no. 670.
[54] Baumann, "Schwaben und Alamannen," 562–4.
[55] On Schaffhausen, see Schib, *Geschichte*, 131–43; on Mulhouse (Mülhausen), see Dierauer, *Geschichte*, 2:183–8, and Bischoff, *Gouvernées et gouvernants*, 54–61.
[56] G. Franz, *Quellen*, 61–2, no. 13.
[57] Even as mediators, the confederates seem to have treated rebels more mildly than others did. Rosenkranz, *Bundschuh*, 1:16–18. Two hundred persons implicated in a 1491 rebellion at Kempten took refuge with the Swiss. Baumann, *Geschichte des Allgäus*, 2:83.

"actions against one's subjects in concert with the League, . . . supression of every scrap of sympathy for rebels, and enforcing obedience to the demands of the Empire and the League."[58] The very process of deliberation and negotiation with princes and nobles awakened among the urban politicians a desperate urge to be regarded as fully competent rulers (*Obrigkeiten*), and the nobles' skepticism that burghers could truly be lords, illustrated by the League's internal debate over the term *commune*, only intensified the desperation.[59]

True lordship, however, meant hostility to rebels and to their friends. In this light, it is significant that the refounding of the Lower Union in 1493 coincided with the first Alsatian *Bundschuh*, the initial wave of rural uprisings that would culminate in 1525.[60] It began with an aborted revolt at Sélestat and continued through plots in the bishopric of Speyer in 1502, at Lehen in the Breisgau in 1513, and at numerous places in 1517. The disturbances troubled relations between Upper Rhenish and Swiss authorities. It was assumed in 1493, for example, that the ringleader, Burgomaster Hans Ulmann of Sélestat, had fled with the other conspirators to Switzerland, where they presumably hoped to get aid for their insurrection. The learned abbot Johannes Trithemius (1462–1516) fixed the connection by describing how the conspirators of 1502 near Speyer swore solidarity "in the Swiss manner" and were determined "to remove the yoke of servitude from everyone through force and to get themselves free by armed might in the Swiss way."[61] In 1513, the government of Freiburg im Breisgau thought that only action by the confederates, on whom one could not count, might dash the Breisgau rebels' hopes for success.[62] It was also widely believed that Joss Fritz, the shadowy leader of the *Bundschuh* from 1502 until 1524, went to

---

[58] Naujoks, *Obrigkeitsgedanke*, 26–7.
[59] Maschke, " 'Obrigkeit' im spätmittelalterlichen Speyer," 8–10 (also in his *Städte und Menschen*, 122–4).
[60] Rosenkranz, *Brundshuh*; G. Franz, "Zur Geschichte des Bundschuhs," 1–23; idem, *Der deutsche Bauernkrieg*, 53–62. For the recent literature, see Scott, "The Peasants' War," 708–10, plus Bischoff, *Gouvernées et gouvernants*, 116–18.
[61] The quotes are taken from Rosenkranz, *Bundschuh*, 2:89–90, quoting his *Annales Hirsaugienses* (St. Gallen, 1690), 2:589–91. On the Swiss involvement, see Rosenkranz, *Bundschuh*, 1:17–18, 21, 36, 54, 58.
[62] Rosenkranz, *Bundschuh*, 1:175, 180. Koenigsberger writes that "the peasant movement itself started in the Black Forest, close to the Swiss cantons with their infectious antiprincely and antinoble traditions. "Reformation and Social Revolution," now in his *Estates and Revolutions*, 216. See also F. Meyer, *Beziehungen*, 86.

56

Switzerland in 1513 to seek armed aid; and his captured comrades confessed that if the emperor would not recognize them, they intended to seek Swiss help.[63] The confederates seemed the natural allies of rebels. The urban governments had to decide whether they could tolerate the growing strength of the idea of turning Swiss among the common folk, or whether they should make common cause with other lords, especially the greatest lord of all in the German South. Their choice helped to bring on the Swabian War.

The Swabian War, 1499

> Die Schweizer han ir sach nit recht betracht,
> dasz sie haben selber ritter gemacht
> selbs in iren taten;
> dar an han sie nit recht getan,
> sie heten es wol underwegen gelan,
> es hat inn niemands geraten.[64]

"They have made themselves knights!" This charge against the Swiss suggests the deep social resentment that fueled one of German history's oddest wars, the Swabian War of 1499. One traditional explanation holds that the Swiss, having refused to obey the enactments of the Imperial Diet of Worms in 1495, simply left the Holy Roman Empire, an act viewed by German historians as a regrettable and permanent loss, but by Swiss ones as an inevitable consequence of the Swiss path to nationhood.[65] King Maximilian did charge the confederates with rebellion, but they were in fact no more disobedient than were many other powers on the Empire's periphery. The Swiss townsmen in particular confessed

---

[63] See Burgomaster and Senate of Freiburg im Breisgau to Jakob Villinger, Nov. 15, 1513, in Rosenkranz, *Bundschuh*, 2:180. Fritz's claim to be a native of Stein am Rhein was almost certainly false. Ibid., 126–7, 142, 145, 161, 183–4, 193, 197; G. Franz, *Der deutsche Bauernkrieg*, 66; Mommsen, *Eidgenossen*, 284; G. Franz, "Der Kampf um das alte Recht," 105–7. For interrogations, see Rosenkranz, *Bundschuh*, 2:133, 186, 195.

[64] "It is not right for the Swiss to make themselves into knights, on account of their own bold deeds. It is not a proper thing to do, and they should have let it lie, for no one advised them to do it." Liliencron, *Volkslieder*, 2:386, no. 202, stanza 14.

[65] For expressions of each of these views, see Peyer, *Verfassungsgeschichte*, 20–1; W. P. Fuchs, "Das Zeitalter der Reformation," 55. The war of 1499 is called the "Swiss War" by German historians and the "Swabian War" by Swiss ones; it seems fair to allow the victors to name it.

themselves "pious Germans," who "belong directly to the Holy Roman Empire, which we haven't the slightest intention of leaving."[66] This war's antecedents lie deeper, buried in

> the hatred that broke out with such seeming suddenness at the end of the 1480s between the Alemannic-speakers on both sides of the Rhine, a feeling that fed on hostilities between nobles and peasants, South German and Swiss mercenary soldiers, Swiss and Swabian cities, and many other groups. It lent the war the wildness and bitterness that made it much like a civil war.[67]

For years before 1499, the borderlands seethed with raids and insults. "Cow-Swiss," screamed the Austrian garrisons over the Rhine, while the nobles took up the old refrain: These "peasants" should be "given a lord."[68] King Maximilian fully agreed, and his edict against them, issued at Freiburg im Breisgau on April 22, 1499, called them "crude, wicked, contemptible peasants, who have no virtue, no noble lineage and no moderation, but only sensuality, faithlessness, and hate," and he mocked their "dishonorable origins."[69] The chief targets of this abuse were hardly the patricians and merchants of the Swiss cities, but rather the rural federations, the bitterest foes of noble lordship and Austrian power; its vehemence flowed not from a desire to conquer the Swiss uplands but from the fear that the specter of men who were "their own lords" would sweep northward and eastward. The Swabian War was thus a kind of preventive social war against the spread of masterlessness into Tyrol, Vorarlberg, Swabia, and the Upper Rhine, and it belongs to the prehistory of the Revolution of 1525.[70]

A variety of forces drew the free cities' governments toward the Habsburg cause on the eve of the war. In Alsace, it was fear of France, that land of "Latin servitude," whose king, as self-nominated guardian of German particularism, was tempting the Swiss with pensions and re-

---

[66] Quoted by Peyer, *Verfassungsgeschichte*, 19. See Mommsen, *Eidgenossen*, 64–96; Sigrist, "Reichsreform und Schwabenkrieg," 123–30; Wiesflecker, *Maximilian*, 2:319–21.
[67] Sigrist, "Reichsreform und Schwabenkrieg," 136.
[68] Dürr, *Politik der Eidgenossen*, 487. See Ulmann, *Maximilian*, 1:720; Wiesflecker, *Maximilian*, 2:331.
[69] Wiesflecker, *Maximilian*, 2:334–5.
[70] Sigrist, "Reichsreform und Schwabenkrieg," 129; Hegi, *Die geächteten Räte*, 416. This suggests that Mommsen's emphasis on the Imperial patriotism of the Swiss, which rests on urban sources, ought to be qualified. Mommsen, *Eidgenossen*, 284; Schib, "Zur Geschichte der schweizerischen Nordgrenze," 6–14.

cruiting contracts.[71] All along the border, Maximilian tried to anchor the free cities to the Empire, as he pressed the new Imperial tax, the Common Penny, with special vigor upon Sankt Gallen, Schaffhausen, Mulhouse, Basel, Rottweil, Buchhorn, Wangen, and Constance.[72] Constance was torn as was no other city, pressured by both Austria and the bishop, admiring the Swiss but fearing they might take the Thurgau, the region south of the lake, from Constance. Finally, in 1498 Constance joined the Swabian League; the next year it became a center of Imperial military operations; and the Swiss seized the Thurgau, a blow from which Constance's economy never recovered. This bitter experience lay behind the remark a generation later that "if you ask a native Constancer whether he is a Swabian, a Thurgauer, or a Swiss, he replies, No, and wants to be merely a Constancer."[73]

In the dead of winter, in the Upper Engadine and in the Vinschgau, where the Etsch/Adige River springs, the Swabian War began in December 1498. Here the three Rhaetian leagues faced a confident Tyrolean regime in Innsbruck, which was determined to bring them to obedience.[74] Each side called on its allies, the Rhaetians on the Swiss and Innsbruck on the Swabian League, and by mid-January the stage was set for a creeping, vicious war on a front all the way from its point of origin, where today Italy, Switzerland, and Austria come together, across the Silvretta Chain of the High Alps into the High Rhine valley, down the Rhine to Lake Constance, across the lake and down the Upper Rhine to Basel's territory, and then on into the Sundgau on the Rhine's west bank. It was neither a "Swabian War" nor a "Swiss War" but a South German civil war among the peoples from Tyrol to the Burgundian Gate, and it soon involved peoples – Alsatians and Breisgauers, Solothurners, and Hegauers – who neither knew nor cared what was happening under the snowy towers of the Rhaetian Alps.[75] Soon enough,

---

[71] This is the major theme of Mertens, "Reich und Elsass." See also Bischoff, *Governées et gouvernants*, 93–6.

[72] Sigrist, "Reichsreform und Schwabenkrieg," 130, 136–7. On Constance, see Feger, "Konstanz am Vorabend," 41–4; Rublack, "Aussenpolitik," 56–69; Bender, *Reformationsbündnisse*, 116–17; Feger, *Geschichte*, 3:332. The city may have been influenced in joining the League by the bishop's negotiations with the Confederacy, for which see Chmel, *Urkunden*, 185–7, no. 163.

[73] Rublack, "Aussenpolitik," 56.

[74] Wiesflecker, *Maximilian*, 2:330; Dierauer, *Geschichte*, 2:396.

[75] On the Swabian War in general, see Wiesflecker, *Maximilian*, 2:350–7; Ulmann, *Maximilian*,

however, everyone knew what was happening in the far South. As all attempts at mediation failed, as the Tyrolean and Swabian armies were beaten along the High Rhine, and as the peasants behind the front began to chant "Swiss! Swiss!" with each new setback, Maximilian hurried from the Netherlands to transform an Austrian war into an Imperial one. He stopped briefly at Mainz on April 9 to declare the Swiss outlaws and rebels, who had gobbled up nearly fifty counties and thrice as many noble seats, and he rushed on to the Swabian front.

Voices from three different sources illuminate the free cities' roles in the Swabian War. Hans Ungelter's dispatches to Esslingen give us a look into the experiences of the Swabian League's towns. The actions of Basel and Strasbourg show how the war disrupted the Lower Union. And the writings of Willibald Pirckheimer, Nuremberg's commander, offer a townsman's view from outside the new Habsburg system.

Not so long ago, in 1491, the Swabian League had sent the Confederacy an offer of alliance, but by 1497 it was preparing for war, and the Lake Constance towns pressed as hard as the Hegau nobles did for the League's renewal in 1498.[76] When the Innsbruck regime called for aid, the League declared war on the Confederacy at Constance on January 20 and ordered two thousand foot to Feldkirch to aid the Austrians.[77] The formula for this levy probably did not differ from those of June and July, by which the cities supplied respectively 209 horse and 4,740 foot and 193 horse and 3,873 foot.[78] Augsburg and Ulm sent about one-third of the cities' share, the next largest twelve cities provided one-half, and the fourteen lesser towns the remainder – all in all less than a quarter of the League's entire army.

Hans Ungelter represented Esslingen in the League's council and reported the entire war from the Swabian front. From the first, he had little good to say. The princes, he noted, were not keen on the war, and the nobles had little stomach for battling the tough confederates, once

---

1:649–903; Dierauer, *Geschichte*, 2:375–451; Schaufelberger, "Spätmittelalter," 342–8. On the background, see also Sablonier, *Adel im Wandel*, 254–9.

[76] Ueberlingen, April 9, 1497, in Klüpfel, *Urkunden* 1:223–5. The 1491 offer is in *EA*, 3,1:389, no. 416a (Zug, Aug. 1, 1491). See Ulmann, *Maximilian*, 1:664–6.

[77] Klüpfel, *Urkunden*, 1:272–3. The plan of campaign featured Constance as the assembly point for League and Imperial forces. See Büchi, *Aktenstücke*, 3–4, 106 n. 2; Klüpfel, *Urkunden* 1:305, 308; *EA*, 3,1:601b; Wiesflecker, *Maximilian*, 2:334.

[78] Wiesflecker, *Maximilian*, 2:354–5, and see 348.

the first heat of fury died away.[79] This agrees with Pirckheimer's report from the Vinschgau that the nobles fled before the wail of Uri's great war horn. "This is the king's war," wrote Ungelter sadly. "There are neither money nor supplies here, and even if the cities stick together, the nobles will go home if the king does not find provisions, as the League's constitution requires him to do. We also have no experienced soldiers."[80] By early March, he thought that the Esslingers had served long enough, and a month later he wrote that "it is very tough for the cities, and no one can hold like this in the long run."[81] The Augsburgers even argued that the war had really begun before the League's renewal, when Augsburg and others had first joined it, and so it was not their war at all. When Maximilian arrived at the front at Ueberlingen on April 27, Ungelter thought that "if the king doesn't change the matter, I think he will be driven out, and then it will be every man for himself."[82] From all fronts, from the Engadine, Vorarlberg, and the Hegau, came news of Austrians and Leaguers beaten or driven off by the Swiss. By early May, Ungelter wrote home about "our ruin," and a month later he wrote in despair, "It's a miserable affair – no guns, no powder, no supplies. The king has nothing and can procure nothing. And so we must wallow here in our shame and throw away what little we have."[83]

Events justified Ungelter's gloom. The Tyrolean army was beaten in the Vinschgau on May 22, and in June the fighting shifted to the central front along the Rhine–Lake line, as the king seemed to prepare for a decisive strike from his headquarters at Constance.[84] Though nearly fifteen thousand troops had gathered here, nothing was undertaken, and

---

[79] Ungelter to Esslingen, Jan. 31 and Feb. 1, 1499, in Klüpfel, *Urkunden*, 1:279–80. See Pirckheimer, *Schweizerkrieg*, 94. This is Hans Ungelter "der Jüngere," who was a senator of Esslingen in 1491–2 and *Richter* in the senate (*Rat*) in 1493 through 1515; he was burgomaster in 1494 and died around 1515. His father, Hans, Sr., held office both before and after the son. Both men are mentioned in Klüpfel, *Urkunden*, 2:84. My thanks for this information go to Hans-Christoph Rublack and Inez Bechinger, who in 1981 prepared the lists from the *Bürgerbuch*, 1482ff., in StA Esslingen, F 28 II.

[80] Ungelter to Esslingen, Feb. 14, 1499, in Klüpfel, *Urkunden*, 1:286.

[81] Ungelter to Esslingen, March 9 and April 7, 1499, in ibid., 300, 312 (quote). The Augsburgers' argument is in his letter of April 18, 1499, in ibid., 319.

[82] Ungelter to Esslingen, April 24, 1499, in ibid., 324. See Wiesflecker, *Maximilian*, 2:335–7.

[83] Ungelter to Esslingen, May 9 and June 2, 1499, in Klüpfel, *Urkunden*, 1:334, 343–4.

[84] Büchi, *Aktenstücke*, 529, no. 697; Wiesflecker, *Maximilian*, 2:340–2, 344–8, who gives a clear account of the Swabian front; and Ulmann, *Maximilian*, 1:771–8, who gives a much clearer picture of the strategy and what was wrong with it.

when the king heard reports of pro-Swiss sympathies among the Upper Swabian peasant and urban commons, he hurled his glove to the ground in disgust and declared, "One cannot fight Swiss with Swiss!"[85] The Villingen chronicler lamented, "There was no heart in it," while Ungelter sighed, "His [Maximilian's] approach is baseless and childish."[86] The decision toward which events reeled, however, came not on this front but much further westward, on the Upper Rhenish front.

From the beginning, the western allies had less taste for the war. The men who ruled the Alsatian cities wanted nothing less than war against their former comrades, and many still alive remembered when men of Strasbourg and Uri, Colmar and Bern, Basel and Lucerne had marched, fought, bled, and died on the fields of Grandson, Murten, and Nancy. Most cruelly affected was Basel, which lay right at the front, bordered by its own bishop, Austria, Bern, and Solothurn.[87] Within the walls, there were plots and intrigues "to murder the nobles" and seize the government. A strong pro-Swiss party grew among the commons, for "the Swiss were seen as the foes of prince and noble and as deliverers from the oppression of the lords, and they naturally had the Common Man's sympathy."[88] As the pressure from both sides on Basel mounted, the council decided to remain neutral between the Upper and Lower unions, but it was suspected by each side of secretly aiding the other.[89] When the fighting swirled around and through its territory, Basel's castellans reported the spread of pro-Swiss feelings. "Although some of your subjects," reports one of them, "say to me that I'm not a good Swiss, I don't care. For whatever you, my lords, are and wish to be, I

---

[85] Wiesflecker, *Maximilian*, 2:347, quotes Maximilian's disgusted comment. It helps to explain an item on the agenda of the Austrian estates assembled at Ensisheim on May 8, 1499: "Vnd als vil verrattern im land, wider vnd für got, daz man do in stetten niemans in, noch in dorffern frömde ligen lass, sunder gut acht vff solh verrattern hab, die anzunemen vnd zu verkuntten" (Schreiber, *Urkundenbuch*, 2:658). There is also evidence of popular anti-Swiss feeling in the Austrian Sundgau, where the people of Mulhouse were insulted with the typical anti-Swiss epithet, "Cow Swiss," or by blowing a horn, "Als ob sy kuh werend." Georges Bischoff connects this with the meaning of "sodomites" (*Gouvernées et gouvernants*, 214, 242).

[86] Hug, *Chronik*, 14, also quoted by Wiesflecker, *Maximilian*, 2:347; Ungelter to Esslingen, July 24, 1499, in Klüpfel, *Urkunden*, 1:366.

[87] F. Meyer, *Beziehungen*, 84. See the superb map in Gasser, *Die territoriale Entwicklung*.

[88] R. Wackernagel, *Geschichte*, 2,1:155; see also 147–57. Bischoff (*Gouvernées et gouvernants*, 214) relates that in 1502 two young Baselers got into a fight, "Da wolt einer ein Oesterricher sein, und der annder wolt ein Schwitzer sein." At the beginning of the Swabian War, several powers were called to aid by both sides, e.g., St. Gallen. *EA*, 3,1:600, no. 640bb.

[89] R. Wackernagel, *Geschichte*, 2,1:157–74; F. Meyer, *Beziehungen*, 84–6.

am, too. And I want to die as a good Basler. I am here, and here I'll stay, so long as you want me to; and don't worry about this castle."[90] The victors' prestige was irresistible, and when the Peace of Basel on September 22, 1499, ended the war, Pirckheimer thought it was already too late to hold Basel out of the Confederacy.[91] Eighteen months later, on March 21, 1501, Basel turned Swiss and opened to its confederates the high road into the entire Upper Rhenish plain.

The same forces tore at Basel's Alsatian sister, Strasbourg, though less strongly, for a broad strip of Austria separated Lower Alsace from the Confederacy. Recognizing the Lower Union's faint enthusiasm for the war, Count Heinrich of Fürstenberg, who was one of Maximilian's commanders, wrote to his brother from Antwerp on March 3, 1499, "that the Lower Union, in accordance with the instruction of which a copy is enclosed, should come into the [Swabian] League, for that would be useful both to the League and to us. His Royal Majesty also favors this step."[92] The Lower Union did not agree. Since February, its envoys had been busily trying to head off the escalation of the Swiss–Austrian conflict into a general war. At this stage, as Basel wrote to Strasbourg, it was difficult to tell just who was fighting whom.[93] As the king had not yet arrived from the north, Queen Bianca Maria, a Sforza princess from Milan, sent to the chief towns of the Lower Union and warned that "the Swiss have rebelled without cause and, with rash ambitions, have mobilized all their forces. Therefore," she continued,

we wish that you . . . as obedient Imperial subjects mobilize your whole forces of cavalry, infantry, and artillery, plus provisions, to aid His Royal Majesty and those lands [Western Austria] and resist the rash undertaking of said Swiss. And we wish that you move without delay toward the four Rhenish towns [Rheinfelden, Säckingen, Laufenburg, and Waldshut] and do your best to save

---

[90] Jakob Iselin, Basel's castellan at Fransburg, to the Burgomaster and Senate of Basel, May 3, 1499; quoted by F. Meyer, *Beziehungen*, 85.
[91] Pirckheimer, *Schweizerkrieg*, 131–3 (book II, chap. 8, para. 17–20), who notes an incident during the Te Deum sung at Basel for the signing of the peace: "Et hic clamor manifestum prae se tulit indicium defectionis ab imperio, quae mox est secuta."
[92] Riezler, *Fürstenbergisches Urkundenbuch*, 4:228, no. 253.
[93] Basel to Strasbourg, Feb. 5, 1499, in Witte, "Urkundenauszüge, I," m73. On the Lower Union's efforts at mediation, see Bishop Albrecht of Strasbourg to Queen Bianca Maria, in response to her letter to the Lower Union of Feb. 15, 1499, in ibid., m67–8, m72, m78, m85; Büchi, *Aktenstücke*, 492 n. 1. See Klüpfel, *Urkunden*, 1:241, 300.

the land and the people, together with the other subjects and servitors of His Royal Majesty and the Holy Empire.[94]

The Lower Union forces were meant to move on the Rhine below the lake from the west, the Swabian League's army from the east.

To Strasbourg, the queen sent special envoys, one of whom was Peter Völtsch, a knight of Strasbourg and since 1496 a Habsburg official.[95] When they heard that the queen was afraid to come to the Alsatian cities, "because Her Royal Highness had received no reply and didn't know how she should regard us," the senators grew angry,

for they always were, and are now, prepared to behave properly toward His Royal Majesty or Her Highness at all times. And if Her Royal Grace had come to us, we would have treated her as loyal subjects, just as we have always done.

The senators responded to the queen's mobilization call that "the envoys of the princes and cities [of the Lower Union] are meeting at this very time, and we hope that Her Majesty has received the [Lower Union's] reply; if not, she will soon." They avowed that Strasbourg would do its duty, though on February 19 they again urged the queen to seek mediation:

And being such as would like to see peace and prosperity in the land, we have sent our embassy and given it solemn instructions to ride out to the camps and the armies with the envoys of the other powers [of the Lower Union], to aid, to search for, and to work for a peaceful settlement to this matter. And we trust that God Almighty will grant His grace that the quarrels and conflicts may be peacefully settled, which we desire from the bottom of our hearts. We would also welcome and hear with rejoicing and pleasure whatever will promote the pleasure, welfare, and honor of His Royal Majesty and Your Royal Highness.[96]

The Strasbourgeois were trying, with their pleas, to warn the queen to make peace while she yet could, for they knew better than most what redoubtable warriors the confederates were. Then, too, Strasbourg was caught, as its allies were, between its obligations to the king and to the

---

[94] Queen Bianca Maria to the Stettmeister and Senate of Strasbourg, Freiburg i. Br., Feb. 15, 1499, in AMS, AA 313, fol. 20ʳ.
[95] On Peter Völtsch, see Brady, *Ruling Class*, 81, 81 n. 91; Mertens, "Reich und Elsass," 251–2; Janssen, *Frankfurts Reichscorrespondenz*, 2,2:590, no. 755. The record of this discussion is in AMS, AA 313, fol. 21ʳ, from which the following quotes are taken.
[96] Wilhelm Böcklin, Stettmeister, and the Senate of Strasbourg to Queen Bianca Maria, Feb. 19, 1499, in AMS, AA 313, fol. 22ʳ.

Swiss, who wrote from Zurich in mid-February about "damaging, dishonorable attacks, actions, and pressure against our folk, our liberties, and our traditions," asking the Strasbourgeois "as our faithful allies... that you regard us loyally and show us that loyalty... "[97]

When Strasbourg sent envoys to the Lower Union's assembly at Colmar on February 25, 1499, the government's instruction recapitulated the correspondence with both sides in such a way as to emphasize the fierce pressures from the queen and the Swiss.[98] "Thus the matter does not seem amenable to arbitration," the senators wrote, and the queen's agents reminded them that

> our lord, the King of the Romans, is head of the Holy Empire, and we ought to know very well what effort His Majesty has made from his desire to protect the Empire and its peace. We ought also to consider the command as coming from the King of the Romans and not from an Austrian prince, and we ought to render him help and aid, as the Diets have decreed.

The agents also pressed to know what troops Strasbourg would send to the Alsatian Vicar (*Landvogt*) at Altkirch, the mustering place in the Sundgau.

The cities' dilemma was not apparent to everyone. A Fribourgeois writing from the other Freiburg (im Breisgau) in February 1499 claimed to have discovered that "the Strasbourgeois, the Count Palatine and the duke [of Württemberg], each wants to run this war and is willing to back it with all his might. And everyone wants to subdue you, Swiss peasants, so that you will have to become tame."[99] Two months later, however, the Milanese ambassador to Maximilian's court correctly reported that the Elector Palatine and the cities of Strasbourg and Basel tried to keep clear of the war and submitted only after Maximilian

---

[97] The Swiss Assembly (*Tagsatzung*) to the Stettmeister and Senate of Strasbourg, Chur, Feb. 1499, in AMS, AA 313, fol. 19ʳ⁻ᵛ. The Lower Union's failed mediation efforts may be followed in *EA*, 3,1:593, 596, 599, 601, 604, 606, 617–18, 629.

[98] Wilhelm Böcklin, Stettmeister, and the Senate of Strasbourg to Stettmeister Friedrich Bock and Altammeister Jakob Wissbach at Colmar, Feb. 25, 1499, in AMS, AA 313, fol. 23ʳ, from which the following two quotes are taken. The envoys had assembled at Colmar before Feb. 13, as Basel reported to Strasbourg on that date, but had gone home again when they heard the (false) report that the war was over. Bishop Albrecht of Strasbourg then called them to Colmar on Feb. 20. Witte, "Urkundenauszüge, I," m78, m85.

[99] Büchi, *Aktenstücke*, 459–60, no. 608. The Milanese envoy's report is in ibid., 166–7, no. 230. Mertens, "Reich und Elsass," 233, notes that the Lower Union, minus the city and bishop of Basel, joined the Imperial side by March 26, 1499.

unfurled the Imperial war banner. The king came to Freiburg on April 21, and on the twenty-seventh his commander on the Upper Rhenish front, Count Heinrich of Fürstenberg, reported that Strasbourg's troops were expected shortly at Altkirch.[100] Come they did, led by Hans von Kageneck and bringing the great gun, "Strus," which would now lay its hard eggs on old comrades turned foes.[101]

When, in early July, Count Heinrich moved against the Swiss, he decided to use Castle Dorneck, high on the Jura's wall south of Basel, as a base of operations against Bern, Solothurn, and Fribourg.[102] With fifteen hundred tough veterans of the Burgundian Guard, who had come with Maximilian from the Netherlands, seven thousand other foot – Austrian subjects from the Upper Rhine and Lower Union forces – and two thousand horse he laid siege to Dorneck. On July 22, a force of Berners, Solothurners, and Zurichers surprised the besiegers and killed nearly thirty-five hundred of them, including the commander. Had the Guard not stood and covered the retreat, perhaps no allied soldier would have survived.[103] The "Strus" was lost, plus the great gun "Kätterli von Ensen" (Kathy of Ensisheim), and this double loss – a Strasbourg and an Austrian cannon – summed up symbolically what the partnership of Habsburg and Lower Union had achieved. Basel chose neutrality and

---

[100] Count Heinrich of Fürstenberg to King Maximilian, Freiburg i. Br., April 27, 1499, in Büchi, *Aktenstücke*, 165, no. 229. He was the brother of Count Wolfgang, one of Maximilian's commanders in Swabia. By May 7 they were at Mulhouse. See Fürstenberg to the Strasbourg commanders at Mulhouse, May 7, 1499, in Riezler, *Fürstenbergisches Urkundenbuch*, 4:253, no. 268. On the mobilization in Upper Alsace, see Bischoff, *Gouvernées et gouvernants*, 99–105.

[101] Hans von Kageneck (d. before 1508), a Strasbourg cavalry commander in the Burgundian Wars, was knighted on the field of Murten in 1476. Niedersächsische Staats- und Universitätsbibliothek Göttingen, Ms. Hist. 154, fol. 13ᵛ. He was a patrician senator at Strasbourg in 1473–4 and 1476–7. Hatt, *Liste des membres*, 465. Wimpheling wrote of him around 1508 that "Joannes de kageneck miles nominis magni, et persona elegantis in exilio periit." Chicago, The Newberry Library, Ms. 63 (on this manuscript, see Herding, "Zur einer humanistischen Handschrift," 153–87).

[102] See Wiesflecker, *Maximilian* 2:348–9, who attributes the plan of campaign to Count Heinrich, whereas Ulmann, *Maximilian*, 1:778, ascribes it to the king.

[103] Büchi, *Aktenstücke*, 380–3, 389–91, 462–4; Pirckheimer, *Schweizerkrieg*, 115–6, who blames Heinrich's failure to take precautions. On the fighting qualities of the troops from these Austrian lands, see Schreiber, *Urkundenbuch*, 2:657–8. At an earlier time, they had said, "Sumus similes Switzenzibus, nullam volumus dare pecuniam ad procurandum cum Switzensibus expedicionem" (Knebel, *Diarium*, 1:249, as quoted by Bischoff, *Gouvernées et gouvernants*, 79). On the Battle of Dorneck, see the song printed by Tobler, *Volkslieder*, 2:90, whose author "hat mengen Swaben erstochen/und mit den Strassburgern gerungen." The Strasbourg banner captured at Dorneck may be seen in the Schweizerisches Landesmuseum at Zurich.

gained safety; Strasbourg chose, though haltingly, the king and got shame and defeat.

Nuremberg had no reason to fight the Swiss. Fifty years before, when the city dismissed a thousand Swiss mercenaries who had fought the margrave's men, their commander had said that "if Nuremberg had need of them in the future and asked for a thousand Swiss, ten thousand would gladly come."[104] When, instead, war came against the Swiss, the council tried to stay neutral, and the commons sympathized with the Swiss.[105] To the king, the Nurembergers denied that they were running guns and money to the Swiss; to the Swiss, they denied that they had sent troops to the League and asked for release of confiscated Nuremberg goods. In fact, Nuremberg had never joined the Swabian League, despite royal orders and threats, chiefly because of the city's Bavarian alliance.[106] Once Maximilian declared an Imperial war, however, Nuremberg had to obey. On May 1, 1499, three hundred Nuremberg foot, thirty-two horse, and four guns left Nuremberg for the Swabian front under the command of a tall, twenty-eight-year-old, Italian-educated patrician, Willibald Pirckheimer. After a stop at Ulm, whence he reported that three-fourths of the allied troops had deserted or been withdrawn,[107] Pirckheimer found the king at Tettnang, in Montfort territory north of Lake Constance, where Swabian officers chided him for bringing so few troops – Ulm had twice as many. The Nuremberger replied that "they ignore the fact that the Swabians' situation differs markedly from that of the Nurembergers: Whereas they make war on the Swiss voluntarily, we do so only in obedience to the emperor's commands."[108] The Nurembergers, who lived far from the frontier, had

---

[104] Quoted by Reicke, "Willibald Pirckheimer," 157; and see idem, *Geschichte*, 428. Erhard Schürstab's account in "Nürnberg's Krieg gegen den Markgrafen," 217–18, 220–1, 226, contradicts Reicke's remark that these Swiss never saw action.

[105] Reicke, "Willibald Pirckheimer," 143–7. On Nuremberg's mediation efforts, see *EA*, 3,1:602, no. 643b, and for Nuremberg merchants in Switzerland, see ibid., 360, 380, 455, 506, 600.

[106] Reicke, "Willibald Pirckheimer," 143. E. Franz, *Nürnberg*, 53, wrongly assumes that the city belonged to the Swabian League (it joined in 1500) and gives the wrong figures for the Nuremberg contingent (for correct figures, see Reicke, "Willibald Pirckheimer," 148–9; idem, *Geschichte*, 479).

[107] Pirckheimer to the Senate of Nuremberg, Ulm, May 8, 1499, in Pirckheimer, *Briefwechsel*, 1:77, no. 7. He doubtless took pleasure in reporting that many of the margrave's men were among the deserters.

[108] Pirckheimer, *Schweizerkrieg*, 93–4, (book II, chap. 4, para. 5, 10). Anton Kreuzer, a Nuremberger, saw the troops march through Ulm and wrote that "viel Leut" had died in the war,

scant reason to hate the confederates. Whereas Ungelter wrote that, should the Swiss break through the Rhine–Lake line into Württemberg, "It is to be feared that the peasants would all join them,"[109] no one in Franconia had to fear that subjects would turn Swiss in this direct sense. Even Pirckheimer occasionally sympathized with the enemy.[110]

Pirckheimer also recognized the social character of this war, in which heralds were not used and prisoners rarely ransomed.[111] He and his Franconians (he also led troops of Schweinfurt, Weissenburg, and Windsheim) also campaigned against Klettgau peasants, who had risen for the Swiss.[112] Of the nobles he had no high opinion. He tells how his colleague, Hans von Weichsdorf, defended the Nurembergers against noble charges of cowardice before the king.

> But why didn't those, who now charge us after the fact with cowardice, attack the enemy alone? They, who were cavalry against mere infantry; they, who had superior numbers against an inferior enemy [i.e., Schaffhausers]; they, who are nobles against those whom they are pleased to call "peasants" . . . ?[113]

Such folk, he went on, "are renowned only through their empty titles of nobility and their knighthood; for in courage they can scarcely compare with common soldiers, not to speak of veterans!" The theme of noble incompetence and faintheartedness runs like a red thread through Pirckheimer's history.

The king liked the well-spoken Nuremberger and won his admiration. Pirckheimer was nevertheless not blind to Maximilian's incompetent conduct of the war. He relates the campaign to the Engadine in late May and June 1499 as one great piece of hopeless effort, a ride among

---

"und sunderlich viel Schwaben, die waren am ersten auf und wolten die Schweizer alein fressen, aber sie assen den tot an inen" (Reicke, "Willibald Pirckheimer," 156).

[109] Ungelter to Esslingen, April 25, 1499: "Denn sollten sie weiter vorziehen, und in Herzog Ulrichs Land kommen, so sei zu besorgen, die Bauern würden sich alle zu ihnen schlagen" (Klüpfel, *Urkunden*, 1:325). See Wiesflecker, *Maximilian*, 2:336.

[110] Reicke, "Willibald Pirckheimer," 139.

[111] He notes that the Swiss could rarely (he writes "never") be taken alive and that neither side used heralds in this war. The Swiss decreed that all prisoners should be killed, "Als vnser fromen Altvordern allweg brucht haben." *EA*, 3,1:600, no. 640gg. See Feger, "Probleme der Kriegsgefangenschaft."

[112] Pirckheimer to the Senate of Nuremberg, Lindau, May 19, 1499, in Pirckheimer, *Briefwechsel*, 1:82–3, no. 9. See Reicke, "Willibald Pirckheimer," 184.

[113] Pirckheimer, *Schweizerkrieg*, 127–8 (book II, chap. 7, para. 47). The phrase "rusticis, ut illos appelant" clearly refers to the nobles' habit of calling all Swiss "peasants." The following quote is at ibid., 128 (book II, chap. 7, para. 51).

the starving ghosts of innocent women and children, whose ghastly plight brought tears to the young patrician's eyes. Then came the fruitless climb over the Umbrail Pass to Bormio to fetch provisions sent up the valley by Lodovico il Moro (1451–1508), the doomed duke of Milan, who was the only Imperial prince to give Maximilian genuine support in this war.[114] The provisions did not arrive, and the Nurembergers trudged back over the pass, oppressed by the shimmering heat and the glare from the icy peaks.

Back at Ueberlingen on the lake, Maximilian held a council of war on July 7.[115] Here "those expert in war" advised him to besiege a leading Swiss town, lure the Swiss forces into a decisive battle, and beat them with his superior guns and cavalry. "The more timid ones," however, advised a war of attrition along the Swabian front, and they held the day. Pirckheimer, at least in hindsight, knew this was wrong. His judgment on the conduct of the war agrees,[116] on the whole, with the devastating comments of Ungelter, the Esslinger, who grumbled that the burghers might as well "throw our money into the Lake." The war's outcome proved these voices right. The Rhaetian Leagues now federated with the Swiss; the emperor lost his influence south of the Rhine–Lake line; and his faithful ally, Duke Lodovico of Milan, was dragged off into French imprisonment. The costs of this miserably conducted war, which fell on the Austrian lands and the free cities, plus the humiliation of defeat might well have wrecked Maximilian's system.

Instead, the Habsburg system survived and grew stronger. The Swabian League was renewed in 1500 and acquired a more fixed form than before.[117] Now, too, the first Upper Rhenish members – Strasbourg and Wissembourg – joined (the latter out of fear of the Elector Palatine),[118] and the League set out to embrace the entire Lower Union. Nuremberg,

---

[114] Ibid., 98–9 (book II, chap. 4, para. 33–9), 99–101 (para. 40–50). See Reicke, "Willibald Pirckheimer," 160–5. Bormio (German: Worms) lies in the Valtellina, just over the Umbrail Pass from the Graubünden. On Duke Lodovico and the war, see Wiesflecker, *Maximilian*, 2:338–9; on Maximilian and Pirckheimer, see Reicke, "Willibald Pirckheimer," 178–80.

[115] Pirckheimer, *Schweizerkrieg*, 109–10 (book II, chap. 5, para. 46–9). He distinguishes those "qui ...rei bellicae erant periti" from those "qui timidiores erant."

[116] Ibid., 117 (book II, chap. 6, para. 38). For Ungelter's comment on the conduct of the war, see his letter to Esslingen, Aug. 13, 1499, in Klüpfel, *Urkunden*, 1:374.

[117] Klüpfel, *Urkunden*, 1:409–19 (Sept. 29, 1500). See Bock, *Der Schwäbische Bund*, 86–108.

[118] Klüpfel, *Urkunden*, 1:407–8 (June 23, 1500), 411 (Sept. 29, 1500), 427–8 (Jan. 7, 1501); Wiesflecker, *Maximilian*, 2:370, 399.

too, came in, and the cities now organized a separate Urban Diet of the League and their own League treasury.[119]

The princes, in their negative way, also helped to solidify the Habsburg system, when at the Imperial Diet of Augsburg in 1500 they "totally emasculated" the king.[120] They created the Governing Council under their own control and denied him a standing army, a permanent tax, and the right to make war; and they treated the cities just as roughly. Like a blackbird stuffed with ant eggs, the Nurembergers bitterly reported, Elector Berthold of Mainz sang as sweetly as a nightingale, but he kept no promises. The sparrow hawk (Maximilian), for his part, paid as little heed to Nuremberg's rights as he did to those of the other cities. The Frankfurters echoed the Nurembergers' despair. When the Diet once again excluded the urban envoys, however, and fixed the taxes, as it seemed, unfairly, the towns decided that the safety of the League under the patronage of a king who was no eagle but merely a sparrow hawk, with newly clipped wings at that, was preferable to the Diet.

Not only the Diet, but also cities' quarrels with individual princes, pulled the urban governments closer together.[121] The years following the Swabian War were rich in such feuds. The most spectacular one was Nuremberg's struggle against Margrave Frederick V of Brandenburg-Ansbach (1460–1536), the handling of which at Augsburg in 1500 occasioned the remarks about blackbird and sparrow hawk.[122] Besides other Nuremberg feuds against nobles, Cologne fought its archbishop, Worms and Speyer their bishops, and Wissembourg the Elector Palatine.

Despite these pressures from the princes and nobles, the southern lands did not slide politically toward the Swiss after the war, nor did the confederates move into Vorarlberg, the Allgäu, the Hegau, the Klettgau, the Breisgau, or the Sundgau. A few cities did turn Swiss – Basel in 1501 and Mulhouse in 1511 – but confederates no longer dreamed of glory in Swabia or on the Upper Rhine. The fall of Milan to France pulled them inexorably into the struggle for North Italy, thus giving the

---

[119] Klüpfel, *Urkunden*, 1:409 (July 23, 1500), 421–22 (Sept. 4, 1500). On the nobles, see ibid., 391–2, and Bock, *Der Schwäbische Bund*, 78–80.

[120] See Wiesflecker, *Maximilian*, 2:364–82, especially 373: "Der König war tatsächlich völlig entmachtet." See also Janssen, *Frankfurts Reichscorrespondenz*, 2,2:659–60, no. 813.

[121] Hölbling, "Maximilian I. und sein Verhältnis," 204–84, recounts eleven such quarrels.

[122] Klüpfel, *Urkunden*, 1:392–6; Pirckheimer, *Briefwechsel*, 1: nos. 18, 25, 47bis, 119, 123, 142; Wiesflecker, *Maximilian*, 2:370; Reicke, *Geschichte*, 538.

frontier, so threatened in 1499, time to harden.[123] It hardened also because the urban oligarchies were becoming more concerned about rural unrest, and Maximilian knew how to exploit their fears. When the *Bundschuh* flared up again in 1502, he portrayed it to the Swabian League as a direct continuation of the recent war,

and specifically on account of the secret, devious actions, past and present, of the Swiss against us, the Holy Empire and the Swabian League. We especially expect a surprise invasion by the Swiss up here [i.e., in Swabia] and on the Rhine. For the Swiss hope through an invasion to set the peasants against the clergy, the nobility, and the other lords.[124]

The League met again at Ulm on Saint John's Day (June 24), and the king called the urban delegates into the Deutsches Haus and explained the situation after his own fashion. The entire affair, he warned them, was a French plot, for it was clear "that the king of France has undertaken to stir up all over the Empire violence, dissension and rebellion; and in order to allow the Swiss to conquer Constance, Basel and other places, he has caused to be started a *Bundschuh*, called *monita*."[125] Downriver in the Netherlands, he continued,

just recently a *Bundschuh* broke out, called "Cheese and Bread." And now a *Bundschuh* is trying to develop on the Rhine, which, despite its name, is directed against the priests and the nobles, although through the king's aid it has for the moment been quieted. The aim of all such rebellions is to gather together and then share out all property equally, to rich and poor alike. And the king of France has caused all this in order to gain the Imperial crown.

Maximilian's response to the conspiracy of Joss Fritz in 1502, therefore, should not be seen as an overreaction to a minor rural plot – a hundred conspirators were caught and executed[126] – but as part of a preventive war to keep South Germany from turning Swiss. "We have been told" he wrote against the *Bundschuh* in 1502,

that some of our subjects and the Holy Empire's, inspired by an evil, capricious arrogance and a desire to collaborate against their duties and honor, have formed

---

[123] Wiesflecker, *Maximilian*, 2:358–63. On French influence and the beginnings of the Italian Wars, see Gagliardi, "Mailänder und Franzosen," parts 1, 2.
[124] Klüpfel, *Urkunden*, 1:468; Wiesflecker, *Maximilian*, 3:18–19.
[125] Klüpfel, *Urkunden*, 1:470–1; and there, too, the next quote.
[126] G. Franz, *Der deutsche Bauernkrieg*, 68.

with one another a conspiracy and a league. Which league... could possibly result in the annihilation and suppression of all authority, spiritual and temporal, also the clergy, the entire nobility and all quality of honor, peace, law and the common weal.[127]

Humiliated and thwarted by one Switzerland, Maximilian grimly determined there would be no others.

Underlying the cities' renewed commitment to the defeated Habsburg system, therefore, lay the oligarchies' stake in the solidarity of lordship. The warrior stockmen of the Swiss uplands had liberated themselves piecemeal and then allied with the cities of the valleys; but out on the plains further north, the land was not defensible, and its folk could become free only with the aid of the towns. The time for such an alliance was, however, long in the past, and the urban ruling classes thought rather to escape both rural insurrection and princely predation through an alliance with the greatest lord of all. Though it had failed against the Confederacy in 1499, this logic had worked against the Bavarians in Swabia in 1492; and it would work against the Palatine Wittelsbachs in 1504.

The Bavarian War, 1504

Es thūt den Behem nymmer gūt,
dass sy das aller edelst blūt,
von seinen vier änen ain küng,
haben gewegen also ring.

. . . .

Sy griffen an margraf Fridrich;
das ganz birg habent sy verbrant
wolten ziehen in das Bairland.
Der küng tet sich bald bewegen,
zoch mit herskraft yn entgegen,
des gleich herzog Albrecht, noch mer:
margraf Friderich hynden her,
herzog von Brunswyg an den spitz,

---

[127] G. Franz, "Zur Geschichte des Bundschuhs," 16–17 (Ulm, July 10, 1502). See Mommsen, *Eidgenossen*, 284: "Den Schwabenkrieg müsste man dann vielleicht als eine Art präventiven Bauernkrieges ansehen."

die von Nürnberg mit vil geschitz;
Augspurg das fiert die grienen bier,
was auch da mit macht und zier;
die von Strassburg warn och dabei.[128]

The Bavarian War of 1504 began when Duke George of Bavaria-Land-shut died on December 1, 1503, leaving his lands – which by Wittelsbach house custom and treaty should have gone to his cousin, Duke Albrecht IV of Bavaria-Munich – to his daughter, Elisabeth, and son-in-law, Count Palatine Ruprecht (d. 1504), son of Elector Palatine Philip.[129] The intradynastic struggle between Munich and Heidelberg over Lower Bavaria and other lands then grew into a general South German war. Maximilian played the royal mediator between quarreling vassals, but he demanded from Albrecht as a Habsburg "interest" a considerable chunk of Wittelsbach lands. Maximilian could look with some satisfaction on strife within the Wittelsbach clan, his most dangerous rivals in South Germany.

It was a brief war. When Ruprecht, backed by his father at Heidelberg and by the Bohemians, refused to accept Maximilian's proposal and a judgment by the High Court – both favorable to Albrecht – war became inevitable. Maximilian's strategy called for a holding action in Bavaria and an energetic strike against the Palatine lands on the Upper and Middle Rhine, followed by a campaign of decision in Bavaria with the combined forces of the Empire, the League, and Duke Albrecht. The king's vigor in the conduct of this war presents the greatest possible contrast to his bumbling in that of 1499. While Ruprecht and Albrecht sparred in Lower Bavaria, Maximilian took an Imperial and Austrian army over the Black Forest and down into the Upper Rhine, seized the

---

[128] "The Bohemians should never have tried to fight against our king, who is of the noblest blood of all. In all four lines he comes from kings ... They struck at Margrave Frederick, burned the Bavarian Forest, and began to invade the Bavarian land. Then the king got after them with all his fighting men, along with Duke Albrecht and others. And the margrave came up behind with the Brunswicker in the van. The Nurembergers brought their many guns, and Augsburg flew its fircone flag. They all came with might and main, and the Strasbourgeois came, too." Liliencron, *Volkslieder*, 2:540, no. 242, lines 15–19, 30–41.

[129] The best monograph on this war is Hruschka, "König Maximilian I. und die bayrisch-pfäl-zischen Erbfolgehandel von 1503–1507." I depend also on Wiesflecker, *Maximilian*, 3:164–205; Riezler, *Geschichte*, 3:580–638; A. Kraus, "Sammlung der Kräfte," 291–4; and Bock, *Der Schwäbische Bund*, 51–2.

73

strong Palatine position on the right bank, and drove Philip from Alsace. By August, with the Palatine power on the Upper Rhine utterly broken, Maximilian moved his army eastward across Germany toward Bavaria and a decision. Ruprecht's death proved an omen, for the king won a great victory on September 12, 1504, over the Palatine and Bohemian forces near Regensburg.[130]

What did this war mean to the southern free cities? It meant different things, clearly, to different cities. The major winner was Nuremberg, which grabbed off big chunks of Wittelsbach lands and kept them.[131] To the Swabian cities, however, the war brought new danger, in the east, where Augsburg, Nördlingen, and the Allgäu towns viewed with anxiety any growth of Bavarian might; and in the west, where Württemberg's duke gobbled up Palatine possessions. This is why, when the League's assembly was meeting under the royal eye at Ulm in early April, Hans Langenmantel of Augsburg, who still hoped for mediation, told the Esslingers that the king "is well disposed toward the League; but it is uncertain how long he will remain so, for the majority of the League's councillors favor Ruprecht."[132] Maximilian already had their promise of aid in his pocket, and on April 15 the Leaguers assembled on the banks of the Lech River, some fourteen thousand foot and twelve hundred horse.[133] One can imagine the town governments' enthusiasm for a war in which the king's princely allies – Württemberg, Hesse, and Brandenburg-Ansbach – devoured whatever they could grab.[134] The

---

[130] See the judgments of Press, *Calvinismus*, 168–9, looking backward, and Cohn, *Rhine Palatinate*, 15, looking forward. Wiesflecker, *Maximilian*, 3:174, calls this war "ein Ereignis, das grösste Auswirkungen auf die gesamtdeutsche, ja auf die europäische Geschichte hatte."

[131] Reicke, *Geschichte*, 521–4; E. Franz, *Nürnberg*, 65. Lazarus Spengler later remarked that it would have been much cheaper to buy these lands than to conquer them. For Augsburg's position, see H. Lutz, *Peutinger*, 46.

[132] Hans Langenmantel to Esslingen, March 22 and April 12, 1504, in Klüpfel, *Urkunden*, 1:501, 503. Of the king's motives, he wrote on March 9, 1504, "Es gehe seltsamlich zu; ihn bedunke, der römische König hätte auch gern etwas vom [Duke George's] land" (ibid., 499). See also Ungelter and Langenmantel to Esslingen, Jan. 1–April 11, 1504, in ibid., 494–505. Both men hoped that the war would be headed off, and Langenmantel did not give up hope until April 11. Ibid., 494–5, 503.

[133] Barth, "Erbfolgekrieg," 10–12. See Langenmantel to Esslingen, March 22, 1504, in Klüpfel, *Urkunden*, 1:501; Wiesflecker, *Maximilian*, 3:165–6.

[134] Ungelter to Esslingen, in camp near "Farenzhausen," May 22, 1504, in Klüpfel, *Urkunden*, 1:508. Duke Ulrich even ordered the nearby free cities to send their League levies to him. Ibid., 507–9, 511.

League's army nonetheless held the eastern front while Maximilian marched another army to the Upper Rhine.[135]

Maximilian's invasion of the Upper Rhine in 1504 pushed forward a penetration of the region that had begun with the Burgundian Wars and the Burgundian marriage. The region contained no other major power, though candidates such as Lorraine, Württemberg, and the Palatinate ringed it round. The Wittelsbachs had begun to move into Alsace a century ago, in 1408, when King Ruprecht had first granted the Imperial Vicariate (*Reichslandvogtei*) to his son, Count Palatine Louis. In 1423, the vicariate was mortgaged to the same family for 50,000 fl.[136] This important office carried remnants of sovereignty over the Alsatian Decapolis, and it became the Wittelsbach spearhead into Alsace. The elector harrassed the city and abbey of Wissembourg and acquired the Alsatian lordship of Geroldseck and a strong position in the Ortenau (Middle Baden), where he shared the vicariate with the bishop of Strasbourg and got the strongest castles.[137] By 1500, the Upper Rhine valley was split between a dominant Austria in the south and an expanding Palatine power in the north.

Too big and too strong to be directly troubled by the Palatine advance, Strasbourg maintained, for the most part, excellent economic, political, and cultural relations with Heidelberg. The Rhine Palatinate lay squarely across the Strasbourg merchants' route down to the Frankfurt fairs, and they needed the elector's safe-conducts to get there.[138] The elector, in return, borrowed very large sums at Strasbourg, which was second only to Cologne among his urban creditors.[139] As Wittelsbach influence crept through Alsace, Strasbourg nobles took service with the elector, and Palatine vassals married into Strasbourg families. The elector's deputy in Alsace, for example, was Jakob von Fleckenstein (d. 1514), from the

---

[135] I deduce this from the reports of Hans Ungelter, who was with the League's army in the field. Ibid., 508–16 (May 22–Aug. 31, 1504). See Wiesflecker, *Maximilian*, 3:175–82.

[136] Cohn, *Rhine Palatinate*, 60–7; Stenzel, *Politik*, 21–73.

[137] Cohn, *Rhine Palatinate*, 61–3; Stenzel, *Politik*, 24, notes how the electors sought to bring the lesser nobles under their influence.

[138] AMS, IV 33/7, 9, 14.

[139] Brady, *Ruling Class*, 153–7; Cohn, *Rhine Palatinate*, 117–18, 162, plus a document in AMS, IV 68/128 (1507), which lists Palatine creditors at Strasbourg. For Strasbourgeois in Palatine service, see my *Ruling Class*, 80, 83–4, 87–9, 134, 137.

far north of Alsace, whose daughter in 1507 married a rising young Strasbourg politician, Hans Bock von Gerstheim (d. 1542). One of their daughters, in turn, married a Palatine chancellor, Florenz von Venningen (d. 1538).

Palatine power came, in the days of Elector Frederick the Victorious, to stretch from Frankfurt and Heilbronn to the borders of Lorraine and from the Moselle and Lahn valleys southward to central Alsace and Baden. Except during the Burgundian Wars, Strasbourg tried, beginning with the alliance of 1457, to keep good relations with Heidelberg. Two Wittelsbach princes in the see of Strasbourg from 1440 to 1506 did nothing to weaken the dynasty's influence there; and although the city's government disapproved of the harrassment of Wissembourg by the elector, it did not answer King Maximilian's call to arms on the tiny town's behalf.[140]

Cultural ties reinforced others, as during the 1490s Heidelberg became a preferred university for young Strasbourgeois. This flow increased after Jakob Wimpheling resigned his Heidelberg professorship and came to tutor well-born lads at Strasbourg. One of them was Jacob Sturm (1489–1553), the future politician, who was a student at Heidelberg when the Bavarian War began.[141]

Strasbourg's situation may stand for those of the other independent Upper Rhenish powers as well. Heidelberg or Freiburg? Palatinate or Austria? Wittelsbach or Habsburg?[142] Tradition spoke for the elector, but the times spoke for the king. Maximilian, indeed, aimed to supplant the Elector Palatine on the Upper Rhine, and he acted on the advice of the Alsatian noble who after the war became Deputy Imperial Vicar in Alsace, Kaspar von Mörsberg,[143] who recommended that the king redeem the vicariate from the Wittelsbachs and bring all the region's powers into obedience. With such lands, he wrote, the Austrian position

---

[140] Stenzel, *Politik*, 22, 43, 45–6, 251–5; Rapp, *Réformes*, 171–9.

[141] Rapp, "Les strasbourgeois et les universités," 14–15. On Wimpheling, see Knepper, *Jakob Wimpfeling (1450–1528)*, 93–181.

[142] When Maximilian offered to join the Lower Union, Ammeister Peter Schott (d. 1504) proposed to admit the Elector Palatine as well. Mertens, "Reich und Elsass," 210–11. On Schott, see my "Aristocratie et régime politique," 19–20.

[143] Mertens, "Reich und Elsass," 223–47, has uncovered the crucial document. The vicariate remained in Habsburg hands from 1504 until 1530, when it was again mortgaged to the Elector Palatine. Ibid., 280–7; Schäfer, "Der Anspruch der Kurpfalz," 265–329.

on the Upper Rhine "would be comparable to a kingdom," and the king could then deal with the Rhenish electors. Enclosed within its mountain walls, the wonderfully rich plain on both sides of the Rhine fairly begged to be made the central seat of a powerful state.

The war began on the Upper Rhine on May 17, 1504, when the king's outlawing of Count Ruprecht was announced to the free cities there. Maximilian called on Strasbourg and Wissembourg to send their Swabian League levies to his army, and he sent his agents, local men mostly, to persuade the other cities to back the king.[144] Strasbourg, which was not permitted – as some Upper Rhenish princes were – to stay neutral, tried unsuccessfully to negotiate downward its contribution to the League.

The long, sinuous valley of the Kinzig River offers the easiest route over the central Black Forest from the Upper Neckar valley, where Maximilian mobilized in Austrian lands, into the Upper Rhine. Here lay three of those tiny free cities that always get lost in any discussion of South German cities: Zell am Harmersbach, Gengenbach, and Offenburg, in ascending order of size. The towns, which had been mortgaged to the Elector Palatine and the bishop of Strasbourg, smelled freedom and made contact with the king, who on May 27 declared them free again. An interesting light on the political culture of these small cities – Zell may have had four or five hundred citizens – is shed by their inquiry to the law faculty at Freiburg about the validity of the king's release, which the professors of this Austrian university duly confirmed.[145] When Maximilian came down the Kinzig in early August, leading eight to ten thousand men from Tyrol and Western Austria, plus heavy guns from Innsbruck, he found the cities' gates open.[146]

The Wittelsbach position on the Upper Rhine rested on Castle Ortenburg, high above Offenburg at the Kinzig's exit from the mountains,

---

[144] Mertens, "Reich und Elsass," 259–61; Ulmann, *Maximilian*, 2:211.
[145] King Maximilian to Gengenbach, Augsburg, May 27, 1504, in Barth, "Erbfolgekrieg," 49–51, with the (undated) reply of the Kinzig valley towns.
[146] Ibid., 21–7; Wiesflecker, *Maximilian*, 3:182–3, who reckons the army at 8,000. Heinrich Slebusch, city secretary of Cologne, estimated from Rottenburg am Neckar, August 2, 1504, that the king had "bi de 10 dusent auss alle sinen erblanden und anderswa." Höhlbaum, "Kölner Briefe," 20, no. 2. Ungelter reported to Esslingen, July 31, 1504, that the king had called up 6,000 Austrians. Klüpfel, *Urkunden*, 1:512–13. The detail about the guns comes from Hug, *Chronik*, 164.

and Castle Hohengeroldseck, the strongest place in Middle Baden.[147] Neither Frenchman nor Swiss came to their aid, and as the Austrian guns were coming up into position, Maximilian crossed the Rhine to Strasbourg, which had sent him five hundred men and, rumor had it, 20,000 fl.[148] On the evening of August 9, 1504, the king entered in full armor by torchlight the city his queen had feared to visit in 1499. Next day, stuffed with gifts, he visited the arsenal. Money and guns, they were the good things cities could supply. On the eleventh, the king recrossed the river to besiege the Ortenburg, which had been built before the coming of cannon and was commanded by a neighboring height; he took it in two days. Now he divided his forces, leaving part to besiege the much stronger Hohengeroldseck, sending another downstream to link up with the Hessians and Württembergers, and taking a third back across the river into Alsace.[149] He hoped to impress the cities there, to whose envoys his spokesmen at Hagenau on August 18 soothed fears of Heidelberg's vengeance and promised that the king would "plant a rose garden around them with his own gracious hands and protect them with both wings of the eagle."[150] This was perhaps more royal care than they wanted, for in return their guns were wanted for a siege of Castle Lützelstein, and Strasbourg had to offer him another loan.

The Upper Rhine now lay under the Habsburg eagle's wings, the path downriver lay open, and Maximilian toyed with the notion of crushing his foes for good. But news came of Count Ruprecht's death and

---

[147] Cohn, *Rhine Palatinate*, 62–3; Barth, "Erbfolgekrieg," 16–17; Mertens, "Reich und Elsass," 262–79.

[148] Heinrich Slebusch to Cologne, Rottenburg am Neckar, Aug. 2, 1504, and Horb, Aug. 4, 1504, in Höhlbaum, "Kölner Briefe," 20, 21. He reports "etlige fil hondert zo voet und perde," whereas the king himself estimated to the Hessian landgrave that he had 500 from Strasbourg and 1,000 Ortenauers. Strasbourg, Aug. 17, 1504, in Ulmann, *Maximilian*, 2:215 n. 1. Peutinger reports that 500 Strasbourg infantry, four guns, and some cavalry arrived at Augsburg on May 27 and left two days later to join the Imperial army. Conrad Peutinger to Elector Berthold of Mainz [Augsburg], June 1, 1504, in Peutinger, *Briefwechsel*, 29–30, no. 15. The League's commander from the cities, Hans Langenmantel of Augsburg, had ordered Strasbourg on Dec. 22, 1503, to send troops. AMS, AA 344, fol. 8.

[149] King Maximilian to Strasbourg, Offenburg, Aug. 15, 1504, in AMS, AA 319, fol. 114; Heinrich Slebusch to Cologne, Strasbourg, Aug. 21, 1504, in Höhlbaum, "Kölner Briefe," 22–4, no. 4. Maximilian lodged, as usual, with the Knights of St. John "zum grünen Wörth." Barth, "Erbfolgekrieg," 32. On the division of forces, see Ulmann, *Maximilian*, 2:215–16.

[150] Quoted by Wiesflecker, *Maximilian*, 3:185. The king stayed at Strasbourg Aug. 9–11, 16–17, and 19, and he collected many gifts. Höhlbaum, "Kölner Briefe," 26, no. 4; Barth, "Erbfolgekrieg," 32.

of a Bohemian invasion of Bavaria, and, leaving his agents to treat with the broken-spirited elector, the king hurried eastward.[151] Near Regensburg, on September 12, 1504, the Habsburg system had perhaps its finest hour. In the central "shock troop" (*Gewalthaufen*) were the Swabian Leaguers from the towns, Nurembergers, Augsburgers, Regensburgers, and Strasbourgeois, who followed the king's own wild charge against the Palatine lines and broke the Bohemians' wagon fort. "The Bohemians were manly folk," sang a bard later, "and they stood fast like walls," but the Leaguers' storm "slew them like hogs, . . . and a great stream of crimson blood flowed across the broad field."[152] In two hours, the king's men won the day. Two days later, Elisabeth, Ruprecht's booted and spurred widow who had fought in the defeated army, died in the night. The war was over, and it remained only for Maximilian to collect his "interest."[153]

The Bavarian War went as well for the king as the Swabian War had gone badly. It brought him, "despite his miserable penury, to the height of his political success."[154] The old Palatine elector and his party were beaten; Elector Berthold of Mainz was dead and his reform party dispersed; and the smoking ruins in Lower Bavaria and on the Rhine warned other potential rivals of the Habsburg power in the South. "The king's power in the Empire is so great," reported Vincenzo Quirini to Venice, "that no one dares any longer to oppose him." Hans von Königsegg, longtime Habsburg envoy to the Swiss, exulted about future Habsburg lordship over all Europe, plus Asia and Africa. Such was the psychological effect of the victory for Maximilian, for the House of Austria, and for the South German system. Part of the victory rested, true, on the allied princes, but the system's constant heart – cash and credits, guns and gunners, and all sorts of provisions – lay in the free cities.

---

[151] Ulmann, *Maximilian*, 2:216–18; Wiesflecker, *Maximilian*, 3:185–6. On the Bavarian campaign of Sept. 1504, see ibid., 186–92.
[152] Ibid., 186–8; and Liliencron, *Volkslieder*, 2:540, no. 242, lines 38–41. The following quote is in ibid., 544, no. 243, stanza 11 (Wiesflecker, *Maximilian*, 3:189, gives a paraphrase).
[153] See Ulmann, *Maximilian*, 2:221, on Elisabeth, Duke George's daughter. On the declaration at Cologne, see Wiesflecker, *Maximilian*, 3:198–203.
[154] Wiesflecker, *Maximilian*, 3:204, and there, too, the basis of the following lines, with the two quotes from p. 205.

3

∞∞∞

Maximilian and his cities, 1493–1519

Maximilian I was a truly prodigal king. During his final decade, he dribbled away in the ruinously expensive Italian Wars most of what he had gained in the Bavarian War. Most, but not all, for his system of clientage and federation in South Germany endured through thick and thin, nourished by the financial and political bonds between cities and monarchy. Just after the emperor's death, his system won a spectacular victory over Württemberg in 1519, their final triumph.

King and cities in the Habsburg system

> Der römisch küng hat sich wol bedacht,
> die reichstett all zūsamen bracht,
> so gar in kurzen weilen;
> er ist gezogen nacht und tag,
> gen Regenspurg thet er eilen.[1]

> Der römisch künig het gar kain ru,
> die fürsten zugen im pald zu,
> die ritterschaft mit kreften;
> die rechstet zu der selben frist,
> was in dem pund zu Schwaben ist,
> mit eren wol behefte;[2]

---

[1] "The King of Romans had a good idea to bring the towns all together as quickly as he could. On the road both day and night, he rode to Regensburg." Liliencron, *Volkslieder*, 2:538, no. 241, stanza 3.

[2] "The King of Romans never rests. The princes ride into camp, and then the knights with all their men and the cities on the spot. All the Swabian League's allies honor their word to him." Ibid., 543, no. 243, stanza 6.

80

Maximilian and his cities

One time, some Amsterdamers came to Maximilian to beg his permission for their city to build new walls.[3] A silken thread would suffice to protect the city, he replied, and this about sums up the emperor's attitude toward cities. He was their patron and their customer, but not their friend. Cities supplied him with so many things he needed or just wanted: money and guns, powder and shot, gems and books, armor and hunting weapons, jurists and secretaries, artists and artisans, mistresses and funerary monuments. Like his distinguished predecessor, Frederick I Barbarossa, Maximilian objected not to cities as such, but to free cities.[4] This attitude was rooted in both royal tradition and personal experience. At Augsburg in 1474, when Frederick III could not pay for his court's room and board, the proud burghers mocked the courtiers and the young prince in the streets and threw dung at them.[5] In the Netherlands, Maximilian moved into the inherited struggle between his wife's house, the Valois dukes of Burgundy, and the great communes. In the great wave of anticentralist feeling that swept the ducal lands on the death of Charles the Bold in 1477, the "three members of Flanders" – Ghent, Bruges, and Ypres – led the movement to recover local liberties. At Bruges, the prince was taken prisoner and guarded by troops of the "three members," while his courtiers were tortured and his supporters executed before his eyes. Maximilian made war on the rebels and eventually (1492) recovered much of what he conceded.[6]

The need for urban financial power was especially strong in South Germany, both because the Austrian lands were weak in urban capital and banking skills, and because much of the Austrian domain, especially the mines, was mortgaged to mining and trading firms, leaving Maximilian no more than a tenth of the 1.5 million florins his mines annually produced.[7] To the extent that the king kept his financial head above water, he did so by mortgaging future revenues for current income from loans, raised where and when he found them. Again and again, to his

[3] Wiesflecker, *Maximilian*, 1:70; for his hatred of the Venetians, see ibid., 3:443.
[4] Hölbling, "Maximilian I. und sein Verhältnis," 294; Boos, *Städtekultur*, 4:145–6. The comparison with Frederick Barbarossa's views is based on Munz, *Frederick Barbarossa*, 154; Skinner, *Foundations*, 1:4–8.
[5] Wiesflecker, *Maximilian*, 1:106.
[6] Ibid., 113–227; Pirenne, *Histoire de Belgique*, 3:43–55.
[7] Wiesflecker, *Maximilian*, 3:397–9, treats finances for the years 1500 through 1508 and promises to deal with the entire subject in vol. 5. See Benecke, *Maximilian I*, 101–2, 138–46.

councillors' disgust, he resorted to the urban bankers, and Austria supplied the lion's share of the revenues to keep this patchwork practice afloat – twenty times more than the Empire, the king estimated in 1507. Hand-to-mouth finance worked tolerably well until 1508, when the Italian Wars threw royal finance into chaos.

In the free cities, Maximilian borrowed from both public and private sources. A by no means complete compilation of his debts to urban governments reveals that he owed them at least 100,000 fl. when he died, of which a quarter each was held by Strasbourg and Nuremberg; 15,500 fl. by Basel; 8–9,000 fl. each by Augsburg and Freiburg im Breisgau; and smaller sums by Speyer, Worms, Cologne, and Ulm.[8] He borrowed mostly on short term, usually three to twelve months, and as time went on his credit with the urban governments sank.

Such sums were small potatoes beside what Maximilian owed the great private banking houses. In this, as in so many other respects, Augsburg functioned as the unofficial capital of Maximilian's realm,[9] whence came the capital to work his mines and the cash to pay for his wars.[10] His biggest creditors were the Fuggers, with whom he began to deal in a big way after 1490, and who from 1512 to 1518 supplied an average of one-quarter of his annual income. At his death, Maximilian owed the Fuggers at least 1,300,000 fl., plus another 230,000 fl. to the Paumgartner and smaller sums to other firms.[11] The loans were secured by concessions in the mines and foodstuffs trade with Austria, and the total may have reached 3,000,000 fl. by 1518, mainly in long-term loans against royal revenues. Investigations would likely yield a similar, if smaller, pattern of borrowing at Nuremberg, Strasbourg, and Ulm.

The sums he got from the cities doubtless whetted Maximilian's appetite for urban wealth as a whole. The free cities paid 20 to 25 percent of Imperial levies, but they vehemently opposed for many years the schemes to finance Imperial government and wars through a direct levy on property (the Common Penny enacted in 1495).[12] By 1507, when

[8] Hölbling, "Maximilian I. und sein Verhältuis," 174–81. I can add from AMS, IV 68/122, an acknowledgment of 3,000 fl. owed by Maximilian to Strasbourg in 1498.
[9] Hölbling, "Maximilian I. und sein Verhältnis," 187–97; Ehrenberg, *Zeitalter der Fugger*, 1:90–1; Pölnitz, *Jakob Fugger*, 1:chaps. 5–17; Benecke, *Maximilian I*, 41, 119.
[10] Pölnitz, *Jakob Fugger*, 1:174.
[11] Wiesflecker, *Maximilian*, 1:96; the figures are supplied by Hölbling, "Maximilian I. und sein Verhältnis," 193–7.
[12] Hölbling, "Maximilian I. und sein Verhältnis," 134–72, gives a clear, useful discussion of the

the Diet of Constance voted him a mere 120,000 fl., half of what he asked for, toward his Italian project, he tried in desperation to tap the big trading firms.[13] Twice he ordered the principal companies to send agents to him at Ulm, alleging that the Diet had authorized him to treat with them about a loan, and he ordered firms from Nuremberg, Augsburg, Ravensburg, and Memmingen to advance him about 80,000 fl. for the Italian campaign.[14] He offered them large deliveries of copper if they did so and prosecution through the courts if they refused. Most of the firms' governments resisted, though the Nurembergers bought off Maximilian with a gift, for they feared the king's assertion of a direct royal jurisdiction over commercial firms, just like that over the Jews. At the Urban Diet at Speyer on June 24, 1508, the free cities' envoys declared that

His Roman Majesty, our most gracious lord, has sent to some firms in the Swabian free cities and ordered them to contribute a large sum of money to his Roman [i.e., coronation] journey, alleging that the merchants' firms belong to His Majesty and the Empire alone, not to the cities in which the merchants reside, etc. This is a demand and an innovation unheard of in the Imperial free cities and among the firms and businesses of their merchants; and we fear that if it is successful, it will bring grave damages and disadvantages to the free cities and to their merchants and commercial firms.[15]

This affair, and especially the king's failure to get what he wanted, illustrates how advantageous it was for the urban rich to be citizens of free cities rather than the king's directly ruled subjects.

Besides the urban governments and the commercial firms, Maximilian tried to find the sums he needed, and which the Imperial Diet denied him, through the Swabian League. At the beginning of 1508, for example, he ordered the Leaguers to hold ready a thousand men for the coming war against Venice. "The matter does not especially concern the League," they replied, "but rather the whole Empire," and, in fact,

---

forms of Imperial taxation. See also G. Schmidt, *Städtetag*, 331–51; Rowan, "Imperial Taxes and German Politics," 207–8, 215–16.
[13] Wiesflecker, *Maximilian*, 3:372–7, 441.
[14] Based on Gumbel, "Berichte, I," 278 n. 2, and "Berichte, II," 142 n. 2. The incident is not mentioned by Wiesflecker. The scheme was hatched already at the Diet of Constance in 1507. Janssen, *Frankfurts Reichscorrespondenz*, 2,2:714, no. 909.
[15] Klüpfel, *Urkunden*, 2:16–17 (June 24, 1508).

"it is not the League's affair at all."[16] Besides, they noted, the request constituted double taxation, since they had to pay Imperial war taxes as well. The incident shows that, even at the height of his power, Maximilian could not rely on his clients to open their purses for his projects outside the region the League had been organized to protect.

Maximilian knew the free cities and their burghers as did few German monarchs before and none after him. The royal presence is revealed by his itinerary: He spent nearly a quarter of his entire twenty-six-year reign in free cities, and almost half of that (about 995 days in twenty-eight visits) in Augsburg.[17] Altogether his travels back and forth across Germany, from Austria to the Netherlands, from Diet to war, brought him on about 186 visits to around forty free cities. This "royal locust" left a trail of creditors and unpaid bills; but he also left behind orders and commissions for all manner of goods and services. The extremely familiar terms he maintained with the burghers probably help to balance psychologically his bad debts and the bad impression his penury made. The favors he strewed so liberally in his path helped even more.

The king's relations with Strasbourg illustrate the varieties of his favors. Maximilian asked the civic government to receive homage as his proxy for Imperial fiefs held by Strasbourgeois;[18] he asked privileges for his councillors; and he frequently intervened in someone's favor before one of the local courts.[19] In May 1503, the king asked the Stettmeister to be royal proxy at the baptism of a child of Claus Jörger, a local cloth merchant and self-made man, and his wife, and he later sent the baby a baptismal gift.[20] As often as he could, Maximilian sent a local man, such as Peter Völtsch, to deal with local people and the local government.[21] How many and which councillors he drew from the free cities

---

[16] Ibid., 14–15 (Jan. 8, 1508).
[17] Based on Stälin, "Aufenthaltsorte" and V. von Kraus, "Itinerarium Maximiliani I." The phrase "royal locust" is from Benecke, *Maximilian I*, 128, who also analyzes the king's itinerary.
[18] AMS, AA 309, fols. 76, 157, 166, 171, 175–6, 179 (1494–8).
[19] King Maximilian to the Stettmeister and Senate of Strasbourg, Augsburg, June 16, 1500, in favor of Heinrich Reyff, a long-time Austrian sevitor. AMS, AA 319, fol. 14. Examples of the king's intervention in suits are in ibid., fols. 23, 24, 55, 61–6.
[20] King Maximilian to the Stettmeister and Senate of Strasbourg, Ensisheim, May 24 and June 10, 1503, in ibid., fols. 75–7. On Claus Jörger, see my *Ruling Class*, 129–30; Rapp, "Préréformes et humanisme," 213.
[21] On Peter Völtsch, see Chapter 2, note 95. The king wrote from Innsbruck to Strasbourg on Jan. 10, 1502, that Völtsch had resigned from "unnser Fiscal Ambts...dieweil er dem swere halb seins leibs nit ausgewarten mag" and asked that Völtsch be allowed to settle in his native

is, in the absence of research, impossible to tell. Certainly there were many, and some outstanding ones, such as Jörg Gossembrot of Augsburg and Jakob Spiegel (1483–c. 1547) of Sélestat, Wimpheling's nephew.[22] Through such men and through grants of fiefs and coats of arms, ennoblements, and pensions, a dense network of familiar bonds grew up between the royal court and the urban upper classes. Through this network the king drew into his patronage, too, the writers who glorified him and his reign.

Though many of them were born in and served free cities, the German humanists made no connection between the ancient autonomous polis and the German free cities but rather developed a defense of the idea of monarchy that was "saturated by a conservative, in many respects even restorationist, ideology."[23] They ransacked German and Roman history to justify the passage of the Roman imperium into German, and specifically Austrian, hands and developed an ideological hull for what may be called "the Habsburg system in South Germany."[24] The full dimensions of Maximilian's recruitment of such men and their services to him and his dynasty are not yet known, but the point will be illustrated with two outstanding examples, Sebastian Brant and Conrad Peutinger, city secretaries respectively of Strasbourg and Augsburg. Brant early on set himself on the king's side, having defended Maximilian against the princes and supported the Common Penny, even though the urban governments mostly opposed it.[25] In 1502, Maximilian appointed him a royal servitor (*diener*), presumably with a pension, later asked that he be permitted to come to court on royal business, and eventually granted

city. AMS, AA 319, fol. 35. Völtsch was active in Habsburg service in 1503. Ibid., fols. 70 (May 18, 1503), 72 (May 16, 1503). Another Strasbourgeois who worked for Maximilian was Mathis Wurm von Geudertheim, father of the celebrated pamphleteer (my thanks to Jean Rott for identifying him for me). Ibid., fol. 93; Rott, "De quelques pamphlétaires nobles," 139–44. One of the king's physicians was Dr. Hieronymus Baldung, whose brother, the father of the celebrated artist, settled at Strasbourg. Another son, Caspar, became city attorney there. AMS, AA 319, fol. 129 (March 18, 1496); Brady, "Social Place," 303–4.
22 Wiesflecker, *Maximilian*, 2:406; Ehrenberg, *Zeitalter der Fugger*, 1:190–2.
23 H. Lutz, *Peutinger*, 134–5.
24 I owe this insight to Mertens, "Reich und Elsass." Still useful are Gothein, *Volksbewegungen*, and Knepper, *Nationaler Gedanke*. See also Waas, *Legendary Character*; and Benecke, *Maximilian I*, 7–30.
25 Wuttke, "Sebastian Brant," and "Wunderdeutung und Politik." A modern book on Brant, along the lines of H. Lutz's on Peutinger, is a pressing need. On his politics, nothing later than Knepper's book (1898) is of much help.

Turning Swiss

him in fief the house "Zum Nesselbach" in Strasbourg. In return, Brant
worked on a never-finished history of the Habsburgs and made propaganda for the old idea of the king as *imperator mundi*.[26] Peutinger, too,
became a royal servitor about the time, late in 1506, when he began to
write his "Book of the Emperors," a repertory of emperors from Julius
Caesar to Maximilian I. He finished neither this nor his Habsburg
genealogy, but he continued until the king's death to advise him on
political and literary matters.[27]

A genuine historical insight tempered these humanist politicians' enthusiasm for the monarchy. When, during the Bavarian War, they ex-
changed views on the future of the German imperium, Peutinger wrote
of his fear that this war would disrupt order enough to bring the Germans
"under a foreign yoke," for nothing guaranteed that the imperium would
remain forever in German hands.[28] Too true, Brant replied, "nor is the
Roman imperium so bound to German soil that it might not come into
other hands."[29] The Germans could lose it, just as the Assyrians, Medes,
Greeks, and Romans had, "for when Fortune should wish it, no one
can gainsay it." This was a far more pessimistic note than the one Brant
had struck in 1486, when he had greeted Maximilian and his father as
the founders of a new Golden Age.

The humanists' praise for the Habsburgs flowed from the realistic
insight that the king was the most likely ally, if the cities were to preserve
their autonomy and defend their merchants' interests. This was the
political calculation of the oligarchies, and, as sincere as it certainly was,
it ought not to be mistaken for the sentiments of townsmen as a whole.[30]
The cities must have contained many witnesses to Maximilian's visits
who were more impressed by his eternal penury, his scrounging, and
his wheedling for money than by the pomp and display of his entries.

---

[26] King Maximilian to the Stettmeister and Senate of Strasbourg, Innsbruck, Jan. 24, 1502, in
AMS, AA 319, fol. 34; AMS, V 137/16 (April 1, 1521); Seyboth, *Das alte Strassburg*, 183;
Knepper, *Nationaler Gedanke*, 105.
[27] H. Lutz, *Peutinger*, 42–3, 120–1.
[28] Peutinger to Sebastian Brant, Augsburg, July 13, 1504, in Peutinger, *Briefwechsel*, 32, no. 17.
[29] Brant to Peutinger, Strasbourg, after mid-July 1504, in ibid., 34, no. 18. See H. Lutz, *Peutinger*,
47; on Brant's mood in 1486, see Knepper, *Nationaler Gedanke*, 157.
[30] Schröcker, *Die Deutsche Nation*, 124, correctly distinguishes between popular views and those
of the humanists. In Alsace, upper-class urban opinion swung sharply against the Swiss after
1500. Feller and Bonjour, *Geschichtsschreibung*, 1:123.

86

Maximilian and his cities

His attentions to the burghers' wives and daughters cannot have heightened his popularity.[31]

In the city halls, there can have been few illusions about the king's person and his legendary thirst for gifts, loans, and bribes. At Maximilian's death, Wilhelm Rem of Augsburg reflected on the king's character.

The emperor was Austria's lord, he was pious but not especially intelligent, and he was always out of money. In his own lands he had given away so many cities, castles, rents and dues, that very little came to him.

His councillors were genuine scoundrels, and they completely dominated him. Almost all of them grew rich, while he was poor. And whoever wanted a favor from the emperor, such as a privilege or other type of charter, he had to pay bribes to the councillors, who got it done. When, however, an adversary came to court, they also took money from him and gave him charters which contradicted the earlier ones. The emperor stood by and let it all happen.[32]

Venality lubricated the life of Maximilian's court. Dr. Erasmus Topler (1462–1512), provost of Sankt Sebald in Nuremberg, spent the last five years of his life at court, and his letters paint a dreary picture of the *finanzen* that greased the cogs of political business there. The market in privileges reached right to the top, he wrote in 1512, and the king told him to warn the Nurembergers not to worry about a privilege the Augsburgers had acquired, "for it is a *finanz*."[33] "As I have earlier told you several times," he sighed, "the nature of this court [is] dedicated to *finanzen*."

Maximilian did not always get what he wanted. The Baselers in 1492 resisted his pressure for a loan, though in the end he got 2,000 fl., which they immediately wrote off as a bad debt.[34] The more pliable government of Metz lent him some 60,000 fl. during the 1490s. In return, Maximilian distributed privileges with a lavish hand, measured according to the size and needs of the city. To Nuremberg, for example, the king confirmed

---

[31] Waas, *Legendary Character*, 53–4; Boos, *Städtekultur*, 4:36.
[32] Rem, "Cronica newer geschichte," 99–100.
[33] Dr. Erasmus Topler to the *Ältere Herren* of Nuremberg, Trier, March 13, 1512, in Gumbel, "Berichte, II," 218. The following quote is from his report from Mainz, May 24, 1508, in ibid., 148.
[34] R. Wackernagel, *Geschichte*, 2,1:140. Between 1473 and 1492, Basel loaned about 67,609 fl. to monarchs. On Metz's loans, see Rem, "Cronica newer geschichte," 99 n. 2, for the years 1492 through 1498.

in 1507 "the freedom concerning merchant affairs," which allowed summary proceedings in suits for less than 600 fl. Little Turckheim in Upper Alsace had no use for such a grand privilege, but in 1498 it got the right to levy a duty on goods entering the city, to tax foreign landowners in the district, and to move the date of its annual fair.[35] The fiscalization of royal justice and administration was as old, perhaps, as the German monarchy, but Maximilian raised it to notorious new heights.

The urban governments also wanted the king's support and protection in their quarrels with neighboring princes. Maximilian failed to save Boppard, true, but he did force Duke Albrecht to disgorge Regensburg, and though he sometimes put royal governors into free cities, his interventions were always temporary.[36] His behavior toward Worms is perhaps typical. Worms, like Speyer, lay under heavy pressure to recognize the bishop's governing rights, to escape which Worms took in June 1494 the unusual step – for it had never been a royal city – of performing homage to the king. When the bishop objected, Maximilian promptly restored episcopal rights; then, on the city's appeal, he reversed himself. Finally, he turned the case over to a group of princes for arbitration. Now began a fierce, grotesque struggle between Worms's government and Bishop Johann von Dalberg, in which numerous judgments were handed down but none enforced by the king. Worms stayed neutral during the Bavarian War, when the Hessians burned right into its suburbs, but later Maximilian took the city under his own protection – naturally, for a cash payment. As the quarrel wore on, an exasperated secretary wrote on the cover of a record of the negotiations, "Whoever would build his house on sand, he should lend to nobles and trust the priests."[37] Although in the end both sides had to compromise, the bishop's priests reentered the city, and the friars, who had manned their pastoral posts during the long struggle, had to leave. The story illustrates a hard lesson of German politics: No free city could be sure of the king's aid, even when he was well paid for it. The king himself was no

---

[35] Gumbel, "Berichte, I," 278 n. 2, and "Berichte, II," 142 n. 2. On Turckheim, see Scherlen, *Histoire*, 57–8.

[36] I follow Hölbling, "Maximilian I. und sein Verhältnis," 204–94. The rest of this paragraph is based on Boos, *Städtekultur*, 4:35–40, 53–7, 78–81, 89–116.

[37] "Wer zu verderben wil bauwen / Soll edeln lyhen und pfaffen getrauwen etc." Quoted by Boos, *Städtekultur*, 4:101.

threat to urban liberties, it is true, but his policies toward cities elsewhere – in the Netherlands, for example – suggest that in South Germany his resort to federation and clientage grew out of necessity rather than principle.

The long-range prospects for the free cities from their association with Maximilian depended to a very great degree on what became of Austria, which sooner or later had to pay most of the bills for the emperor's grand designs.[38] In 1518, the last year of his life, he decided to make a virtue of necessity and undertake a major centralization of the Austrian lands as a step toward bringing the entire Empire more closely under his control. This "Austrian way to a German monarchy," though it remained a paper project at his death, shows the direction of Maximilian's thinking.

By 1518, Maximilian had little left. The Italian Wars had wrecked his credit, the Tyrolean mines and foundries were pledged, the Austrian domain was sold or mortgaged, and he owed the Augsburgers about 2 million florins.[39] Tyrol stood open to a French strike from Milan, and the king still dreamed of a great crusade against Sultan Selim the Terrible.[40] Maximilian's cruel penury, nourished by years of overspending, thriftless administration, shortsighted finance, and broken promises of fiscal reform, had driven him, already in 1516, to consider centralization of Austria itself as a possible step. Peutinger had even helped to draft a plan for the creation of a separate hereditary kingdom of Austria, to be ruled by Maximilian's younger grandson, Ferdinand, though the plan had foundered on the opposition of the king's chief heir, Charles of Burgundy.[41]

Two years later, Maximilian tried centralization by another route. He called delegations from the Austrian territorial estates (a *Generallandtag*) in January 1518 to Innsbruck, where they sat until May 24.[42] These

---

[38] Wiesflecker, *Maximilian*, 3:405–6, 443–6, and 4:494–7.
[39] Ibid., 305; see 289–305 for the war's effects on Austria.
[40] Ibid., 229–32. He was not responding to Turkish pressure, for at this time Sultan Selim I (r. 1512–20) was deeply engaged in his conquests of the Safavid kingdom and the Mamlūk state. Shaw, *Empire of the Gazis*, 82–5.
[41] H. Lutz, *Peutinger*, 122–3; Koller, *Das "Königreich" Österreich*; Wiesflecker, *Maximilian*, 4:302–3, who suggests that the Austrian estates opposed the idea; and Fichtner, *Ferdinand I of Austria*.
[42] The sources are printed by Brandis, *Landeshauptleute*, 446–9; and Zeibig, "Ausschuss-Landtag," 205–7. See Fellner, "Zur Geschichte," 267–8; Wiesflecker, *Maximilian*, 4:305–20.

men represented lands and towns from the Hungarian border to Alsace, and the emperor meant to win them for a centralizing scheme that promised to restore his shattered finances. That it was to be a step toward the harnessing of the Imperial Diet is suggested both by its timing – just before the Diet of Augsburg – and by its originally announced meeting place, Donauwörth in Swabia. Twice before, projects for a permanent supreme council over the Empire, the Governing Council (*Reichsregiment*) of 1500 and Maximilian's own aulic council (*Hofrat*) in 1502, had come to nothing.[43] The emperor was nonetheless determined to remedy through structural reform the gross overburdening of Austria for what were, in effect, Imperial tasks, such as the Italian Wars and war against the Turks. It was this prospect, that Austria should no longer bear the lion's share of the costs, that made the centralization attractive to the king's Austrian subjects.

Having promised the Austrian estates to make no new war without their consent, Maximilian proposed to the assembly a closer relationship between Austria and the Empire. "To the purpose of promoting our own welfare and that of our lands and subjects," he told them, "we are decided to negotiate and establish, at the proper time and place, a neighborly union, agreement, and league with the estates of the Holy Empire; or, if that is impossible, at least with the principalities, cities, and lords that border on our Austrian lands."[44] This was nothing less than an expanded, more closely integrated version of the Swabian League. Its supreme organ was to be an aulic council (*Hofrat*) of eighteen members: five from the Empire, five from the Lower (eastern) Austrian lands; two each from Tyrol and Western Austria; and four royal officials (chamberlain, marshal, chancellor, and treasurer).[45] Maximilian agreed to hand over to this council, whose members would serve for six months, all judicial and financial affairs, "except for our own secret and weighty

---

[43] See Wiesflecker, *Maximilian*, 3:208–13 (Diet of Cologne, 1505), and 4:274–5 (Diet of Trier-Cologne, 1512); see also 3:1–15, 247–49, 375. On the Governing Council, see Wolgarten, *Reichsregiment*.

[44] Dated May 24, 1518, printed by Brandis, *Landeshauptleute*, 456–83, here at 470. There is a much better, though abridged, text in Fellner and Kretschmayr, *Zentralverwaltung*, 1,2:91, no. 10. Maximilian's instruction is in Brandis, *Landeshauptleute*, 449–56.

[45] Brandis, *Landeshauptleute*, 470–1; Fellner and Kretschmayr, *Zentralverwaltung*, 1,2:84, lines 20–9; and see Zeibig, "Ausschuss-Landtag," 227.

matters."[46] The members of the Council, which would supervise the governments of the individual Austrian lands, were forbidden "any interest, share or participation in mercantile firms or minting syndicates in our lands, nor may they pursue any trade which might redound to disadvantage of our silver and copper sales, or of us or our lands in any way."[47] The king also agreed to establish a central treasury and accounting office at Innsbruck, plus a commission charged with recovering and reorganizing the ducal domain, and he promised to form three provincial regimes at Vienna, Innsbruck, and Ensisheim.[48]

The Austrians were wary. The deputies approved the plan, seeing in it the promise "that a large part of our concerns and grievances can be satisfied,"[49] but they also demanded an end to all venality at court and the exclusion of all non-Austrians from deliberations on Austrian affairs. They sensed, perhaps, that the king's much slighter control over the Empire than over Austria would prevent him from shifting much of the financial burden to the non-Austrian parts of the Empire. They needn't have worried, as it turned out, for though the approved project was published on May 24, 1518, the emperor's death in January 1519 frustrated its execution. The ensuing anticentralist reaction in Austria was smashed by Archduke Ferdinand, who in 1527 gave Austria its first centralized administration.[50] The differences between the two documents illustrate the passage from one age to another: Whereas Maximilian's plan was merely centralist and aimed at integrating Austria with Habsburg clients, Ferdinand's was centralist, absolutist, and limited to Austria.

The old emperor did try once more to secure from the Imperial Diet a permanent executive organ for the Empire and a standing army. Once more, however, the princes defeated his plans at Augsburg in 1518,

---

[46] Brandis, *Landeshauptleute*, 471; Fellner and Kretschmayr, *Zentralverwaltung*, 1,2:85, lines 30–31.

[47] Brandis, *Landeshauptleute*, 472, and see 483–5; Fellner and Kretschmayr, *Zentralverwaltung*, 1,2:86, lines 33–40.

[48] Brandis, *Landeshauptleute*, 476–7; Fellner and Kretschmayr, *Zentralverwaltung*, 1,2:90. On the domain and debts, see Wiesflecker, *Maximilian*, 4:329.

[49] Zeibig, "Ausschuss-Landtag," 225; ibid., the following quotes at 234, 238.

[50] King Ferdinand's *Hofordnung* of Jan. 1, 1527, in Fellner and Kretschmayr, *Zentralverwaltung*, 1,2:100–16. See Fellner, "Zur Geschichte," 271–7, who calls 1527 "das Geburtsjahr der österreichischen Centralverwaltung (277)"; Lhotsky, *Zeitalter*, 214–16.

after the Innsbruck assembly.[51] The Diet of Augsburg also heard the first notes of a great new theme that would disrupt and then shatter Maximilian's South German system. The mortally ill emperor left Augsburg for the last time on September 23, 1518. Two weeks later, a university professor from Wittenberg in far Saxony arrived for an interview with the papal legate, Cardinal Cajetan. His name was Martin Luther.

Triumph in Württemberg, 1519

Vater unser:
Reitling ist unser.
der du pist in den himmeln:
Ehing und Essling wölln wir auch pald gewinnen.
geheiliget werde dein nam:
Hailprunn und Weil wölln wir auch han.[52]

Maximilian's failed plan for a centralized government built more or less on the system he had organized in South Germany. This system, too, suffered erosion during the emperor's declining years. The western wing had always been the system's weakest part, and Maximilian began to surrender his gains on the Upper Rhine almost immediately after the Bavarian War. He mortgaged the Imperial Vicariate of the Ortenau to Count Wolfgang of Fürstenberg; and though he announced his intention to redeem the Wittelsbach mortgage on the Vicariate of Alsace, he could not produce the price, 80,000 fl.[53] The Alsatian vicariate in particular had great value to the Austrian position on the Upper Rhine, Maximilian explained to his heir in 1518, and must by no means fall into other hands.[54] The emperor could do nothing, however, to prevent the Lower Union from fading away into oblivion.[55] Strasbourg, which extricated

---

[51] Wiesflecker, *Maximilian*, 4:287, 289, 392–404.
[52] "Our Father (Reutlingen is ours), Who art in heaven (we'll soon have Ehingen and Esslingen, too), hallowed be Thy name (and then get Heilbronn and Weil der Stadt)." Liliencron, *Volkslieder*, 3:239, no. 313, known as "Duke Ulrich's paternoster."
[53] Barth, "Erbfolgekrieg," 31–2; Mertens, "Reich und Elsass," 280–3.
[54] Maximilian I to Charles V, May 18, 1518, in Le Glay, *Négociations diplomatiques*, 2:127.
[55] Matzinger, *Zur Geschichte der niederen Vereinigung*, 572–3. Maximilian tried to revive it in 1509 and 1512.

itself from the Swabian League in 1512, began once more to court its old comrades in arms in the Confederacy, though from these contacts came no concrete ties, no more than they did from the efforts of the pro-Swiss party at Constance.[56] Still, Maximilian's system was weaker on the Upper Rhine and in the lake region than in the heart of Swabia, and the old alternative of turning Swiss was by no means dead.

The 1510s were terrible years in Southwest Germany, wracked by famine and social unrest. A tremendous social paroxysm sped through the free cities in 1511–14, engulfing at least nine towns in movements more radical and resentful than the historic guild revolts of an earlier age.[57] Maximilian's feeble interventions, as at Speyer in 1512, did little to restore order to the towns or a sense of confidence to their oligarchies. Then, in 1514, the Poor Conrad movement in Württemberg brought rural and urban rebels together in a new way, giving a foretaste of 1525.[58] The emperor could, or would, do little to aid the oligarchies against their own subjects, though some help was had through the Swabian League.

The League was renewed in 1512[59] after negotiations over the defense of Tyrol, which were so hard that Maximilian proposed scrapping the League for a new alliance of Tyrol and Western Austria and the cities.[60] The free cities, which opposed the Italian Wars' disruption of the Venetian trade, eventually gave in and even voted a levy for the defense of Tyrol.[61] Truth to tell, the urban governments had become accustomed to regular participation in the life of the Swabian League, which encouraged confidence and solidarity among the urban politicians and promoted the internal administrative competence and efficiency of the member governments.[62] They also became accustomed to dealing with the League's increasing number of princely members. Indeed, Duke William of Bavaria (r. 1508–50) learned how to take advantage of the

---

[56] Ulmann, *Maximilian*, 2:610 n. 4; Rublack, *Einführung*, 3–9.
[57] Kaser, *Bewegungen*, 34–184.
[58] G. Franz, *Der deutsche Bauernkrieg*, 19–30.
[59] Klüpfel, *Urkunden*, 2:22–3 (June 1, 1508); see also Bock, *Der Schwäbische Bund*, 141–6.
[60] Klüpfel, *Urkunden*, 2:27–8, 35–6, 50; Bock, *Der Schwäbische Bund*, 98, 143–4. Although Venice assured the South German cities that trade would not be molested, Maximilian suspended all trade with Venice – except, of course, for favored firms. Gilbert, *The Pope*, 19–20.
[61] Klüpfel, *Urkunden*, 2:70–1 (June 26, 1513).
[62] Naujoks, *Obrigkeitsgedanke*, 27–8.

League, which had been a straitjacket for his father, and he offered alternative support and leadership to the free cities of the League when they found themselves at odds with the emperor.[63]

It was the combination of Bavaria and the free cities in the Swabian League that produced the last great triumph of Maximilian's system, the conquest of Württemberg in 1519. The old emperor died on January 12, 1519, at Wels in Upper Austria. The news of his passing unleashed the ambitions of his South German rivals, chief among them Duke Ulrich (r. 1503–19, 1534–50) of Württemberg, one of the great princely predators of the age. A cruel, violent, and imperious prince, Ulrich had married in 1511 Sabina, Duke William's sister, whose mistreatment at her husband's hands bred mortal emnity between Stuttgart and Munich.[64]

Duke Ulrich's relations with the free cities, which lay so richly strewn in and about his lands, are summed up in the "Württemberg paternoster":

> Our Father:
>   We've got Reutlingen;
> Who art in heaven:
>   We'll soon grab Esslingen;
> Hallowed be Thy name:
>   Then we'll get Heilbronn and Weil, too;
> Thy kingdom come;
>   Ulm is next;
> Thy will be done on earth as it is in heaven:
>   Schwäbisch Gmünd will become our shooting blind;
> Give us this day our daily bread:
>   Our guns have no equals;
> And forgive us our debts:
>   We serve the king of France;
> As we forgive our debtors:
>   We'll shut the Swabian League's mouth;
> And lead us not into temptation:
>   And maybe snap up Bavaria, too;
> But deliver us from evil:

[63] Kraus, "Sammlung der Kräfte," 297–304.
[64] There is no full biography of Ulrich newer than Heyd, *Ulrich*, published in 1841–4.

Perhaps we'll soon wear the Imperial crown.
Amen.[65]

This rich litany lacks only one name, that of the Swiss Confederacy. Württemberg and the Confederacy had been allies for more than a decade when Ulrich left the Swabian League in 1511.[66] This anti-Habsburg coalition contained great risks for Ulrich's power, as Württemberg gained increased importance as a supplier of foodstuffs to the confederates and a borrower of their money, for the Confederacy remained the natural refuge of all beaten groups and smaller powers who fled or feared princely power. The refugees of the broken Poor Conrad movement in 1514, for example, fled to Zurich and Schaffhausen, where "they wanted to enjoy the benefits of the godly law."[67] The smaller powers around Württemberg also looked to the Confederacy for protection they did not expect from the emperor. When news came of Maximilian's death in January 1519, the Rottweilers, associated with the Swiss since 1503, sought associate membership in the Confederacy. Here, high on the Neckar and far from the nearest Swiss power, the Rottweilers chanted, "Here is Switzerland, land and soil!"[68] The same solution attracted the abbot of Sankt Georgen in the Black Forest, who in 1502 fled to Rottweil "and was a good Swiss," much to the disgust of the Württembergers.[69] So long as Constance did not turn Swiss, a move prevented by the Austrian power,[70] the Confederacy lacked the natural bridgehead into Swabia. The confederates' natural interests in the region nonetheless made them a dangerous ally to Ulrich, even while they served the same anti-Habsburg cause.

Ulrich proved an especially dangerous neighbor to the free cities. He quarrelled with Rottweil and had more or less standing conflicts with Esslingen, Schwäbisch Gmünd, Weil der Stadt, and Reutlingen. It was his grab for Reutlingen, a metalworking and cloth town of some fifty-

---

[65] Steiff and Mehring, *Lieder und Sprüche*, 130–2, no. 35, a composite of five versions. There are others in Heyd, *Ulrich*, 1:529 n. 26; Liliencron, *Volkslieder*, 3:239, no. 313.
[66] Hug, *Chronik*, 17; Bock, *Der Schwäbische Bund*, 154.
[67] Hug, *Chronik*, 57. On the idea of godly law, see Blickle, *Revolution von 1525*, esp. 145–9 (English: *Revolution of 1525*, 91–93); Becker, " 'Göttliches Wort' "; Bierbrauer, "Das Göttliche Recht."
[68] Hug, *Chronik*, 19–20; Vater, "Beziehungen," 26–63. See Feyler, *Beziehungen*, 50–7.
[69] Hug, *Chronik*, 40–41; Feyler, *Beziehungen*, 26–38.
[70] Rublack, *Einführung*, 3–9; idem, "Politische Situation," 316; idem, "Aussenpolitik," 56.

Turning Swiss

four hundred citizens on the Neckar, that brought the duke's downfall.[71] At the news of Maximilian's death in 1519, Ulrich appeared before Reutlingen's walls on January 21 and entered the city on the twenty-eighth. His actions show that he intended the city's full, permanent subjugation: He received the citizens' homage, removed their treasures to his castle at Tübingen, called them his "subjects," gave them a new coat of arms and banner and destroyed the old ones, and installed a governor and a garrison of some three thousand men. His appetite whetted, Ulrich turned next to the somewhat larger (ca. seven thousand) free city of Esslingen.[72]

Reutlingen and Esslingen – and perhaps other free cities – were saved by the Swabian League, though only after much Bavarian prodding. Duke William's chancellor, the tough Leonhard von Eck, described to him the urban delegates' behavior at Ulm after Reutlingen's fall.

I've already written to you about how terrified the cities have been. They all believe that had Duke Ulrich advanced, he would have conquered all the free cities in his territories – there are four or five of them – and even taken Ulm.[73]

Eck pressed them, however, and the cities responded.

Twenty thousand strong, the army left Ulm on February 27 under Bavarian command, streamed over the Swabian Jura, and began to reduce one by one the great fortresses that perched on the spurs of that ancient, deeply cleft upland's northwestern face.[74] During April, they took the chief Württemberg towns on the Middle Neckar, Stuttgart and Tübingen; and when Duke William entered Castle Hohentübingen to take custody of Sabina's and Ulrich's children, the victory was complete. The "prince of thieves," as the humanist hebraist Johann Reuchlin (1455–1522) of Pforzheim had once called Ulrich,[75] was nowhere to be found. Soon he turned up in Switzerland, where his pleas for aid were countered by an Austrian agent, a Brabantish nobleman named Maxi-

---

[71] Based on the colorful account by Heyd, *Ulrich*, 1:525–8, and on the very full treatment by Ulmann, *Fünf Jahre*, 124–30. For the long-range consequences, see my "Princes' Reformation vs. Urban Liberty."
[72] Klüpfel, *Urkunden*, 2:164–5; Kittelberger, "Herzog Ulrichs Angriffspläne."
[73] Jörg, *Deutschland*, 29 n. 2; and see Ulmann, *Fünf Jahre*, 131 n. 21. For literature on Eck, see Kraus, "Sammlung der Kräfte," 299 n. 1.
[74] Ulmann, *Fünf Jahre*, 148–67, is the best account.
[75] Quoted by Frey, "Das Gericht," 247, and see 249, 274.

milian van Bergen.[76] The Swiss politicians, haunted perhaps by the recent horror at Marignano, had recalled their troops from Ulrich's service, and they sent him no more. A brief, initially successful effort in August to recover his lands with Palatine Wittelsbach aid also ended in failure.

Contemporary voices saw in Ulrich's fall the work of the free cities. To one songster, it proved the irreducible conflict between urban and noble interests:

> I warn you princes and nobles,
> Who disapprove this deed,
> Do not ally with cities,
> Who'll desert you in your need.
> You princes must ever be in the van,
> While the towns send only a boy and a man
> The one a servant, the other a lad,
> And no rich burgher is to be had.
> ....
> The text alone I offer here,
> You yourself can supply the gloss.
> The towns will flourish, you'll have but loss,
> Just as you've seen in Württemberg –
> Lords, people, and land – all gone.[77]

Another writer addressed the conquered land, groaning under the unworthy lordshop of commoners from the League's free cities:

> O Württemberg, you poor land,
> Long and loudly I protest your fate.

---

[76] Feyler, *Beziehungen*, 100–34; Ulmann, *Fünf Jahre*, 141–4. See also letters of the Commanders (*Hauptleute*) and Councillors of the Swabian League to Maximilian van Bergen, lord of Zevenberghen and Orator of the King of Spain, March 12, 1519, and Maximilian van Bergen to the Swabian League's envoys at Constance, March 26, 1519, both in StA Augsburg, Litteralien-Sammlung, at dates. Bergen and his colleagues arrived at Zurich on or before Feb. 9, and on March 3 they joined the League's envoys in asking the Swiss not to aid Duke Ulrich. *EA*, 3,2:1134, 1136, 1139–40, 1141, 1142, 1147–8, 1149–50, 1164–5, 1167, 1169, 1175, 1176–7, 1417–21.

[77] Liliencron, *Volkslieder*, 3:252, no. 318; there is another version in Seckendorff, *Reimchronik*, 80. This opinion was probably widespread, for Nördlingen instructed its envoy to the Urban Diet at Esslingen, May 18, 1519, to express his surprise, "dass Fürsten, Adel und Prälaten dafür halten wollen, dieser würtembergischen Krieg sei allein den Städten zu gut fürgenommen worden, besonders Reutlingen wegen ..." Klüpfel, *Urkunden*, 2:169. See also Sattler, *Geschichte des Herzogtums*, 2: Beilagen, 49–50.

97

Turning Swiss

The bath attendant from Ulm is your lord,
From Nördlingen the cloth-dyer,
And from Weil der Stadt the tanner,
The fancy baker from Nuremberg,
And Augsburg's weaver lord it over you.
And then the papermaker from Ravensburg,
The patrician, too, from Schwäbisch Hall,
The Kempten teamster, he's there, too,
And from Aalen the shepherd in the Hertfeld,
From Wimpfen the fellow who cuts the hay,
And from Isny the pastry gobblers,
From Lindau, too, the shipbuilders,
Along with Giengen's baker of crullers.
There are others whom I won't name here,
For the gang is big, and I weary of it.
. . . .
These and others I leave unnamed,
They now rule o'er poor Württemberg.[78]

Another ducal loyalist chimed in to suggest a plot between Ulrich's subjects and the treacherous free cities:

There were some in his own land,
Who conspired to bring him down,
And their infamy will live forever.
Chosen they were by the twelve cities;
With lies and untruths beyond compare,
They sealed the evil pact with their pals
And thereby lost all honor.[79]

The same thoughts troubled South German princes, among them Count Palatine Frederick, brother to Elector Louis in Heidelberg, knight of the Golden Fleece, and former tutor to King Charles of Spain. From Spain he wrote on January 4, 1520, to Margrave Casimir of Brandenburg-Ansbach, another bitter foe of the cities:

---

[78] Liliencron, *Volkslieder*, 3:252–3; there is another text in Seckendorff, *Reimchronik*, 81–2, where 25 cities are named.
[79] Heyd, *Ulrich*, 2:22 n. 42.

It is thus urgent that we heed the example of Württemberg's duke, who has now lost land and subjects, as indicative of the bent of the free cities, who strive ceaselessly to wipe out us princes... You know that some years ago the emperor wanted to punish the Württemberger, but the League, and especially the cities, would not agree to it. But then, when he attacked the cities, especially when he grabbed Reutlingen, he was driven from his lands.[80]

Duke Ulrich, for his part, had by no means resigned himself to this outcome. From his lands in Montbeliard, he attacked the trade caravans of "the Leaguers," and rumor had it that he would do the same from Swiss territory.[81]

The free cities' governments had good reason to be pleased with their handiwork in Württemberg, though thoughtful observers noticed that the campaign had not advanced the political goal of strengthening the monarchy. One was a Nuremberger, Anton Tucher, who wrote to the elector of Saxony on April 30, 1519,

I believe it would have been good and useful, that when the duke of Württemberg decided to overcome an Imperial and League city, Reutlingen, by force, someone from among the heads of the Empire, especially those to whose office it pertains, should have intervened; then it would never have come to this general rising. But since the duke had his way without resistance, one inept action produced another, so that right down to the fruitful ending the very truce itself could seem unsatisfactory.[82]

Tucher's sober judgment befit a Nuremberger, whose Franconian hometown lay "in the midst of wolves," as he said.

And so the old emperor's reign closed just before the last great triumph of his system. The system rested less on conquest than on the recovery of royal rights and titles, such as the Vicariate of Alsace, and on the federations of smaller powers as Habsburg clientele. It aimed to protect its members from the princes of the opposition – Bavaria, the Palatinate, Württemberg – and the entire region from Swiss penetration and influ-

[80] Count Palatine Frederick to Margrave Casimir of Brandenburg-Ansbach, Molins de Rey, Jan. 4, 1520, in *RTA, jR*, 2:120. On Frederick, see Scheible, "Fürsten," 381–2.
[81] Brady, "Princes' Reformation vs. Urban Liberty," 269–70, based on HStA Stuttgart, A 149/ 1. For the rumor of attacks from Swiss territory, see Burgomaster and Senate of Nuremberg to Schultheiss and Senate of Fribourg, Nov. 22, 1519, in StA Basel, Politisches L 1, at date; H. Lutz, *Peutinger*, 160.
[82] Kamann, "Ratskorrespondenzen," 248; the following quote is from 253.

ence. The urban oligarchs, who had few illusions about either the ultimate object of Maximilian's aggrandizement or the venality of his regime, led their communes into the system and, with some important exceptions, kept them there. It proved for them the safest course, safer than the Diet, safer than the princes, and safer than the Swiss.

In the interim between Maximilian's death and Charles's election, the cities and the League stood watch over the system's interests. Even as the Swabian League mobilized against Ulrich, Maximilian's councillors campaigned furiously to secure the succession for his grandson, the king of Spain. Two elements of the old emperor's system played important roles in this campaign: While the House of Fugger produced a river of gold to secure the electors' favor for Charles, the League sent its army downstream from Stuttgart toward the lands that divide the lower Neckar basin from the lower Main valley. When the electors on June 28, 1519, voted to take Charles as the next emperor, the army lay not far away at Höchst on the lower Main River[83] – a silent witness to the ancient election rite and a reminder to these great princes that Maximilian had formed in the South an alternative to the centralized monarchy they had denied him.

---

[83] Boos, *Städtekultur*, 4:148–49.

4

∽∽

Charles V and his cities, 1519–1523

> Carle haist er mit namen,
> er ist iez ausserkorn,
> das römisch reich zū besitzen,
> und alle zū beschützen
> mit allen seinen witzen,
> die ganzen cristenhait,
> der künig hochgemait.[1]

When King Charles of Spain, a nineteen-year-old heir to much of the known world, succeeded to the lordship of Austria and the Imperial crown in 1519, there was every chance that he would continue his grandfather's policies in South Germany. Or so thought Count Palatine Frederick, who, having borne the news of Charles's election to the king in Spain, wrote to Margrave Casimir about the mood at court, "that the courtiers who advise His Majesty esteem the cities more highly than they do the princes; that such folk want to preserve the Swabian League, to which most of the cities belong, against the future day when it might be used to force a prince into obedience; and that there are very few Imperial princes who have no quarrels with cities..."[2] The fate of the poor Württemberger, Frederick mused, should be a lesson to us all. The count's judgment may well have been colored by the success of a Nuremberg embassy, which had trailed him to Spain.

---

[1] "Charles is his name, and he is elected to guard the Roman empire, to protect all its folk, and to do the best he can for the whole of Christendom, this wondrous, mighty king." Liliencron, *Volkslieder*, 3:230, no. 309, stanza 8.
[2] *RTA, jR*, 2:119, lines 19–26. See Naujoks, *Obrigkeitsgedanke*, 48.

Turning Swiss

The Nurembergers were once more at odds with a margrave of Brandenburg-Ansbach, this time Casimir, whose service to the Habsburgs had brought him little profit, though his brother, Hans, stayed at court, married Germaine de Foix (1488–1538), King Ferdinand the Catholic's widow, and became governor of Valencia.[3] Nuremberg, hoping to get Charles to nullify his grandfather's grant to Casimir of a duty on wine, dispatched Dr. Christoph Scheurl and a companion to Spain, where they found the court at Molins de Rey near Barcelona shortly after Frederick's arrival. The king suspended the toll until his own arrival in the Empire, confirmed Nuremberg's liberties, and promised to hold his first Imperial Diet there. Scheurl left a fulsome account of his sixty days at court. "Unless I am blind and deaf and have learned nothing," he wrote, "the mind and mood of His Majesty and the councillors favor granting our city, insofar as they can, its wishes and a favorable decision, with which we would be fully satisfied."[4] The courtiers told him "that fortunately we came just at the right time," which confirms Frederick's gloomy observation, but he also warned that "the emperor must at the same time seek ways and means of maintaining the friendship of his kinsman, Margrave Hans [of Brandenburg-Ansbach] and the princes, and not set them against himself." Back in Nuremberg, Scheurl boasted that he had accomplished far more than his masters had expected, and his confidence may well have become infectious.

Five urban embassies from Augsburg, Nuremberg, Worms, Speyer, and Strasbourg greeted Charles when he landed at Ghent on June 6, 1520, hoping that the young king would continue Maximilian's South German policy. More specifically, the cities wanted him to settle the disposition of Württemberg, to renew the Swabian League (due to expire in 1522), and to protect them and their commerce from nobles, princes, and the Imperial Diet.[5] On these expectations, relations between the free cities and their new monarch grew up.

---

[3] Gumbel, "Berichte, I," 262–66; J. Müller, "Botschaft," 302–28; Soden, *Beiträge*, 92–104; Bebb, "Scheurl," 102–4; Headley, *Emperor*, 79–80. On Margrave Casimir, see Scheible, "Fürsten," 379–81.

[4] Scheurl to the Burgomaster and Senate of Nuremberg, Dec. 21, 1519, in J. Müller, "Botschaft," 318 n. 2; the following quotations are at 319 n. 1, 321. Charles abolished the wine toll when he came to Germany. *RTA, jR*, 2:25 n. 2.

[5] *RTA, jR*, 2:72; F. Roth, *Reformationsgeschichte*, 1:94; H. Lutz, *Peutinger*, 160–3. Ulm hesitated and then sent an embassy to the Netherlands on Dec. 3. *RTA, jR*, 2:105 n. 2, and see 75.

Charles V and his cities

Maximilian van Bergen and the Austrian way

O Karole, du edels blūt,
halt [Württemberger] land und leut in diner hūt!
behalts bi deinen edlen handen,
bi andern osterrischen landen;
ist es dir glich ietzt nit vil nuz,
villicht so ists dir für ain truz,
der dir möcht gegnen mit der zit.[6]

Württemberg presented Charles with his first major German issue. The League's constitution provided for equal division of spoils among the members, which in this case was patently impossible, as the impoverished land lay crushed with debts and open to Duke Ulrich's intrigues for Swiss, French, and Palatine aid.[7] At Esslingen in May 1519, the Leaguers yielded to Bavarian pressure and Duchess Sabina's pleas and decided to place the land in joint Bavarian-Austrian trust for the heir, Duke Christoph.[8] Well and good, but who was to pay the 300,000 fl. of war costs? By means of this question, the duchy came to the House of Austria.

The idea of bringing Württemberg to Austria probably originated among Charles's German and Netherlandish councillors, more specifically with Maximilian van Bergen, lord of Zevenberghen.[9] His family, which took its name from the city of Bergen-op-Zoom in North Brabant, had come to form, with the Egmonds and Nassaus, the core of an Imperial party at the Burgundian court, where they opposed the Burgundian "national" party led by Guillaume de Croy, lord of Chièvres.[10]

---

[6] "Oh Charles, you of royal race, hold land and folk in your embrace. Keep the land in your noble grasp with the other Austrian lands. If it now does you little good, perhaps it's meant to be a challenge to test you in the future." Steiff and Mehring, *Lieder und Sprüche*, 204, no. 48, lines 879–85.

[7] Ulmann, *Fünf Jahre*, 169; Feyler, *Beziehungen*, 169–216. See Maximilian van Bergen to Johann Schad von Mittelbiberach, Oct. 8, 1519, in StA Augsburg, Litteralien-Sammlung, at date.

[8] Klüpfel, *Urkunden*, 2:170; Ulmann, *Fünf Jahre*, 167–71; Wille, "Uebergabe," 525–6.

[9] See the (unsigned) article "Bergen, Maximiliaan van," in *Nieuw Nederlandsch biografisch woordenboek*, IX: 51–2; Slootmans, *Jan metten lippen*, 197–200; Walser, *Zentralbehörden*, 141–2. This man is called "Zevenberghen" in the modern literature, after a property his mother left him. The German documents call him "der herr zu Siebenburgen" and the French documents "de Berghes," but I will call him simply "Bergen."

[10] Slootmans, *Jan metten lippen*, 147–87; Walther, *Anfänge*, 6–10, 17–18, 25, 137–8, 166; Bernhardt, *Zentralbehörden*, 734–5; Tracy, *Politics*, 11–22, 77, 83. On the parties around Philip, see Wies-

Turning Swiss

The Imperial party was weakened by the growth of French influence around Archduke Philip the Handsome (1478–1506), who sent the brothers Jan and Henry, bishop of Cambrai, home from Spain in disgrace in 1502. The Bergens moved heavily into Netherlandish prelacies, and they advanced large sums to the Habsburg regime, which by 1515 owed them, the Egmonds, and the Nassaus at least 600,000 fl.[11]

Maximilian van Bergen came to Germany in 1518 to work against French influence in Switzerland. Hard work, he reported, for the Swiss, like the Apostle Thomas, believed only what they could touch.[12] When the old emperor died, Bergen plunged into Charles's election campaign, and he tried from the very first to turn the Württemberg campaign to Habsburg advantage.[13] He urged Archduchess Margaret to send Ferdinand, Charles's younger brother, to the front at once with a thousand horse, for everyone awaited the young prince there.[14] Ferdinand did not come, but Bergen toiled on. It was he who deterred the Swiss from further aid to Duke Ulrich's cause and thereby saved the Swabian League from a headlong collision with the Confederacy.[15]

The idea of a Habsburg Württemberg first appeared in Bergen's instruction for an envoy to Charles in Spain at the end of July 1519.[16]

<hr/>

flecker, *Maximilian*, 3:255–71. Jan van Bergen (Jean de Berghes) on Oct. 5, 1506 sent King Maximilian a (first?) report that Philip had died. Chmel, *Urkunden*, 257, no. 201.

[11] Walther, *Anfänge*, 18; Pirenne, *Histoire de Belgique*, 3:161–2, 188. On Bergen loans to the Habsburg regime, see Le Glay, *Négociations diplomatiques*, 2:234; Tracy, *Politics*, 83.

[12] Roesler, *Kaiserwahl*, 51. For sources, see Le Glay, *Corréspondance*, 2:372; idem, *Négociations diplomatiques*, 2:159; Gachard, *Lettres*, 2:151, 155. On Bergen's activities in Switzerland, see *EA*, 3,2:1134–1252, especially the places cited in Chapter 3, note 76.

[13] Roesler, *Kaiserwahl*, 79, 81, calls him "die stützende Säule des österreichischen Interesses in Deutschland" and "die Seele aller Bemühungen um das grosse Ziel." Walser, *Zentralbehörden*, 142, calls him "die eigentlich treibende Kraft" of the election campaign.

[14] Maximilian van Bergen to Archduchess Margaret, Augsburg, Feb. 1, 1519, in Le Glay, *Négociations diplomatiques*, 2:189–93. Her reply is in Mone, "Briefwechsel," 27–32. See also *RTA*, *jR*, 1:181, no. 20.

[15] Bergen did the main work of persuading the Swiss to abandon Duke Ulrich, for which see Chapter 3, note 76. Bergen wrote to Johann Schad von Mittelbiberach on Oct. 8, 1519, that Ulrich's pleas for 8,000 Swiss foot had been rejected, "Nun lassent sich die Eigenossen mercken, das sy übel zufriden seyen, das der Bundt ire Boten nit gehört hab, unnd glaidt abgeschlagen, So wer gut, das der Bundt inallweg sich gerüst hielt und gewarnet wer" (StA Augsburg, Litteralien-Sammlung, at date). See Seckendorff, *Reimchronik*, 83–4; Sattler, *Geschichte des Herzogtums*, 2: Beilagen, nos. 41, 43.

[16] Wille, "Uebergabe," 551. In a letter of Jan. 17, 1520, Charles said that the envoys in Germany had broached the idea through a messenger, Hieronymus Brunner. Ibid., 554; and see *RTA*, *jR*, 2:11.

By October 4, 1519, when rumor was flying through Germany that "Austria wants that land,"[17] Charles instructed Bergen to conclude a treaty with the Swabian League, "so that this same principality of Württemberg, all other lands conquered from Ulrich, and the duke's children be placed in our custody; and that in return the members of the League be promised and assured a tolerable and appropriate sum on our behalf."[18] Bergen and his colleagues then had their headquarters at Augsburg, where they dealt with the League's cities through Peutinger.

No one had argued more vigorously for the Habsburg cause during the anxious weeks of early 1519 than had the Augsburgers. There were other ideas among the urban governments – such as a five-year alliance among Nuremberg, Augsburg, and Ulm; a general urban league; and an alliance of Nuremberg with the Swiss – but at Augsburg Peutinger and Ulrich Arzt boosted the Habsburg cause, begging Margaret through Bergen for Netherlandish aid, "so that Madame Margaret and our land may be protected."[19] Arzt voiced his fears privately to Peutinger that "we will be pushed from behind toward the Swiss. Then the saying will come true, that when a cow stands on the bridge at Ulm and moos, she'll be heard in the middle of Switzerland."[20] To Bergen, however, Arzt, who was one of the commanders of the Swabian League, boasted that the League could take care of the French king, too, and "If God would only send us the king of Spain, we would have no trouble to make him King of the Romans."[21] Indeed, if Charles "will give us the sum of money he now gives the Swiss, we would make him king without fail [*in parfortz*]." Bergen fell in completely with this idea and wrote to Margaret that "concerning the Swabian League, Madame, I have always thought that it is the readiest instrument through which the king, if God so wills, will gain his goal."[22] The central idea of Maximilian's South

---

[17] Peter von Aufsäss to Elector Frederick of Saxony, Sept. 4, 1519, quoted by Ulmann, *Fünf Jahre*, 189 n. 225. Aufsäss was councillor to the bishop of Würzburg. Ibid., 178 n. 194. For further evidence that the idea was discussed as early as July 21, 1519, see H. Lutz, *Peutinger*, 158; Klüpfel, *Urkunden*, 2:174.

[18] Charles V's powers (*Gewalt*) for his agents in Germany, dated Barcelona, Oct. 4, 1519, is in Sattler, *Geschichte des Herzogtums*, 2: Beilagen, no. 42. On what follows, see H. Lutz, *Peutinger*, 154–60; and Puchta, *Herrschaft*, 3–23.

[19] H. Lutz, *Peutinger*, 147. The cities' league is described in ibid., 150–1.

[20] Arzt to Peutinger, Feb. 9, 1519, quoted in ibid., 147.

[21] Ibid., 149, and there, too, the following quote.

[22] Mone, "Briefwechsel," 293, quoted by H. Lutz, *Peutinger*, 376 n. 19.

German system, that the free cities and the Habsburgs formed a community of fortune embodied in the Swabian League, was thus pressed on the young king from the first.

The Bavarian proposal, that Württemberg be held in trust for Ulrich's son, lost much ground through Duke Ulrich's quick strike into the duchy in August 1519. Ulrich Arzt framed the alternatives: If Charles took Württemberg from the League, the cities would be rid of the hated Württemberg toll and recover much of the war's costs; if not, the conquered land would be a burden and constant source of danger.[23] On November 30, 1519, the League's assembly at Augsburg decided to transfer Württemberg to King Charles, if he met their financial terms. During the next three months, Bergen tried to persuade Charles that this solution was a grand bargain.

Bergen's instruction from Charles could not have been clearer. "It seems to us," Charles had written in September from Barcelona, "that of all the proposals concerning the fate of Württemberg, the best is the final one: namely, to negotiate with the Swabian League that the land be put into our hands, and that we not only accept it but also take the young duke into our custody... and then to satisfy the League with 300,000 fl., of which 60,000 fl. will return to us as Austria's share and the remainder be paid over eight or ten years."[24] Clear enough, but where was the money? Bergen had come just before Christmas from Innsbruck, where he had tried to reform the regime and find money, but armed insurrection was sweeping through the Tyrolean valleys, and the five Lower Austrian duchies lay on the brink of rebellion.[25] At Augsburg, on the other hand, waited Charles's massed creditors. First in line stood Jacob Fugger, for whose crucial role in Charles's election Bergen was partly responsible, and Fugger wanted securities for the final 122,000 fl. of the more than half-million he had advanced.[26] Bergen recommended

---

[23] Arzt to Esslingen, Dec. 31, 1519, in Klüpfel, *Urkunden*, 2:181. On the Bavarian plan, see A. Kraus, "Sammlung der Kräfte," 307. On the League's decision at Augsburg, Nov. 30, 1519, see Klüpfel, *Urkunden*, 2:177.

[24] Charles V to his Commissioners in Germany, Barcelona, Sept. 24, 1519, in Wille "Uebergabe," 551. Bergen's arrival in Augsburg is noted in his letter to Charles V, Augsburg, Dec. 27, 1519, in HStA Marburg, PA 389, fols. 79ʳ–90ᵛ.

[25] Bergen to Charles V, Augsburg, Dec. 27, 1519, in HStA Marburg, PA 389, fol. 80ᵛ. See Pölnitz, *Jakob Fugger*, 1:432. Conditions in Austria after Maximilian I's death are described by Lhotsky, *Zeitalter*, 85–99.

[26] Bergen to Archduchess Margaret, Augsburg, Feb. 26/7, 1519, in Mone, "Briefwechsel," 32–

payment in Spain and bombarded the Augsburger with new pleas for cash. After all, he pointed out, Fugger had made good business through his financing part of the Württemberg campaign.[27] Next in line stood the two Saxon rulers, Elector Frederick with his bill for 33,000 fl. and Duke George wanting his 25,000 fl., but Bergen made them wait, for he spent the only cash he could raise, a paltry 4,800 fl., on mercenary troops.[28]

Bergen's most pressing need was for money to pay off the Swabian League and close the Württemberg deal. "But since we must have the aforementioned 100,000 fl. for this purpose," he wrote to Charles, "which cannot possibly be raised in the Austrian lands, we most humbly pray ... Your Royal Majesty to send us immediately and as soon as possible the 100,000 fl. in letters of exchange... Without this money we can accomplish nothing, and the whole affair will slide into ruin."[29] He also needed the 122,000 fl. for Jacob Fugger, for otherwise "Your Royal Majesty will lose much credibility and reputation among the German nation; and we would consequently lose all our credibility as well. There is no way we can ourselves pay out this enormous sum without destroying our own future ability to serve Your Royal Majesty, either financially or in other ways."[30]

It was not just Charles's credit with the South German bankers that worried Bergen, for just as Württemberg might prove a great boon to the Habsburg position, its loss might be catastrophic. "Your Majesty should be thoroughly convinced," he wrote to the King at Christmastide 1519,

that this land of Württemberg is a large and important territory, and that Your Royal Majesty can procure no greater advantage than to bring it into Your

---

6, summarized in *RTA, jR*, 1:308–13, no. 100, here at 311–12. See Le Glay, *Négociations diplomatiques*, 2:283, no. 77; Pölnitz, *Jakob Fugger*, 1:427–8.

[27] One reason, as he confessed to Duke George of Saxony, was that Ulrich had menaced Fugger's county of Kirchberg. Pölnitz, *Jakob Fugger*, 1:434, 438. Heiko Oberman has uncovered another reason. Dr. Gregor Lamparter (d. 1523), who had fled Württemberg for Habsburg service in mid-November 1516, was married to Fugger's illegitimate daughter. Oberman, *Werden und Wertung*, 181–3; on Lamparter see also Grube, *Landtag*, 102, 104, 114. On Charles's debts to Fugger, see HStA Marburg, PA 389, fol. 87[r] and Pölnitz, *Jakob Fugger*, 2:430, who also analyzes the election costs at 416–23.

[28] Bergen to Charles V, Augsburg, Jan. 10, 1520, in HStA Marburg, PA 389, fol. 96[r-v]; and Pölnitz, *Jakob Fugger*, 1:436–7, and 2:426–8. On the loan of 4,800 fl., see HStA Marburg, PA 389, fol. 86[r-v].

[29] Bergen to Charles V, Augsburg, Dec. 27, 1519, in HStA Marburg, PA 389, fol. 82[r-v]; Petri, "Herzog Heinrich," 128.

[30] HStA Marburg, PA 389, fol. 88[r], repeated on fol. 102[r] (Jan. 10, 1520).

Majesty's hands. This is so, because it lies in the middle of the Holy Empire and borders on some of Your Royal Majesty's hereditary Austrian lands. If Württemberg is added to them, then Your Royal Majesty would have, as archduke of Austria, adequate power vis-à-vis the disturbers of the peace in the German lands. Your Majesty should also consider that he could thus all the better maintain law and order in the Holy Empire, and that the common folk in Württemberg wish nothing more than to join the obedience of Your Royal Majesty and the House of Austria.[31]

Otherwise, he feared, Württemberg would drift toward the Swiss Confederacy: "If, on the other hand, Württemberg does not come into Your Royal Majesty's hands, it will certainly come into those of the Swiss. Although the Swiss are not yet quite their own lords, they will become such if they gain control of Württemberg." Not only would a Swiss Württemberg become Charles's and Austria's bitter enemy, Bergen continued, "but I am convinced that some of the League's cities, too, are only waiting for the conclusion of these negotiations to join the Swiss, which will surely endanger all of your Royal Majesty's hereditary western Austrian lands." It would be a terrible blow both to Charles's Imperial dignity and to Austria.

As the negotiations dragged on, largely because Bergen had strict instructions to drive the price down,[32] the Leaguers began to lose interest in protecting Württemberg from Ulrich, for whose restoration there was still Swiss pressure. The League, Bergen wrote to Charles on January 10, 1520, "secretly and without telling us, withdrew the embassy they had sent to Switzerland to combat the intrigues of Duke Ulrich there"; and true friends of Austria had informed Bergen "that if the negotiations are not soon concluded, they will brook no more delay and will deal with the Swiss."[33] Bergen painted for the king the consequences of straining the League's patience: "Your Royal Majesty would lose all your good friends in the League and in the Holy Empire, plus their dependents, and your reputation; and then for certain the League will

---

[31] Bergen to Charles V, Augsburg, Dec. 27, 1519, in ibid., fols. 81ʳ–82ʳ, for this and the following two quotes.
[32] I agree with Adolf Wrede (in *RTA, jR*, 2:13 n. l, against Wille, "Uebergabe," 553–4) that Charles was convinced before the transfer of the need to take Württemberg.
[33] HStA Marburg, PA 389, fols. 106ᵛ–107ʳ.

deal with the Swiss and bring the land of Württemberg into their power . . ."[34]

The threat that Württemberg and the free cities might turn Swiss may have been partly a mere device to persuade the king, but it also rested partly on a genuine appreciation of the situation.[35] After the terrible defeat at Marignano in 1515, the confederates had concluded an "Eternal Peace" with France and formulated a policy of nonentanglement in the Habsburg–Valois struggle. Bidding for their support became intense, and though the Swiss withdrew their early support for Ulrich against the Swabian League, they nonetheless continued to exert diplomatic pressure in his favor.[36] There were, as Bergen recognized, important economic ties between Württemberg and the Confederacy. The duchy, along with Burgundy and Alsace, supplied much of the grain needed in the Confederacy since the shift from mixed farming to pastoral economies.[37] The Swiss also had lent Ulrich a lot of money. Ulrich was a notorious spendthrift,[38] whose debts had not been fully covered by the Treaty of Tübingen's provision, on July 8, 1514, of 24,213 fl. annually to help cover 950,000 fl. of ducal debt. Bergen told the Swiss that service on Ulrich's foreign debts would require 60,000 fl. annually, which suggests a principal of more than a million florins.[39] Some of this was owed to Swiss creditors, and when Bergen negotiated the transfer of Württemberg to Charles V, he promised the Swiss that their notes would be paid and that the free trade southward in grain and wine would not be disrupted.[40] These economic and financial dependencies do not mean that Württemberg was fully ripe to turn Swiss, but it is worth noting that the social structure of the duchy, a land of small towns and villages,

---

[34] Bergen to Charles V, Jan. 28, 1520, in ibid., fol. 137ᵛ.
[35] Bergen to Matthäus Lang, bishop of Gurk, and Jakob Villinger, Zurich, March 21 and 24, 1519, in *RTA, jR*, 1: 474 n. 2, 454 n. 1; *EA*, 3,2:1141i. Dierauer, *Geschichte*, 3:22–8, sketches the international situation; for details, see Gisi, "Anteil," and Fueter, *Anteil*.
[36] See their appeal to the Swabian League, Nov. 24, 1519, in Sattler, *Geschichte des Herzogtums*, 2: Beilagen, no. 47; and Feyler, *Beziehungen*.
[37] Rundstedt, *Regelung*, especially 29–43; Muralt, "Renaissance und Reformation," 395–6, identifies Alsace, Burgundy, and Upper Swabia, plus Lombardy and the Piedmont, as the "granaries of Switzerland."
[38] Carsten, *Princes*, 10–16; Grube, *Landtag*, 74–113; Hamburger, *Staatsbankrott*.
[39] StA Basel, Politisches 2,1, at Feb. 10, 1520 (noticed in *EA*, 3,2:1228, no. 8100).
[40] StA Basel, Politisches 2,1 at March 5, 1520 (noticed in *EA*, 3,2:1228). See Wille, "Uebergabe," 561.

lay well within the range already represented in the Confederacy.[41] The territorial diet was controlled by small-town notables (*Ehrbarkeit*), not by nobles and big merchants, and their opposition to the duke made them natural allies of some outside power, either Austrian or Swiss. Ulrich's former chancellor, Dr. Gregor Lamparter (d. 1523), had already entered Austrian service.

The essential fact, Bergen recognized, was the fundamental social instability of southwestern Germany, about which he warned the king on February 7, 1520. "The League has many members," he wrote, "and not all of them are rich; some have a strong inclination toward the Swiss. Had they known that the treaty would . . . be so long delayed, or that we had no plenipotentiary powers, . . . the matter would long ago have been settled in a Swiss sense."[42] He thought that through careful diplomacy the duchy's transfer could be managed without war,[43] but he feared that the attraction of the Confederacy was palpable, wherever communal institutions flourished. This meant a much wider region than Swabia alone, as he told Charles, who had meanwhile landed in the Netherlands, by messenger in late April 1520, well after the treaty of transfer had been signed on February 6.[44] Charles had hesitated to sign the treaty, which would pledge him to pay 220,000 fl. of the war debt, and Bergen warned him that the entire structure of Habsburg power in South Germany lay in jeopardy. The Swabian League, he urged,

upholds law and order, and because of it all the powers of the Empire – princes, Swiss, or others – must respect Your Royal Majesty more than they otherwise would do. We know well, however, that some princes oppose the League and intrigue to make a league of princes, through which they could shove the cities aside and enjoy a "free government" in the Empire. Your Majesty can well imagine how much obedience you would then command! Also, once the cities see what is happening, His Majesty can be assured that nothing less will happen than that all these cities will join the Swiss, and thereafter the whole land of

---

[41] Grube, "Dorfgemeinde"; Blickle, *Revolution von 1525*, 97–8, 184–5 (English: *Revolution of 1525*, 63–4, 117). On the notables' opposition, see Grube, *Landtag*, 5–6, 74–107.
[42] Bergen to Charles V, Feb. 7, 1520, in HStA Marburg, PA 389, fol. 165^{r-v} (printed by Wille, "Uebergabe," 557). About this time, Margrave Casimir proposed a princes' alliance to replace the Swabian League. *RTA, jR*, 2:119, lines 26–9.
[43] HStA Marburg, PA 389, fol. 219^v. See Wille, "Uebergabe," 560, 563.
[44] Instructions for envoys to the lord of Chièvres, Augsburg, April 20, 1520, in HStA Marburg, PA 389, fols. 215^r–23, 253^r–55^r (Wille, "Uebergabe," 559–67). By 1533, only 10,000 fl. of this debt had been paid. Klüpfel, *Urkunden*, 2:357.

Swabia and the Rhine Valley all the way down to Cologne would join as well. God grant that it might go no further [the Brabanter thinks of the Netherlands]! We are firmly convinced that the princes who thus intrigue do not sufficiently consider what they do; for if it develops so far in this direction, they will be expelled by their own subjects, who would then join these others; and in the end the whole German land would become one vast commune, and all the lords would be expelled.[45]

On the upper Rhine in particular, he continued, the Vicariate of Alsace "is a great and important thing" (precisely the words he had earlier used of Württemberg), which should never be restored to the Elector Palatine, "for otherwise the ten free cities who stand under this vicariate would, for a variety of reasons, join the Swiss; and what Strasbourg would then do, may well be imagined." Then the tiers of lands north of the Confederacy would fall southward, like stacks of dominos, "for the land of Württemberg lies near the Swiss, and should it join them and they admit it, then the other lands – Tyrol and Inner and Outer Austria – would also be lost, and also all Swabia and the regions down to Cologne. Bavaria, too, would then doubtless fall."[46]

Bergen doubtless exaggerated when he maintained that "the whole German land would become one vast commune, and all the lords would be expelled," if Charles refused Württemberg and the duchy joined the Confederacy. Still, his analysis rested on his correct estimation that Switzerland was not just another star in the European political constellation, whose shapes and structures were all familiar to him. Its social character made the Confederacy a powerfully attractive model, whereas its military might made it a highly desirable ally. Far beyond its borders, the density of communal institutions contained a potential danger to lordship in the possibility of joining or imitating the confederates. The urban oligarchies might prefer the protection of a strong monarch, but they would turn Swiss if they could, rather than be left helpless prey to the princes. Monarchy was preferable to confederation among men who ruled others, so long as the monarch did not threaten particularism, and Bergen wanted Charles to exploit this natural monarchism. He should

---

[45] HStA Marburg, PA 389, fols. 254ʳ–55ʳ (Wille, "Uebergabe," 566–7), for this and the following quote. See the remarks by Cardinal Albrecht of Mainz, in *RTA, jR*, 1:844, lines 4–10, no. 379, also quoted by Endres, "Zünfte und Unterschichten," 152 n. 3.
[46] Wille, "Uebergabe," 570.

make Württemberg into a strong new block in the arc of Habsburg power that marched with the curve of the Confederacy's northern boundary, and he should secure it through the alliance of Austria and the free cities. If they were forced to choose, however, the cities' oligarchs feared the masterless men, who were equal partners with the Swiss city-states, less than they did the masterful men who ruled most of the South German countryside.

In the end, both the Confederacy and the princes accepted, if grudgingly, the transfer[47] of Württemberg to Charles V, who promised to repay the Leaguers' war costs. His agents now faced three tasks: the installation of a Habsburg regime in Stuttgart, the integration of Württemberg into Austria, and the renewal of the Swabian League.

Charles named Bergen "Statthalter of our principality of Württemberg"[48] and charged him with the organization of the duchy's new administration. Bergen instructed a committee of the territorial diet to begin the awesome task of making the duchy solvent, in the first place through the compilation of a budget (*ain Stat*).[49] Under the Austrian regime, Württemberg acquired the parliamentary institutions it was long to retain, the Large and Small committees, plus a collegial financial body controlled by the territorial estates. Austrian models combined with native traditions to strengthen the governmental role of the estates, and thus the political power of the Württemberg notables, during the Habsburg era (1520–34). For the upper classes, at least, Austrian rule was a relief after Ulrich's chaotic reign.

Württemberg's integration into Austria was linked to the broader problem of Austrian centralization. Charles's chief contribution was to send Austria a resident lord. On January 30, 1522, he appointed his brother, Ferdinand, his viceroy in all the Austrian lands.[50] In the fol-

---

[47] Abbot Johann of Au wrote to Abbot Gerwig Blarer of Weingarten on Nov. 12, 1520, that the duchy had been transferred, not sold, though he doubted the debt would soon be paid. Blarer, *Briefe und Akten*, 1:5, no. 7.

[48] HStA Stuttgart, A 2, Bd. 396, fol. 7ʳ. On the reform of the Stuttgart administration and relations with the estates, see Carsten, *Princes*, 15–16; Grube, *Landtag*, 114–30.

[49] Charles's Instruction for Bergen as Statthalter is in HStA Stuttgart, A 2, Bd. 396, fols. 6ʳ–11ʳ, from which the following details are drawn. See Carsten, *Princes*, 16; Kothe, *Der fürstliche Rat*, 49–52, for the basis of the rest of this paragraph.

[50] W. Bauer, *Anfänge*, 149–51, 247–9; Puchta, *Herrschaft*, 24–7; Laubach, "Nachfolge"; and Ficht-

lowing year, Württemberg envoys attended the Tyrolean diet, and in
1524 there was some cooperation among the administrations at Innsbruck, Stuttgart, and Ensisheim.[51] Such activities pale, however, beside
a plan to centralize and coordinate the Austrian lands, which is the best
evidence for an appreciation in Charles's entourage for the idea of the
"Austrian way" to a German monarchy.

Shortly after Charles acquired Württemberg, someone drafted a project which repeated the essentials of Emperor Maximilian's ill-fated 1518
plan for Austrian centralization.[52] It recommended an integrated judicial
system with four courts at Wiener Neustadt, Innsbruck, Stuttgart, and
Ensisheim, with Innsbruck to have appellate jurisdiction over Württemberg and Alsace. Over this system would rule an aulic council (*Hofrat*)
"as a supreme government for the House of Austria."[53] The plan repeated the idea of 1518 "that the Imperial government might be made
dependent on this State Council," which was to include "a prominent,
able person from the Netherlands."[54] "For concerning the government
of the Empire," the plan suggested, "it may be made dependent on the
aforementioned State Council, though we cannot yet know with cer-
tainty, before the Diet meets [at Worms], just what this government will
look like."[55] To the courts and State Council, the plan added a central
treasury (*General Rait Cammer*), which together might have freed Charles
and Ferdinand from the Imperial Diet and given them effective tools
of government in both Austria and the rest of the Empire. All in all, the
plan was a blueprint for the "Austrian way."[56]

The authorship of the plan is uncertain, though the only known copy
comes from the archives of Bergen's regime in Stuttgart and may well

---

ner, *Ferdinand I of Austria*, 17–20. Ferdinand's entry into Stuttgart in May 1522 is described
in Seckendorff, *Reimchronik*, 91–3.
[51] Hug, *Chronik*, 99; Grube, *Landtag*, 132–3; Carsten, *Princes*, 17.
[52] HStA Stuttgart, A 2, Bd. 396, fols. 70ʳ–74ʳ; an edited version appears in Appendix B. It belongs
between Maximilian's "Innsbrucker Libell" of 1518, which it closely resembles, and Ferdinand's
Hofordnung of Jan. 1, 1527 (Fellner and Kretschmayr, *Zentralverwaltung*, 1, 1:108, no. 12 I A).
[53] HStA Stuttgart, A 2, Bd. 396, fol. 70ʳ, for this and the following quote.
[54] This illustrates Charles's Netherlandish perspective on the Empire, for which see Press, "Die
Erblande," 62.
[55] HStA Stuttgart, A 2, Bd. 396, fol. 74ʳ⁻ᵛ.
[56] Press, "Die Erblande," 48–50, sees in Austria's unification the "basis of Imperial policy," which
is what I mean by "the Austrian way."

stem from his pen. It can be dated to the time between the transfer of Württemberg on February 20, 1520, and the opening of the Diet of Worms on January 27, 1521.[57] The project presents an alternative, based on the situation in 1520, to the Empire as a republic of princes: an Imperial monarchy based on a centralized Austria, allied to the financially potent free cities and the other smaller southern powers. In some respects its central idea, the domination of Germany from a consolidated Austrian South, resembles the de facto dominations of Britain by England and of Iberia by Castile. The project was never realized, not least because the dramatic new advance of Ottoman power westward during the 1520s robbed the Austrian lands of the time to grow together.

In the eyes of the smaller southern powers, including many free cities, the transfer of Württemberg was linked to the renewal of the Swabian League. Just after the Württemberg campaign, more than two years before the old treaty expired, Charles's agents began to work toward this end.[58] During the spring of 1520, however, there arose in Upper Swabia an opposition group of smaller towns, whose governments feared that the League's center was shifting too far northward through the admission of Württemberg and even more "distant" (*weitläufig*) states, such as Hesse.[59] They refused to discuss renewal of the League until Charles came in person to hear their grievances.

The Swabian League nonetheless continued in its old role as rival governmental power to the Imperial Diet and the Governing Council (reconstituted in 1521) in South Germany.[60] The League continued to aid members' merchants against marauders, and its court formed an important point of entry for Roman law and written judicial procedure into southern Germany.[61] The court, which distinguished itself through its adaptability and openness to change, sat at Tübingen (1503–12) and Augsburg (1512–33), and its judges gave "few grounds for complaint."[62]

---

[57] Wohlfeil, "Wormser Reichstag," 78.
[58] Klüpfel, *Urkunden*, 2:180 (Nov. 30, 1519).
[59] Ibid., 183, 198, 201, 205, 210, The cities were Memmingen, Biberach an der Riss, Ravensburg, Pfullendorf, Wangen, Isny, Leutkirch, Buchhorn, and Ueberlingen.
[60] Bock, *Der Schwäbische Bund*, 170–8.
[61] Examples are in Klüpfel, *Urkunden*, 2:156, 187, 199, 204, 208, 218, 224, 228, 233; Frey, "Das Gericht," 228–9.
[62] Frey, "Das Gericht," 239, 260. The jurists' opinion is in StA Augsburg, Litteralien-Sammlung, at Feb. 10, 1526.

The smaller powers found in the League the redress and executive power the Imperial government rarely could supply; and as the League grew together, its jurists began to argue for the League's direct jurisdiction over members' subjects.

The reign of Charles V thus opened on a major victory for Austrian power and its clients in South Germany. The subjugation and conquest of Württemberg not only rid them of a major opponent, it also dampened, for the time being, the charm of the confederates as model neighbors. If the Rotweillers chanted, "Here is good Swiss land and soil," the Württemberg notables replied that "Here is Austrian land and soil!"[63] The issue between the monarchy and the Confederacy was hardly settled, and the existence of dissatisfaction among the urban upper classes is suggested both by the Upper Swabian opposition to the Swabian League's renewal and by the ephemeral projects for separate alliances in 1519. These were but small shadows on a horizon of brilliant prospects during the first days of 1521, as the young king moved toward the – to him unknown – German South.

Charles V and the cities of his realms

Ist Carolus genennet
von gottes gnaden zart,
romischer kung erkennet,
neulich erwelet ward,
und auch kunig noch mere:
in Hispanien herre
zū Castilien ferre,
zū Arragonien,
gib ich euch zū versten.[64]

The man who now came to order his German dominions was just entering his third decade of life. Reared at Brussels in northern Europe's most densely city-strewn landscape, Charles grew up amid the scions

---

[63] Hug, *Chronik*, 77; Grube, *Landtag*, 126–9.
[64] "Charles he is called, chosen by God's grace to be the Roman King through royal high election. He has many other crowns, Lord of Spain is he and king of far Castile, and also of Aragon or, so I've been told." Liliencron, *Volkslieder*, 3:229, no. 309, stanza 2.

115

of the Burgundian and Netherlandish upper nobility. His heritage brought him the centralist ideal of the great Valois dukes rather than the particularism of his Netherlandish subjects, and it steeped him in the neo-chivalry of the Burgundian court rather than the culture, either vernacular or neo-Latin, of the urban upper classes.

The formation, development, and content of Charles V's political mentality is a much-disputed subject.[65] What is certain is that the proudest imperial ideal represented in his immediate entourage derived neither from his Austrian-German heritage nor from Burgundian ideals, but from Italy, that shattered political landscape of wrecked city-states and powerless petty nobilities. Mercurino Arborio di Gattinara (1465–1530) was a Piedmontese nobleman and university-educated lawyer who had entered Archduchess Margaret's service while she was still the wife of Savoy's ruling duke.[66] In 1518, he succeeded the lord of Chièvres as Charles's Grand Chancellor, and he undertook to educate the young king to the ideal of universal monarchy. "Sire," he wrote to Charles in late 1523,

your grandeur and the security of your affairs do not consist in directly holding Milan nor any other place that you may later conquer but rather consist in winning the hearts of men and causing through them that kings, dukes, princes and potentates come to your devotion and obedience and recognize you as their superior. This is the way by which the Romans and others had the monarchy of the world, and to which you ought to conform in order to attain thereto.[67]

Gattinara, who believed in a universal Christian imperium ruled by "the supreme Charles, more fortunate than Augustus and more virtuous than Trajan,"[68] pleaded with Charles in 1519 to accept the Imperial crown, against those who thought he would thereby overreach his grasp and endanger his hereditary lands.

Then Mercurino alone demonstrated their error; for the Imperial title is the most suitable for winning rule over the entire earth, because this title was established by God, predicted by the prophets, preached by the apostles, and

---

[65] Yates, *Astraea*, 20–7; Koenigsberger, *Habsburgs and Europe*, 10–11; Brandi, *Kaiser Karl V.*, 2:42–4; Tracy, *Politics*, chaps. 1–3; Menéndez Pidal, "Formácion," 144–66.

[66] Walser, *Zentralbehörden*, 161–77; Headley, "Gattinara," 64–98; idem, "Habsburg World Empire," 93–127; idem, *Emperor*, 1–14.

[67] Quoted by Headley, "Gattinara," 70–1.

[68] Ibid., 66–7.

confirmed by Our Savior, Jesus Christ, in word and deed. At stake is the establishment of peace throughout the earth, which cannot be attained without a world monarchy. As God's servant Charles can easily achieve such a monarchy.[69]

Gattinara was also a Ghibelline, who believed in the emperor as sole heir, against the papal claims to temporal power, of Rome's imperium, and he liked to cite on Charles's behalf – "Charles the Greatest," he called him, who would complete the work begun by Charles the Great – the favorite Ghibelline text: "That there may be one shepherd and one flock" (John 10:16).[70] He even tried to persuade Erasmus to publish Dante's *De Monarchia*, a Ghibelline classic, but the Dutch humanist, no friend of universal imperium, demurred and left the task to a later hand.[71] It may well be true, as has been said, that a vast imperial system such as Charles's threatened local liberties less than did the smaller, centralizing monarchies of the time, but this does not mean that Charles sympathized with particularism in any way.[72] Three events of his reign suggest his appreciation for local urban liberties. The first was the great revolt of the Castilian *comuneros* in 1520, led by Toledo, which was brutally crushed in the king's name.[73] The second incident was the pacification of Ghent in 1540, when Charles besieged the recalcitrant commune, stoutest defender of Flemish particularism, and stripped it of its self-government.[74] The lesson of Ghent impressed German city governments no less than the falls of Mainz, Regensburg, and Boppard in the previous century had done. At Strasbourg the government noted the event: "Reflect on the example of Ghent; in every way we should be more careful."[75] The third event occurred after Charles beat the German Protestants in 1546–7. In 1548 and 1552, his councillors altered the constitutions of more than thirty free cities, expelling guildsmen in favor of presumably more loyal patricians.[76] Charles and his councillors, most of them great nobles from Burgundy, the Netherlands, Germany, and

---

[69] Quoted by H. Lutz, *Peutinger*, 15.
[70] Headley, "Habsburg World Empire," 97–102.
[71] Tracy, *Politics*, 23–47; Headley, "Gattinara," 78–9; Duchhardt, *Kaisertum*, 8–10.
[72] Wallerstein, *World-System*, 1:172–3. This can be seen in Gattinara's idea of empire, which was not absolutist. See Headley, "Germany, the Empire and *Monarchia*," 15–30.
[73] Haliczer, *Comuneros*.
[74] Pirenne, *Histoire de Belgique*, 3:114–25.
[75] AMS, RP1540, fol. 188ʳ.
[76] On the *Hasenräte*, see Chapter 6, section titled "Reprise: Nuremberg under the eagle's wing."

Castile,[77] naturally believed that rule belonged to those born to rule. To the South German communes, therefore, the new king might be, like his grandfather, an ally and patron, but never a friend. More, even, than his rearing, his councillors, and his mentality, the vast assemblage of lands that had come to the young king through dynastic marriages and genetic accidents, plus the varied constitutions, interests, strengths, and weaknesses of these lands, stood in the way of Charles's simply resuming his grandfather's patronage of the South German free cities. Charles began as a Burgundian Netherlander, who tended all his life to view German affairs from a Netherlandish perspective rather than an Austrian or Imperial one.[78] His succession to the crowns of Spain, however, plus the French assault on Italy and the Turkish pressure right across the Mediterranean, made the Hispano-Italian realms his imperial heartland. At one point in the mid-1540s, Ferrante Gonzaga, a Mantuan prince, even recommended that Charles surrender Germany and the Netherlands and form the rest into an integrated Hispano-Italian kingdom.

From the very first, South Germany nonetheless figured importantly in Charles's vision of his realms, for thence came much of the fiscal glue that held the realms together. Later, of course, Castile and the Netherlands would become the financial pillars of this great, ramshackling empire, but during the desperate days after Maximilian's death, "no other place in the world came near, in its importance for the financial history of the western world, the significance of the city on the Lech. Augsburg is the economic gatehouse of the world."[79] Other South German houses also served the Crown, and other South German bankers also bore the title of "Imperial Councillor," but the Fugger bank of Augsburg emerged as "the economic arsenal of the Habsburgs."[80]

The spectacular role of Augsburg money in his election must have

---

[77] Rosenfeld, "Governors," 257–60.

[78] Press, "Die Erblande," 62. For Gonzaga's proposal and the end of this paragraph, see Chabod, "Conttasti interni," 57–9.

[79] Pölnitz, "Der Kaiser," 41. On the structures and finances of Charles's empire, see C. Bauer, "Machtgrundlagen," 218–29; Elliott, *Imperial Spain*, 197–9; Näf, "Strukturprobleme," 167–72; Baelde, "Financiële politiek"; Koenigsberger, *Habsburgs and Europe*, 27–55.

[80] Pölnitz, "Der Kaiser," 41. Among the other bankers who became Imperial councillors was Friedrich Prechter of Strasbourg, on whom see F.-J. Fuchs, "Les foires et le royonnement économique," 307–13.

enhanced the king's appreciation for South German financial power, which seems in turn to have shaped his broader view of the South German cities. For several generations, South German commercial firms had been active not only in Charles's native Netherlands but also in Iberia.[81] Augsburgers and Nurembergers gradually surpassed the Great Ravensburg Company in South German investments, which migrated from Venice and Aragon toward Portugal – seemingly a safe bet after the Portuguese beat a combined Egyptian-Gujurati fleet off Diu in 1509 – to Castile around 1508. Nurembergers contributed to the Solis expedition along South American shores in 1508, and Augsburg helped outfit Magellan's great circumnavigation in 1519–22. In December 1522, Charles's government lifted the prohibition on foreign participation in Spanish voyages and drew even more Nuremberg and Augsburg capital from Lisbon to Seville. Charles thus knew of the South Germans chiefly as traders and financiers, men who had money to lend and who could supply guns and men for war. He lacked his grandfather's familiar ties to the German cities, none of which ever bound itself to his power so closely as Augsburg had to Maximilian's.[82]

From his heritage and from the structures of trade and finance in his realms, Charles V thus tended to see the South German cities in a financial, not a political, light. He might have learned more about them but for the emergence of two challengers, King Francis I of France and Sultan Suleiman the Magnificent, who distracted him from German affairs from an early point in his reign. No one could foresee that these rivals, and not German issues, would come to dominate Charles's nights and days – not in 1521, when he came to be crowned, to view and be viewed by his German subjects, and to preside over his first Imperial Diet.

The struggle against monopolies

Carle der wirt regieren
in grosser strengikeit,

---

[81] This paragraph is based on Kellenbenz, "Beziehungen," 456–93; idem, "Finanzierung," 153–81; idem, "Verbindungsplätze," 1–37; and Werner, "Beteiligung," 494–524.
[82] Lehmann, "Kaisertum," 77; C. Bauer, "Machtgrundlagen," 228.

die grechtigkeit wird er zieren,
zū kriegen sin bereit;
kein ungrechtigkeit wirt er nit lon,
ir richstet thūnd euch fröwen
dass es ist darzu kon.[83]

The historical image of the Imperial Diet of Worms in 1521 will always be dominated, even overwhelmed, by the confrontation between Charles V and an obstreperous professor of theology from Wittenberg, Martin Luther.[84] Without benefit of hindsight, however, the Diet's leading theme might well have been the emergence of an aggressive new spirit among the princes against the free cities and their merchants, for which the leading cities' envoys were quite unprepared. One of the cities' two speakers, Hans Bock von Gerstheim of Strasbourg, came to Worms prepared to secure Charles's confirmation of Strasbourg's own liberties, especially the right to grant citizenship to other lords' subjects (*Pfahl-bürgerrecht*).[85] Peutinger, the other speaker, came from Augsburg to work against a paragraph in the new law on the High Court, which seemed to threaten trade.[86] They did not work together. When some nobles attacked Strasbourg's position on citizenship, and when the cities' House of the Diet formed a committee to draw up a statement on the issue, Peutinger tried to insert his (utterly unrelated) matter into the document. Bock objected, and Peutinger threw into the fray the proxies of twenty-three other cities of the Swabian League – and won.[87] So much for urban solidarity at Worms. The cities were quite unprepared to face the challenge of a new Governing Council, in which they got two seats – no improvement since 1500 – and of which Count Palatine Frederick became deputy-president.[88] Far more serious than this development, however, was the reappearance at Worms of the deadly monopoly question.

---

[83] "King Charles will now govern, with sternness he'll be just. He will give us justice and make war if he must. He'll favor no injustice, and so, you cities, now rejoice that he is on the throne." Liliencron, *Volkslieder*, 3:235, no. 311, stanza 4.

[84] Wohlfeil, "Wormser Reichstag," 61–6.

[85] On Bock, see Brady, *Ruling Class*, 88–90, 161–2, 210–11, 227, 302–3. He was not a doctor (as Wohlfeil, "Wormser Reichstag," 76, 81), nor was he a humanist (as Kohls, "Humanisten," 416). His instruction is lost.

[86] Peutinger's instruction is in H. Lutz, *Peutinger*, 180–2. Most of what Kohls, "Humanisten," 423, writes about these urban politicians is swathed in fantasy.

[87] *RTA, jR*, 2:246; *PCSS*, 1: no. 79.

[88] *RTA, jR*, 1:866; E. Franz, *Nürnberg*, 78. See Baron, "Religion and Politics," 407.

"Monopoly"[89] was a name for all the merchants' ways of manipulating and controlling the market, which were widely held responsible for the price inflation that set in during the last third of the fifteenth century. Monopoly fed the power of money in the world and the power of the urban rich both inside and outside their cities, and it was nearly universally believed to be inimical to the common good. Monopoly nourished the belief that the growing power of money was strangling the old values and virtues of both nobles and commons. "Everything has gone bad," explained a Bamberg singing master named Muskatblüt,

> Who has the money, now gets the honor,
> Though in former days he would have been
> A robber and a usurer.[90]

Nonetheless, protested Hans Armbruster in der Brandgasse of Strasbourg decades later, but still before 1500, "he whom God has granted wealth, also wants honor." Resentment of the rich was part of the urban commons' way of life, but the truly explosive potential of antimonopoly sentiment came from its power to unite the princes and nobles with the urban commons.[91] In this, it was the antiusury sentiment reincarnate.

Urban antimonopoly sentiment developed as a defense of old, corporate, and collective values against the invasion of privileged wealth. This was the burden of the critique by John Geiler of Kaysersberg, one of South Germany's greatest preachers, from his wonderfully carved stone pulpit in Strasbourg's cathedral. "To those who buy as cheaply as possible," he thundered, "and to those who sell as dearly as possible, the Holy Sacrament should be refused . . . for this is against brotherly love. You should add a modest profit, also your trouble and effort, but to buy as cheaply and sell as dearly as you can, that is false!"[92] Geiler

---

[89] See Blaich, "Reichsstädte"; idem, *Reichsmonopolgesetzgebung*; idem, *Wirtschaftspolitik*; Höffner, *Wirtschaftsethik*.

[90] Quoted by Burger, *Renaissance*, 67.

[91] Höffner, *Wirtschaftsethik*, 64–101; De Roover, "Monopoly Theory," 274–9. On Hans Armbruster in der Brandgasse, see my *Ruling Class*, 58.

[92] These quotes are from Geiler's *Brösamlein*, ed. Johannes Pauli (Strasbourg: Johannes Grüninger, 1517) and are quoted by Strieder, *Studien*, 62, 189–92. On Geiler, see Rapp, "Jean Geiler," 25–32.

thus wielded the teaching of Thomas Aquinas against unrestrained pursuit of profit, which violated all norms of justice, love, and corporate solidarity.

Look at the human body, how each member serves the whole. My eye sees for my feet, the feet walk and bear the whole body; the mouth eats for the belly, and the belly receives the food and distributes it to the whole body and its members. And if you have a sore on the shoulder which is dangerous to the whole body, which supports all the other members, you cut it away and say: "Why should it remain?" But I say: we here at Strasbourg are all one body, and you and I are the members. If one member is a merchant, a forestaller, who damages the other members, . . . such a sore should be cut away and entirely removed.

Now Geiler moved from corporate metaphor to everyday life:

Monopolists are all those who buy up goods cheaply, or try to. And then they secure a privilege, a sealed charter, from a prince of the land or a king. These are monopolists properly speaking, who want [exclusive right] to sell something. The other sort of monopolists are those who don't want to sell at all, but who make secret agreements with one another to fix the price at which they will sell, and no lower. So they withhold [forestall] the goods, according to the oaths they've sworn. Such men want all the profit and will let no one buy cheaply, as they did themselves. They stand alone in the trough like a sow, who won't let the other hogs in. They want sole control over the goods, and everyone else must light his lamp from theirs. For they conspire together, so that no one can buy an ell of cloth, or anything else, cheaper than their price. Dearer, but not cheaper . . .
   Why is this forestalling improper? Because, though it seems an honorable transaction, it in fact damages the common weal [*gemeiner Nutz*]. How? It robs the market of its freedom. Here and elsewhere there is a free market, so that each may sell his goods as he pleases. This freedom is taken away by forestalling . . . Therefore, forestalling damages the common good.

Geiler's critique of monopoly illustrates two aspects of contemporary social thought. First, his defense of both "a modest profit" and "a free market" suggests the confusion into which business practices and power had thrown the defenders of traditional, corporate norms. Secondly, his views exemplify the vital connection between scholastic theology and everyday life, which ranged over such questions as tithes, usury, witchcraft – and monopoly. The lines of critical debate ran from the scholars' studies and pulpits of the pre-Reformation era directly into the radical pamphleteering of the 1520s.[93]

Critical social ideas found their resonances in humbler milieux. The idea that the big firms and their monopolistic charters damaged the common good went back at least to the *Reformation of Emperor Sigmund* in the earlier fifteenth century,[94] and it emerged later in many ordinary places. At Basel, for example, the political triumph of the guilds in 1515 led to the abolition of big firms, and an ordinance of 1526 assured the artisans' restrictive hegemony over the local marketplace.[95] During the heady days of 1524–6, it surfaced in several programs. The Tyrolean coppersmiths complained "that the firms make iron and copper dearer," and Michael Gaismair's *Tyrolean Constitution* proposed to socialize the mines and foundries, "which [now] belong to the Fuggers, the Höchstetters, the Paumgartners . . . and the like."[96] Further north, the *Heilbronn Program* of 1525 demanded "that the firms, such as the Fuggers, Höchstetters, and Welsers and the like be abolished, for they are able to control all goods and to oppress poor and rich alike."[97]

Monopolies did provoke poor and rich alike, and such views were more or less shared or advanced by princes and nobles. Hans von der Planitz, Frederick of Saxony's representative in the Governing Council, wrote to his lord in 1524 about a new Augsburg monopoly at Lisbon, "from which they hope to clear 150,000 fl. The common man has to pay every bit of it. It is said that Dr. [Hans] Rehlinger gave away more than 10,000 fl. at the last Imperial Diet, most of it to [Jean] Hannart, in order to retain the privileges."[98] The Bavarian dukes' instruction for the same Diet urged Hannart, Charles's commissioner, to regulate the firms, "so

[93] See in general Oberman, *Werden und Wertung*, with massive documentation, to which should be added Zimmerman, *Die Antwort der Reformatoren* (my thanks to Peter Blickle for this reference).

[94] Höffner, *Wirtschaftsethik*, 50–6.

[95] Strieder, *Studien*, 88; R. Wackernagel, *Geschichte*, 2,1:525ff.; Füglister, *Handwerksregiment*, 282–94.

[96] Wopfner, *Quellen*, 120; G. Franz, *Quellen*, 289; Laube and Seiffert, *Flugschriften*, 142. Art. 6 of the grievances drawn up at Augsburg during the Schilling affair in Aug. 1524 reads: "Sixthly, all monopolies should be abolished, and everybody should work for himself." Quoted by Broadhead, "Internal Politics," 151, from StA Augsburg, Urgichten 1524, Knöringer. See also the Merano Articles of 1525, in Wopfner, *Quellen*, 41. For an overview of the sources, see Blaich, *Reichsmonopolgesetzgebung*, 54–5.

[97] G. Franz, *Quellen*, 380; Laube and Seiffert, *Flugschriften*, 78.

[98] H. von der Planitz, *Berichte*, 626, lines 1–7 (April 27, 1524). See Richter, *Reichstag zu Nürnberg 1524*, 48 n. 1; and *PCSS*, 1:89.

that the discontent and unrest, which they might engender, could be prevented."[99] The Swabian League warned the Bohemian estates in 1525 of the misery and grief that would surely come from letting "the firms, with their monopolies and fast practices," into the kingdom of Bohemia, and the free knights of Franconia petitioned the Imperial Diet in 1522 against "the big merchants' firms," which damage all levels of society "with their monopolies, associations, and agreements, concerning how dearly each item should be sold."[100] It is important to recognize that these voices did not condemn privilege or price fixing, which were fixed parts of everyday life, but the power of the large commercial firms to endanger livelihood and social order for the sake of profits. At Strasbourg, where Geiler claimed there was a free market, the artisan masters in fact struggled against "merchant freedom" (*freie koufmanschaffi*) for the big traders.[101]

By the opening years of Charles V's reign, "monopoly" had become a watchword against the leading firms.

In the pamphlets and broadsides, in satirical poems and carnival jokes, this exotic expression appeared as a curseword and polemical slogan; but also in the sermon literature, in the acts of the Imperial Diets and in the textbooks of the jurists and theologians, monopoly played a significant role. In those days, especially among the townsmen, it must have had much the same ring as "capitalism" has had during the past one hundred years. It was the most frequently heard political-economic slogan of the age.[102]

This must be kept in mind, if we are to judge correctly the campaign the princes conducted against the urban monopolists. Some princes used very hard language. Count Palatine Frederick, for example, said that the merchants "damage the land and the people more than the clergy do, and they selfishly export all the gold and silver out of Germany. Nothing on earth damages Germany more in this respect than do the merchants and their firms."[103] "In the past," he continued, "nothing

---

[99] Jörg, *Deutschland*, 115–16; and there, too, the following quote.
[100] Ibid., 21–4, 39, 45, 116–17; the full text is in *RTA, jR*, 3:695–726, no. 113, and the passage here quoted at 724, lines 1–10.
[101] Brady, *Ruling Class*, 116–17. See De Roover, "Monopoly Theory," 284–5; and Blaich, "Reichsstädte," 212–13, on antimonopoly laws enforced against artisans.
[102] Höffner, *Wirtschaftsethik*, 7.
[103] Count Palatine Frederick's instruction for P. Probst to the Diet of Augsburg, Oct. 17, 1525, printed by Friedensburg, *Reichstag zu Speier*, 513–15, here at 514, and the following quote at 515.

has damaged Germany more than the failure to foster the common good and law and order [*gut polliceien*]. Therefore, the best thing would be to abolish and dissolve all firms, large and small, in the Empire, outside the mining districts, where many mining firms are needed." Unlike John Geiler or the Franconian free knights, Frederick sat in the Imperial Diet. And so did his kinsman and friend, Margrave Casimir, who at Worms in 1521 proposed to shift the tax burden to the cities and establish an import duty on luxury goods, which, he alleged, would hurt the big firms and aid the small merchants.[104]

What the princes wanted to suppress was not big capital but big *independent* capital, just as they objected not to cities but to politically autonomous cities. A clue to this motive appears in Count Frederick's exception to the proposed abolition, mining firms. He permitted, in fact, his tin mines in the Amberg-Sulzbach region of the Bavarian Nordgau to be exploited by a stock company.[105] Behind the great upsurge in metals production after 1470 lay an alliance between the rulers' control of mining, based on a regalian right, and the capital and organizing abilities of urban investors; the pamphleteer surely hit the mark who said the big merchants were the princes' "bedfellows."[106] The Habsburgs were the Empire's greatest mining lords, as under Maximilian Augsburg capital had come to control the Tyrolean copper industry and much of the Austrian trade in foodstuffs.[107] In Saxony, the mines came during the later fifteenth century into the hands of capitalist *Gewerke*, associations of (mostly Saxon) townsmen, and Duke George the Bearded chartered in the 1490s a "Society for Tin" in the mines of the Erzgebirge.[108]

The monarchy had no choice but to protect the monopolists, both because powerful princes wanted chartered monopolies to exploit their mines and because the Habsburgs themselves depended so heavily upon the urban rich who were both lenders to the Crown and investors in monopolistic companies. Charles's brother, Ferdinand, for example, was party to the monopoly in the Idrian mercury trade,[109] and he and Charles

---

[104] *RTA, jR,* 2:404–5.
[105] Strieder, *Studien,* 145–7, 269–70.
[106] The pamphleteer is quoted by Höffner, *Wirtschaftsethik,* 51. See Strieder, *Studien,* 362–3; Laube, *Studien,* 272–8.
[107] Strieder, *Studien,* 79; Ehrenberg, *Zeitalter der Fugger,* 1:190; Wiesflecker, *Maximilian,* 2:411–12, 3:232–5.
[108] Laube, *Studien,* 82–181; Strieder, *Studien,* 220, 226–7, 414–15, 424–7.
[109] Strieder, *Studien,* 78–81.

had to protect their creditors and partners. This was the most fundamental partnership between the Habsburgs and the South German free cities, and it warns us not to identify the interests of the big firms entirely with those of "the cities." Even where the coincidence of wealth and political office was most nearly complete, at Nuremberg, the government could not regard the interests of the rich alone. The scale of monopolistic commerce and investment also varied enormously from city to city, and the defense of the firms against charges of "monopoly" thus became a very divisive issue in urban ranks.

Augsburg's government defended monopoly with heart and soul, but no other city dared follow its lead. In November 1522, the Governing Council canvassed southern cities about commercial firms in preparation for the Second Diet of Nuremberg.[110] Ulm replied that "the big firms, as presently constituted, are damaging and intolerable to the Holy Roman Empire of the German Nation and the common good, and they should be abolished." Firms should further be limited to a father and son or son-in-law, and a special import tax should be levied on all imported metals, silks, spices, wax, and other goods. The Augsburgers, by contrast, though they admitted there were abuses, rejected all restrictions on firms and argued that, in general, unrestricted trade promoted the common good. The burden of this defense fell on Peutinger, who noted that price fixing and the primacy of private over the common good were not peculiar to the big firms. "It is not alone by the large firms," he wrote, "that monopoly, as it is called, and forestalling are practiced. If you look around, you will find that all buying and selling, large-scale and small, by persons of the highest to the lowest degree, is carried on in pursuit of private good, not common weal or brotherly love . . . "[111] In his defense of the social utility of the pursuit of private gain, Peutinger advanced down a trail that Johann Eck (d. 1543), who had also served the Augsburg firms, had blazed in his defense of interest taking during the 1510s.[112] Though they lagged behind such Italian

---

[110] *RTA, jR*, 3:556, no. 100, probably also sent to Frankfurt. The Nuremburg government's reply to the Governing Council on monopolies, which agrees substantially with the Ulm opinion quoted here, is summarized by M. Meyer, "Haltung," 204–5, from an unpublished dissertation by N. Heieck.

[111] *RTA, jR*, 3:559–60. Strieder, *Studien*, 79, believed that the opinion was influenced, if not written, by Peutinger.

[112] C. Bauer, "Durchbruch,"; idem, "Gutachten"; H. Lutz, *Peutinger*, 106–9. On Eck, see Oberman, *Werden und Wertung*, 174–86 (English: *Masters*, 130–43).

humanists as Poggio Bracciolini (1380–1459),[113] who had attacked the Christian ideal of evangelical poverty in the name of private accumulation of wealth, the South German apologists for big capital made enormous strides in this single generation. Wherever the practical needs of the great firms were being explained, wherever their freedom required defending, wherever the case was argued for letting the market set prices, and wherever the so-called selfish manipulations of the firms were clothed in the common good, the pen of Peutinger, the learned and Welser-connected politician, could be found at work. He noted that mining and selling metals required a concentration of capital,[114] an echo of Count Frederick's views, and he argued that the monopolists' profits were justified by the great risks to capital and health and by unceasing work, a novel argument in a society whose ruling classes lived chiefly from rents. Occasionally, Peutinger came close to the wisdom of a later age, that private selfishness necessarily promotes the common good, and though he never quite took that final step, yet he did his best to undermine the traditional corporate view that private must yield to public good.[115] The "freedom of the market" meant something quite different to him than it did to John Geiler at Strasbourg. It was not that Strasbourg's intellectuals ignored the business world,[116] but that the big merchants there were not powerful enough to procure a public identification of their private freedom with the common good.

Cities under attack

Er [Charles V] wil sein glick zum friden
wenden und einigkeit
in des reiches geliden,
darzū ist er bereit.[117]

---

[113] Baron, "Franciscan Poverty." The key text, Poggio Bracciolini's *De avaritia*, is translated by Kohl and Witt, *Earthly Republic*, 231–89.

[114] See Strieder, *Studien*, 70 n. 4, 82 n. 1.

[115] C. Bauer, "Durchbruch"; H. Lutz, *Peutinger*, 136–41. For a contrary view, see De Roover, "Monopoly Theory," 285–7.

[116] Schott, *Works*, 1:255–6, which relates a discussion of a business contract.

[117] "The king will try his best to bring peace and unity to all his German subjects, as best he ever can." Liliencron, *Volkslieder*, 4:5, no. 421, stanza 5.

The campaign against monopolies began with the Imperial Diet of Cologne in 1512, which noted the appearance "recently" (*in kurtzen Jahren*) of many large firms, which attempted to control the markets in spices, metals, cloth, and other goods.[118] This damaged "the Holy Empire and all its members" and violated the common law and the principle of honor. Such firms' goods were to be confiscated and their members forbidden safe-conducts, though "no one shall hereby be forbidden to join in a firm or to buy and sell goods where he pleases; but he should not try to bring a single kind of ware all into one hand and then set the price as he pleases..." When Charles V was elected at Frankfurt on June 28, 1519, he had to promise to enforce this 1512 law against monopolies.[119] A generation of steady inflation of prices, especially of foodstuffs, made the issue ever more pressing, and antimonopoly legislation now became the centerpiece in a campaign against the great firms and the financial independence of the free cities, which certain princes conducted through the first four Imperial Diets of Charles's reign at Worms (1521) and Nuremberg (1522, 1522–3, 1524).

At Worms, the Small Committee of the Diet debated whether "the merchants' firms should be abolished" and decided that the new Governing Council "should diligently collect information about these matters from those who are experienced in and knowledgeable about them."[120] The Council returned the results of its survey to the Small Committee of the Diet of Nuremberg in 1522, whose collection of information on commerce and monopolies became an arsenal on which antimonopolists would draw for years to come. It was to this committee that the Franconian free knights complained that the big merchants, "with their sneaking ways, doubtless damage the German nation more in one year...than all the other bandits could do in ten."[121] "There sit the foes of the cities and the merchants," Peutinger wrote home, "who would not be so diligent, were

---

[118] Schmauss, *Neue und vollständigere Sammlung der Reichs-Abschiede*, 2:144. See Blaich, "Reichsstädte," 202–3, and *Reichsmonopolgesetzgebung*, 10–11, on the statute's enactment.
[119] *RTA, jR*, 1:872. See Blaich, "Reichsstädte," 202. The common political actions of the free cities between 1522 and 1526, plus the issues that brought them together, are reviewed by M. Meyer, "Haltung," 181–235, a very useful, if excessively polemical, study. Despite a promise (185) to review radically the conclusions of "bourgeois historiography," his final assessment is modest and quite balanced.
[120] *RTA, jR*, 2:354, no. 30, here at lines 24–6. See C. Bauer, "Gutachten," 152.
[121] *RTA, jR*, 3:725, lines 3–5.

the target highwaymen."[122] Other townsmen shared his view of the committee's motives: "first, envy; secondly, hatred of law and order; thirdly, error and misunderstanding; fourthly, fickleness; and fifthly, the desire to diminish or even wipe out ordinary trade." As if to confirm the drift of things at the Diet, at the turn of the year to 1523, while the Diet was still sitting, the Imperial prosecutor, Dr. Caspar Marth, began a suit under the law of 1512 against the Nuremberg firm of Peter Imhof on the grounds of remarkably large capitalization, the attraction of foreign capital, and a spice monopoly.[123] Similar suits followed against the Augsburg houses of Fugger, Welser, Höchstetter, and some others.

Why did this gathering storm not break in 1523? Hardly anyone, except for Peutinger and his Augsburg masters, defended the big firms outright. The Small Committee at Worms had divided between those who thought "that aforesaid forbidden monopolies cannot be abolished, unless all merchants' firms are suppressed," and those who argued "that such a suppression of firms would do the whole German nation more harm than good."[124] Both sides agreed that the big firms were harmful and thought the urban governments were in league with them. "The merchants' governments," the committee had written, "which are chiefly those of the free cities, where most of the violations occur, are hand-in-glove with the merchants and are therefore interested parties. The governments are partisan and far too much compromised to supervise the trade or regulate it justly. Other, strict enforcers of the law are needed." There was scant comfort for monopolists here. And yet the Diet did not act. The committee's only urban member was Hans Bock von Gerstheim from Strasbourg, though his son-in-law, Florenz von Venningen (d. 1538), chancellor of the Palatinate, also sat in the committee, and his lord, Elector Louis, apparently did not share his younger brother's animus against the cities.[125] A more important clue is provided by the Large Committee's report on the Small Committee's recommendations, which acknowledged the need for monopolistic practices in mining and marketing met-

---

[122] Peutinger, *Briefwechsel*, 331, no. 203. The following quote is from Blaich, *Reichsmonopolgesetzgebung*, 12.
[123] Blaich, *Reichsmonopolgesetzgebung*, 12–13. Marth was a native of Worms.
[124] *RTA, jR*, 2:354, lines 5–9; the following quote is at 352, lines 31–6.
[125] On Bock, see note 85 in this chapter. On Venningen, see Press, *Calvinismus*, 29–30; Brady, *Ruling Class*, 302. On Elector Louis, see Press, *Calvinismus*, 168–80.

als. Strict construction of the law of 1512 would make this impossible, "as can be learned from My Gracious Lord, Duke George of Saxony."[126] George the Bearded probably did as well from mining as his cousin, Elector Frederick, who got more from his silver mines than from all the rest of his lands.[127] The Diet's failure to act against monopolistic firms, despite the powerful sentiment against them, must be attributed to the objections of the great mining lords, especially the Wettins of Saxony and the Habsburgs, who needed such firms to exploit their mines.

No such considerations stayed the Diet's hand in matters of taxation. The Diet had granted no new major tax since 1512 and undertaken no reapportionment since 1505. When the Diet of Worms acted, it shifted the tax burden perceptibly toward the cities, which had been assessed up to 25 percent of the total in Maximilian's time but bore 30 percent of the new apportionment.[128] The next Diet drafted a proposal for a levy of 5 percent on property and income, the proceeds to be used against the mounting Turkish threat.[129] The princes, nobles, and other rulers would pay 1 percent on their *incomes*, the urban populations up to 1 percent on their *total assets*. The urban governments had always objected to such taxes, which would provoke "notable and unheard of rebellion and discontent" in their communities, as the Swabian League's cities had written in 1513.[130] A decade later, their opinion had not changed, for in 1522 they complained that the levy, "insofar as it concerns the cities and their people, can be neither approved nor paid, for it is not only unbearable and intolerable, but we cannot pay it, for evident and sufficient reasons detailed below."[131] Such taxes were not customary in Germany and would lead in time to "a perpetual servitude."

---

[126] *RTA, jR*, 2:361, lines 6–8. On Duke George as a mining lord, see Strieder, *Studien*, 73, 214–15, 220, 226–7, 414–15, 424–7; Blaschke, *Sachsen*, 38–46; and Laube, *Studien*. On the duke himself, see Scheible, "Fürsten," 390–7.

[127] Laube, *Studien*, 77–81.

[128] *RTA, jR*, 2: no. 56; Hölbling, "Maximilian I. und sein Verhältnis," 137–8, 168. On taxation and the cities, see Isenmann, "Reichsstadt," 66–89, especially the table on 70 n. 184; G. Schmidt, *Städtetag*, 352–420; Eitel, *Reichsstädte*, 12–15; Dollinger, "Charles-Quint," 183–92.

[129] *RTA, jR*, 2:412–19, no. 53. On the urban governments' attitudes toward such taxes, see Hölbling, "Maximilian I. und sein Verhältnis," 136–7, 172.

[130] Hölbling, "Maximilian I. und sein Verhältnis," 138; Klüpfel, *Urkunden*, 2:75. They also opposed levies in money rather than troops, for which see ibid., 2:1.

[131] *RTA, jR*, 3:456, lines 17–21; the following quote is from 188–97, no. 35 (April 30, 1522). The cities' critique is in ibid., 366–69, no. 71, composed by the Urban Diet at Nuremberg in Oct. 1522 and based on the recess of Esslingen. See F.-J. Fuchs, "Guerre et économie," 123–33.

The urban governments were no happier about a tax to support the Governing Council and the High Court, especially as Margrave Casimir had proposed to free the princes altogether from this obligation and to introduce an import duty on luxury goods.[132] Temporarily torpedoed by Peutinger, the plan was revived by the Governing Council over the cities' objections. Nuremberg's council held the project "to be the most grievous measure against the Holy Empire, and especially the honorable free and Imperial cities, within memory."[133] The free cities' envoys protested that the scheme "is regarded as so grievous and throughly injurious, that we think it will in time prove ruinous to all powers, but especially to the honorable cities. It is therefore impossible and intolerable that this tax be enacted."[134] The Governing Council nonetheless proposed the duty to the Second Diet of Nuremberg, arguing that only seven cities – Nuremberg, Augsburg, Strasbourg, Ulm, Cologne, Metz, and Lübeck – had extensive trade outside the Empire, and their interests must yield to Germany's common good.

The princes were split by this proposal. Although a general import duty would relieve the pressure of taxation on them and their subjects, in would also, as Leonhard von Eck pointed out, provide a large, steady income to the emperor. "Truly," he wrote to Duke William of Bavaria in mid-1522, the duty will be established "to the suppression of all the princes and other powers, for this money, which will come to many hundreds of thousands of florins, will go to the House of Austria and stay there; and with it he [Charles V] will introduce the Latin and French style of obedience and bring them under the yoke, which will be intolerable for the princes."[135] The import duty would also "destroy the [Swabian] League and bleed the German lands dry... The cities, I understand, will never approve this duty."[136]

Against these taxes, which were proposed to the Imperial Diets of the years 1521 to 1523, the urban governments had few weapons, es-

---

[132] Scheible, "Fürsten," 382.
[133] Quoted by Zophy, "Christoph Kress," 52–3. See F. Roth, *Einführung*, 129; Baron, "Religion and Politics," 407–8. For other attitudes, see *PCSS*, 1:48–9, no. 86, and 80, no. 140; H. von der Planitz, *Berichte*, 162–3, no. 70.
[134] *RTA, jR*, 3:530, lines 14–23, no. 96. For the Council's action, see ibid., 765, lines 32–5, no. 119.
[135] Eck to Duke William, July 17, 1522, in Jörg, *Deutschland*, 14.
[136] Ibid., 23(March 28, 1523); H. Lutz, "Das konfessionelle Zeitalter, I," 302–6.

pecially as the princes and electors continued to refuse them more than a consultative role in the Diet's deliberations. When, for example, the urban envoys at Worms in 1521 asked to see the assessments before consenting to them, their betters replied that "what the electors, princes, and other powers have decided, the cities must accept. Our view is that the cities are bound to give their consent; and if they don't, then we shall be obliged to inform the emperor who it is that is to blame."[137] The Imperial constitution simply provided the free cities with no remedy for their intolerable position.

By contrast, in those areas in which the urban governments and their merchants *wanted* action, the Diet did little or nothing. The Sickingen feud against Trier and the Knights' Revolt in 1523 had to be put down by the princes, for the Imperial executive authority proved powerless. On the Empire's highways reigned conditions described in a supplication penned to Charles V by some merchants assembled at Frankfurt in 1521.[138] They drew a grim picture of their plight:

Although the common artisan, who builds and uses the Holy Empire's highways, ought to be able to pursue his trade and affairs with trust and security, in the past the public peace had been broken not only against our governments, but also against our own persons and goods. Both ours and other governments of other free and Imperial cities of the Holy Empire have for a long time been the objects of wars and other attacks, to the extent that there are very few honorable cities who have not, in the time since the public peace was established [1495], suffered damages or violence. The contempt and disdain for the law on the part of many in the Holy Empire have produced a state of lawlessness and violence against us, which we can hardly bear and which will push us into ruin.[139]

They described the perils of a merchant's life: violence, mutilation, kidnapping, ransom, robbery, imprisonment; and they begged Charles for relief.

Not the Governing Council or the Diet but the Swabian League gave the merchants relief. During the spring of 1523, the League sent its

---

[137] *PCSS*, 1:49, no. 86.
[138] AMS, AA 374b, fols. 5^{r-v} (not in *RTA*, *jR*). This document is printed in Appendix C.
[139] AMS, AA 374b, fol. 5^{r-v}.

army into the wilds of Franconia to burn out the worst noble predators.[140] Though the chief target was Thomas von Absberg, the unruliest spirit in an unruly land, the army hit many other folk as well. Then the troops marched into Nuremberg, right under the noses of the Governing Council.[141] "The said Governing Council and the Swabian League cannot possibly agree," wrote Archduke Ferdinand to his brother, "for they are totally opposed to one another,"[142] but he had to admit that the League was effective: "The Swabian League acquitted itself well against the Franconians, destroying up to twenty-three castles and chasing their lords from the land." Once again, the League had proved the surest enforcer of the law and guarantor of urban interests.

The rise of the urban front

O Carle, du edler keiser werd,
zeuch auss dein keiserliches schwert,
mit deinem brüder Ferdinand
beschütz teutsch und welsche land,
lass nicht lenger stecken in der scheid,
beschirm die heilig christenheit
in der welt weit und preit,
damit du die ewigen seligkeit
erlangen mügestt mit fürsten und herren![143]

A brief but remarkably vital renaissance of the free cities' political solidarity occurred during the first four years of Charles's reign. Inspired by the Swabian League's successes, emboldened by the apparently benign attitude of the new monarch, and pressed to defend their particular liberties, their wealth, and their far-flung economic interests against predatory nobles and ambitious princes alike, the governments of the leading

---

[140] Klüpfel, *Urkunden*, 2:225–39, 243–4, 272–5; Baader, *Verhandlungen*. See Bock, *Der Schwäbische Bund*, 185–6.

[141] H. von der Planitz, *Berichte*, 548; Reicke, *Geschichte*, 804–5.

[142] W. Bauer and Lacroix, *Korrespondenz*, 1:84, no. 50, para. 9 (Dec. 18, 1523), and the following quote is at 87, para. 18.

[143] "Oh Charles, emperor of noble blood, draw now your imperial sword and with your brother, Ferdinand, protect both German and Latin lands. Don't let your blade unsheathed lie, protect the Christian folk in this world both far and wide, so that you may enter heaven with other princes and lords!" Liliencron, *Volkslieder*, 4:3, no. 420, lines 132–40.

southern free cities tried to establish a regular forum for political con-sultation and a system of collective security. Their pursuit of these two goals, in which they attained the former but not the latter, may con-veniently be summed up under the term *the urban front*.[144]

The cities obtained a forum for consultation through the revitalization of the Urban Diet. This assembly of all free cities arose during the 1470s but went into eclipse at the rise of the Swabian League. When the Cities' House at the Diet of Nuremberg in 1522 decided to call an Urban Diet to Esslingen on July 25, no Urban Diet had met since 1508.[145] The League, however, also formed the indispensable prelude to the urban front, for the League cities had acquired the habits of consultation and deliberation, managed their own assemblies, and evolved the custom of empowering the larger cities to represent them all in the Imperial Diet.[146] These habits of solidarity flowed into the activities of the Urban Diet, which met ten times between 1522 and 1525 and was often better attended than were the Imperial Diets.[147]

The Urban Diet, more even than the Cities' House of the Imperial Diet, was a southern assembly. All four "corresponding cities" – Augs-burg, Strasbourg, Frankfurt, and Nuremberg – which handled com-munications for free cities in four different sectors of the Empire, were southern, and all of the meeting sites – Nuremberg, Speyer, Esslingen, and Ulm – lay in the South. Furthermore, among the thirty most fre-quently attending cities between 1495 and 1545, only one, Cologne, lay north of the region defined in this study as South Germany.[148] Still, is remarkable that envoys should have ridden from Cologne to Esslingen or Ulm to meet for one or two days with representatives from the southern towns.

Just as in the Cities' House of the Imperial Diet, in the Urban Diet the cities were formally equal and in fact divided into the few large towns who led and the others who followed. The middling towns were only once called on to play a special role, when five of them were

---

[144] G. Schmidt, *Städtetag*, 146.
[145] Based on Appendix A below; see G. Schmidt, *Städtetag*, 17–146, on the Urban Diet.
[146] For instances of common representation, see Klüpfel, *Urkunden*, 2:36 (1510), 206 (1521); *RTA, jR*, 2:742–3, no. 101, and vol. 3:484, no. 88.
[147] G. Schmidt, *Städtetag*, 54, and 36–9, 47–8, for attendance by city and meeting.
[148] Rublack, "Politische Situation," 333–4; G. Schmidt, *Städtetag*, 38–9, 94–7.

appointed to audit the accounts of the Spanish embassy sent in 1523.[149] The smaller towns often gave their proxies to larger patrons. The issues discussed by Urban Diets of this era, however, concerned cities of all sizes and levels of power: decisions by past and agendas of future Imperial Diets; disruptions of the public peace in general and threats to particular cities; and the religious question. Although the Urban Diets often met in close connection with Imperial Diets, and sometimes met during the latter, yet they were truly independent assemblies, largely removed from influence by other Imperial powers and institutions.[150]

For all their limitations, the Urban Diets of the first half of the 1520s were imposing assemblies, both in size and composition. Grandest in numbers was the Urban Diet held in March 1523, when envoys from forty-four cities, who also brought proxies for five more, assembled at Speyer on the Rhine.[151] This and the other Urban Diets of these years brought together the political cream of the urban upper classes, the men who gave the oligarchies their tone. There were big men from big towns, such as Christoph Tetzel and Bernhard Baumgartner of Nuremberg, Peutinger of Augsburg, Dr. Peter Bellinhusen of Cologne, Bernhard Besserer of Ulm, and Daniel Mieg of Strasbourg; substantial men from middling towns, such as Hans Holderman of Esslingen, Bartholomäus Botzheim of Hagenau, and Joss Weiss of Reutlingen; and big fish from small ponds, such as Martin Hoheloch of Schweinfurt and Johann Gustenhofer of Offenburg.[152] Those who were not patrician rentiers or merchants were secretaries or lawyers, and the youngest of them was close to forty years of age. More than any other institution, the Urban Diet contributed to the exchange of ideas and knowledge among the urban ruling classes far beyond the bounds of individual regions.

Despite the successes of regional federations, such as the Swabian League, the idea of a general urban league to protect the public peace never died. The very successes of the Swabian League, in fact, reawakened the notion among the Rhenish towns late in Maximilian's reign, and the project was taken up by the revitalized Urban Diet in March 1522 at Speyer, and in August of the same year at Esslingen,

---

[149] Klüpfel, *Urkunden*, 2:256–8; *PCSS*, 1:80, no. 140. See G. Schmidt, *Städtetag*, 110–11.
[150] G. Schmidt, *Städtetag*, 33–5.
[151] Ibid., 47.
[152] Ibid., 117–32.

where the urban envoys deliberated on how the cities "could erect a secret, honorable, effective, and appropriate alliance [*verstand*], through which they might resist whatever troubles might afflict one or more cities."[153] What such troubles might be appears in a Nuremberg instruction, "for through such an alliance the cities can all the better secure peace, right, and their liberties and customs and protect them from violence and the presently threatening uprisings [*aufrur*]."[154] During the following year, a treaty of alliance was drafted, but it could not be enacted, chiefly because of the economic discrepancies among the cities. The large cities would not form an alliance without firm commitments by the smaller cities to share the costs, which the smaller towns would not give. The idea was revived as the religious question got hotter in 1524 and 1525, but it all came to nothing. The urban politicians surely dreamed of the great urban leagues of the past, through which their ancestors had won glory and secured their communes' liberties, but the world had clearly changed since then. The idea of an urban military league was discussed, debated, revived, and referred until the last Urban Diet dissolved in 1671.

The urban front crystallized politically at the Second Imperial Diet of Nuremberg, whose Small Committee attacked the big firms, which – as any fool could see in Nuremberg's spice shops – had driven prices sky-high and were provoking rebellion. The Diet approved a limit on the size and capitalization of firms and revived the project for an Imperial customs duty.[155] The prosecutions of monopolists also continued, and the urban envoys gathered in a grim mood at Speyer on March 22. The limits on firms, they declared, "if they are enforced, may in time well achieve the annihilation of general trade and exchange through the ruination of all the honorable free and Imperial cities."[156] They agreed to continue discussing a military alliance and poured out their grievances to Charles V:

---

[153] Recess of the Urban Diet at Speyer, March 22, 1523, in StA Ulm, A 521, fols. 15^v–16^r, 20^r–21^r. The quote is from G. Schmidt, *Städtetag*, 149.

[154] Quoted by G. Schmidt, *Städtetag*, 149. On the fate of the alliance idea during the 1520s, see ibid., 149–64; Bog, "Betrachtungen," 91.

[155] *RTA, jR*, 3:575–82. See also ibid., 752–3, no. 117, and 522–41, no. 108; H. von der Planitz, *Berichte*, 248, no. 113.

[156] *RTA, jR*, 3:522, lines 11–14; the following quote is at 530, lines 14–23.

Among these [grievances] the worst is the customs duty, which is to be levied and paid on all goods and wares exported from or imported into Germany. Which duty... is considered to be so grievous and entirely injurious, that we think it will in time prove ruinous to all powers, but especially to the honorable cities. It is therefore impossible and intolerable that this duty should be approved.

The customs duty, which was a much more broadly based grievance than the prosecutions for monopoly, sparked the decision to lay the urban grievances before Charles V in Spain. Seven weeks later, the largest Urban Diet in Charles's reign met at Speyer from March 22 to April 2, 1523, to prepare the Spanish embassy.

The list of grievances the cities sent to Spain opened with the 1522 levy for the Turkish war, which assessed the cities "five or ten times as high as other estates."[157] Secondly, they protested once more their lack of full voting rights in the Imperial Diet. In third place came the most pressing issue, the customs duty, on which they "unanimously" [*einhelliger meinung*] declared, "that this duty is impossible, insufferable, intolerable, unacceptable, and unbearable; that is, unless they and their subjects want to bring about their own certain and total ruin and plunge themselves into irreparable and certain decline." On monopolies, the fourth point, the Urban Diet trod the path blazed by the Ulmers. Although they admitted the existence of abuses, they strove to prevent the catchword "monopoly" from being applied to all trading firms. If the present anticommercial campaign continued, they said, "no free, legitimate, honorable trading would be allowed, but this project would lead in a short time to the extinction of all trade, large-scale, medium, and small, and it would wreck the free cities and their citizens." They would tell Charles the truth about monopolies, so that "whatever is legal and just and serves the common good, and therefore is not a monopoly, will be permitted." The fifth grievance concerned the Governing Council, which "in its present form is in several ways burdensome, damaging, and intolerable to all the honorable free and Imperial cities, and to other powers as well, and not just because of a few individual cases," but because the Council utterly disregards the cities' freedoms and customs, which "could lead to contemptuous and disobedient attitudes toward

[157] Klüpfel, *Urkunden*, 2:245–6, for this and the other quotes in this paragraph.

the government, rebellion in the cities, and the ruin of all the free and Imperial cities and their citizens and subjects..." If the Governing Council and the customs duty were abolished, nothing more than "a proper, prestigious, and reliable High Court" was needed in the way of an Imperial government. Sixthly and finally, the cities protested all Imperial tax assessments as too high for the cities. All in all, the grievances suggest that Nuremberg and Ulm led urban opinion into the most widely useful path: protection of trade from duties, citizens from taxes, and cities from the Governing Council, but not the big firms from the Imperial antimonopoly law.

The cities' embassy of appeal from the Imperial Diet to the emperor was organized by Augsburg, Nuremberg, Strasbourg, and Metz, which drafted instructions and credentials, arranged for French safe-conducts (through the French-speaking Messins), and provided money for the envoys' expenses. As speaker, Nuremberg sent Dr. Christoph Scheurl, veteran of the 1519 mission to Spain, and Clemens Volckamer; Augsburg sent Simon Seitz, former Welser factor in Portugal and Spain and presumably master of Iberian tongues; from Strasbourg came Bernhard Wurmser von Vendenheim (d. 1540), a noble Stettmeister of no great distinction; and Metz supplied a patrician, Philippe d'Esch.[158] They left Strasbourg in mid-May 1523, came to Lyons on June 3, and reached the Imperial court at Valladolid on August 6, where they laid the urban front's case before their sovereign.[159]

The embassy to Spain, 1523

Ganz Spanien thūt er zieren
und trägt auch uf ir kron,
Napels thūt er regieren,
darzū auch Arragon,

---

[158] On Scheurl, see note 3 in this chapter. On Simon Seitz (d. by 1526?), see Pölnitz, *Jakob Fugger*, 1:148, 2:133. He is not identical with Simon Magnus (Mang) Seitz (1482/3–1544), a wool merchant who held office from 1527 until his death (my thanks to James E. Mininger for this information). On Wurmser, see my *Ruling Class*, 356–7. Preparations for the embassy can be followed in *PCSS*, 1: nos. 140, 143–5, 147–8; see also H. von Schubert, *Lazarus Spengler*, 408–9.

[159] Senate of Strasbourg to the VII of Metz, April 20, 1523, in *PCSS*, 1:81, no. 143. The envoys' route is given from the Frankfurt copy of their report by Baumgarten, *Geschichte*, 2:306–7, which I have checked against the copy in StA Augsburg, Litteralien-Sammlung, at Aug. 24, 1523.

Charles V and his cities

in Granaten gwaltiger künig und herr,
mit gwalt so müss im dienen
das künigreich von Nawerr.[160]

Though perhaps not a "triumph for the free cities,"[161] the Urban Diet's embassy to Charles V in the summer of 1523 certainly brought the free cities' governments and their emperor to the brink of a new political understanding, in which the cities might have traded financial aid for a centralized regime in Germany. On the surface, at least, the townsmen could not have arrived at Valladolid at a better moment.[162] A very docile Castilian *cortés* had just adjourned, proof that the monarch had mastered the *comuneros'* fearsome insurrection. Nine days before the German embassy arrived, Charles had clinched a great anti-French league with Pope Adrian VI, Venice, Florence, Genoa, and England, and the king, "faced with the torment of penury, perpetual as hell," was moving toward the decisive moment in his struggle with Francis I.

After an initial royal audience on August 9, punctuated by Dr. Scheurl's address in Latin, Grand Chancellor Gattinara's reply, and the envoys' formal submission of the urban grievances, negotiations of substance took place from August 11 through 14 with a party of councillors.[163] Jean Hannart (d. 1539), lord of Likerke, First Secretary and Vice-Chancellor, headed the commission, and he was assisted by Gérard de Plein, Sieur de la Roche, another Netherlander.[164] The other two members were Germans: Balthasar Merklin (c. 1479–1531), provost of Waldkirch and an Alemannic-speaker from the Breisgau,[165] and Max-

---

[160] "He rules the whole of Spain and also wears her crown. He rules the realm of Naples and Aragon as well. He is Granada's king and lord, and holds in his obedience the kingdom of Navarre." Liliencron, *Volkslieder*, 3:235, no. 311, stanza 5.

[161] Baron, "Religion and Politics," 409.

[162] Brandi, *Kaiser Karl V.*, 1:171–2; Vercauteren, "Notes," 97–101. Just then, Spanish overseas expeditions were opened to foreign investors. Kellenbenz, "Finanzierung," 168. On Charles V's attitude toward the monopolies, see in general Kellenbenz, "Das Römisch-Deutsche Reich," 41–6. The quote at the end of this paragraph is from Carande, *Carlos V*, 1:140 (here translated by Wallerstein, *World-System*, 1:179 n. 2).

[163] This account is based on the envoys' report in StA Augsburg, Litteralien-Sammlung, at Aug. 24, 1523. See Baumgarten, *Geschichte*, 2:307–13; Kluckhohn, "Handelsgesellschaften"; H. Schmidt, "Reichsstädte," 184–91 (based on StA Ulm, A 526, fols. 2–52); and G. Schmidt, *Städtetag*, 173–7, 431–3, 444–8.

[164] Headley, *Emperor*, 33, 68, 81.

[165] On Merklin, see Hasenclever, "Balthasar Merklin."

imilian Transsylvanus (d. 1538), a humanist secretary.[166] After the exchange of courtesies and the bestowal of gifts on the courtiers[167] – this much had not changed since Emperor Maximilian's day – the grievances were delivered and negotiations began. On August 13, the embassy was told through Merklin that two of the six points must be rejected out of hand: The cities' claim to vote in the Imperial Diet was "an innovation ... which never was before,"[168] and the Imperial tax for the Turkish war derived from "unavoidable necessity."[169] As for the customs duty, the free cities should tolerate it "for a little while, with assurances that it will eventually be abolished ... for certain incomes are necessary for the maintenance of law and order."[170] The justice of the other urban grievances was admitted, and the cities were offered two seats on the High Court.

Matters were not to end so simply and cheaply, for the urban envoys rejected Merklin's remarks and made a new proposal:

> If a King of the Romans were elected, and some other arrangements were made, then we wouldn't need a Governing Council. The manner of appointment of this body and the High Court, indeed, was arranged at the electoral assembly at Frankfurt [in 1519], where the electors were able to control the Empire. In time, therefore, not only would this practice damage the House of Austria, it would also bring more harm than good to the Empire.[171]

---

[166] Not to be confused with Maximilian van Bergen, whom the Germans called "Siebenburger." On this German humanist and royal secretary, see Roersch, "Maximilian Transsylvanus."

[167] A note to the envoys' report gives the sums of 200 ducats for "Von Rosch" (La Roche), 300 for Waldkirch, and 200 for Transsylvanus. StA Augsburg, Litteralien-Sammlung, at Aug. 24, 1523, fol. 20ʳ. Strasbourg's share of the gift for Hannart came to 125 gold florins. AMS, IV 40/20. On the entire subject of gifts and bribes, see Koenigsberger, "Patronage and Bribery," 166–75; G. Schmidt, *Städtetag*, 177–80.

[168] StA Augsburg, Litteralien–Sammlung, at Aug. 24, 1523, fols. 28ᵛ–29ʳ: "Und erstlich, warumb die Stett allererst bei Regierung dises jungen kaisers dise newrung ins Reichs Rat stÿm und session zu haben, so vor allters nie gewesen, furnemen."

[169] Ibid., fol. 29ʳ: "Zum dritten, der furgenomen Turckhen hilff widerreten sich die Stet unpillich, dhweil solichs die hochst unvermeidenlich notturft ervordert ... "

[170] Ibid.: "Darum soltn die Stet den furgeschlagen zol ein klaine zeit auff genugsame versicherung, das der alsdann entlich fallen solt, oder zum wenigsten von hundert zween zu zolen, bewilligen, oder aber ander weg bedencken und antzaigen, diweil sunst niemant nichts thun wolt, von dannen ein statthafter Stathalter und Cammergericht im Reich underhalten werden mochten."

[171] Ibid., fol. 30ʳ: "Im fall, das ein romischer konig erwelt wurde und ander villerlai ursachen, das kains Regiments von notten, und welcher mass dasselb, als wol als das Commergericht gestallt, besetzt und gelegen sei. Was auch in der wal zu Franckfordt practiciert sei, wo ein Churfurst das Reich zu underhalten vermugend gewesen were, derhalb diser zol nit allain dem hawss osterreich mit der zeit nachtailich sein mocht, sunder auch dem Reich ... mer verderbens dan aufrung verursachen wurde ... "

The point of this odd passage is that a customs duty would provide the money for Council and Court in their current form, that is, under the control of the princes, thus thwarting Charles and the cities alike. This was a cue for the talks' shift from the individual grievances to the discussion of a new order of power in the Empire, and Merklin, who showed that he understood the cue by conceding that the customs duty was "the most important and chief article,"[172] responded with the decisive point: "that the envoys should further declare, what the free cities would expect from His Majesty, and what they would do for him, should His Imperial Majesty take the government into his own hands and abolish both the customs duty now proposed and the Governing Council."[173] Surprised, perhaps, by Merklin's bold directness, the envoys replied that they would show their instructions, "which contain nothing more than what we read to you; and we have no power to agree to anything more, for we are only envoys [*bevelchhaber*]."[174] Merklin coaxed them, assuring that "His Imperial Majesty is himself, as an honorable prince, disinclined to establish the customs duty, which is a disagreeable thing, or to maintain this Governing Council, and he places the greatest trust in the free and Imperial cities, far more than in the other Imperial estates."[175] He also warned them that some of Charles's advisors, including Dr. Gregor Lamparter, favored the customs duty. The emperor himself "is burdened now with very great and unexpected war costs, and he must have help," and, after all, the cities had given Charles no special aid at the inception of his reign, as they had to his grandfather and great-grandfather. The urban envoys were not to be lured, though they, not Charles's men, had first shifted the subject of the discussions from the satisfaction of individual grievances to a new, direct royal government in Germany in return for some form of direct financial support by the cities.

No formal agreement was reached, though during the final audience

---

[172] Ibid., fol. 31ʳ: "Und achteten den zol fur den wichtigsten und haupt artikel ..."
[173] Ibid.: "Im fall, das kai. Mt. die Regierung zu iren handen nemen, das Regiment und den furgenomen zol entlich abstellte, wess si sich zu gemainen Steten versehen sollte, und was si bei irer Mt. thun woltn."
[174] Ibid., fol. 31ᵛ: "Erpietent, ir instruction furzulegen, weiters nichts inhaltend, dann wie si gehort were, verner hetten si zu bewilligen weder bevelch noch gewalt, si weren gleich wol mer nichts dann bevelchhaber ..."
[175] Ibid., fol. 32ʳ⁻ᵛ: "Die kai. Mt. als ein loblicher furst sei fur sich selbst zu aufrichtung dises zols, als eines hessigen dings, als wenig als zu erhaltung dess Regiments nit vasst genaigt, si stell und setz irn furnemsten trauen vor andern Reichs Stenden auff die Frei und Reichs Stet."

with Charles on August 19, Merklin tightened the screw on them. The emperor regarded the customs duty and the restrictions on commercial firms as the "chief and most important articles,"[176] and he would order the Diet and the Governing Council not to enforce the laws against monopolies and firms without his prior knowledge and permission, "for His Majesty in no way intends to diminish commerce or do it any damage." Further, he would quash the customs duty "and take the government into his own hands and establish an effective vicar and a proper High Court, so that peace, law, and order might be maintained in the Holy Empire."[177] Of course, Merklin added, if the customs duty and the tax for the High Court and Governing Council were suppressed, Charles would need revenues from new sources – not to speak of the war costs.[178] There it was again: the promise of direct royal government against the cities' financial commitment.

The screw tightened one more turn. Pope Adrian, Merklin said, had complained to Charles about the cities of Augsburg, Strasbourg, and Nuremberg, "that they, more than others, adhere to the execrable, damnable, seductive, false, heretical Lutheran doctrine, to the contempt of both papal and Imperial edicts; and they allow the sermons and other Lutheran pamphlets to be printed and sold, rather than having them burned."[179] Charles would bring the whole matter before the Diet, when he sent Hannart to Germany. The envoys twisted and squirmed – the religious question had not been broached before – they denied that Lutheran printers were tolerated and pleaded that the books were being smuggled in from other places. Their masters were not to blame for the

---

[176] Ibid., fol. 35ʳ: "Zum dritten, hat ir Mt. ausserhalb bemelts abschids weiter vertraulich und in gehaim zuerkennen geben lassen, ir Mt. achtet den zol und kaufmans handlung fur die haupt und wichtigsten artikel."

[177] Ibid.: "Nun were si [Charles] den Frei und Reichsteten vor andern Stenden mit sundern gnaden gnaigt und derhalb ir gemut und maynung keins wegs den furgenomen zol in sein wirkung komen zulassen und zubewilligen, sunder die Regierung zu iren handen zu nemen und einen dapferen Statthalter sampt einen statlichen Cammergericht zuverordnen, damit im heiligen Reich Frid, Recht, Execution, etc., erhaltn werden mocht ..."

[178] Ibid., fol. 35ᵛ: "Nun sei aber ir Mt. diser zeit mit schweren und unversehen kriegs leufften hart beladen ..."

[179] Ibid., fol. 36ʳ⁻ᵛ: "Das sich Bepstliche hailigkait durch ein Brieve, so er in handen hielte, bei Kai. Mt. uber die drei Stett, Augspurg, Strassburg und Nurenberg, hochlich beschwerdt und jemerlich beclagt hett, darumb das si vor andern der verworfen, verdampten, verfurischen, falschen, ketzerischen, lutterischen leer zu verachtung Bepstlicher und kaiserlicher gepot, anhiengen, die predigten, die lutterischen puchlein druckten, verkaufften liessen und nit verprandten etc."

spread of Lutheranism, and "it is also pertinent that the Common Man thirsts after the Bible and asks that it be preached to him; and he holds human teachings in much less esteem than he used to..."[180] Merklin warned them one last time about the Edict of Worms, at the same time promising action, if not too openly, against the customs duty. Two envoys held further secret talks with Merklin, apparently about a loan to the emperor – earlier 40,000 fl. had been mentioned – and all further action was put off until Hannart came to Germany.[181] The envoys left Valladolid on August 24 in high spirits, conscious of having secured their most important points.

While Scheurl veered off at Genoa to try his (bad) luck with a sea voyage, the other envoys paused at Lyons for an audience with King Francis and stopped at Basel. Here they recounted the story of Pope Adrian's charge against their cities of complicity with the Lutherans, which they seem at this point not to have taken too seriously.[182] Having spent a mere 1,300 fl., the envoys brought their masters the promise of a rich return, which the cities could hope to realize when the Imperial Diet assembled again at Nuremberg in January 1524.

How seriously ought we to judge these events as a potential new departure in Charles's German policy and in the cities' relations with their monarch? Charles's promises through Merklin certainly lay in the direction he had already intended to go. When he promised to "take the government into his own hands" – though only after the urban envoys suggested it – to appoint a vicar in the Empire, and to reform the Governing Council and High Court, he revealed a goal toward which something had already been accomplished: the establishment of a stronger Habsburg monarchical presence in the Empire. He had already provided, for example, a viceroy in the person of Archduke Ferdinand.[183] At Worms on April 28, 1521, he had named Ferdinand heir to the

---

[180] Ibid., fol. 38ʳ⁻ᵛ: "Dann gleich woll nit on were, den gemainen man durstet nach dem Ewangelio und der Bibl, pette im auch dieselb zu predigen und hielt menschen leer fur menschen leer nit als hoch als vor jaren ... "
[181] StA Augsburg, Litteralien-Sammlung, at Aug. 24, 1523, fols. 39ᵛ–40ʳ. See Hamann von Holzhausen to Frankfurt, Nuremberg, Feb. 12, 1524, in *RTA, jR,* 4:673, no. 187, lines 1–36.
[182] StA Augsburg, Litteralien-Sammlung, at Aug. 24, 1523, fol. 40ᵛ. See Soden, *Beiträge,* 165. The stay in Basel is recorded by Vögeli, *Schriften,* 1,1:139–40, and 2,2:1010 n. 291.
[183] On this entire question, see W. Bauer, *Anfänge*; Lhotsky, *Zeitalter*; Laubach, "Nachfolge"; Castrillo-Benito, "Tradition und Wandel"; Fichtner, *Ferdinand I of Austria.*

Austrian lands, and by two acts during the first half of 1522 he had announced him as vicar in both Austria and the Empire, where Count Palatine Frederick was to be his deputy. By the following summer, the rumor was being traded about that Count Henry of Nassau had come to Germany to sound out the electors and see "if Charles should make Ferdinand King of the Romans."[184] Ferdinand might have made a very capable German monarch. Reared at the court of his grandfather, King Ferdinand the Catholic of Aragon, a much stricter school of rulership than the lax court at Brussels, Ferdinand was more even in temperament, less prey to personal vices, steadier in judgment, and better educated than was Charles. What is more, the pattern of his travels during these first years as Charles's vicar, before the Jagellonian inheritance of Bohemia and Hungary distracted him eastward, resembled Maximilian's familiar wanderings through the free cities of South Germany.[185] It was not to be, for not only did Ferdinand get no free hand in Germany, he had to wait eight more years, until 1531, to become King of the Romans.

A second hindrance to Ferdinand's resuming Maximilian's ways lay in the Austrian problem. Not only did the archduke arrive at a time of open revolt in the Lower Austrian duchies, which the freedom he allowed his Spanish councillor, Gabriel Salamanca, did nothing to calm, but Ferdinand was and remained "only in a certain sense lord of the hereditary lands."[186] He lacked the authority to press immediately for the consolidation of the Austrian lands, and without pressure there was to be no Austrian centralization. The Tyrolean estates, for example, and those of Austrian Swabia opposed Württemberg's incorporation into Austria, because the duchy was so heavily indebted.[187] Lacking his elder brother's full confidence, which his detractors in Charles's entourage did their best to keep from him,[188] Ferdinand nonetheless did undertake an Austrian consolidation by 1527, when he gave the hereditary lands their first central administration. By then, however, the time for a fully

---

[184] Hans von der Planitz to Elector Frederick of Saxony, Nuremberg, July 16, 1523, in H. von der Planitz, *Berichte*, 491. See Laubach, "Nachfolge," 7.

[185] Ferdinand's itinerary is in Stälin, "Aufenthaltsorte," 384–95. Fichtner, *Ferdinand I of Austria*, 27–39, makes progress toward a revision of our picture of Ferdinand during the 1520s.

[186] Press, "Die Erblande," 52; also see 57–8 for what follows.

[187] W. Bauer, *Anfänge*, 98–9; Quarthal, *Landstände*, 68.

[188] W. Bauer, *Anfänge*, 163–5. For Hannart's hostility to Ferdinand, see Lanz, *Korrespondenz*, 1:106–7; *RTA, jR*, 4:692–4, 765–9; Laubach, "Nachfolge," 7 n. 30; Headley, *Emperor*, 129.

western-oriented Austria was past, as the great Turkish invasion of Hungary during the previous year had riveted Ferdinand's attention on the task of getting and keeping two crowns of his own.

Charles V had a great capacity for half-measures, as he displayed once more in his treatment of the Governing Council. The cities wanted it abolished, and by the autumn of 1523 Christoph Kress of Nuremberg was reporting that "the Governing Council is extremely weak here, and it is in fact almost dead."[189] Rather than risk the princes' resistance, however, and place all his bets on Ferdinand and the cities, Charles sent Hannart to Germany with instructions to reform the Council and translate it to Esslingen, closer to a center of Habsburg power. It is quite understandable, of course, that with the French war looming ever nearer, and in view of his Netherlandish subjects' reluctance to vote new taxes, Charles declined to provoke his German princes through aggressive measures.[190]

Moving to more directly financial matters, Charles's actions seem more positive concerning what he had, through Merklin, identified during the final audience with the townsmen at Valladolid as the "chief and most important articles," the customs duty and the measures against commercial firms. On the customs duty, the king was as good as his word. At the Third Diet of Nuremberg in 1524, the townsmen interpreted Hannart's instruction from Charles to mean that the project was dead, and the Diet in fact dropped the customs duty and agreed that the Diet and the emperor would each cover half the costs of the Governing Council and the High Court.[191]

In making good on his promise to provide relief for commerce, Charles took the Augsburg path rather than that marked out by the urban front, which wanted to sacrifice the big firms to protect commerce in general from the antimonopolists. To what degree Charles's policy was influenced by an opinion passed to his councillors at Valladolid by Simon Seitz of Augsburg, and perhaps drafted by Peutinger, is impossible now to say, though the assumption that the Augsburgers had somehow subverted the embassy later set the other towns against them.[192] Whatever the

[189] Christoph Kress to Gerwig Blarer, Nuremberg, Nov. 7, 1523, in Blarer, *Briefe und Akten*, 1:26, no. 44, line 27.
[190] On Charles's financial situation, see Vercauteren, "Notes," 95–101.
[191] G. Schmidt, *Städtetag*, 448–9; H. Schmidt, "Reichsstädte," 195.
[192] See G. Schmidt, *Städtetag*, 431–3.

reason, the emperor moved to protect the leading trading firms, when, on September 15, 1523, three weeks after the urban envoys left his court, he ordered Marth, the Imperial prosecutor, to stay the monopoly suits against the Fuggers and other Augsburg firms.[193] His next action fell as the news arrived at Madrid of the great Imperial victory over the French at Pavia (on February 24). Charles's "epoch-making" edict affirmed the right of all firms, large and small, to conduct their affairs without interference and limited prosecution under the law of 1512 to conditions most favorable to the big firms.[194] Peutinger, and behind him Jacob Fugger, may also have had something to do with this edict.[195] Be that as it may, eight days later, on March 18, 1525, Charles issued special decrees to protect leading Augsburg and Strasbourg firms from prosecution under the law of 1512 by placing monopolistic contracts in the mining and metals sector outside the law's definition of "monopoly." This is precisely what princely foes of the free cities, such as Count Palatine Frederick, had wanted, an abolition of monopolies except where they were useful to the princes. Finally, an edict of May 13, 1525, publicized the new immunities and made the argument that the freedom to trade, including the freedom to establish monopolies, was vital to the common good and prosperity of the Empire.[196] One needs to imagine the financial straits that led this Burgundo-Hispanic monarch, who believed devoutly in his God-given Christian imperium, to allow over his own signature this sponsorship of Peutinger's radical argument that the unrestrained pursuit of private profit promotes the common good. It is important to recognize that, although Charles interpreted protection for commerce in a sense congenial to the great monopolists, an interpretation perfectly in keeping with his predominantly financial view of the

[193] The text is printed by Strieder, *Studien*, 370–1, and by Vercauteren, "Notes," 104–5. Brandi, *Kaiser Karl V.*, 1:138–9, mentions Vercauteren's text but not Strieder's. On Jakob Fugger's influence, see Pölnitz, *Jakob Fugger*, 1:527–8.
[194] The text is printed by König, *Peutingerstudien*, 169–71; for comments, see Strieder, *Studien*, 75–6, and Pölnitz, *Jakob Fugger*, 1:555–6, who calls it "epoch-making." The date of arrival at court of news from Pavia is given by Knecht, *Francis I*, 172.
[195] This was first suggested by Aloys Schulte. See Pölnitz, *Jakob Fugger*, 2:538; H. Lutz, *Peutinger*, 220–2. This opinion rests on a comparison of the edict with Peutinger's memorials on monopolies, printed by C. Bauer, "Gutachten," 3–14. Pölnitz believes that Duke George of Saxony was Peutinger's intermediary at court.
[196] The text, dated Toledo, May 13, 1525, is printed by Strieder, *Studien*, 375–81. For commentary, see ibid., 82–5; Pölnitz, *Jakob Fugger*, 1:555–64; Blaich, *Reichsmonopolgesetzgebung*, 13.

German cities, he nonetheless did make good, in his own way, on his 1523 promise to provide that protection. His efforts to satisfy, at his own pace, the grievances the cities' embassy had presented in August 1523 are, on the whole, fairly impressive.

What of the urban governments back in Germany? Official notification of the embassy's report came in January 1524 at Nuremberg, where an Urban Diet convened during the early days of the Imperial Diet. The leading towns clearly expected to resume negotiations with Charles's commissioners, who included, besides Jean Hannart, two of the other negotiators at Valladolid, Balthasar Merklin and Maximilian Transsylvanus.[197] The Urban Diet decided to offer Hannart 500 fl. and an annual pension of 100 fl., plus 200 fl. for Waldkirch, to be borne by the cities as a whole, and they concluded "that we should negotiate with Hannart how we can establish a treaty with His Majesty, so that the grievances presented in Spain can be settled and satisfied; and for this purpose 30,000 fl. seems like enough."[198] Some of the politicians were disappointed – the Frankfurters, for example[199] – that the grievances had not been settled in Spain, but the decision to vote 30,000 fl. shows that the Urban Diet expected much from future negotiations.

The one cloud on the horizon at this point promised to trouble the urban front's solidarity, not its relations with the Crown. It arose from the Spanish embassy's report that Charles promised to send "a proper deputy" to Germany and that "if the cities grant His Majesty an appropriate tax and aid, they will quickly get from him or from his deputy [Hannart] a gracious and honorable decision, reply, and eventual repeal of the customs duty."[200] The only concrete action they could report, however, was the edict of September 15, 1523, staying the suits against the monopolists. This, plus the news that Simon Seitz had submitted at Valladolid a promonopoly memorial, which contradicted the urban front's petition of grievances, let the cat out of the bag and precipitated a series of bitter scenes, unparalleled in the history of the Urban Diet. As Hamann von Holzhausen reported to Frankfurt, the townsmen "re-

---

[197] *RTA, jR,* 4:263, 263 n. 1.
[198] Ibid., 263. See Anton Forner to Nördlingen, Nuremberg, Jan. 25, 1524, in ibid., 654, no. 178.
[199] *RTA, jR,* 4:263, no. 30.
[200] Hamann von Holzhausen to Frankfurt, Nuremberg, Jan. 28, 1524, in ibid., 654, no. 178.

gard this article on monopolies to be the main matter from which all the enmity of the princes and nobles against the cities has arisen," and hence they had worked hard "to abolish these same monopolies."[201] He added somewhat later that

the delegates of all free and Imperial cities . . . represented here at Nuremberg believe . . . that the great firms should be abolished; and that this should be done with the aid of the electors, princes, and other estates . . . But the Augsburgers said openly before everyone that, so far as monopolies are concerned, they and their government dissent and will not abide by our decision.[202]

How fervently the other urban governments, especially those of Nuremberg and Ulm, had hoped to appease the antiurban and anticommercial sentiments by feeding the great Augsburg firms to the princely and noble antimonopolists, appears from the heat of their politicians' attacks on Simon Seitz and the drafter of the embassy's instruction, Dr. Hans Rehlinger of Augsburg.[203] Bernhard Besserer, Ulm's political boss, led the assault.[204] His anger focused by the foreboding that the cities were about to pull ruin down upon themselves, Besserer lashed out at Rehlinger:

[First], Augsburg negotiated for herself on monopolies behind the backs of the other envoys. [Then], the memorial on monopolies was submitted without authorization to His Majesty, thereby violating the recesses and agreements made at Speyer and Esslingen [Urban Diets in 1523]. Thirdly, we city men have worked hard to suppress this thing called "monopoly," which is against the law and all equity – but this was not done. There is in truth little difference between what the other estates want and what we want. In the past the free cities have shown little regard for the common good. Indeed, if the thing is rightly looked at, we have done more against the common good than for it.[205]

Rehlinger struck back on January 28, denying that his masters had violated the agreements made last year and warning that if the Urban Diet now changed its mind, "he would on no account approve it."[206]

---

[201] Ibid., 655.
[202] Holzhausen to Frankfurt, Nuremberg, Feb. 12, 1524, in ibid., 673, no. 187.
[203] The evidence is reviewed by G. Schmidt, *Städtetag*, 431–2.
[204] On Besserer, see now Brecht, "Ulm," 98. His speech repeated his government's position in the instruction for the Urban Diet at Esslingen, June 18, 1525, in Klüpfel, *Urkunden*, 2:265.
[205] *RTA, jR*, 4:257, lines 10–24, from Hans Schultheiss's report to Memmingen.
[206] Ibid., 258.

"Besides," he sneered at the small-town men, "none of the envoys can say what a monopoly really is, but for that the merchants themselves must be asked." "Oh, no," replied Worms's envoy, "we know quite well what monopoly is – evil engrossing by certain parties in the great firms, to their profit alone and to the damage of many others." Hamann von Holzhausen chimed in that the Frankfurters, too, "knew what monopoly was." Rehlinger counterattacked Besserer's charge of partisanship with the remark that "he regards all of us as partisans, and he will never approve measures designed to aid the small merchants and to damage his own lords." As payment for his sneers, discussion of Rehlinger's compensation (he had drafted the embassy's instruction) was tabled, on a motion by the Ulmers and Esslingers.

The next day, Rehlinger was denied a further hearing, and the assembly deliberated passing an antimonopoly memorial to the Electors' House, clear evidence of their wish to shed all responsibility for protecting the monopolists.[207] When Rehlinger accused the authors of this proposal, the Nurembergers, of dishonesty, their chief, Christoph Kress, rose to the attack. Though descended from merchants, Kress was a well-educated and worldly warrior diplomat, an imposing, aristocratic figure among these small-town politicians and secretaries. He denounced Rehlinger and demanded passage of the antimonopoly memorial, and he was supported by Worms, Hagenau, "and other cities." On January 31, the Nuremberg memorial was read and approved, Augsburg dissenting, and, though Nuremberg later patched up the quarrel with Rehlinger's government, it never approved the payment for his service to the Spanish embassy.[208]

The bitter clash over monopolies troubled the cities' influence in the Diet, but so did their sparse attendance. Only a handful appeared for the Urban Diet in January; thirteen cities were still represented on March 27 and eleven on April 2; and only seven signed the Imperial Diet's recess.[209] The big cities were there, however, and theirs was the burden of securing the dividend from the investment represented by the Spanish embassy.

---

[207] Ibid., 259–61. On Kress, see Zophy, "Christoph Kress" and "Lazarus Spengler."
[208] Burgomaster and Senate of Nuremberg to Christoph Kress, April 22, 1524, in *RTA, jR*, 4:778–80, no. 264.
[209] Ibid., 232, 612–13, 746–7.

Turning Swiss

The third Imperial Diet of Nuremberg witnessed not the end of the beginning of a new relationship between free cities and Crown but the beginning of the end of their traditional partnership. Jean Hannart wrote to his master on March 13 from Nuremberg that, despite Charles's gracious treatment of the embassy at Valladolid, the urban envoys "have been most difficult about consenting to support the Governing Council and the other matters that were dealt with."[210] The decision to reform the Governing Council and remove it to Esslingen,[211] though it may have disappointed the Council's most committed foes among the urban politicians, does not explain why Hannart found them sulky and un-cooperative. Nor does the monopoly question, which the Diet agreed to place in the emperor's hands.[212] No, the real reason is revealed in a remark by Hannart to Charles just after the passage quoted above. "The city of Augsburg," he wrote, "has nonetheless shown itself most willing in these matters, except for the Luther affair, on which all the cities agree and with which all are tainted."[213] The "Luther affair" had, in-deed, finally emerged to trouble Imperial politics, and the urban governments were mostly willy-nilly engaged in the fate of what Cardinal Matthäus Lang of Salzburg called "the Lutheran sect."[214] The chief reason, therefore, why the achievements of the Spanish embassy bore no fruit is to be sought in the advance of the Reformation in the free cities of the South.

---

[210] Jean Hannart to Charles V, Nuremberg, March 13, 1524, in Lanz, *Korrespondenz*, 1:98–113, no. 52, here at 105. Hannart repeated his opinion in an instruction for Michel Gilles to Charles V, Nuremberg, April 26, 1524, in ibid., 128, no. 55. See Baumgarten, *Geschichte*, 2:330–1; Richter, *Reichstag zu Nürnberg 1524*, 42–4.

[211] Jean Hannart to Charles V, Nurembrg, March 13, 1524, in Lanz, *Korrespondenz*, 1:111–12. See the recess in *RTA, jR*, 4: no. 149, para. 1–3; and Mogge, "Studien," 87.

[212] *RTA, jR*, 4: nos. 110–11, 115, 117–19, 144, 149; Blaich, *Reichsmonopolgesetzgebung*, 12–13; Mogge, "Studien," 99–100.

[213] Lanz, *Korrespondenz*, 1:128, no. 55.

[214] Förstemann, *Neues Urkundenbuch*, 184, no. 64.

5

∽∽

The Reformation of the Common Man, 1521–1524

In 1871, the founding year of the Prussian-German empire that arose on the ruins of the Holy Roman Empire, a Bavarian jurist described the free cities' liberating role in the German Reformation: "The Reformation was not simply prepared in the cities, there it was also first put into practice. There, where civil freedom was greatest, in the free cities, came the earliest reforms. Then, from the cities the spirit of the Reformation and the Reformation itself spread out in ever widening circles."[1] A century of research has placed beyond doubt the cities' role as the nurseries of the Reformation movement, where the Evangelical cause was transformed from a provincial issue into a mighty German movement. After it came the "Princes' Reformation," which gave German Protestantism its historic shape,[2] but which also drew institutions, personnel, values, and symbols from the "urban Reformation."[3]

When Charles V set a new, hard policy on the religious question in

---

[1] Quoted by Rublack, "Forschungsbericht," 10 n. 7, who notes that Maurer wrote one hundred years before A. G. Dickens's celebrated comment that "the German Reformation was an urban event." Dickens, *German Nation*, 182. The massive literature on the urban Reformation is surveyed by Rublack, "Forschungsbericht"; G. Müller, *Reformation und Stadt*; and Greyerz, "Stadt und Reformation" (my thanks to Kaspar von Greyerz for letting me read it in typescript). For a briefer overview, see Brady, "Social History," 167–72.
[2] Dickens, *German Nation*, 221. Whereas Dickens laments the subsequent domination of the Lutheran princes, which he believes fostered "legalism rather than...religious and political liberty," Oberman contends that, despite "the acute disadvantages" of the princes' reform, intellectual freedom was better served by the Lutheran reformation than the urban one. *Werden und Wertung*, 346, 361–7 (English: *Masters*, 272, 284–8). Heinz Schilling's very important conclusions (*Konfessionskonflikt*, 387–91) to some degree parallel Oberman's, though he makes far less of theology. All three scholars agree on the role of the cities as the nurseries of German Protestantism.
[3] See Press, "Stadt und territoriale Konfessionsbildung," 251–96; Schilling, *Konfessionskonflikt*, 168–76.

1524, he put tremendous pressure on the urban governments, within whose communes Luther's followers were stirring vigorous social movements: groups of committed persons united in collective actions with a common consciousness, who wanted or attempted rapid and immediate changes to the existing religious order, sometimes through noninstitutional means.[4] Calling themselves "Evangelical," they wanted to free Christianity from centuries of "human additions" to the Bible. By 1524, the size and militancy of such movements made it impossible for their governments, whatever the oligarchs' personal views, to enforce strictly the Imperial ban on Luther's works and ideas.[5]

In this massive and unprecedented intervention, the Common Man made history. Already by 1524, before the great insurrection on the land was fairly underway, popular action had inspired or frightened urban governments into defying the emperor and the law, thereby damaging severely and irreparably the old partnership between Crown and cities. By the deep winter of 1524–5, when the valleys and uplands of the South seethed with incipient revolution, the latest form of the Habsburg system's urban wing, the urban front, was already a wreck.

The Common Man in the urban reformation

> Das evangeli frone
> auss gotts gnad fürher bracht
> Martinus Luther schone,
> das vor lang was veracht,
> mit füssen was vertreten
> und lag ganz in dem staub;
> das hat er sauber gjeten,
> wie wol in nit hat beten
> der romanisten raub.[6]

---

[4] See Moeller, *Reichsstadt*, 19–34 (English: *Imperial Cities*, 54–69); Dickens, *German Nation*, 102–34; Scribner, "Social Movement," 54, 77–8, on whose definition I depend here. On the movement's phases, see Blickle, "Social Protest," 5–7.
[5] Wohlfeil, "Wormser Reichstag," 148–51.
[6] "It has come from God's own grace that the wondrous Martin Luther has restored the Gospels' splendor; for long years it was despised, trod under the feet of men, and left lying in the dust. He did this with great skill, despite the strong objections of the robbing Roman horde." Liliencron, *Volkslieder*, 3:510, no. 393, stanza 3.

When the Edict of Worms was issued on May 8, 1521, the southern urban governments hardly rushed to publish it locally, nor did they hurry to censor the printers.[7] The tide of books, pamphlets, and broadsides quickly became a flood, as printers, illustrators, and authors rushed to promote Luther as a holy man and his cause as a holy cause, drawing upon symbols and language that were "deeply embedded in the culture and belief of those brought up in the old faith."[8] The cities, centers of all communication – oral, visual, and written, learned and lay – became the breeding ground for a mighty movement, though for a few years "the Luther affair" seemed to disappear from the stage of Imperial politics.[9] The rulers of the towns, however, knew quite well what was going on within their walls, and it troubled them.

From the very beginning, the Evangelical movement had to be a matter for public attention, because "the concern for the sustaining of the civic commonweal gave even the forms of piety a public relevance, which from the first necessarily made the issues of the veneration of saints and of images especially pressing."[10] One may go further and say that clerical involvement also made the movements public, for clergy were public persons, and the movement began as an attack of one group of clergy on another. The Evangelical leaders were well-educated clergymen from urban backgrounds, sons of patricians, merchants, and artisans.[11] They gained hearings largely because they offered answers to long-posed questions, and they sowed seed on long-prepared soil. Even where such answers and such seed were not, from the preachers' perspective, central to their gospel, they hoped that by addressing such questions – usury, tithes, clerical immunities, clerical indiscipline – they would win a hearing for pure doctrine. Luther showed the way by trying to touch every sensitive nerve of his day, at the price of sowing unclarity about his message, though not about his person. Some of his partisans came to see the world through his central message; others did not. But in these

---

[7] Brecht, "Wormser Edikt," 476.

[8] Scribner, *Simple Folk*, 245. For very different approaches to printing and the Reformation, see Moeller, "Stadt und Buch," 25–39 (and Scribner's critical "How Many Could Read?"); Chrisman, *Lay Culture*, chap. 7. The current state of research on pamphlets is accessible in Köhler, *Flugschriften*.

[9] Noted by Brecht, "Wormser Edikt," 479.

[10] Oberman, *Werden und Wertung*, 238 (English: *Masters*, 188).

[11] Scribner, "Practice and Principle," 99–106.

years their cause was a common one.[12] The urban preachers sensed this and tried skillfully to adapt Luther's message to the hegemonic corporate-communal values of their fellow citizens.[13] The building of followings, however, no matter how militant, was but the first step in a process that had to end with the support and protection, willing or grudging, of the urban oligarchies, who alone could shield the movement from its enemies.

The Evangelical preachers' freedom to act grew out of the pre-Reformation clergy's freedom from reform, which had flowed from the many checks on a bishop's power to discipline his clergy.[14] This clerical freedom, rooted in the pre-Reformation deadlock over control of the Church, often threatened good order and civic peace, a fact many oligarchs, engaged or not, Lutheran or Catholic, recognized. At Strasbourg, for example, Augustin Drenss (d. 1552), a big man in the Gardeners' guild, complained that the wooing of his sister by the young preacher Caspar Hedio (1494–1552) was merely one more case of a lustful priest violating the sanctity of an upright Christian home. It mattered little to Drenss that Hedio called himself an "Evangelical."[15] At Nuremberg, Christoph Kress, a Lutheran, complained that "nothing bothers me more than to see the escaped monks and priests running about. If I had my way, they could go to the Devil."[16] And at Augsburg, Ulrich Arzt, a Catholic, wrote amid the upheaval of 1525 that "we townsmen are to blame, and I fear it will bring down the honorable cities. Had we got rid of these preachers and allowed their own superiors to punish them, as is just, these things would now be settled and overcome."[17]

If such opinions were common among the oligarchs, one may fairly ask, how did the Evangelical movement ever succeed in the cities? The

---

[12] Oberman believes that, at this point in the history of the movement, Luther was more significant as symbol than as teacher. Oberman, "Gospel of Social Unrest," 43. I agree.

[13] This conclusion of Moeller, *Reichsstadt*, esp. 34–55 (English: *Imperial Cities*, 69–90), has been heartily seconded by Schilling, *Konfessionskonflikt*, 45, 142–3. Both Moeller ("Stadt und Buch," 38–9) and Schilling (*Konfessionskonflikt*, 376 n. 17a) have criticized my view of the sacral commune as both a leading idea, in the Marxian sense, and a shared value, which at times could be defended by the commons against their rulers, as happened at Strasbourg in 1548 (Brady, *Ruling Class*, chap. 8) and Lemgo in 1609 (Schilling, *Konfessionskonflikt*, 241–71).

[14] This is superbly documented by Rapp, *Réformes*.

[15] Brady, *Ruling Class*, 231–2, 307 (May 1524).

[16] Kress to Gerwig Blarer, Nuremberg, Nov. 7, 1523, in Blarer, *Briefe und Akten*, 1:26, no. 44, lines 21–4.

[17] Vogt, "Correspondenz, I," 367, no. 123.

social character of the urban Reformation has, indeed, long been a hotly debated subject. According to a thesis formulated for northern Germany and subsequently extended to the southern cities, "The Reformation was never the work of a town council," and there was "a general antipathy to the Reformation especially among the patricians."[18] That is much too categorical, for the early Reformation movement

embraced various forces and interests. They included oligarchs and humanists, artisans and journeymen, clergymen and artists, peasants and plebians, who differed from one another in their views on both the theoretical and practical aspects of the Reformation, and who reacted differently to different situations.[19]

These groups briefly saw in the Evangelical movement a common vehicle for liberation from an oppression that they, for the moment, sensed to be a common one, though later the movement began to break into different, sometimes opposed, streams. At the beginning, however, from all classes were recruited "Evangelicals," that is, men and women who believed that, for the sake either of individual salvation or the integrity of Christian life in this world, or both, the rightly understood Bible required the abolition of certain religious traditions and the curbing of ecclesiastical power.

Townsmen of good family had, to be sure, special reasons for opposing such a movement, ranging from career advantages in the old Church to familial attachments to religious orders to native oligarchical conservatism.[20] Wealthy and politically powerful men nonetheless emerged as early patrons of and participants in the Evangelical movement, before it moved from the monasteries and private homes to the pulpits, shops, guildhalls, and taverns. In a few southern cities, true, such as Rottweil and Schwäbisch Gmünd, ruling patricians closed ranks against the Evangelicals, especially when they also took up the cause of political reform.[21] In most other cities, however, the upper classes did little to defend Catholicism in an organized way after about 1526.

There was much in the reformers' messages to attract the urban oligarchs. The pure gospel "could be understood by burghers and peas-

---

[18] Lau, "Der Bauernkrieg," 119; Moeller, *Reichsstadt*, 25, 27 (English: *Imperial Cities*, 60–1, 63).
[19] Vogler, *Nürnberg*, 323.
[20] See Brady, *Ruling Class*, 215–30; Christensen, *Art*, 71–2.
[21] Brecht, "Rottweil"; Naujoks, *Obrigkeitsgedanke*, 60–4, 96–102.

ants as the common good translated into theological terms,"[22] which justified liberating the urban churches from external authority and bringing whole sectors of clerical activity under welcome governmental control: poor relief, schools, marriage law, clerical citizenship and guild membership, parish organization, and the administration of parish and monastic properties. Through cooperation with the popular movements and the preachers, the town councils expanded and intensified their sovereignty over churches and citizens, and this domestication of urban religion converted the ecclesiastical order from a disruptive into an integrative element in civic life.[23]

As it moved out into the churches, shops, and taverns, however, the movement developed clearly dangerous forms of action, such as iconoclastic riots, and it pressed the governments to clearly illegal measures, such as the dissolution of religious houses. The preachers had a nose for exploiting existing grievances, such as demands for greater political participation, and the urban commons gradually became the motor of the movement, as large numbers – we need not assume undocumented majorities – of ordinary folk supported through their guilds the program of religious change.[24] Where the guilds embraced very large shares of the adult-male population – about thirty-five hundred at Strasbourg, a city of some twenty thousand, and almost twenty-three hundred in slightly smaller Ulm[25] – the governments had to deal with the movements through negotiation rather than coercion. The movements had nonetheless to be mastered in the name of the historic civic norms of peace, justice, and unity.

The true danger from the Evangelical movement for the oligarchies lay in the fact that, even where the clergy could be controlled, the principle of biblicism stayed to haunt the governments. The identification of the Bible, understood as the *lex Christi*, with the common good admitted of different interpretations, according to whether the Bible was used to legitimize or to criticize existing social structures and practices. Just this ambiguity turned Christoph Fürer (1481–1537) of Nuremberg against the Evangelicals, who "are making the common people so godless

---

[22] Blickle, *Reformation im Reich*, 131.
[23] Scribner, "Sozialkontrolle"; Wettges, *Reformation*, 66–8.
[24] Wettges, *Reformation*, 117. For the example of Basel, see Füglister, *Handwerksregiment*.
[25] Rott, "Artisanat," 158; Nebinger, "Abstimmungslisten," 26.

that they will lack all good discipline and human morals."[26] The realism of his fear is suggested by the remarks of Ott, an Augsburg ropemaker, who was overheard in 1524 to damn the "dishonorable priests and the rich..., who pile up goods and money and keep the truth from us." "We have always been Evangelicals," Ott blurted out, "and we still are today. But, truly, we have been fed many lies. If we truly followed the gospel, we would all have to be like brothers."[27] Why should the Bible slice through the lordship of bishop and priest but stop at that of artisan master, landlord, and town councillor? Should Christians not also treat their fellow citizens as "brothers" in Ott's sense? Had the movement for "godly law," "Christian commonweal," and fraternal cooperation won out, revolution would have come to the village, the town hall, the guildhall, and the shop. Whether one calls this program "the gospel of social unrest" or "biblicism vs. feudalism,"[28] it could be tolerated by no one who believed that peace, justice, and unity could be established and preserved only from above.

The common challenge the Evangelical movement posed to the urban governments is symbolized by the common measure they first used to gain control of it, the preaching edicts of 1523 and 1524. These laws commanded the clergy to preach "nothing but the gospel" and leave off "all provocative and insulting comments, including everything which tends to rouse the Common Man to anger or confusion or to a rebellion against his rulers, lay or ecclesiastical..."[29] Between January 29, 1523, and April 5, 1524, such laws were issued at Zurich, Worms, Basel, Bern, Mulhouse, Augsburg, Strasbourg, Constance, Frankfurt am Main, and Sankt Gallen.[30] Their family resemblance derived both from consultation and from a common descent from the Imperial Diet's decree of February 9, 1523, by which preachers were to be ordered "to shun everything that might stir up the Common Man against the rulers or

[26] Quoted by Reicke, *Geschichte*, 839.
[27] StA Augsburg, Urgichten 1524, Produkt 3, at Sept. 27, 1524 (my thanks to Hans-Christoph Rublack for this text).
[28] The first phrase is Oberman's, the second Blickle's.
[29] Moeller, "L'édit strasbourgeois," 58. On the origin of the crucial phrase, see Augustijn, " 'Allein das heilig Evangelium,' " 150–65.
[30] Moeller, "L'édit strasbourgeois," 51–61; Vögeli, *Schriften*, 1:154–5; Rublack, *Einführung*, 244 n. 21; H. Lutz, *Peutinger*, 227; Jahns, *Frankfurt*, 35; Oberman, *Werden und Wertung, 250–1 (English: Masters*, 196–7).

confuse the ordinary Christian; but they should preach and teach only the holy gospel as interpreted by the writings that the holy Christian Church has approved and accepted."[31] Such laws were proof not of an official partisanship for Evangelical religion but of the urban governments' determination to bring the internal divisions under control through the exercise of their *jus pacificandi*.[32]

This cause, bringing the Evangelical movement under control, became the duty of every oligarch pledged to preserve peace, justice, and unity, though growing dispute about God's honor and the common good made the duty's discharge ever more difficult. Gradually, however, the town councils went beyond the biblicist minimum of the preaching edicts and began to claim divine authority for their actions. Memmingen's council wrote in 1527, for example, that "because we wish to defend God's honor, and because we have received our authority from God Himself, we are inclined and determined to issue a law forbidding concubinage and prostitution to all our citizens, both clerical and lay."[33] Specific changes ought to be seen less as inevitable products of individual politicians' conversions[34] than as actions of urban governments, which, pushed from below by their commons and harangued by the preachers, came to see that the new gospel offered welcome solutions to nagging old problems. The revolutionary events of 1524 and 1525, as Christoph Kress once admitted, pushed the governments farther than they had ever intended to go.[35] Few urban politicians dreamed, however, that with the preaching edicts they had embarked on a course that would make them arbiters of Christian doctrine and sole enforcers of Christian morals, a role for which little in their traditions, education, or experience had prepared them.[36]

Urban oligarchies and Reformation movement, 1524

Nun wirt das bletlein umbgekart
und fürgewänt ain ander art.

---

[31] *RTA, jR*, 3:747–8, no. 117. The Governing Council's enforcing edict of March 6, 1523, is in ibid., 447–52, no. 84.
[32] Oberman, *Werden und Wertung*, 241–50; the following quote is at 249 (English: *Masters*, 196).
[33] Burgomaster and Senate of Memmingen to Ambrosius Blarer, Nov. 27, 1527, in Schiess, *Briefwechsel*, 1:143, and also in Dobel, *Memmingen*, 2:50–1.
[34] Brecht, "Politik."
[35] Leonhard von Eck to Duke William of Bavaria, Feb. 27, 1525, in Vogt, *Die bayrische Politik*, 399.
[36] See Brady, *Ruling Class*, 192–3; Broadhead, "Politics and Expediency," 55–70.

The Reformation of the Common Man

Ich main si all, die sölicher gestalt
erheben sich gaistlicher gwalt
in reichtumb, bracht und übermüt,
zern von des armen schwaiss und blüt,
den si mit unrecht oft und vil
thün zwingen zü irem bübanspil
zü geben alls was er vermag.

. . . .

Wo man vom evangeli sagt,
So hat man in gar bald verjagt.[37]

By the early months of 1524, the fabric of established authority in many a free city was creaking under the strain of maintaining law and order. Though some have written of a "victory" or "breakthrough" of the Reformation in 1524, the movement's destructive or purgative phase culminated only with the abolition of the central act of Catholic worship, the Mass, which happened at Zurich in 1527, at Memmingen, Strasbourg, and Basel in 1529, at Ulm in 1531, and at Augsburg, Ravensburg, and Biberach an der Riss never.[38] During the first months of 1524, by contrast, the movement was in most southern cities just exhibiting its muscle in public for the first time.

Rarely did solid oligarchic opposition keep the Evangelicals from sweeping rapidly to victory, though at a few places – Regensburg was one – the government did indeed plod after the popular movement.[39] In most of the larger cities, however, rich and powerful individuals and families lent protection and aid to the Evangelical movement from the first. Nowhere was this aid more decisive than at Nuremberg, where,

---

[37] "Now the page is turning to show another side. I mean to show up them all, who make themselves priests, who live in wealth, luxury, and arrogance and feed on the poor man's sweat and blood. They do so much harm themselves and force others as well to give them all they have.... Wherever the Gospel has its say, they've been driven all away. Liliencron, *Volkslieder*, 3:366, no. 352, lines 25–33, 43–44.

[38] On the victory thesis, which I discussed in *Ruling Class*, 204–5, much new light is shed by Rublack, *Nördlingen*, especially 263; and Abray, *Laity's Reformation*, who shows that none of the fundamental issues was settled at Strasbourg during the 1520s and 1530s. See Oberman, *Werden und Wertung*, 348 (English: *Masters*, 273), on the Reformation's geographical limitations and "loss of substance," comments he repeats in "Stadtreformation," 88. Bolder is Ozment, *Age of Reform*, 437–8, though his gloomy conclusion rests on theological rather than historical criteria.

[39] Wettges, *Reformation*, 53.

even before a truly Lutheran presence emerged, the cream of local society had gathered around Johann von Staupitz (d. 1524), the reform-minded General Vicar of the Augustinians. Anton Tucher was there, and Hieronymus Ebner, along with Caspar Nützel, Hieronymus Holzschuher, Endres and Martin Tucher, and Sigmund and Christoph Fürer, representatives of a "typical South German Christian humanism, shaped by Erasmian biblicism, which is repeatedly and justifiably regarded as an important point of contact for the Reformation in the cities."[40] The senate of Nuremberg, though it did temporize, also called the first Lutheran preachers to the city in 1522 and protected them from the bishop of Bamberg. By early 1523, Hans von der Planitz was reporting to Elector Frederick that a serious official move against the preachers would provoke an insurrection; soon Nuremberg was gaining a reputation for heresy.[41] The presence of the Governing Council and the High Court,[42] plus the staging of three Imperial Diets at Nuremberg between 1522 and 1524, may well have heightened the senate's caution, and the growth of radical stirrings in the countryside, where many Nuremberg patricians had substantial seigneurial holdings, prompted careful reflection about following words with deeds.[43] The government therefore both protected Lutheran preachers against the bishop and Catholic ceremonies against the Evangelicals, though there can be no doubt about the deep penetration of Evangelical ideas into the best homes. Many of the officeholders, for example, who marched in procession on Corpus Christi and Saint Sebald's Day, 1524 – the last ever held at Nuremberg in this era – probably did so from respect for tradition

[40] Seebass, "Reformation in Nürnberg," 254. This account is based on ibid., 252–69 (English: "Reformation in Nürnberg," 17–40); idem, "Stadt und Kirche in Nürnberg," 66–86; Vogler, *Nürnberg*, 33–134; Strauss, *Nuremberg*, 154–74; and Wettges, *Reformation*, 23–7, 33–8, 62–5, 97–102. Engelhardt, *Reformation in Nürnberg*, is useful for details but narrowly confessional in perspective.
[41] Planitz is cited by H. von Schubert, *Lazarus Spengler*, 379–83. See Vogler, *Nürnberg*, especially 95–118. On Nuremberg's reputation, see Abbot Georg Truchsess of Wernitz-Anhausen to Gerwig Blarer, Jan. 9, 1524, in Blarer, *Briefe und Akten*, 1:28, no. 45; Strauss, *Nuremberg*, 174.
[42] The attitude of the Governing Council toward the Evangelical movement is not clear. See Engelhardt, *Reformation*, 1:129; H. von Schubert, *Lazarus Spengler*, chap. 8; Richter, *Reichstag zu Nürnberg 1524*, 12. Archduke Ferdinand wrote to Charles V, Innsbruck, May 12, 1523, about "aulcuns, et en especial de cellui qu'est au lieu du duc de Saxe, nommé Plains [Planitz], lequel avec plusjeurs ses adherans sans aucune craincte de dieu ne vergoigne du monde s'emploient tres detestablement..." W. Bauer and Lacroix, *Korrespondenz*, 1:59, no. 36, para. 10.
[43] Vogler, *Nürnberg*, 27–8, 83–134.

rather than conviction.[44] The senate also tolerated as its public spokesman the notoriously Lutheran city secretary, Lazarus Spengler (1479–1534), whose efforts Luther compared with the labors of the prophets of old.[45] The situation at Nuremberg during the Imperial Diet of 1524 thus suggests that the transitional phase of discussion and tolerance of parties would come to an end, once Nuremberg escaped the limelight of Imperial government.

Events at Augsburg ran a similar course at a slower pace.[46] Some very big men early joined the typically clerical circles of initial Evangelicals, including three of the four burgomasters – Georg Vetter (d. 1536), Ulrich Rehlinger (d. 1547), and Hieronymus Imhof (1468–1539) – plus such other leading politicians as Conrad Herwart, Lucas Welser, and the younger Martin Weiss. Against them stood an "old guard" headed by the fierce Ulrich Arzt, and between the parties Conrad Peutinger pursued his "middle way," tending and mending Augsburg's lines to the Imperial court.[47] A report of 1522, that half the Augsburgers supported the Evangelicals, surely exaggerated; but two years later Clemens Sender, a Benedictine chronicler, noted that "in the year of Our Lord 1524 Lutheranism grew very rapidly at Augsburg, and heresy got the upper hand."[48] This was close enough to the truth that the papal legate, Cardinal Lorenzo Campeggio (1474–1539), was advised in March 1524 that he should enter Augsburg at noontime, when the craftsmen were indoors eating lunch.[49] Despite the growing number of Evangelicals in the government, however, the intense external pressures on Augsburg – from the Habsburg courts, the Bavarian dukes, and the bishop of Augsburg – made its magistrates more cautious and reluctant to act than their Nuremberg counterparts. This inertia was to lead to the movement's getting out of hand during 1524.

---

[44] Soden, *Beiträge*, 159–60.
[45] *WA TR*, no. 5426. H. von Schubert's unfinished biography is by no means superseded by Grimm, *Lazarus Spengler*, but Bernd Hamm's forthcoming work will put the subject on a new basis.
[46] To the fundamental work by F. Roth, *Reformationsgeschichte*, should be added Broadhead, "Internal Politics" (of which there is a useful extract in his "Popular Pressure"), and Wettges, *Reformation*, 27–31, 38–49, 102–7.
[47] F. Roth, *Reformationsgeschichte*, 1:53–73, 87–94, 136; H. Lutz, *Peutinger*, 222–8.
[48] Sender, "Chronik," 154.
[49] Rem, "Cronica newer geschichte," 144, translating "handwercksvolck" as "craftsmen" rather than "laborers" (as Broadhead, "Popular Pressure," 80).

Turning Swiss

Outside the Confederacy, no other large city of South Germany moved so swiftly to accommodate the Evangelicals as Strasbourg did.[50] By the end of 1523, the movement had gained powerful patrons and adherents, such as the Ammeisters Claus Kniebis (1479–1552), Martin Herlin (d. 1547), and Daniel Mieg (c. 1484–1541), the future Ammeister Mathis Pfarrer (1489–1568) – who was also Sebastian Brant's son-in-law – the rich merchant Conrad Joham (d. 1551), and Egenolf Röder von Diersburg (1475–1550), a prominent nobleman with important connections in Middle Baden.[51] Hot words over religion flew in the senate chamber during 1523, and the memorial Mass for Ammeister Heinrich Ingold just before Christmas was the last such Mass ever sung in Strasbourg's cathedral.[52] When the new senators took office in January 1524, the Evangelicals – militants and moderates together – held a majority, and on January 25 they liquidated the clergy's ancient immunity and began to attack the monasteries. There were nonetheless very cautious men among the oligarchs, such as Jacob Sturm, whose judgment on the religious parties was that "both sides are Christians, may God have mercy!"[53] External pressures and influences were much weaker here than at Augsburg or Ulm. The one Imperial councillor in the government, for example, was Friedrich Prechter (d. 1528), the Fugger agent in Alsace, but he played a very minor role in public affairs.[54] All in all, Strasbourg appeared in early 1524 to be the major free city sailing most nearly in Zurich's wake.

Though somewhat smaller in size, Ulm resembled Strasbourg in social structure and politics.[55] Religious change came slowly to this capital of the Swabian League, though the Evangelicals did win over prominent laymen, among them Bernhard Besserer, who was as conservative and cautious as Strasbourg's Sturm. During 1523, the government's attitude began to soften, and by December it was reported that the new religion "has so rooted and grown in the people, that even with force it would be very hard to put down."[56] Ulm had no outstanding clerical figure to

---

[50] This is based on Chrisman, *Strasbourg*; Lienhard, "La Réforme à Strasbourg, I–II."
[51] Brady, *Ruling Class*, 209–10.
[52] Ibid., 205, 229.
[53] Brady, " 'Sind also zu beiden theilen Christen,' " 76.
[54] F.-J. Fuchs, "Les foires et le rayonnement économique," 307–13; Feyler, *Beziehungen*, 178.
[55] On Ulm, see Geiger, *Reichsstadt Ulm*; Naujoks, *Obrigkeitsgedanke*; Brecht, "Ulm"; Walther, "Bernhard Besserer."
[56] Quoted by Naujoks, *Obrigkeitsgedanke*, 53.

162

lead popular pressure against the government, which moved no faster than events forced it to do.

The story of a fifth large city, Frankfurt am Main, contrasts neatly with that of Strasbourg.[57] The patricians, who had surrendered only one-third (versus Strasbourg's two-thirds) of the offices to the guilds, still dominated the town's economy through the chartered fairs, which drew merchants from far and wide. The three collegial churches also enjoyed Imperial protection. The archbishop of Mainz maintained a much greater authority at Frankfurt than did the bishops – Bamberg, Augsburg, Strasbourg, and Constance – whose jurisdictions covered Nuremberg, Augsburg, Strasbourg, and Ulm. The external pressures on Frankfurt's government were thus relatively strong. Lutheran ideas first spread here, as elsewhere, among humanist clergymen, and the movement was greatly aided by the patronage of two leading patrician politicians, Philipp Fürstenberger (1479–1540) and Hamann von Holzhausen (1467–1536). Later than in other cities, the movement spilled out of patrician homes and monasteries into the churches and shops, but by early 1524 it had mounted little or no direct action.

This survey of five larger towns may be supplemented by views of three middling ones, Constance, Esslingen, and Nördlingen. Constance, squeezed between bishop and Austria, had lost the rich Thurgau in 1499 and its chance to turn Swiss in 1510, and, having no stable past to which to cling, proved very open to change.[58] One sign of this openness was the early and strong movement of leading patricians into the Evangelical party, such as Burgomaster Bartholomäus Blarer (d. 1524) and Hans Schulthaiss (d. 1538), the richest man in Constance.[59] The special intimacy, indeed, that developed here between preachers and politicians rested on the fact that the two leading preachers, Ambrosius Blarer (d. 1564) and Johann Zwick (d. 1542), were natives who had brothers in the government. Very early, these circles split from the Erasmians at the episcopal court and provoked some of the earliest episcopal countermeasures in all of South Germany. When Archduke Ferdinand demanded action against Lutheran literature in early 1524, the council

---

[57] This is based on Jahns, *Frankfurt*, 16–36.
[58] This is based on Rublack, *Einführung*, 20–6, 34–7; idem, "Aussenpolitik"; idem, "Politische Situation"; Moeller, *Johannes Zwick*; Bender, *Reformationsbündnisse*, chap. 2.
[59] Rublack, *Einführung*, 16–17, 62–6; Buck, *Anfänge*, 60–9, 519–22.

expelled his local agent, whom the Evangelicals regarded as "an enemy of human salvation."[60] Constance's situation meant that every Evangelical action drew strength from the nearness of Zurich, whereas every counteraction must be tarred with episcopal or Austrian brushes, so that by early 1524 Constance had become, after Strasbourg, the most nearly Evangelical urban government.

The movement came to Esslingen later than to Constance, though its leading politicians, Hans Holdermann, wondered already at Worms, "as to what will become of the monk's affair, I believe that no one really knows, for I think that it contains a wholly new understanding of things, which not everyone can yet see."[61] The movement developed slowly at Esslingen, though the government kept a careful watch on its growth in other towns. The town council protected Catholic clergy and services without suppressing the Evangelicals, and, with one eye on the Habsburg regime at Stuttgart and the other on the Swabian League, remained master in its own house all through the 1520s. The transfer of the Governing Council and High Court, which freed the movement from some constraints in Nuremberg, retarded its growth in Esslingen and allowed the council to pursue a temporizing policy "more for the security of public order and civic unity than for loyalty to the Church."[62] Pressure from below nonetheless emerged in mid-January 1524, when some citizens asked for Michael Stifel's restoration to his pulpit and for regular Sunday preaching in the convents. As late as the end of April 1524, Esslingen's government boasted that the town had no "Lutheran disturbance," though a few days later began the first expulsions for anticlerical agitation.[63]

Nördlingen, a final example, was a Franconian cloth town of middling size (about seven thousand).[64] The Evangelical movement surfaced here in 1522 with anticlerical agitation, tithe resistance, and breaches of the fast. Although the government expelled a local Carmelite, Kaspar Kantz, when he married a butcher's daughter in 1523, it took no other action

---

[60] Rublack, *Einführung*, 36–7.
[61] This is based on Naujoks, *Obrigkeitsgedanke;* Borst, *Geschichte*, 218–19, 224–6; Rublack, "Reformatorische Bewegung," from which the quote is taken, p. 196.
[62] Rublack, "Reformatorische Bewegung," 203.
[63] Krabbe and Rublack, *Akten*, 18–20, nos. 2–4.
[64] This is based on Rublack, *Nördlingen*, 94–100.

until the anticlerical demonstrations of 1524. As in Esslingen, in Nördlingen the presence of Evangelical sympathizers in the town council did not lead to official action, beyond bare toleration, until after the first popular demonstrations.

This survey of eight cities to early 1524 confirms a recent judgment that the situation from 1521 to the end of 1523 "has the marks of a transition or advent," which was characterized by "the expectation, that something must and would change," though nothing was yet decided.[65] The Evangelical movement had developed out of its original milieu, monasteries, patrician parlors, and printshops, into public places; it had taken shape under clerical leadership and petitioned for protection of Evangelical clergymen, but it had not yet moved to disturbances of the civic peace. The degree of official cooperation with popular demands for change seems to have related directly to the strength and intensities of external pressures on the oligarchies: from the bishops and neighboring princes; from the two Habsburg courts; from the privileged status of vital economic operations, such as trading firms and fairs; and from the presence of organs of Imperial government – the Diet, the Governing Council, and the High Court. Such forces kept the oligarchies from acting, no matter how deeply the new ideas penetrated powerful families, until in 1524 there arose a kind of political scissors, of which one blade was the urban commons' direct pressure for religious change, and the other was Charles V's new determination to scotch the Lutheran heresy. The convergence of these two blades made it impossible for most urban governments to continue the policy of benign inaction. The pressure from the commons developed more or less dangerously, depending on whether the social distance between oligarchy and commons was relatively great (Nuremberg, Augsburg, and Frankfurt) or small (Strasbourg, Ulm, and Constance), and on whether there were politically significant guilds (Strasbourg, Ulm, Constance, and Esslingen), relatively weak ones (Augsburg, Frankfurt), or none at all (Nuremberg). In the absence of guilds, even in the presence of great social differences, the craftsmen and tradesmen had no established institutions through which to press their grievances and demands on their governments. Where the social gap was wide and the guilds prominent, as at Augsburg, the oligarchy

---

[65] H. Schmidt, "Reichsstädte," 290; and see his excellent summary on 123–61.

was the least mobile and the Evangelicals most likely to take their message into socially sensitive areas. Each of these factors – external forces, social structure, and constitution – contributed to the urban governments' variegatedly common situation.

Though some of the town council's early acts on religion could be justified by its mandate to keep the peace and interpreted as well within the local traditions of church–state relations, by the early weeks of 1524, when the Third Imperial Diet of Nuremberg convened, the limits of tradition were being overstepped, or soon would be, at Strasbourg, Constance, and perhaps Nuremberg. Each new challenge by or to episcopal authority brought closer the day when the Edict of Worms would be enforced. The edict was no dead letter. The Governing Council's supplementary enforcing edict of February 20, 1522, [66] had been published by Duke George the Bearded in his parts of Saxony and by the bishop of Freising, and Stuttgart's own edict was to be followed by others in Western Austria. The Swabian League had nonetheless not yet been stirred to become the guardian of orthodoxy in South Germany, though it very soon would be,[67] and the free cities' governments felt as yet a palpable threat neither from above nor from below. This situation was about to change.

The "Luther affair" surfaces, Nuremberg, 1524

> In steten sind aufgstanden
> vil predicanten frum,
> hand dwarheit gnommen zhanden
> und forchten in nit drum,
> erboten zdisputieren
> menglichem in der welt;
> ob iemants könd probieren,
> dass sie das volk verfüren,
> solt helfen sie kein gelt.[68]

---

[66] *RTA, jR*, 3:21–4. See Brecht, "Wormser Edikt," 476, against Borth, *Luthersache*, 132, who calls it "mild." On its enforcement in South Germany, see Brecht, "Wormser Edikt," 477–8; Oberman, *Werden und Wertung*, 305–8 (English: *Masters*, 241–2) on "the onset of the Counter-Reformation."

[67] Rublack, *Nördlingen*, 139–45.

An odd calm about the Luther affair had prevailed in Imperial politics since the Diet of Worms in 1521. The Second Diet of Nuremberg in 1522–3 had reformulated the German powers' grievances against the papacy, bishops, and clergy and had listened to Pope Adrian's somber confession of the clergy's contribution to the current disorders and laxity.[69] Nor, to judge from the extant acts, did the religious question disturb the Urban Diet's deliberations during four sessions between July 1522 and the following June.[70] The subject did surface, however, at the Urban Diet of Speyer in November 1523, when the government of Wissembourg asked for advice about the excommunication of two of its clergymen by the bishop of Speyer. The cities decided not to aid Wissembourg, for the bishop's action was justified by the Governing Council's mandate of March 6, 1523, against divisive preaching, and an opinion to this effect was signed by envoys from Strasbourg, Frankfurt, Nuremberg, and Ulm in the name of all the free cities, who "still stood on the ground of the Church."[71] For the urban oligarchies, as for the German ruling classes as a whole, down to the end of 1523 the religious question had not disturbed the traditional patterns of politics.

When the Imperial Diet opened ceremoniously at Nuremberg on January 14, 1524, no sign showed that this calm would not prevail. The Diet's agenda, drafted for Archduke Ferdinand by the Governing Council, gave highest priority to the reorganization and financing of the Governing Council and High Court.[72] What no one at Nuremberg knew, and especially not Ferdinand, was that Jean Hannart had come from Spain with a secret instruction, which raised the Luther affair once more to prominence and demanded that the monk's doctrine "must be suppressed and not allowed to spread."[73] Apparently – the initiative is still unclear – Charles had decided to bring the religious question to a head

---

[68] "In the cities has arisen many a pious man to preach God's own true Gospel without the slightest fear. They've offered to debate it with anyone at all. If any can now prove that they lead the folk astray, they'll get nothing as their pay." Liliencron, *Volkslieder*, 3:510, no. 393, stanza 5.

[69] G. Müller, *Kurie*, 14; Oberman, *Werden und Wertung*, 305–6 (English: *Masters*, 241); H. Schmidt, "Reichsstädte," 191–230.

[70] H. Schmidt, "Reichsstädte," 182–3.

[71] Ibid., 231–40, with new documents; the quote is from 240.

[72] *RTA, jR*, 4:273, no. 32. See Rublack, *Nördlingen*, 133; and H. Schmidt, "Reichsstädte," 291–335, whose account is fullest and clearest.

[73] *RTA, jR*, 4:295, para. 3. Headley, *Emperor*, 129, sheds new light on Hannart's instruction.

and solve it through the Diet's reaffirmation of the Edict of Worms. Perhaps he was responding to the complaint, voiced by Pope Clement VII's German legate, Lorenzo Campeggio, that "the Edict of Worms is not obeyed by many lay and ecclesiastical princes. How that could happen in the Empire, he [Campeggio] doesn't understand."[74] Whatever the background, Charles's action was certainly spectacular, if not quite "revolutionary,"[75] for he demanded "that every ruler make sure that his subjects live according to His Majesty's edicts."[76] The Diet eventually declared itself willing to enforce the edict, but only to the extent that "the Common Man" was thereby given no cause for "rebellion, disobedience, murder, or slaughter"[77] – a qualification that effectively took back with one hand what it gave with the other – and asked for a "national" council of the Church in the Empire to meet at Speyer in September.[78] The Diet acted thus less out of sympathy for Luther than from instinctive resistance to the emperor when he operated, as Charles now did, hand in glove with the pope, and from a fine sense for the mounting unrest among their subjects.

The Cities' House displayed a remarkable solidarity in the discussions of the religious question, which began only after the arrival of Cardinal Campeggio in mid-March and continued until April 19.[79] Although they heartily approved the idea of a "national" council, the cities protested en bloc against the reinstatement of the Edict of Worms, and their representatives refused to sign the Diet's recess. In their memorial to the rest of the Diet, the cities raised above all the specter of revolt,

because now the Common Man everywhere thirsts after God's Word and the Gospel, which . . . have recently spread much more widely than before . . . If we accept, approve, or allow to be enforced even the slightest barrier to the Gospel's spread, the honorable free and Imperial cities . . . could not only not enforce

---

[74] *RTA, jR*, 4:487, no. 106. See Mogge, "Studien," 88–9. There are new perspectives on Charles's religious policy during the 1520s in Reinhard, "Vorstellungen," and Rabe, "Befunde," especially 101, who notes that the religious question did not play a large role in the emperor's correspondence.
[75] Borth, *Luthersache*, 147, based on *RTA, jR*, 4:500. See Brecht, "Politik," 189.
[76] *RTA, jR*, 4:295, no. 34. See H. Schmidt, "Reichsstädte," 292–3.
[77] *RTA, jR*, 4:507, no. 113. This echoed the urban governments' argument that they couldn't enforce the law for fear of the Common Man.
[78] Ibid., 301, no. 36. See Mogge, "Studien," 91; H. Schmidt, "Reichsstädte," 299–305.
[79] H. Schmidt, "Reichsstädte," 305–33; G. Schmidt, *Städtetag*, 479–83.

such a law, but they would doubtless provoke widespread disturbances, rebellion, murder, bloodshed, yes, total ruin and every sort of evil... The honorable free and Imperial cities, whom these developments would cause the greatest harm, damage, and ruin, must prevent them and protect themselves and their people from such injury and ruin.[80]

This document set the keynote for all subsequent efforts to keep the urban front together despite the division over religion: Without taking formal sides with either Evangelical religion or Catholicism, the cities stressed the futility of all outside attempts to suppress the former, in view of the Common Man's support for the Evangelical cause and his propensity for rebellion. The cities thus took de facto a pro-Evangelical position without taking sides on doctrinal grounds.[81] The policy was formulated by a committee with a pro-Evangelical majority from Nuremberg, Strasbourg, and Ulm, but it was weakened by removal of positively pro-Evangelical elements to accommodate Cologne and other Catholic governments.[82]

The actions of the Cities' House of the Diet at Nuremberg provide the first evidence that pro-Evangelical governments and politicians were beginning to set the tone in the urban front. Only nine cities took much active role in the deliberations, and Nuremberg and Strasbourg seem to have taken the leading parts. On the question of the council, the cities decided to follow Strasbourg's Hans Bock rather than Nuremberg's Spengler. Spengler counseled delay, believing that "the longer it goes on, the more, praise be to God, the Word of God will spread to and take root in all parts of the land, so that nothing can be undertaken against it."[83] The current dilemma was a test for the city folk, "whether or not they are Christians," and if they stood fast, Christ would defend his own, "for I am certain that Christ is Lord also over his enemies and thus is mighty enough to sustain this cause...against many foes."[84] "However mighty, awesome, or powerful they might be," he declared,

---

[80] *RTA, jR,* 4:506–8, no. 113, here at 507, lines 27–37, and 508, lines 1–6. The call for a council is at p. 508, lines 20–2.
[81] G. Schmidt, *Städtetag,* 481; Scribner, "Cologne."
[82] G. Schmidt, *Städtetag,* 482–3, who found the document at Frankfurt.
[83] *RTA, jR,* 4:491, no. 107.
[84] Ibid., 238–9, no. 28, and see 50 n. 1.

the opposition "cannot hitch the stirrup one notch higher than where God long ago ordained and decreed it to be."[85] The danger of a council, he warned, was that it might rule against the Evangelicals.

Strasbourg's government, by contrast, wanted the religious question referred to a council. This policy, first broached by the Imperial Diet at Nuremberg in January 1523,[86] had been taken up at Strasbourg no later than the following December, before the Evangelicals had a clear majority.[87] Bock's instruction for Nuremberg had lamented the misunderstandings and disputes over religion, which only a free, public hearing of the preachers could dispel; "whatever a free council or Christian assembly [*gemein*] would then decide, the government and commune of Strasbourg, which have ever been and still are an obedient, Christian member of the Holy Roman Empire, would support and accept."[88] The urban envoys at Nuremberg endorsed this policy and rejected the reinstatement of the Edict of Worms as unenforceable. This formula, which united Evangelical and Catholic envoys and thus preserved urban solidarity, "was neither a theological demonstration nor a beacon, but a decision based on considerations of political utility."[89]

During the spring and summer of 1524, the popular movement in the free cities "reached its first peak."[90] At Strasbourg five parishes, those of the "little people" – fishermen, gardeners, and craftsmen – moved to select their own preachers; and by summer's end the government ordered the purge of all religious images from the churches.[91] At

---

[85] Ibid., 490, lines 14–15, 27–36, and see 492–3 for his rejection of a council. The document is summarized by Brecht, "Politik," 188, who exaggerates Spengler's role.

[86] *RTA, jR*, 3:424, lines 23–5, no. 79. See Bernhard Wurmser von Vendenheim and Daniel Mieg to the Stettmeister and Senate of Strasbourg, Nuremberg, Feb. 4, 1523, in ibid., 924, lines 7–8, no. 250.

[87] The instruction for the Urban Diet at Speyer in Dec. 1523 is in *Annales de Sébastien Brant*, no. 4484. Moeller, "Zwinglis Disputationen, II": 222, is properly cautious about drawing conclusion from it about religious policy, but Brecht, "Politik," 188–9, is not. On the context, see my *Ruling Class*, 205–8.

[88] *PCSS*, 1:87–8, no. 162; there is a better text in Bucer, *Deutsche Schriften*, 1:345–7. Brecht, "Politik," 189 n. 33, believes that the idea may have come from Bucer, but this cannot be proved. For discussions at Strasbourg, see *Annales de Sébastien Brant*, no. 4495; *PCSS*, 1: no. 166.

[89] G. Schmidt, *Städtetag*, 482, who criticizes Brecht, "Politik," 190–1.

[90] H. Schmidt, "Reichsstädte," 464, who surveys the subject on 444–64.

[91] Chrisman, *Strasbourg*, 114–16, 138–40, 144; Brady, *Ruling Class*, 166–8; Bornert, *La réforme protestante*, 133–4.

Augsburg, the government's immobility brought the city to the brink of an uprising over the dismissal of Johann Schilling, who preached that "if the government will not act, the commune must."[92] After nearly eighteen hundred Augsburgers gathered before the city hall on August 6, shouting for their favorite, on the ninth the senators appeared in full armor and cowed the crowd outside, and they sealed their courage by sending two old weavers "with bloody hands from life into death."[93] Jacob Fugger closed his office, buried his cash, and fled to Biberach an der Riss. At Ulm, the government called in June the first official Evangelical preacher, Konrad Sam (1483–1533), after a citizens' petition on May 22 had demanded that Catholic preaching be prohibited.[94] At Constance, where matters were more advanced, the preachers and their Catholic opponents were already squaring off for a disputation à la Zurich.[95] There were riots and demonstrations against the Catholic clergy in many towns, not least in Frankfurt am Main.[96]

No other city seethed more tumultuously during the summer than did Nuremberg, whose population, now relieved of the Imperial government's presence, took up the Evangelical cause in all seriousness. Lutheran preaching had already become an everyday matter, and it was said during Easter Week 1524 that "the preachers here preach more sharply than ever before against the pope, cardinals, and bishops."[97] Important changes were made in Catholic ceremonies during these weeks, and Andreas Osiander (1498–1552) turned his rhetorical guns on both clerical and lay authorities. "He is now also attacking the lay authority," one report ran, "to the degree that the subjects might well rise up against it."[98] In truth, peasants around nearby Forchheim had recently rebelled, and Nuremberg artisans were joining them.[99] The movement's first peak

---

[92] H. Lutz, *Peutinger*, 235; F. Roth, *Reformationsgeschichte*, 1:155–70; Wettges, *Reformation*, 104–6; Broadhead, "Internal Politics," 114–63. To the sources listed by H. Lutz, *Peutinger*, 392 n. 1, should be added Hans Ungelter's report of Aug. 13, 1524, in Klüpfel, *Urkunden*, 2:279–80.
[93] H. Lutz, *Peutinger*, 235.
[94] Keim, *Reichsstadt Ulm*, 64–6, 86–8; Naujoks, *Obrigkeitsgedanke*, 57–8; Brecht, "Ulm," 98.
[95] Rublack, *Einführung*, 40–1.
[96] Jahns, *Frankfurt*, 35–6.
[97] Quoted by Vogler, *Nürnberg*, 58; see 58–63.
[98] Quoted in ibid., 59.
[99] Pfeiffer, "Einführung," 112–33; Seebass, "Stadt und Kirche in Nürnberg," 73. On the rural disorders, see Vogler, "Vorspiel."

also created painful stresses within Nuremberg's oligarchy, dividing families and friends. Susanna Stromer, a nun of very good family, poured out her distress to Katharina, widow of Caspar Kress:

Ursula Topler has no good reason for leaving her convent, only that she was treated too laxly and that her monk and friends sent her Lutheran books. I've not had such a bad life in the convent, and I've never wanted to take a husband. ... Dearest Auntie, I trust that you will stick to the old ways and won't forget entirely the poor nuns here. God searches out his own in all classes of society, finds good and bad everywhere; and the good shouldn't be wiped out because of the bad. This is God's punishment on the clergy, and I hope that His divine goodness will yet turn things around and make them turn out for the best.[100]

Yet the movement could not be held back at Nuremberg, and soon Huldrych Zwingli was saluting the Nurembergers as comrades in arms.[101]

The rumblings in their own commons did not disrupt the urban front – not yet. The cities came together again in an Urban Diet at Speyer in mid-July 1524. Although the agenda contained six separate points, yet, as Nuremberg pointed out, it "is true that among other articles this matter, which has been called the new, misleading doctrine, is not the least, in fact, we would call it the most important, the principal matter."[102] It had, in other words, replaced the customs duty, monopolies, and the Spanish embassy as the most pressing subject. The leadership of Strasbourg and Nuremberg, established at the recent Imperial Diet,[103] still held, though the two governments could not agree on a policy. Nuremberg wanted the cities to frame another appeal to Charles V – their favorite tactic – to ask for a more moderate law, and they insisted that each city should prepare its own case for the national council at Speyer in the fall. The Strasbourgeois, however, were instructed to urge the cities to form a stronger unity and to put their houses in order through stricter censorship and firmer controls on preaching, so "that nothing should be presented and preached but the holy divine scriptures, to the enhancement of God's honor and love of neighbor, and brotherly con-

[100] Pfeiffer, *Quellen*, 306–7 (after Dec. 4, 1524).
[101] Zwingli to Willibald Pirckheimer, Zurich, Oct. 24, 1524: "Futurum arbitror, ut Norimberga et Tigurum aliquando in eodem iungantur foedere..." Ibid., 293, from *Z*, 8: no. 349.
[102] Quoted by H. Schmidt, "Reichsstädte," 465.
[103] Simon Reibeisen to the bishop of Strasbourg, April 17, 1524, in *RTA, jR*, 4:173, lines 27–32, no. 25. The published sources for the Urban Diet of Speyer, July 13–18, 1524, are collected by Brecht, "Politik."

cord should be preserved. And all other doctrines, which contradict the holy scriptures and lead to rebellion and discord, should be abolished."[104] The cities must also face the national council as one body, and they "should prepare a common memorial to justify the chief points: that the priests are taking wives; that the Eucharist is received by laymen under both species; and that no one is bound by church law to confess sins, to fast, and other such things." As to the Edict of Worms, the emperor must be told that enforcement "is not possible," and that "where it is enforced, it would lead to great rebellion and conflict between commune and government, and between clergy and laity."

Probably the Strasbourgeois tried to make the urban front more decidedly Evangelical than was possible, especially as concerned the preparations for the national council.[105] The Urban Diet could nevertheless agree that the Edict of Worms, restated and given teeth by a mandate from the Governing Council, was simply unenforceable in the cities, and Strasbourg, Nuremberg, Frankfurt, and Ulm agreed to represent this refusal of full obedience to the Governing Council.[106] Some other cities were not willing to go this far, and none was willing to join Strasbourg and Ulm in planning an urban military league to defend the cities in religious matters.[107] The time was unripe for an *Evangelical* urban front. The Urban Diet's letter of grievance to Charles V, however, spoke of a fear every urban officeholder could share:

In the past the honorable free and Imperial cities . . . have always shown every possible form of obedience to the Roman emperors and kings . . . yet this edict is so framed that many of them cannot enforce all of its articles without provoking serious uprisings, the destruction of law and order, and dissension between commons and regimes and between clergy and laity. This will all lead to murder and bloodshed, and the honorable free and Imperial cities will thereby be alienated from His Imperial Majesty, and the Holy Roman Empire will be pushed toward certain ruin.[108]

---

[104] *PCSS*, 1:92, no. 171, and there, too, the following quotes.
[105] H. Schmidt, "Reichsstädte," 467.
[106] The recess is in StA Ulm, A 527.
[107] G. Schmidt, *Städtetag*, 485–6.
[108] Förstemann, *Neues Urkundenbuch*, 1:211, no. 855, dated to July or early Aug. but almost certainly drafted about July 18, 1524. For the Ulmers' position, see Naujoks, *Obrigkeitsgedanke*, 57; the Nurembergers' policy is noted by Brecht, "Politik," 196, from Pfeiffer, *Quellen*, 158–63.

As these lines were written, armed peasants were already patrolling the valleys in the southern Black Forest, harbingers of the coming revolution.

These summer months were the urban front's Indian summer. To be sure, the advance of the Evangelical movements in some prominent cities gradually shifted the tone in the Urban Diet in a pro-Evangelical direction, but not so strongly that the cities had been split by the religious question. The urban commons were nevertheless pushing their governments farther and farther into illegality and open heterodoxy. The appeal to a national council, which had been framed by the entire Imperial Diet, preserved, for the moment, the urban governments' freedom of action to meet the pressure from below with concessions. This could continue, probably, so long as the other blade of the scissors did not begin to close.

The fall of the urban front

> Also ists vast aufgangen
> in allem deutschen land,
> zu Wittemberg angfangen,
> den Entchrist bracht in shand.[109]

While in Germany the Luther affair was developing from the disobedience of a provincial professor into a movement of tremendous power, at Charles V's court in Spain it could not even be discussed. Or so wrote Margrave Hans of Brandenburg in mid-1525 to his brother, Casimir, confessing that he knew little about the new doctrine, about which no one at court would enlighten him, for fear of angering Charles.[110] Charles himself did not have to rely on ecclesiastical channels for his knowledge of heresy's progress, for Archduke Ferdinand's letters expressed mounting concern about it.

One of the most important things Ferdinand had learned since his arrival in 1522 was that the Habsburg power in Germany was truly in danger. He entered an Austria aboil with unrest and rebellion. His agents

---

[109] "The movement come from Wittenberg has spread on every breeze through the whole German land and brought Antichrist to his knees." Liliencron, *Volkslieder*, 3:510, no. 393, stanza 4.
[110] Friedensburg, *Vorgeschichte*, 104 n. 2.

in Tyrol met armed resistance from country folk, who demanded to be put directly under the emperor, while radicals convened their own assemblies in the Lower Austrian duchies and called for death to the nobles.[111] Some of his subjects warned him, he reported, that they had to have a natural prince or else they'd turn Swiss.[112] The shade of Maximilian van Bergen, who had not lived to see Ferdinand's Austrian progress, must have smiled. Ferdinand also seems to have comprehended that the unrest racing through his and his brother's lands represented the common desire to extend to entire lands the principles of communal-federal life as learned in the village, district, mining, and urban communes and in the territorial diets. It was with good reason, therefore, that he congratulated Charles on the smashing of the Castilian *comuneros*, whose ultimate demand might very well have suited his own Austrian subjects: "The notions of the nobles and heathens belong to the past; the entire kingdom should live as one commune in peace and justice under one king and one law."[113] As a prince of strong dynastic consciousness, but also as a younger brother who very much wanted authority independent from an elder one, Ferdinand strove to convince Charles that conditions in Germany required Ferdinand's election as King of the Romans and successor to Charles, if the decline of Habsburg prestige there were to be arrested.[114]

In reporting to Charles the progress of the German heresy, Ferdinand added to his other motives a desire to protect the religion of his ancestors. "Sire," he wrote to Charles from Nuremberg at the end of 1523, "the Lutheran sect reigns so thoroughly in this land of Germany that the good Christians hardly think they can declare themselves and be known as such."[115] At Constance, heresy was being openly preached, "and such is no less preached here in Nuremberg and in all the other Imperial

---

[111] V. von Kraus, *Zur Geschichte Oesterreichs*; Lhotsky, *Zeitalter*, 81–92, 98–104; Fichtner, *Ferdinand I of Austria*, 22–5.

[112] Archduke Ferdinand's instruction, Nuremberg, Nov. 1522: "Ains disent vouloir avoir seigneur naturel out aultrement ilz se rendront Suysses..." W. Bauer and Lacroix, *Korrespondenz*, 1:23, no. 21. Somewhat later, it was said in the Governing Council, "Dass auch etzlich reichsstett sich zu den schweiczern schlahen [könnten]." Quoted by Grabner, *Reichsregiment*, 101.

[113] Quoted by Brandi, *Kaiser Karl V*, 1:121–2 (English: *Emperor Charles V*, 148), the saying comes from the Valencian Germanía. Ferdinand's congratulation is in W. Bauer and Lacroix, *Korrespondenz*, 1:31, no. 23, para. 2. See Haliczer, *Comuneros*, 131, 176–9, for the *comuneros'* ideals.

[114] Laubach, "Nachfolge," 6–10.

[115] W. Bauer and Lacroix, *Korrespondenz*, 1:89–90, no. 50, para. 26.

cities. Also, the people refuse to pay tithes, eat meat on Friday, take the sacrament without first confessing, and do other things of that sort."[116] Charles reacted to these and other reports with his "great displeasure, that the Lutheran sect dominates in all Germany."[117] The Third Diet of Nuremberg was just about to end, and Ferdinand fanned the flame by adding – and here the truth gave blessed support to his own ambition – that "in the Lutheran matter... [there is] the greatest moment and danger."[118] He then clinched the argument through a messenger he sent to Charles in June 1524, suggesting that the Germans might force "the electors to elect a new [i.e., a Lutheran] king."[119] Charles, who had paid dearly for the Imperial candidacy of Elector Frederick the Wise of Saxony in 1519, knew what that meant.

Charles, meanwhile, in the spirit of his current policy and convinced, apparently, that the leading southern free cities were indeed fonts of the heresy, wrote to Nuremberg to express his displeasure "that you and the other estates support Luther so much." He charged the government with allowing Lutheran books to be printed and sold, thereby encouraging others to similar acts of disobedience. Nuremberg should abandon Lutheranism, "since most of the others in the Holy Empire will follow your example," and because otherwise the city would lose its liberties.[120] The wisdom of this harder approach was confirmed by Ferdinand in August, when he reported that the free cities, assembled at Speyer (in July), had decided to defend the cause of Luther, "with whose doctrine they are so thoroughly infected that you cannot imagine it."[121] Lest Ferdinand be accused of merely trying to increase the pressure on Charles to give him more independence, Jean Hannart, who was no friend to Ferdinand, reported from Germany in the same vein.[122]

---

[116] Ibid. See Rublack, *Einführung*, 213, no. 50. Fichtner, *Ferdinand I of Austria*, 6–7, 110–17, 141–2, 148–9, 209–17, 228–31, sheds new light on Ferdinand's religious opinions.

[117] W. Bauer and Lacroix, *Korrespondenz*, 1:108, no. 62, para. 14 (Burgos, April 15, 1524).

[118] Archduke Ferdinand to Charles V, Nuremberg, April 27, 1524, in ibid., 115, no. 65, para. 7.

[119] Archduke Ferdinand's instruction for Karel de Bredam, Stuttgart, June 13, 1524, in ibid., 158, no. 76, para. 16.

[120] E. Franz, *Nürnberg*, 87–8. A similar letter from the Governing Council, dated April 18, 1524, went to Strasbourg. *PCSS*, 1:92 n. 1.

[121] Archduke Ferdinand to Charles V, Vienna, Aug. 14, 1524, in W. Bauer and Lacroix, *Korrespondenz*, 1:210–11, no. 85, para. 3.

[122] Jean Hannart wrote on April 26, 1524: "Item il fault grandement peser le fait de ladite secte luterane, pour ce quelle est desia fort esparse en toute la lemaignes ingendrant beaucoup de maulx et desobeissance du peuple, tant contre les gens deglise comme vers les superieurs et

From Charles's perspective, therefore, the southern free cities, which in the late summer of 1523 had emerged as the best potential supporters of stronger Habsburg rule in the Empire, a year later had become the nurseries of a movement that, if successful, would undermine the church whose symbols and authority lent legitimacy to the Habsburg sense of dynastic calling.

It remained to find an instrument to bring the cities in line. The Imperial Diet was unsuitable, because it had called for a national council. The Governing Council lay then in the throes of its transfer to Esslingen, a move that would increase princely suspicion of it.[123] Of the Swabian League, on the other hand, some expected much as a bulwark against the Lutheran onslaught,[124] but the League's council contained a strong voice from the cities, the objects of repression, and it had princely enemies as well. It was never to be an entirely reliable instrument for the defense of Catholicism in South Germany.

The idea of a new military league, the first of those confessional leagues that would dominate German political life until 1648, probably came from Lorenzo Campeggio, the papal legate, and Duke William of Bavaria.[125] It was called the "Regensburg Pact," because of its creation by Archduke Ferdinand, Dukes William and Louis of Bavaria, and twelve South German bishops at Regensburg between June 27 and July 7, 1524. Its aims were enforcement of the Edict of Worms and a church reform to take the wind from Lutheran sails. Though this league fell victim to the anti-Habsburg turn of Bavarian policy in 1525, it had some lasting success in splitting some of the smaller Upper Swabian free cities

---

justices. Et fait sur ce paz a noter, que toutes les villes imperiales ont proteste contre lexecution dudit mandat de Worms, et a ceste occasion non voulu seeller ledit departement et recez." Lanz, *Korrespondenz*, 1:127, no. 55.

[123] Baumgarten, *Geschichte*, 2:330–2. See Jean Hannart to Charles V, Nuremberg, March 6, 1524, in Lanz, *Korrespondenz*, 1:105, no. 52. On the Governing Council's religious complexion at this time, see Archduke Ferdinand to Charles V, May 12, 1523, in W. Bauer and Lacroix, *Korrespondenz*, 1:59, no. 36, para. 10. Ferdinand wrote to Charles from Nuremberg, Dec. 18, 1523, that "d'autrepart led. regiment et la ligue de Zwave [Schwaben] ne s'accordent point bien ne est possibles, car ilz sont totalement contraires..." Ibid., 84, no. 50, para. 9.

[124] Gerwig Blarer to Dr. Johann Fabri, May 18, 1524, in Blarer, *Briefe und Akten*, 1:31, lines 3–4, no. 50. See G. Müller, *Kurie*, 286; Rublack, *Nördlingen*, 139–42. There was also a princely opposition to the League, for which see Salomies, *Pläne*, 36–7.

[125] H. Lutz, "Das konfessionelle Zeitalter, I," 314. On the Regensburg Pact, see Friedensburg, "Regensburger Convent," and Borth, *Luthersache*, 161–8. Many sources for it are in *ARC*, 1:294ff.

– Ueberlingen, Ravensburg, Leutkirch, Wangen, and Pfullendorf – away from the increasingly Evangelical Urban Diet.[126] The Regensburg Pact also threw Duke William, rather than Archduke Ferdinand, into the spotlight as the political leader of a nascent Catholic party in the South. William had come early to the conclusion that the bishops alone could not halt the Lutheran advance,[127] and his role as a leader of the Catholic party happily united the defense of the faith with a weakening of Habsburg influence.

The dreamy calm of Indian summer broke in late September 1524, when Charles's decision on the Diet's request arrived from Spain. There would be no national council at Speyer on Saint Martin's Day; and the Edict of Worms would be enforced to the letter.[128] With this Edict of Burgos fell the death blow, not to the Urban Diet or the tradition of urban cooperation, but to the urban front – that is, to the promise of making urban solidarity effective through a new kind of partnership with the monarch.[129] When Charles's reply to the Diet became known, the Edict of Worms stood alone as valid Imperial law on the Lutheran question. The emperor's decision fell as a hammer blow on the urban front, not so much because the Speyer assembly might have achieved a solution to the religious question – there was little hope of that – but for two other reasons. First, it came at a time when the Evangelical movement was making perceptible progress, week by week, in the cities, pushing the governments further and further toward partisanship for the new religion. Secondly, it found the South on the brink of the greatest social upheaval in German history, the great Revolution of 1525, called "the German Peasants' War."[130]

The movement of the leading urban governments toward public defense of the Evangelical cause was no figment of Archduke Ferdinand's

---

[126] H. Schmidt, "Reichsstädte," 473–6.
[127] Duke William of Bavaria to Duke Ernest of Bavaria, Jan. 2, 1524, in *ARC*, 1:162–3, quoted by H. Lutz, "Das konfessionelle Zeitalter, I," 313 n. 2. The text has a phrase that is usually taken as proof of Evangelical sentiments, "die gottliche ehre und unser heiliger glauben."
[128] The edict is in Förstemann, *Neues Urkundenbuch*, 1:204–5. Brecht, "Politik," 197–202, describes these events, though he elsewhere (193) seems to confuse an edict of April 18, 1524, drafted in Charles's name by the Governing Council, with the edict sent from Spain. Borth, *Luthersache*, 158 n. 233, lists the *three* edicts.
[129] G. Schmidt, *Städtetag*, 478, rightly criticizes me (in "Jacob Sturm and the Lutherans," 202) for construing the effects too drastically.
[130] Oberman, "Gospel of Social Unrest," explains why the term is inappropriate.

imagination. Two Nurembergers, Hieronymus Ebner and Caspar Nützel, described the recent Urban Diet to Elector Frederick the Wise: "The free cities have appeared in great numbers, and others have sent proxies, to a meeting at Speyer [in mid-July], where they decided unanimously to hold to the Word of God, come what may."[131] Count Palatine Frederick, too, noted a new sense of unity in this Urban Diet and thought it meant future trouble for the princes.[132] The surviving documents drafted in free cities for the national council at Speyer reveal an impressive new commitment to Evangelical principles and language, though not necessarily to specifically Lutheran ones, and breathe the strong biblicism native to the urban Reformation.[133]

The news from Spain reinforced the slide toward an urban front committed to the Evangelical cause. This is visible in the Urban Diet that met at Ulm on Saint Nicholas's Day (December 6), 1524. Some small Upper Swabian Catholic towns boycotted the assembly, but most of the big folk were represented: Strasbourg by two Evangelicals, Egenolf Röder von Diersburg and Martin Herlin; Nuremberg by two burgomasters, Christoph Tetzel and Clemens Volckamer; Augsburg by Antoni Bimel, who already stood under Zwingli's influence; Constance by Jakob Zeller, a strongly Evangelical guildsman; and Esslingen by Hans Holdermann, who kept his distance from the Evangelicals without opposing them.[134] The Edict of Burgos frightened away the Frankfurters, who wrote that "we must obey this edict [of Worms] insofar as we are able, so that we cannot send anyone to this meeting without incurring considerable risk."[135] Called at Nuremberg's request, this Urban Diet dealt officially with "Luther's doctrine" for the first time.[136]

It is not true, as has been alleged, that the Urban Diet of Ulm on

---

[131] Förstemann, *Neues Urkundenbuch*, 1:213, no. 87.

[132] Count Palatine Frederick to Counts Palatine Ottheinrich and Philip, Aug. 5, 1524, in Friedensburg, *Reichstag zu Speier*, 10. Under his presidency, the Governing Council began to move against cities for failure to enforce the Edict of Worms. Naujoks, *Obrigkeitsgedanke*, 58.

[133] H. Schmidt, "Reichsstädte," 476–85, who cogently criticizes Brecht, "Politik," 219–20, for making the document too specifically Lutheran.

[134] Brady, *Ruling Class*, 317–18, 342–3. Nuremberg's envoys are listed in the recess, in StA Ulm, A 529, fol. 24ᵛ. See also F. Roth, *Reformationsgeschichte*, 1:88, 102 n. 7; Rublack, *Einführung*, 107–8; idem, "Bewegung," 197; Krabbe and Rublack, *Akten*, nos. 162–5.

[135] Jahns, *Frankfurt*, 36. Frankfurt did send a proxy to Ulm. StA Ulm, A 529, fol. 25ʳ.

[136] The meeting was called at Nuremberg's request (StA Ulm, A 529, fol. 3ʳ) to consider Luther's doctrine (ibid., fol. 2ʳ). Thirty envoys attended (ibid., fols. 3ʳ–4ʳ). The recess is in ibid., fols. 2ʳ–25ᵛ.

December 6 through 13, 1524, displayed "the primacy of the Reformation religious principle in the cities' common policy in 1524."[137] Despite the deliberate absence of a large number of cities, the Diet did not adopt the views of Lazarus Spengler, who criticized his own masters, and those of the other cities, for their timidity.

They should not be so timid in this matter, which concerns not only this government but all the Empire's subjects, and which is not the cause of any one person, but God's cause. They shouldn't start at every carnival mask, such as are used daily to frighten them; but, as Christian people, they should trust God, His word and righteousness, because they seek nothing else than His honor, their subjects' welfare, and the good of all Christendom – not their own interests. If you trust God more than men, He will become your helper in His own good time, and He will never abandon those who trust in Him. Viewed in the light of God's grace, this matter is not so dangerous that the council should abandon those whose hearts are in the right place or do anything that is improper or disadvantageous before God and the world, for the government would otherwise give a public example for abandoning the gospel.[138]

The entire Evangelical movement, Spengler trumpeted, is "a great... courageous... assembly, which will permit no power to wrest it from the gospel and the Word of God," and the best way to defend it is through an embassy to inform Charles V about the conditions in the Empire. The Constancers wanted to go even farther and send "learned and pious men" to Spain to instruct the emperor in the new doctrine and its religious and social benefits.[139]

The Urban Diet at Ulm heard the Edict of Burgos read and then resolved

not to sit by and do nothing, but to act diligently... and, with God's grace, to seek suitable ways, means and assistance in nullifying the severity of said penal edict, or in counteracting it effectively. For if this is not done, the efforts of the free and Imperial cities' grim and hateful foes – especially the fish whose water is removed by the holy, indestructible Word of God [i.e., the bishops] – will produce evil worse than any pen can describe...[140]

---

[137] Brecht, "Politik," 202. See G. Schmidt, "Haltung," 197–8.
[138] Pfeiffer, *Quellen*, 176; the following quote is at 172.
[139] Spengler's memorial is in ibid., 168–77; and the Constance document is printed by Vögeli, *Schriften*, 2, 1:656. See Brecht, "Politik," 199–202; H. Schmidt, "Reichsstädte," 485–502; G. Schmidt, *Städtetag*, 487–90.
[140] StA Ulm, A 529, fol. 4ᵛ; the following quote is at fol. 5ʳ.

The best remedy would be a "Christian letter" [*ein Christenlich schrifft*] to warn the emperor that "it is not humanly possible for the free and Imperial cities to enforce this edict on the Common Man or other subjects or to force them to give up the Word and call of God, without uprisings, ruin, destruction, and bloodshed within our communes." This was the same argument the cities had employed at the Third Diet of Nuremberg and again at the Urban Diet at Speyer in July 1524. This time, however, a new spirit, intensely religious and direct, animated their pleas. "For we confess by our consciences," they wrote to Charles,

and on our souls' salvation, that in this we seek nothing else and ask for nothing more earnestly from God, than that His divine honor, praise and honor of His holy name, and also brotherly love, to be advanced. Also, [we desire] that His authentic Word be preached to all men throughout the whole world for salvation and solace, and that the prosperity, welfare, and prestige of the Holy Roman Empire and of Your Imperial Majesty be increased.[141]

The envoys were careful, to be sure, to distance themselves from Luther and his doctrine.

It has not been, and is not now, our intention, desire, or opinion to defend in any way or to support Luther's person or his doctrine, particularly where the latter is supposed to be against the Word of God and the holy gospel. For we consider Luther to be a man, who can err as other men do. We were not baptized in the said Luther's name or that of any other man. He did not suffer for us, and he did not bear and pay for our sins. But we believe in God the Almighty as our Creator and head of His Christian churches, Who saved us through the death of His only beloved Son, Jesus Christ, and Whose Word and gospel we will support, so long as He gives us grace.[142]

There is nonetheless an unmistakably Evangelical ring to their denunciation of all laws and edicts issued "to forbid us in any way the Word of God, from which alone we have life, through which we must be preserved and be saved, and which alone we want to protect against all human doctrines, teachings, and opinions." Nothing like this, surely, had ever before been submitted to Charles V. The Urban Diet of Ulm also worked out a plan of collective security to aid those cities that were

---

[141] Pfeiffer, *Quellen*, 310, who prints the full text (308–11) from StA Ulm, A 529, fols. 5ᵛ–10ᵛ. See Brecht, "Politik," 200–1.
[142] Pfeiffer, *Quellen*, 308–9, and there, too, the following quote.

being prosecuted for violations of the Edict of Worms, such as those by the bishop of Speyer against Wissembourg and Landau and that of the bishop of Augsburg against Kaufbeuren. It was not the much-discussed urban league, but it was a step in that direction.[143]

While the Urban Diet deliberated and framed conclusions, South Germany rolled on toward revolution. The social landscape sprouted volcanoes, as peasants rose in arms in the bishopric of Bamberg, the southern Black Forest, and Switzerland. At Wendelstein near Schwabach in Franconia, they drove out their pastor and claimed the right to install a new one, and at Thayngen near Schaffhausen they did the same.[144] From its starting point in the Black Forest, the revolt had spread since early summer into the Klettgau and the Hegau, the politically spongy boundary zone between Swabia and the Confederacy.[145] Nowhere did the urban Evangelical movements and the rural uprisings, both nourished by communalism, converge more successfully than along the higher reaches of the Upper Rhine, where Balthasar Hubmaier (1481–1528), a Swabian radical with a strong anti-Jewish record, drew together around Waldshut all the complaints of the Common Man – against the priests, the Jews, the merchants, and the Austrian government.[146]

The fundamental theme of these movements was expressed by the upland subjects of the great abbey of Sankt Blasien in the southern Black Forest, who declared that they simply wanted to be free, like other "peoples" [*Landschaften*] and pay no more dues.[147] The Evangelicals' desire for religious self-rule converged with and mightily strengthened the much broader and older movement for self-rule in general, which had sprung from the erosion and defeat of feudal lordship. Had it not been for the preachers and printers of the early 1520s, who spread common symbols and slogans of encouragement and resistance, possibly the *Bundschuh* actions of 1502 and 1513–17 would now appear as mere

---

[143] StA Ulm, A 529, fols. 11ʳ, 11ᵛ–12ʳ, 12ʳ–17ʳ, 19ʳ⁻ᵛ, 21ʳ–;22. Well over 90 percent of the text deals with this issue.
[144] G. Franz, *Der deutsche Bauernkrieg*, 100–1. See, in general, ibid., 99–112; Blickle, *Revolution von 1525*, 24, 28, 38, 160, 206, 214, 220, 223, 249–50, 277.
[145] G. Franz, *Der deutsche Bauernkrieg*, 104–18; idem, *Bauernkrieg. Aktenband*, 241, no. 83.
[146] G. Franz, *Der deutsche Bauernkrieg*, 110–13; Scott, "Reformation and Peasants' War."
[147] G. Franz, *Der deutsche Bauernkrieg*, 107. On the rural movement's phases, see Blickle, "Social Protest," 7–9.

aftershocks of the Swabian War of 1499, not as preliminary tremors to the Revolution of 1525.

And so, while the urban governments, pressed from below by their own commons, came to the brink of declaring all-out partisanship for the Evangelical cause, and while their sovereign, who was convinced that the cities were nursing heresy, the mother of rebellion, tightened the pressure on them from above, all around the public peace and the self-confidence of lords were melting away before the fires of revolt. This conflagration would reveal both the fundamental weaknesses of the Habsburg power in South Germany and how impotent the free cities were without effective royal leadership.

6

∞∞∞

Cities and Crown in the age of the Reformation

Dreams sometimes come true. They rarely do so, however, so suddenly and unexpectedly as did Charles V's dream of supremacy over his most dogged foe, King Francis I of France. In 1524, the emperor had begun a new war, fraught "with all sorts of inner uncertainties and even contradictions," against the French power in Italy.[1] His gloomy, stoical reflections written at year's end reveal how little he expected a quick, happy solution to this fearsome struggle. Then, during a few hours one February morning in 1525 before the Lombard city of Pavia, the barely dared dream came true: The French were crushed, Francis and many of his nobles were Imperial prisoners, and Lombardy and all Italy lay securely in Habsburg hands. Pope Clement could hardly continue his anti-Habsburg course alone; the costs of occupying Lombardy could be pushed off on France's Italian friends; and the entire peninsula could be restored to peace, prosperity, and obedience. Such were the goals Chancellor Gattinara laid down during the heady days after Pavia.[2] Now the time had come, he reflected, to settle the religious question and secure Christendom, suppress the German heresy, counterattack against the Turk, and begin reform of the Church through a General Council. "Sire," chimed in the faithful Lannoy to Charles, "you will recall that Lord de Berssele once said that God gives each man once in his life a bountiful harvest. If he doesn't reap then, the chance is past."[3]

The year 1525 was harvest time in Germany. Not for twenty years

---

[1] Brandi, *Kaiser Karl V.*, 1:184 (English: *Emperor Charles V*, 223).
[2] Ibid., 185–7 (English: ibid., 224–7).
[3] Ibid., 184–5 (English: ibid., 223). On Charles de Lannoy, a Walloon nobleman who became grand marshal and viceroy of Naples, see Halkin and Dansaert, *Charles de Lannoy*.

would Charles have another opportunity to settle the religious question there, twenty years filled with vacillation, compromise, and endless attempts to pacify the German Evangelicals with words and concessions in exchange for their aid against more resolute foes. For three years, the Edict of Worms had been almost a dead letter, while Charles had wrestled with the revolts in Castile and Valencia, the French problem in Italy, and the Turkish threat on several fronts. During those years, Ferdinand had tried to establish himself as effective lord over Austria and Imperial vicar. His measures against the Lutherans in Austria[4] and Charles's commands to the Imperial Diet in 1524 gave testimony to the brothers' resolution to press forward against the German heretics. And so, the opening months of 1525 saw increasing force from the Imperial side of the scissors, whose blades were popular pressure and monarchical will, that cut ever more deeply into the power and prestige of the South German urban oligarchies.

Two events kept this scissors from closing: the great insurrection in the German South in 1524–6 and the Turkish onslaught on Hungary in 1526. The Revolution of 1525 destroyed much of the urban regimes' remaining influence in the Swabian League; it threatened many a regime from within and even toppled some governments in small towns; and it generally damaged the oligarchies' prestige by tarring them with the brush of rebellion. The revolution also laid bare Ferdinand's weakness as lord of Austria and Imperial vicar; it sparked the beginning of an anti-Habsburg policy in Bavaria; and it confronted South Germany's rulers with a pressing issue, law and order, which temporarily shunted into the shadows the question of Luther's person and doctrine.

Sultan Suleiman's attack on Hungary drew Ferdinand away from the German question.[5] It began in 1522, one year after the fall of Belgrade (August 29–30, 1521), with raids into Carinthia and Friuli. Unlike the Austrian borderlands, at the Hungarian court King Louis II and Queen Mary, sister of Ferdinand and Charles, did little to prepare for the invasion everyone expected. The storm broke in 1526, and Louis led fewer than twenty thousand Hungarians to face Suleiman's gigantic, superbly equipped army. At Mohács, where the River Drava flows into

---

[4] Lhotsky, *Zeitalter*, 160–4.
[5] Ibid., 179–85; Shaw, *Empire of the Gazis*, 91–2, 312; Fichtner, *Ferdinand I of Austria*, 54–65.

the Danube, the king attacked what he falsely believed a portion of Suleiman's force and led the Hungarians to his and their certain death. In accordance with agreements Emperor Maximilian had made, Ferdinand of Austria succeeded to the Jagellonian inheritance, the crowns of Bohemia and Hungary.

The acquisition of the first two of his three royal crowns drew Ferdinand's attention and person from Germany, just as the Spanish crowns drew his brother's attention from his German lands. This double royal distraction weakened, at a critical time, the Habsburg monarchy's pressure on the South German urban oligarchies. The relief came, however, only after many months of deepest crisis.

The cities in the Revolution of 1525

Nach Christi fünf und zwenzig
und fünfzehn hundert jar
das christlich leben wendt sich,
schalkheit ward offenbar.
Die bawern wurden geheufel
und triben hochmuts vil;
die fürsten wurden zweifel,
der reisig flucht den teufel,
doch bleib in still der widerwill
biss zu seim zil
und het der böse teufel
mit Jederman sein spil.[6]

As "the highpoint and zenith of the attempts to construct the state on communal foundations,"[7] the Revolution of 1525 frightened the lords and their followers all over South Germany. Some saw in it an enormous attempt to turn Swiss, as a songster wrote about the Battle of Leipheim on April 4, 1525:

---

[6] "In the Year of Our Lord a thousand five hundred and twenty-five, true Christian life appeared once more, and roguery was unmasked. The peasants came together and showed their arrogance. The princes were beflustered; the knights fled from the Devil, and the old Foe worked secretly his design. And in the end the Evil One caught them all in his snare." Liliencron, *Volkslieder*, 3:471–2, no. 381, stanza 3.

[7] As Peter Blickle, *Untertanen*, 118, puts it: "Der Bauernkrieg von 1525 ist Höhepunkt und Scheitelpunkt der Bemühungen, von der gemeindlichen Grundlage aus den Staat aufzubauen."

The peasants tried to learn
An evil lesson from the Swiss
And become their own lords.[8]

Others, looking closer to home, held the free cities responsible for the entire catastrophe. Margrave Casimir, for example, said "that the peasant insurrection mostly has its roots in the cities."[9] Konrad Mutianus (1471– 1526), a refined Erfurt clergyman, wrote to Elector Frederick of Saxony that he had heard the free cities intended, under the cloak of the gospel, to provoke the peasants and the Jews to annihilate the princes and other high nobles. The townsmen want to abolish the princes altogether, he warned, and to erect a republic in the form of Venice or ancient Greece. Popular sovereignty must be hostile to princely rule, and it was a dangerous error to believe that the peasants aimed to wipe out only the clergy.[10]

The belief, or at least the charge, that the rebellion flowed from urban fonts must have been widespread. Johann Fabri (d. 1541) thought it necessary to defend Constance against suspicion of conspiracy, and Leonhard von Eck accused Memmingen and Kempten of being the instigators of rebellion in the Allgäu.[11] Eck's opinions are instructive, because he knew through his work in the Swabian League in what a predicament the urban governments lay. Sometimes he blamed the Lutherans for the rebellion, sometimes he felt it was a smoke screen for Duke Ulrich's strike to regain his duchy. He came to see, however, that whatever role the Evangelical movement had in touching off the rebels, the insurrection itself aimed at all lordship. "I can't see or judge otherwise," he wrote to Duke Louis from Ulm on February 15, 1525, "than that this affair was begun to suppress the princes and nobles, and it has its origin in the Lutheran doctrines; for the majority of the peasants

---

[8] Steiff and Mehring, *Lieder und Sprüche*, 221, no. 54, stanza 6.
[9] Margrave Casimir of Brandenburg-Ansbach to Count Palatine Frederick, April 9, 1525, quoted by Jörg, *Deutschland*, 135 n. 7. See Friedensburg, *Reichstag zu Speier*, 152–3, 153 n. 2; Sea, "Imperial Cities," 30–7.
[10] Mutianus, *Briefwechsel*, 307, no. 625 (April 25, 1525). See Spitz, *Renaissance*, 130–54; Burger, *Renaissance*, 362–6.
[11] Vögeli, *Schriften*, 2,2:1111–21, with Fabri's defense at 1121; Eck to Duke William of Bavaria, May 25, 1525, in Vogt, *Die bayrische Politik*, 454–6 (also by Jörg, *Deutschland*, 136).

justify their demands from God's Word, the gospel, and brotherly love."[12] Two weeks later, he noted how the rebellion affected the cities: "The peasants' strength grows daily, and they've written to a number of cities, including Ulm, about their attitudes to the cities and how they sympathize with them. For in the towns there is a great split: the poor Lutherans side with the peasants, while the non-Lutherans and rich Lutherans are against the peasants."[13] The fissure ran right through the towns, and Eck sneered at the urban upper classes, "those who thought to rule the world and who told and boasted of their guns, power, and intelligence, are now not safe from their own peasants!"[14] He admitted, however, that the League needed the free cities' support to crush the rebels, for "the peasants are getting stronger very rapidly, though I hope they won't get to enjoy their mischief, if some of the cities, especially Ulm, stand fast."[15] Eck's realistic assessment of the conditions in the cities contrasted vividly with the crude recrimination of Count Palatine Frederick, who charged that the whole city of Nuremberg was on the rebels' side.[16] This was absurd, for the proud Nuremberg patricians believed fervently in the divine right of oligarchy. When the Franconian peasant army in the Aisch River valley asked the senate and the commune of Nuremberg for weapons and food for the fight against Margrave Casimir, the government replied that

we beg to inform you that it is not and has never been the custom here – and would be, in our opinion, incompatible with God's Word and commands – that our commune in this or any other matter would have a part in decisions along with their divinely ordained rulers. This is especially so, as they have been ruled by us in a right and Christian manner, which we have with God's help most diligently and faithfully performed. [To consult them] would mean that

---

[12] Eck to Duke Louis of Bavaria, Ulm, Feb. 15, 1525, in Vogt, *Die bayrische Politik*, 383 (see also 381, 384), and also in G. Franz, *Quellen*, 151, no. 33.
[13] Eck to Duke Louis of Bavaria, March 2, 1525, in Vogt, *Die bayrische Politik*, 402, and also in G. Franz, *Quellen*, 152, no. 33; Matthäus Cardinal Lang, archbishop of Salzburg, noted the same division in a letter to Duke William of Bavaria, May 18, 1525, quoted by Jörg, *Deutschland*, 113.
[14] Eck to Duke William of Bavaria, May 25, 1525, in Vogt, *Die bayrische Politik*, 456, and also in Jörg, *Deutschland*, 153, who reads "Badern" for "Bauern."
[15] Eck to Duke William of Bavaria, Ulm, March 21, 1525, in Vogt, *Die bayrische Politik*, 417, and also in Jörg, *Deutschland*, 120. A Bavarian official at Landsberg wrote to Duke William on April 1, 1525, "Den die Städt' sind Niemand nutz" (ibid., 121).
[16] Count Palatine Frederick to Duke William of Bavaria, Neumarkt, May 5, 1525, in ibid., 154 n. 9.

they would rule us. For this reason we believe it unnecessary to consult with our commune about this matter...[17]

Their rejection of the communal idea, that ordinary folk could govern themselves, could not have been plainer. Most townsmen of wealth, influence, and prestige must have thought similarly, even if it was not always politic to say so. However much they might chuckle at the rebels' humiliation of monks and nobles, they could not want the revolution to succeed.

There was nevertheless some objective truth behind the belief that the revolt on the land had something to do with the cities: first, because their commons sympathized with the rebels and sometimes aided them; second, because the idea and institution of the commune were so very deeply rooted in the cities; and third, because of the urban origin of the ideas and slogans that had catalyzed the rebellion. This complicity with the revolution, deep but unwilled and only sheepishly or secretly acknowledged by the urban oligarchs, lay behind the towns' policy of conciliation. The complicity also explains the initial paralysis with which the cities greeted the rebellions. This paralysis of will impressed Leonhard von Eck, who wrote that "up till now I've seen nothing more frightening than the unheard-of timidity of all rulers... Wherever they've resisted, even a little, the peasants have conquered nothing... In this matter, therefore, the greatest struggle is to bring the rulers to a more manly frame of mind. Then the peasantry is finished."[18] The princes, unconscious of complicity with the rebels or the need to conciliate their sympathizers,[19] recovered their "manly frame of mind" much more quickly than the urban oligarchs did. They took action through the Swabian League.

Since 1500, the princely membership in the Swabian League had slowly grown, until by 1525 it included, besides Charles and Ferdinand (for Württemberg), the archbishop of Mainz, five other South German bishops, six princes from the two Wittelsbach lines, Margrave Casimir,

---

[17] Quoted in ibid., 153 n. 8 (May 27, 1525).
[18] Eck to Duke William of Bavaria, April 13, 1525, in Vogt, *Die bayrische Politik*, 431, and also in G. Franz, *Quellen*, 152, no. 33. Johannes Herolt, a pastor at Schwäbisch Hall, also noted the lords' paralysis. Buchholz, *Regierung Ferdinands*, 2:177 n.
[19] See, however, Elector Frederick's remarkable letter to his brother, Duke John of Saxony, Lochau, April 14, 1525, in G. Franz, *Quellen*, 502, no. 167.

and the landgrave of Hesse. They confronted an Urban House of twenty-six members, led by Augsburg, Nuremberg, and Ulm, and a weak Nobles' House of knights and abbots.[20] When Archduke Ferdinand issued the original call for action in late 1524, asking for aid against his town of Waldshut and the uplanders of the southern Black Forest, the Leaguers at first reacted with skepticism – perhaps under Bavarian influence, for Eck suspected that "the archduke is reaching for the reins; if the emperor or Ferdinand gets them, then Your Princely Grace [Duke William] will be poorer than I am."[21] Bavaria was then still untouched by the storm. What finally spurred the Leaguers to action was the advance of Duke Ulrich's Swiss troops in February 1525, using the rural disturbances as cover.[22]

The League's capital at Ulm lay very near the home district of Upper Swabia's first peasants to rise, the Baltringers, and the city's internal security was questionable. Ulrich Arzt reported to Augsburg that "rumors are going about that the commons at Ulm will not allow hostile action against the peasants,"[23] and he favored mobilizing the League's army. Until that happened, however, and the northern members such as the Franconian bishops and the Hessian landgrave were not yet convinced of its necessity, the League had to negotiate with the rebels when it could, notably on the abbot of Kempten's lands in January.[24] The threat from Duke Ulrich's force – six thousand Swiss foot and three thousand horse – gave the Upper Swabian peasant armies time to unite into the Christian Federation, with which the League had to strike a truce in late March. "When we are finished with Duke Ulrich,"

---

[20] Bock, *Der Schwäbische Bund*, 162–84; Greiner, "Politik," 10–12.

[21] *ARC*, 1:300 (April 1524); Klüpfel, *Urkunden*, 2:281–5. See Scott, "Reformation and Peasants' War," on this theater of rebellion. The League's skepticism is revealed in its decision at Ulm on Oct. 28, 1524, to meet again on March 12, four and a half months later, though the meeting was moved up to Feb. 5. Greiner, "Politik," 17, 19.

[22] Greiner, "Politik," 17–18, 20–1. See Haushofer, "Ereignisse," 268–85, who modifies the conventional view that Bavaria was untouched by the revolution. See also the *Landschreiber* at Ravensburg to the *Landvogt* of Upper Swabia, May 5, 1525, in Baumann, *Akten*, 264–5, no. 266. On Duke Ulrich's invasion, see Feyler, *Beziehungen*, 250–99.

[23] Vogt, "Correspondenz, I," 300, no. 22, quoted also by Greiner, "Politik," 30. See ibid., 24, 29, 88–9; Blickle, *Revolution von 1525*, 173–4 (English: *Revolution of 1525*, 111) for examples of collaboration between townsfolk and rural rebels.

[24] Klüpfel, *Urkunden*, 2:288; Greiner, "Politik," 21–2.

wrote Arzt on March 9, "we must face the peasants."[25] By the end of March, Ulrich's Swiss troops had once more deserted him, and the League's army was marching on Ulm. During April, it crushed or settled with the Upper Swabian peasant armies, one by one, and then moved on to pacify Württemberg and Franconia.

The free cities contributed to the pacification of Upper Swabia only a weak effort to delay a military decision and promote a negotiated peace. "I do not believe that many cities would stand by and do nothing," Leonhard von Eck wrote cynically, "if they weren't concerned for their own property."[26] An exaggeration, perhaps, but the masters of exchange did have to worry about the condition of the producers. All through the critical period in Upper Swabia, from late March until the Treaty of Weingarten on April 24, the Upper Swabian free cities maintained diplomatic contacts with the rebel armies, partly, perhaps, because of the rumblings within their own commons.[27] Their efforts, combined with those of the Governing Council at Esslingen, may have delayed a military decision in Upper Swabia by, at most, a few days.[28] Eck expressed his bemusement with the entire strategy of conciliation:

The good, pious folk in the Governing Council at Esslingen have sent a long letter here to the League, in which they ask us to reflect on these grievous rebellions of the duke of Württemberg and the peasantry. They would be pleased if the latter were invited to arbitration. Which we don't want to do or even think about, much less throw away our time-honored weight and reputation like old whores.[29]

Once the time for delaying was over, Eck and the Austrians encouraged the larger cities to act against their own peasants, just as the League itself was about to move.

Several of the League's middling towns were directly involved in the hostilities. Heilbronn, for example, admitted the Neckar-Odenwald army

---

[25] Vogt, "Correspondenz, I," 363, no. 117. See Greiner, "Politik," 25–50.
[26] Eck to Duke William of Bavaria, Feb. 11, 1525, in Vogt, *Die bayrische Politik*, 381.
[27] See Greiner, "Politik," 55 n. 241, for references. On the cities' conciliation policy, see Klüpfel, *Urkunden*, 2:289–90; Bock, *Der Schwäbische Bund*, 195–6; G. Franz, *Der deutsche Bauernkrieg*, 127–34; Blickle, *Revolution von 1525*, 173 (English: *Revolution of 1525*, 111); Sea, "Imperial Cities," 26–7.
[28] Volk, "Reichspolitik."
[29] Vogt, *Die bayrische Politik*, 408, also quoted by Greiner, "Politik," 61 n. 265, and see 60–5.

of rebels, for which the League later punished it severely. Farther south, Ravensburg and Ueberlingen took strict, repressive actions against their own peasants, whereas Memmingen, in effect the capital of the Upper Swabian revolution, called on the other cloth towns of the region to support its mediation efforts. That such efforts had much influence on the outcome may well be doubted, but still the Upper Swabian cities strove for conciliation until well after the revolution's defeat.[30]

"We city folk are making ourselves a reputation in this war," wrote Arzt to Peutinger at the end of March 1525, "that will long cling to us."[31] They surely did, and the League's princes later tried to revenge themselves on the towns that had not supported the war wholeheartedly. Nuremberg's council worked tirelessly to protect the smaller cities and shore up the cities' battered prestige in the League. No aid was forthcoming from Ferdinand, for the crisis of 1525 had unmasked Austrian weakness, except in concert with the Bavarians, and to the Austro-Bavarian tune the League's cities willy nilly danced. Ferdinand had not supplied the kind of central leadership and vigor the Habsburg system required, and the Governing Council's efforts were merely pitiful.[32]

The Swabian cities in the crisis of 1525 had no alternative to the Swabian League, which the princes now dominated. On the Upper Rhine, things were different. As early as the late summer of 1523, a Habsburg agent reported that Strasbourg's government was intriguing with the Swiss cities,[33] and, when the Edict of Burgos became known, the rumor became reality. Talks began with Basel, Bern, and Zurich in the autumn of 1524, continued through 1525, and, after an interruption, resumed in 1527 and led to the formation of a Christian Federation [*christliches Burgrecht*] two years later.[34]

The crisis of 1525 also drew Strasbourg's rulers more closely into their own region. They became active in negotiations between rebels and their lords all over Lower Alsace and the Ortenau and other right-bank lands, and they pursued conciliation with far greater success than

---

[30] Greiner, "Politik," 56–60, 62–5, 75, 80. For the situation at Memmingen, see Blickle, *Revolution von 1525*, 166–73 (English: *Revolution of 1525*, 106–10).

[31] Vogt, "Correspondenz, I," no. 386.

[32] Lhotsky, *Zeitalter*, 146–67; Greiner, "Politik," 86–8.

[33] Michel Gilles to Charles V, Constance, Aug. 8, 1523, quoted by Baumgarten, *Geschichte*, 2:313 n.

[34] Hauswirth, *Landgraf Philipp*, 157–60; Brady, *Ruling Class*, 209, 239–40.

their Swabian counterparts did. Strasbourg could do nothing, to be sure, to avert the Lower Alsatian peasants' defeat at the hands of Duke Antoine of Lorraine at Saverne on May 18, but on the right bank its politicians mediated a series of treaties (Renchen, Basel) that brought peace without the savage repression that was elsewhere the rule. This was limited success, perhaps, but no other free city achieved anything like so much.[35]

With the Revolution of 1525, the history of the urban front proper comes to a close. This short, lively story contains several lessons. First, there was to be no "Austrian way" to a German monarchy, at least not under Charles V and not in cooperation with the southern free cities. Second, Charles saw in Maximilian's South German system chiefly a source of money, and Ferdinand became distracted, after a few years of rule, by the Jagellonian inheritance. Third, the Swabian League, the system's political hub, passed into princely control and thereby lost its role as an alternative to the Diet. Fourth, though the urban governments were being pushed by their commons toward the Evangelical program, every step deepened the gulf between them and the monarchy. The cities had not lost entirely their former unity, but until some way could be found to remove the religious issue from the usual patterns of politics, they could no longer rely on the monarchy as their obvious partner. Between the great crisis of 1525 and the discovery of such a way lay the next thirty years.

The cities adrift, 1525–8

Auf, auf, ihr werden deudschen stedt,
dass ihr euch ja ietzt nicht verspett,
ihr seit im ober- oder niderland,
das spil in guter acht hand!
Der teufel hat was böses im sinn,
zu treiben meint er ganz gewinn,
weil er so schwinde list erfunden,
dass durch den babst keiser uberwunden
und endlich dahin beredet ist,
sein gewalt zustrecken dieser frist

---

[35] See Blickle, *Revolution von 1525*, 174–8 (English: *Revolution of 1525*, 111–13), and above all the richly detailed study by Rott, "La Guerre des Paysans."

wider ewer glied, die euch beiston;
etlich fürsten deudscher nacion
zu strafen unter diesem nam,
sam werns dem reich ungehorsam,
sei auch keins wegs gesinnet nicht,
der religion unru anzuricht.[36]

The Revolution of 1525 cut the cities adrift. The Swabian League no longer gave sufficient protection, the Habsburgs no longer wanted to lead the cities, and for three or four years the free cities resisted the forces that were splitting the Empire into religious parties and tried to patch together new solidarities out of pieces from the past. Gradually, they began to yield to the logic of parties determined not by estates – cities, princes, nobles – but by religion, and sooner or later most of them joined the Protestant Smalkaldic League, formed in 1531. How they fared in that alliance is a story that cannot be told here.[37] Nor can the story of the last decade of the Swabian League, which expired in 1534, though it is vital to the history of the Swabian and Franconian cities and to the course of the Reformation in South Germany. Nothing illustrates the wreckage of Emperor Maximilian's system better, for example, than does the reconquest of Württemberg for Ulrich in 1534, an apple plucked from a powerless hand.[38] It is enough here to point out that during the early 1540s the old tendencies, both the idea of partnership with the monarchy and that of turning Swiss, revived among the South German free cities, and this scene, with Nuremberg and Strasbourg as its protagonists, ends the story. It needs to be prefaced, however, by an account of how the old ideas and old solutions accompanied the cities, especially the big ones, through the years of drift that followed 1525.[39]

For about one year following the suppression of the great rebellion's

---

[36] "Wake, awake, you noble German towns, don't be caught in bed, in the South or in the Lowlands, take care what is afoot. The Evil One has his game and plans to win it all, for he's caught with cruel cleverness our emperor in the papal snares. Our emperor has been misled to use his might at this time against those who are your friends. Under this design he will punish some German princes who disobey Imperial laws and tell you he has no desire to touch the holy Faith." Liliencron, *Volkslieder*, 4:324, no. 524, lines 1–16.
[37] Brady, "Phases and Strategies," especially 166–73.
[38] Brady, "Princes' Reformation vs. Urban Liberty"; G. Schmidt, *Städtetag*, 211–12.
[39] The following lines depend on G. Schmidt, *Städtetag*, 154–64; and H. Schmidt, "Reichsstädte," 497–511.

main phase, the leading free cities engaged in an intense search for some form of collective security. This activity began with a very poorly attended Urban Diet at Ulm in late July 1525, which Nuremberg, Augsburg, and Ulm called without even consulting Strasbourg and Frankfurt, and it ended for the time being with the Imperial Diet of Speyer in the summer of 1526. Two lines of discussion ran through the meetings: The Urban Diet confronted once more the idea of a general urban military league; and, in between the Urban Diet's sessions, Nuremberg, Augsburg, and Ulm tried to work out a Three Cities' League. The general urban league made very slow headway, because, although the Nurembergers insisted that any such alliance must have the blessing of Charles and Ferdinand, the cities' envoys learned in 1525 that the archduke harbored a deep suspicion of all urban assemblies.[40] This estrangement, which was a fruit of 1524–5, could hardly be made good. The deeper reason, however, for the failure of the general urban league was that the large cities abandoned the idea. This was the import of two meetings of envoys from Nuremberg, Augsburg, and Ulm to discuss a Three Cities' League that were held at Heidenheim and Giengen in northeastern Swabia in August and October 1525.[41] Augsburg's instruction for Heidenheim affords a clear insight into why the large cities shunned a league with the small ones. "Such a league," it ran,

would certainly be disadvantageous and even intolerable to the three cities, and it would lead in time to their ruin, for they would have to be perpetually ready to aid the other, smaller cities. But the latter would not come forth with the aid they owed the large cities. Besides, the free and Imperial cities lie distant

---

[40] G. Schmidt, *Städtetag*, 159; H. Schmidt, "Reichsstädte," 500, 506–8.

[41] G. Schmidt, *Städtetag*, 154–6, 158; H. Schmidt, "Reichsstädte," 502–4, 509–11. I use the Augsburg documents in StA Augsburg, Litteralien-Sammlung, at Aug. 20, 1525, consisting of an instruction (fols. 2ʳ–7ᵛ), notes by an envoy (fol. 8ʳ⁻ᵛ), and the recess of Heidenheim (fols. 9ʳ–18ᵛ). Envoys were Conrad Herwart and Antoni Bimel for Augsburg; Martin Tucher and Clemens Volckamer for Nuremberg; and Conrad Rot, Sebastian Renntz, Claus Greck, and Bernhard Besserer for Ulm. The Ulmers were all members of the V Geheimen. Fabian, *Beschlüsse*, 2:168–71. Heidenheim was then mortgaged by Württemberg to Ulm. Heyd, *Ulrich*, 3:30–2. The Augsburg documents on the meeting at Giengen are in StA Augsburg, Litteralien-Sammlung, at Oct. 28, 1525, consisting of instruction (fols. 2ʳ–6ᵛ) and recess (fols. 7ʳ–18ᵛ). Envoys were Conrad Herwart and Antoni Bimel for Augsburg, Christoph Tetzel and Clemens Volckamer for Nuremberg, and Bernhard Besserer and Sebastian Renntz for Ulm. A very small free city, Giengen lay below Heidenheim in the valley of the Brenz, a left-hand tributary of the Danube.

from one another, and the aid would not be forthcoming... Further, from the tales of former days it seems that when the free and Imperial cities were allied among themselves and took action against a neighboring prince, then the other princes, or most of them, did great damage to the cities.[42]

The Augsburgers dreamed of former days, of the great age of Maximilian's South German system. Not only did they want a new alliance of Swabian free cities with Charles and Ferdinand (though excluding Württemberg, "because it is ever and again attacked by Duke Ulrich"[43]), they also wanted to revive the old Lower Union. One ought to consider, they wrote, "whether then the free and Imperial cities on the Rhine should come to acceptable and honorable terms with His Imperial Majesty and His Princely Grace [Ferdinand] and their western lands – Alsace, the Sundgau, and the Breisgau, as is appropriate – and form a league with them."[44] Strasbourg, which had been proposed as a fourth member of the alliance of Nuremberg, Augsburg, and Ulm, could not be included "because of the distance."[45] Far better that the Rhenish towns form their own alliance with Austria – then the old dual federations would be restored. As for the religious question, the Augsburgers wanted it "to be laid to rest and not allowed to be mixed into this alliance nor entangled with it."[46]

---

[42] StA Augsburg, Litteralien-Sammlung, at Aug. 20, 1525, fol. 5^{r-v}: "Das solhe verainung durchaus den drein Stetten unfurtreglich unnd ganntz beschwärlich, auch mit der zeit zu verderben dienen wurde, dann si den anndern unnd mynndern zu gut mit ir hilff allwegen gespannen sein muessten, unnd die notturfftig gegenhilff von denselben nit erlangt werden mocht. Zu dem, das die Frei und Reichsstett fer von ain ander gelegen, also die hilff nit erspriessen ... Unnd sich aber aus erganngen alten geschichten erfindet, wa die Frei und Reichsstett allain bei ain annder gewesen, unnd gleich wol ettwan ain Fursten bei inen gehabt, das si dannocht von den anndern Fursten zum merer tail grosse beschedigung entpfanngen haben..." The passage concludes, "Dweil meine herren die verainigung, wie die zu Ulm ausgeschriben ist [by the Urban Diet], nit fur gut ansihet."

[43] Ibid., fol. 6^r: "Der gleichen mochten die Schwabischenn Stett mit kayserlicher Majestät und Fürstlicher Durchlaucht und derselben Graveschafft Tyroll und gepirgleuten auch dermassen sich vergleichen, unnd das Wirtgemberg umbganngen wurde, dweil das fur unnd fur von hertzog Ulrich angefochten wird..."

[44] Ibid., fol. 6^r: "Ob dann die Frei unnd Reichsstett am Rhein sich mit kayserlicher Majestät und Fürstlicher Durchlaucht mit iren vordern lannden, Elsas, Sunggaw und Preisgaw, je nach gestalt der sachen, inen leidlich und träglich vertragen unnd mit inen ain verstandt gemacht hette."

[45] Ibid., fol. 6^r: "Meine herren hetten auch davon geredt, unnd wa die [Strasbourg] neher gelegen weren, die auch gern haben wolten. Aber von wegen der ferre mocht ir hilff den dreien Stetten, unnd die drei Stett inen nit wol erschiessen unnd ettwan zuspaet komen..."

[46] Ibid., fol. 4^r: "Ob dann von der Luterischen sache, Newe Lere oder den predigern wolt geredt werden, wissen die gesanndten sich dagegen wol zuhalten und dieselben mit gutem fueg in Ru stellen, und in disen verstannd nit lassen einmischen noch verwickeln."

The envoys of the three cities did draft a treaty at Heidenheim. Besides modest military aid – three thousand foot and some guns – it reflects the revolutionary events of that year: "If it should happen that in one of the three cities disputes should arise between the council and the people, ...the other cities should, upon request from the affected one, send envoys who, with divine aid and grace, shall do everything humanly possible to settle these conflicts."[47] The envoys also firmly admitted that the smaller towns, besides their unwillingness to pay for protection, might become disheartened and put themselves under princely protection.[48] This was a standing complaint of the big-city politicians and the chief reason for their aversion to a general urban league. "With the best of will," wrote Lazarus Spengler to the city secretary of Strasbourg, Peter Butz (d. 1531), some months later,

I have found thus far at Imperial Diets and other assemblies so much mistrust among the cities, that no city has the faintest notion of how it could in extremise depend on the others. Also, as you may well know, the recent disturbances have caused such great trouble ... so that hardly any town government will any longer tolerate God's Word and the holy gospel within its walls ... Each strives to find favor more with a gracious emperor than with a gracious God. But now is the time to decide! Either we are and remain Christians, or we deny Christ. There is no middle ground.[49]

Big talk from Spengler, but in fact his own government wanted the Three Cities' League approved by the emperor and Ferdinand.[50]

---

[47] Ibid., fol. 14ʳ⁻ᵛ (Art. 9): "Item, ob sich (wie der allmechtig mit sonndern gnaden furhietten welle) weitter begebe, das in gemelter dreier Stett, ainder oder mer, zwischen ainem Rate unnd der seinen sich irrungen zutruegen oder ereugten, wie die darrurten, so solten die drei Stett aufferfordern der Stat, in der sich vorgelauter weise irrungen begeben, aber furdelich bei ain annder erscheinenn, unnd vermittel gotlicher hilff und gnaden allen menschlichen und moglichen fleis, fur unnd ankern, damit dieselben spenn guetlich hingelegt, vertragen unnd also die drei Erbern Stett, durch obangezaigt mittel unnd weg, wider Reich unnd den landtfriden an iren oberkaiten, oder in annder weise, von niemandt, wer der oder die wern, beschwerdt und belestigt wirden."

[48] Ibid., fol. 16ʳ⁻ᵛ (Art. 13): "Daneben ist aber je auch zu bedencken, wa sich die drei mer gemelten von gemainen Erbern Frei und Reichsstetten entlich sonndern, und sich mit den selben in ainich weise oder wege nit einlassen, geben oder verstenndigen wolten, oder wollen, das solhs bei gemainen Erbernn Frei unnd Reichsstetten nit klain bewegknus, forcht unnd beschwernus gepern. Sonnder villeicht dieselben zum tail als verlassen verursachen und dahin dringen wirde, nachgedenncken zuhaben, bei Fürst oder anndern irs gleichen, schirm, hilff oder trost zu suchen, etc."

[49] *PCSS*, 1:256, no. 451. See Rott, "La Réforme à Nuremberg et à Strasbourg," 101–2, 124–42, who prints fragments of the Butz–Spengler correspondence.

[50] StA Augsburg, Litteralien-Sammlung, at Aug. 20, 1525, fols. 16ᵛ–17ʳ (Art. 14): "Item, so ist

Even the narrower alliance of big cities seemed hopeless. Augsburg instructed its envoy to the Giengen meeting in October 1525 that the time was inopportune, because an Imperial Diet was about to convene within its walls,[51] and the envoys at Giengen made little progress. One reason was Augsburg's caution; another was Nuremberg's tendency to wax hot or cold about alliance, according to whether the pressure on the Evangelicals intensified or eased. The general league of cities was, for the moment, a dead idea, and when Strasbourg asked in the spring of 1526 that an Urban Diet be called to Speyer, Nuremberg replied that it was inopportune and proposed instead that Strasbourg join the alliance talks of the three big cities.[52]

One reason for the drifting negotiations of these years was the first contacts among Evangelical cities and princes, which would lead in 1531 to the formation of the Smalkaldic League. Ironically enough, Nuremberg, which later boycotted the Protestant league, seems to have been the first city to strive for an understanding with princes based on religion, making contact with princes of Saxony, Brandenburg-Ansbach, and Hesse in October and November 1525.[53] When, however, Elector John of Saxony and Landgrave Philip of Hesse approached the major towns with an offer of alliance, which they did during the Imperial Diet held at Speyer in the summer of 1526, the urban governments rejected the idea of a league with princes of the same religion.[54]

Strasbourg's policies during these years also display the drifting confusion of the situation. Strasbourg's government had broken off its talks with Basel, Zurich, and Bern, once the immediate danger of revolution was past.[55] The situation here, at Constance, and at several Upper

---

von der Erbern Stett Bottschafften ganntz fur fruchtber bedacht, wa man sich obgelawter weise vertrewlich zusamen verpringen, das man solhs mit vorwissen der kayserlichen Majestät oder Fürstlichen Durchlaucht thun solt unnd muest."

[51] StA. Augsburg, Litteralien-Sammlung, at Oct. 28, 1525, fol. 4^r: "Darumb ein Erber Rat acht und es darfur hat, vor endung obgemelter sachenn, der notdurfft nach statlich unnd beschleusslich nit kond noch moge inn diser sach gehandlt werdenn." On the Diet of Augsburg in 1525, see H. Schmidt, "Reichsstädte," 511–19, and there, too, the following remark about Nuremberg at 519.

[52] Strasbourg to Ulm, March 24, 1526; Nuremberg to Ulm, April 2, 1526; both in StA Augsburg, Litteralien-Sammlung, at dates.

[53] H. Schmidt, "Reichsstädte," 513–14.

[54] Fabian, *Entstehung*, 31.

[55] Brady, *Ruling Class*, 240. In my "Jacob Sturm of Strasbourg," 153–4, I misjudged the significance of the religious question to Strasbourg's policy at this point. On Constance, see Rublack, *Einführung*, 120–8.

Swabian cities was complicated by the fact that since the Revolution of 1525 a running quarrel between Saxon and southern Evangelical theologians and preachers had broken out, which would soon split the Evangelical movement into two parties, called "Lutherans" and "Zwinglians." Many of these southern cities found themselves branded "Zwinglian" or "sacramentarian" (from the quarrel over the Eucharist). The charge was true, not because they allowed the reformer of Zurich to guide their reformations, nor because they professed his doctrines, but because his theology best formulated the southern cities' experience of an integrative gospel of cooperation between clergy and laity, church and government, government and commune, and city and city.[56] The Lutheran attempt to link "sacramentarianism" with rebellion expressed, in the psychological backwash of the Revolution of 1525, rulers' fear of the Swiss model's attraction for all South Germans who wanted "to be their own lords."

Neither a Swiss alliance, an urban league, nor a union with the Evangelical princes seemed to satisfy the Strasbourg government's hunger for security in this era of drift. Gradually, Strasbourg fell in with the feeble notion of a big cities' alliance, making it a Four Cities' League, discussions of which came to a head at Geislingen, in Ulm territory, from Sept. 14 through 15, 1528.[57] It was a gala gathering of big-city politicians: Conrad Herwart of Augsburg, Jacob Sturm of Strasbourg, Bernhard Besserer of Ulm, and Bernhard Baumgartner of Nuremberg. They found no ground for unity. The three League cities wanted to except the emperor and the Swabian League from the potential foes; Augsburg wanted religion excluded, and Ulm wanted it included; and Nuremberg wanted to curry Charles's favor. The great stumbling block was the Swabian League, now emerging as a barrier to the free spread of Evangelical religion in South Germany, but which the League cities would not abandon. Jacob Sturm, by contrast, insisted that "the League must be blocked."[58] The deadlock could not be broken, not then and

---

[56] See Locher, *Zwinglische Reformation*, 452–501, who frankly confirms the political character of Zwingli's theology, though his discussion of Zwingli's policy toward the Habsburgs (540–2) is not completely clear.

[57] The recess and other acts are in *RTA, jR*, 7:336–41, 1065–6; the Strasbourg instruction by Jacob Sturm and Peter Butz is in *PCSS*, 1:305–6, no. 536 (before Sept. 13, 1528).

[58] *PCSS*, 1:306. See Augsburg to Ulm, Dec. 9, 1528, in StA Augsburg, Litteralien-Sammlung, at date; *RTA, jR*, 7:336–7, 340 (Ulm), 339–40 (Nuremberg).

not later, when an attempt was made to expand the discussions to five cities through the inclusion of Frankfurt.[59] The idea of a big-cities' alliance simply was not viable, no more than was that of the league of all cities, which cropped up once more, with predictable effect, at the Urban Diet at Esslingen from June 27 through 30, 1528.[60] So far down did the Urban Diet's prestige sink during the years of drift that, when Jacob Sturm and Arnoldt von Siegen of Cologne were appointed as envoys to Ferdinand by the Urban Diet in 1526, both men declined to serve. While the cities' reputation for intrigue and sedition swelled on rumor's wings, their political solidarity and confidence leaked away.[61]

In this atmosphere of confusion and hesitation, the spirit of one urban government stood out. The militancy of Constance's magistrates comes to life in their instruction for Conrad Zwick to the hopeless Urban Diet at Esslingen in July 1528.[62] The princes' refusal of the cities' rights in the Imperial Diet, they thought, made it impossible for the cities to defend themselves there, especially as the Diet now followed the orders of "certain people," the bishops, who strove to crush urban liberties. Their attitude and that of the emperor proved that "an army of Germans and foreigners will be put over the Germans, but first of all over the cities." Then the free cities and the Swiss would share a common fate. The bishops hid this all under the cloak of religion, and when they had mediatized their neighboring cities, "no longer will there be a free, German government, such as our ancestors bequeathed to us, but a government of force and domination, as in other nations."[63] Since the clergy, the emperor, and the king had become partners "and do secret things, so that the clergy have become their confessors and most trusted advisors, the cities can hope for nothing from them – not for law or justice, nor for any peace kept in the Empire."

As the Constancers believed that the real threat was to urban liberty,

---

[59] *RTA, jR*, 7:1062–3; Naujoks, *Obrigkeitsgedanke*, 68; Buck, *Anfänge*, 485.

[60] Klüpfel, *Urkunden*, 2:347; *RTA, jR*, 7:326, 331–2, 1059–64.

[61] *Annales de Sébastien Brant*, no. 4746 (July 27, 1528). For rumors of plots among the cities, see Thomas Gassner to Joachim Vadian, Lindau, June 12, 1538, in Arbenz, *Briefsammlung*, 4:119, no. 526; Governing Council to the Urban Diet, Esslingen, July 24, 1528, and the Urban Diet's reply, July 29, 1528, in *RTA, jR*, 7:326, 331–2, nos. 1234, 1245.

[62] *RTA, jR*, 7:1069–71 (July 15, 1528). See Buck, *Anfänge*, 485–6; Rublack, *Einführung*, 126–7.

[63] *RTA, jR*, 7:1060. See Hans Ehinger to Memmingen, April 15, 1529, who wrote that the division of the cities would make Germany into a "Welschland" and bring the cities into utter servitude. Klüpfel, *Urkunden*, 2:344.

their remedy was an urban league like those of old, "but since the league was dispersed, many cities have been mediatized, lost their freedoms, and become princes' towns." An urban league was now needed far more than in the past, considering "how much more powerful the forces against the cities are now than formerly." Therefore, the cities had to come together, "to protect and to defend each other's land, people, liberties, rights, and privileges, body and goods, real and personal, to assure the rights to buy and sell, and to further their honor and welfare."[64] This league ought not be based on religion, because, as faith "is an undeserved, free gift of grace from God, it is not fitting that any force be used in such matters." Instead, the alliance treaty ought to provide "that each city in its own jurisdiction and lands should arrange matters of faith and ecclesiastical affairs, that is, what concerns the Christian religion and the soul and conscience, in such a way as can be justified before God and Holy Writ."[65] This was nothing more and nothing less than the ruling of the Imperial Diet of Speyer in 1526, that each Imperial estate must proceed, until a General Council met to resolve these matters, "in such a way as can be justified to God and the emperor." It was the ideal solution for the free cities, both because it suited very well their particularist traditions and Zwinglian inclinations in ecclesiastical affairs, and because it removed them from danger by effectively eliminating the enforcement of religious doctrine and canon law from the level of Imperial government.

The Constancers' proposal in 1528 shows that one political effect of the urban reform was not so much to thrust religion into political thinking in a new way as to revitalize traditional urban notions of liberty. This, indeed, was the legacy of the Evangelical movement's religious communalism, of "Zwinglianism," which inspired urban governments to face all their foes squarely, even crowned ones, and which contrasts dramatically with the political quietism of urban Lutheranism. The origin of this difference is probably to be sought less in theology, which merely attempted to explain perceived reality through unperceived truth, than in the relative social distances between rulers and ruled. On the one hand, the oligarchs believed that their own solidarity with their citizens

---

[64] *RTA, jR,* 7:1060.
[65] Ibid., 1060–1. See Friedensburg, *Reichstag zu Speier,* 481–6; Wohlfeil, "Speyerer Reichstag," 15–18.

demanded a defense against all external threats to their liberties; on the other, the oligarchs believed that only their own obedience to higher authority guaranteed their subjects' obedience to them. The difference can only be explained, therefore, in terms of the different social evolutions and social situations of the different urban ruling classes.[66]

The militant Constancers also unmasked the cities' situation more clearly than any other proposal had done. The partnership with the Habsburg monarchy, the heart of Maximilian's South German system, was dead, killed by the advance of the gospel among the townsmen and its rejection by the emperor. The free cities were then back on their own resources, their own united strength, as in the days of the urban leagues of old. They had to defend alone their precious liberties against all foes, bishops, and other princes – but also the emperor and his brother. They had moved squarely into the situation in which their Swiss neighbors had always found themselves, for Austria the friend had become a foe. From Constance's perspective, the coming of the Reformation had turned the free cities Swiss.

Reprise: Strasbourg, Constance, and turning Swiss

Den helden wil ich nennen,
Huldrich ist er genant,
vom gschlecht hat er des namen
Zwingli, euch wol bekant;
den hat allein die ere
des höchsten waren gott
fürgstelt mit syner lere,
damit man hielt syn bot.
Ouch ist im angelegen
ein gemeine eidgnoschaft
domit und nit vergeben
ein christlich burgerschaft,
sich täglich thet berümen,
sam wärents all fromm lüt,

---

[66] I depend greatly here on the discussion by H. Schmidt, "Reichsstädte," 666–81.

ouch schalkheit hüpsch verblümen,
als achtent sys für nüt.[67]

Huldrych Zwingli believed that the expansion of the Gospel was a vital
part of its proclamation, and his message combined the communal principle as the basis of reform with the defense of particularist liberties
against Roman Empire and Roman Church.[68] He warned that Charles
V strove for "a restitution of the Roman Empire," that "one should not
trust the friendship of tyrants," and that "under the guise of religion
the free cities will lose their liberties."[69] Nowhere did this message
dovetail more neatly into civic traditions and native reform movements
than at Strasbourg and Constance, whose guilds had long ago conquered
their respective city halls. Evangelical clergymen began to clothe the
Evangelical message in the language of revitalized civic and communal
ideals, the language of the sacral corporation. The message of the Evangelical urban reformers interacted powerfully with the burghers' communal values, so that "the victory of the 'Reformed' Reformation in the
Upper German imperial cities is finally explained by the encounter of
the peculiarly 'urban' theology of Zwingli and Bucer with the particularly
communal spirit in Upper Germany."[70]

The urban Reformation also unleashed powerful new federal im-
pulses, which radiated from the city of Zurich and threatened to burst
through the boundary that Maximilian von Bergen had counseled Charles
V to keep tight against Swiss expansion. The Evangelical movement
awakened new expansionist dreams in the mind of Huldrych Zwingli.
His first contacts with Strasbourg politicians in 1524 coincided with the

---

[67] "There is a noble hero, Huldrych is his name. He comes from good family, the Zwinglis, as
you know. He it is who teaches in his doctrine true the honor of the Living God, whose
commandments we must obey. He also serves all the Swiss and labors not in vain for a Christian
Federation. The people, however, pride themselves on being pious folk; they give themselves
to mischief and hold his plans for nought." Liliencron, *Volkslieder*, 4:37, no. 431, stanzas 9–
10.

[68] Hauswirth, *Landgraf Philipp*, 65–100; Bender, *Reformationsbündnisse*, 157–62; Locher, *Zwinglische Reformation*, 344–63, with rich literature.

[69] Bender, *Reformationsbündnisse*, 159, quoting Siegfried Rother, *Grundlagen*, 79.

[70] Moeller, *Reichsstadt*, 67 (English: *Imperial Cities*, 103); Oberman, *Werden und Wertung*, 336–7
(English: *Masters*, 267), on the unity of the urban Reformation. It is Moeller's great merit to
have given generalized form and extensive documentation to an interpretation developed by
Wilhelm Bofinger in a Tübingen dissertation, "Oberdeutschtum und württembergische Reformation" (partly published as "Kirche und werdender Territorialstaat").

first alliance talks among the cities, which began and continued under the Ammeisterships of men – Claus Kniebis, Daniel Mieg, Martin Pfarrer, and Martin Herlin – who led the militant faction in Strasbourg's government.[71] The rise of Zwingli's influence among the preachers at Strasbourg coincided with the renewal of political friendship with the old comrades upriver.

The institution through which Strasbourg, Constance, and the leading Swiss cities bound themselves together was the Christian Federation (*christliches Burgrecht*), a religiously colored version of a very old form of association, the *Burgrecht*.[72] The *Burgrecht* was an exchange of the rights of citizenship between two or more powers, more favored by the Swiss cities than by the rural federations. The institution had played a major role in the Confederacy's expansion and was still in use. On December 28, 1518, for example, Bern, Fribourg, and Solothurn concluded such a treaty with the Burgundian free city of Besançon.[73] Constance's treaty with Zurich in 1527 was of quite traditional form, providing that "we together and each for the other receive and accept the loyal citizens and dependents [*schirmsgenossen*] of the other."[74] The one new element in the *Burgrechte* of the Reformation era was the forging of such associations among the regimes alone, and no longer the communes as well, a change that likely reflected the general growth of oligarchy. The *Burgrecht* concluded among Strasbourg, the Swiss cities, and Philip of Hesse on November 18, 1530, was of this untraditional kind.[75]

When the news spread that, as Christoph Kress of Nuremberg wrote, Constance "has already turned Swiss,"[76] there were those who drew the (largely correct) conclusion that movement toward the Confederacy meant looser ties to the Empire and hostility to Austria.[77] At Constance,

---

[71] On the first contacts, see Brady, *Ruling Class*, 209 n. 33, and on the militants, 209–11.

[72] Bender, *Reformationsbündnisse*, 11–52.

[73] Formed at the initiative of Besançon. See *EA*, 3,2:1132, 1135, and the treaty's text on 1421–4.

[74] Quoted by Bender, *Reformationsbündnisse*, 43, from *EA*, 4,1a:1511.

[75] Bender, *Reformationsbündnisse*, 7–10, esp. 9 n. 7. Note, however, that Solothurn's treaty with the county of Montbeliard was also a *Burgrecht*. *EA*, 3,2:1135, 1163, and see 1169, 1173–4, 1180. On the Hessian *Burgrecht*, see Hauswirth, *Landgraf Philipp*, 221–9.

[76] Kress to Gerwig Blarer, Nuremberg, Jan. 2, 1528, and Blarer's reply of Jan. 11, in Blarer, *Briefe und Akten*, 1:106, lines 17–19; 107, lines 12–17; and 108, lines 1–3; nos. 171–2. The latter text supports Bender's interpretation of the *Burgrecht*.

[77] See the Regime at Innsbruck to King Ferdinand, March 26, 1529, in *RTA, jR* 7:609–10, where it is argued that the common religion will lead Strasbourg and Constance from alliance into

Austria was a palpable presence, especially since the religious question had brought Habsburg policy into line with the episcopal aims, and Austrian power was becoming the cornerstone of the effort to save Catholicism in southwestern Germany.[78]

Zwingli, on the other side, had by 1529 evolved a plan to unite the Swiss and Swabian cities through a *Burgrecht*, thereby extending his own gospel and the anti-Habsburg front far to the north, while at the same time gaining the power to break the Forest Cantons.[79] In the following year, sensing perhaps the limited potential of an urban league, he dropped it in favor of an international alliance of all anti-Habsburg powers. In 1529, however, his scheme for a cities' league came just as Lutheran agitation against him was reaching its peak. The Upper Swabian cities, too, were just then searching for some new form of solidarity. An Ulm document spoke of the free cities as "an instrument of God"; an assembly at Memmingen on July 20, 1529, referred to "a Christian alliance in the matter concerning the holy gospel"; and Bernhard Besserer even proposed in September of the same year that the Swabian and Swiss cities "have a Christian and trusting care for one another."[80]

Most zealous in this cause was Constance, which was to some degree Ulm's rival for influence in the other towns – Memmingen, Biberach, Kempten, Isny, and Lindau. "If the free cities go down," the Constancers warned Zurich and Bern in July 1529, "the Swiss will find it hard to resist." Conversely, if the Swiss were crushed, "then the free cities will be mediatized without much difficulty."[81] The pristine urban gospel, with its profound sense of the direct connection between true religion and true liberty, thus revitalized briefly the impulse in free cities to turn Swiss. The cow was not to moo from the bridge at Ulm, however, for

---

full membership in the Confederacy. Constance, however, contended that its pact with Zurich and Bern was established "allain von wegen des globens und was daruss kommen wurd." Fabian, *Abschiede*, 50. See Hauswirth, *Landgraf Philipp*, 130.

[78] See Rublack, *Einführung*, 17, 211 n. 29; Oberman, *Werden und Wertung*, 304–28 (English: *Masters*, 240–59).

[79] Hauswirth, *Landgraf Philipp*, 129–37. The Swabian free cities do not figure in Zwingli's anti-Habsburg "consilium rerum gallicarum" of Feb. 1530, though Constance and Strasbourg do. Ibid., 184–93. In my "Jacob Sturm and the Lutherans," 193–4, I failed to distinguish clearly between Zwingli's two plans. On the Forest Cantons' resistance, see Bender, *Reformationsbündnisse*, 165–8; Locher, *Zwinglische Reformation*, 156 n. 269.

[80] *RTA, jR,* 7:180, no. 346, and 183, no. 352; Bender, *Reformationsbündnisse*, 170, quoting Ernst, "Bernhard Besserer," 93.

[81] *EA,* 4,1b:304–5; *RTA, jR,* 7:197, lines 38–40.

it was Ulm's Besserer who veered around to work against the spread of Zurich's and Constance's influence into Upper Swabia.[82] There were other reasons, of course, why nothing came of the scheme for an urban league. The Ulm–Constance–Zurich axis ran through lands dominated by Austrian Swabia, the Catholic towns north of Lake Constance, and the Upper Swabian nobles – the Montforts and the like. In this respect, little had changed since 1453, except that Austria now lay on the other side, and so did some of the towns. The problem lay, as ever, not in the cities but in the control of the broad lands between the cities, and here the lack of rural communal federations *à la suisse* still blocked the possibility to form urban ones.

One has nonetheless to be impressed by the power of "Zwinglian" Evangelical religion to pump new vigor into the old particularist republicanism. In the influence of their preachings on public ideals and sentiments, the urban preachers of the German South resembled Florence's Savonarola more than they did Wittenberg's Luther. The chief difference lay in the need, given South Germany's different social and political conditions, of the cities for powerful partners if they were to defend their liberties, not to speak of larger institutions more suitable to their interests. The religious issue had deprived them of the traditional partner, the Habsburgs and Austria, and Zwingli's failure to master even the Confederacy and his death at Kappel in 1531 removed another. Once the two traditional alternatives disappeared from realistic political calculations, an alliance with the Protestant princes gained compelling logic.

The Smalkaldic League of Protestant powers, however, could never attract those politicians who clung to the pristine Zwinglian union of true religion and liberty, the latter in the old, particularist, communal sense. At Strasbourg, where Zurich's defeat and Zwingli's death in 1531 removed the idea of turning Swiss from the government's political agenda,

---

[82] Walther, "Bernhard Besserer," 20–7. Armed resistance to the emperor was also a major issue at Ulm, supported by Biberach against Kempten, Lindau, Memmingen, and Isny. The Ulmers asserted that "dan uns wil nit gepurn, [uns] wider *ksl. Mt.* zu setzen. Dan wir finden im rechten, dem kaiser in allem gehorsam [zu] sein, obe er uns gleich unrecht thue." Lindau countered: "Das man sech, das es der pfaffen ding sei ... " *RTA, jR,* 8:219–20, no. 560 (Sept. 5–7, 1529). On the Ulm–Constance rivalry, see Walther, "Bernhard Besserer," 26 n. 2; Buck, *Anfänge,* 494–6. Memmingen, too, seems to have opposed a Swiss–Swabian urban league. See Klüpfel, *Urkunden,* 2:345–6.

this idea lived on in the mind and will of the man who, more than any other, had led the city's Evangelical movement to its remarkable political successes during the mid-1520s. Claus Kniebis or his parents came from the right-bank lands, for his mother was a Rastatt woman, and his name suggests a mountain district in the central Black Forest.[83] He studied law at Freiburg im Breisgau and became a wealthy man through means unknown, though he owned lots of rural property and was one of those who profited from the dissolution of Strasbourg's religious houses. Kniebis took the Evangelical religion, which he perhaps first learned while serving in the Governing Council at Nuremberg in 1522, warmly to heart, though he disapproved of the alliance with the Lutheran princes.

In the early 1540s, when the hostility between princes and cities began to revive both in the Smalkaldic League and in the Imperial Diet, Ammeister Kniebis, clear in mind though plagued by ill health,[84] thought back more than a decade to the glory days of the urban Reformation. Wishing to reawaken the old ties between Strasbourg and the principal Swiss city-states,[85] he approached Bernhard Meyer,[86] burgomaster of Basel, who had conducted secret political talks with leading Strasbourg politicians in 1535 and was to visit the city again in 1542 and late 1547.[87]

---

[83] Brady, *Ruling Class* (see index), gathers most of what is known about Kniebis. His portrait by Hans Baldung Grien is often reproduced, most conveniently by Ficker, *Bildnisse*, no. 4.

[84] What follows is based on the Kniebis–Meyer correspondence, only part of which was published in *PCSS*, 3–4. Katherine G. Brady and I intend to publish the rest. A few more pieces of Kniebis's correspondence are published by Rott, "Un recueil," 778–88, nos. 1–5; and idem, "La Réforme à Nuremberg et à Strasbourg," 112–21, nos. 1–2, 4–8.

[85] Kniebis to B. Meyer, Strasbourg, April 9, 1543, in StA Basel, Politisches L 2,1, fol. 302ʳ.

[86] Meyer (d. 1558), called "zum Pfeil," senator of Basel 1530–48, burgomaster 1548–58, member of the XIII 1540–50. His brother, Adelberg, was senator 1514–58 and burgomaster 1521–47. Füglister, *Handwerksregiment*, 312–13, who also shows (186–205) that Bernhard Meyer was Basel's most active diplomat during the Reformation era. Kniebis's son, Nicolaus Hugo, entered the University of Basel on Aug. 27, 1542. H. G. Wackernagel, *Matrikel Basel*, 2:29. The first extant letter in the Kniebis–Meyer correspondence is dated Aug. 13, 1542 (*PCSS*, 3:302–3, no. 290), and Kniebis first broached his object on Aug. 30, 1542 (StA Basel, Kirchen-Akten A 8, fol. 15ʳ, partly printed in *PCSS*, 3:309–10, no. 297), which replies to a lost letter of Aug. 25.

[87] In 1535, Meyer spoke with Hans Bock, Bernhard Ottfriedrich, Daniel Mieg, Mathis Pfarrer, Matthäus Geiger, Claus Kniebis, Jacob Sturm, Ulman Böcklin von Böcklinsau, and Batt von Duntzenheim – nearly the entire membership of the XIII. StA Basel, Kirchen-Akten A 8, fol. 6ʳ. On a visit around June 3, 1542, he spoke with Martin Herlin, Kniebis, Mathis Pfarrer, and Jacob Meyer. Ibid., fol. 29ᵛ. Finally, in Dec. 1547 he spoke with Kniebis, Herlin, and Meyer. Ibid., fol. 34ᵛ. These men were the political cream of Strasbourg's oligarchy, and they can all be identified with ease in my *Ruling Class*.

Kniebis referred to the ancient tradition of friendship between the two Alsatian cities and assured Meyer that "I and others here have no doubts about you Baselers."[88] Both cities ought to be alarmed by the princes' menacing posture toward the free cities,

and for that reason you and all of us should gather together those who will risk life, honor, and goods to remain free and to struggle against the tyrannical powers. We must not wait until we have been stripped clean of our wealth and no longer have any capacity, or until some of us have been mediatized... For if God in heaven wants us to be prudent, it will happen, by His grace. If we wait, however, "until a roasted dove flies into our mouths," as the saying goes, it will be a sign that God has blinded us, so that we look but don't see. I have no doubts, however, that if we turn to God, and if we care for one another with true brotherly love, then, if someone tries something unjust against us, we will take the trouble of one as the concern of all and support one another's just and equal rights. Then God will look upon us with favor and not withhold His grace from us. For God has given us a love for the highest things, and if we don't follow it, His wrath will come upon us.[89]

These "higher things" included liberty.

Kniebis aimed to revive "the good, old neighborliness, which Strasbourg many years ago had with your friends, the confederates, and especially with your city of Basel, just as you pointed out to me."[90] "We have been betrayed and robbed of our money," Kniebis moaned, and the princes "want the lion's share and treat us without fairness or justice.

---

[88] Kniebis to Meyer, Strasbourg, Aug. 30, 1542: "Und füg üch daruff zü vernemen, das ich und oüch andere an eüch zü basel kein zweyfel tragen ..." StA Basel, Kirchen-Akten A 8, fol. 15ʳ.

[89] Ibid., fol. 15ᵛ: "Dorumb wolt ich, das ir alle und wir alle die, die begeren, fry zu blyben und sich der tyrannischen regierung zu erweren, jetz in dem anfang gedachten lyb, Er und güt züsamen zü setzen, und nit warten bytz harnach, so unss die har in Eyntigem üssgezogen und wir nit mecht hetten und vermochten und ettlich von unss abgeryssen, das wir dann, so die sach verumpt, erst bedencken wolten, woll an wyll gott unser vatter im hymel, das wir fürsichtig syen, wo wurtt es geschehen, und wurtt uns genad erzeygen. Wollen wir aber warten bytz, das unss ein gebrotten tüb in das mül flügt (als man sagt), so ist es ein zeychen, dass wir von gott verblendet, das wir sehen und nit sehen. Aber ich zweyfel nit, wann wir recht uff gott sehen, und umb rechter liebs wyllen einer uff den andern sehen und so jeman solte wyder billichs gegen uns ettwas furnemen, das dann wir liessen solchs unser aller sach syn, und handthaben einander by billichen gleichem rechten, das wurd gott gefallen. Syn genad wyrd unss ouch nit entwichen, dann er hatt die lieb zum hochsten geben, so wir das nit thun, so wurdt ouch syn rach nachgan, do vor unns der her bewar. Amen."

[90] Kniebis to Meyer, Strasbourg, Aug. 13, 1542, in StA Basel, Kirchen-Akten A 8, fol. 39ʳ (not printed in *PCSS*, 3: no. 290): "Die alte güte nachburschafft, so vor vil joren Strassburg mit ewern frynden, die Eidgenossen, gehabt und in sünderoheit mit der Stat basel, wie ir selbs angezeygt ..." The following two quotes are from passages printed in *PCSS*, 3:302.

May Almighty God help us to free ourselves from these raging wolves!"
Kniebis grew furious when he heard of Esslingen's oppression by Duke
Ulrich, whom Strasbourg had helped in 1534 to get his duchy back,
"for the wickedness and disloyalty of the lords is so great, that I believe
Our Lord God is preparing for them a great change [*enderung*]. They
have forgotten God's just punishment in the rebellion of 1525. We could
tolerate the Turk better than we can some of that crowd."[91] In the cause
of liberty, Catholic townsman and Evangelical townsman should stand
together against such predators, no matter what their religion.[92] The
revived "good, old neighborliness" would take the form of an urban
league. "You should seriously consider," Kniebis wrote to Meyer,

whether it were good or bad that Basel and Strasbourg first discuss the matter
alone; or whether it were better that you launch inquiries with your Swiss
friends and see if the idea pleases them. Then you could inform us of the
answer. I wish that we all had the grace to bring all your confederates, plus
Strasbourg and the other cities that lie near your borders, together to discuss
the menacing attacks of those who would love to rule over us as they please
. . .[93]

This dream still lay close to the old man's heart in July 1546 on the eve
of the Smalkaldic War, and though Bernhard Meyer did come to Strasbourg one last time in December of the following year, it was by then
far, far too late for an urban league.[94] The sick old militant had to sit
by and watch with dimming eyes while Jacob Sturm negotiated the
Interim of Augsburg into Strasbourg, while Martin Bucer left for bitter

---

[91] Kniebis to Meyer, Strasbourg, Nov. 12, 1542, in *PCSS*, 3:337, no. 324. On the conflict that
touched off this outburst, see G. Schmidt, *Städtetag*, 210–24.
[92] See *PCSS*, 3:309, no. 297.
[93] Kniebis to Meyer, Strasbourg, Aug. 30, 1542, in StA Basel, Kirchen-Akten A 8, fol. 15ᵛ: "Do
zwyschen wollen ir so vil moglich uch bedencken, ob güt bösser were, dass basel und strossburg
zu erst allein sich besprechen mit einander. Oder ob güt were, das ir als fur uch selbs by andern
ewerer frynden, den Eydgenossen, erfaren mochte, ob in ouch ettwas gelieben wollte oder nit,
uch desselben ouch berichten. Ich wolte, das wir alle die genade hetten, dass alle ewere Eydgenossen und dann strassburg und andre stette, die an üch und ewere Eydgenossen anstossen
und grentzan, sich züsamen thetten und bedachten, die gefarlichen anschlege deren, die gern
uber unss nach irem gefallen herschen wolten . . ." He goes on (fol. 16ʳ) to describe reports
from Sturm in Nuremberg that arrived that day in Strasbourg, among which was surely Sturm's
letter of Aug. 6, 1542, in *PCSS*, 3:292–3, no. 284.
[94] Kniebis to Meyer, Strasbourg, July 26, 1546, in *PCSS*, 4:260, no. 239; Instruction of the
Burgomaster and Senate of Basel for Bernhard Meyer to the XIII of Strasbourg, Dec. 5, 1547,
in StA Basel, Kirchen-Akten A 8, fol. 34ʳ, with Meyer's notes on his visit on fols. 34ᵛ–35ʳ.

English exile, and while the Mass's idolatry rang out once more in Strasbourg's cathedral.[95]

Within the Confederacy, too, the old ideals were passing. Perhaps they began to fade in 1481 at Stans, when the rural federations agreed to respect the lordship of the cities over rural subjects. Perhaps they faded further when Huldrych Zwingli sacrificed the defense of republicanism to his grander anti-Habsburg plans. There did come a time, at any rate, when the defense of liberty became more antimonarchical than antifeudal, and no Swiss aristocrats had better reason to make this transition than did the proud patricians of Bern, who ruled over many thousands of rural subjects. They could appreciate an idea of liberty that united the gospel with the autonomy of lords against the Habsburg monarchy – the idea that animated the Smalkaldic League. Their envoys defended just this idea when Charles V's agents came to the Swiss Assembly at Zurich on July 5, 1546, to persuade the confederates to stay out of the German war.[96] The Habsburg agent argued that the emperor merely intended to punish rebels, no concern of the Swiss. It is essential in these times, replied the Bernese, "not to trust the emperor's smooth words," but to consider that the Habsburgs and their allies "are of one mind and heart against the free, unyoked lords, cities, and communes."[97] Think of the past and the principles, they begged their colleagues, "whence the venerable Confederacy sprang, and what our pious ancestors did to win their freedoms and expel arbitrary force, and how these same freedoms have been maintained until now, praise God, and preserved at the cost of so much blood. And consider how badly the Austrian princes have suffered, whenever they tried to wrest our freedoms from us." Remember, they said, what happened at Sempach and how the Habsburgs were driven from the Aargau; remember how Charles the Bold, the present emperor's ancestor, was beaten at Grandson, Murten, and Nancy; remember the shame and humiliation

---

[95] Brady, *Ruling Class*, chap. 8; Weyrauch, *Krise*, the best study of the subject. See Oberman, *Werden und Wertung*, 302 n. 127 (English: *Masters*, 238 n. 127).

[96] *EA*, 4,1d: no. 301. See Geiser, "Haltung der Schweiz," 171–3. Bernhard Meyer reported (ibid., 191) the arrival of a Strasbourg envoy to seek Swiss aid for the Smalkaldic League. The assembly's recess is in *EA*, 4,1d:640–2.

[97] StA Basel, Politisches M 8,3, fol. 126ʳ⁻ᵛ, and there, too, the two following quotes. The Basel text agrees with the Bernese one printed by Geiser, "Haltung der Schweiz," 239–40, which is the instruction for Peter Imhag and Hans Pastor.

of Emperor Maximilian and his allies in the Swabian War, when they lost the Thurgau; and remember how many have fallen in Italy under the flag of France, fighting this same emperor. He is also of this same House of Austria, and he seeks to repair his ancestors' shame and humiliation by taking revenge on others.

Since the free princes and free cities in Germany have taken heart and example from the Swiss, as to how they can win and keep their freedom... the emperor wants most of all to deprive them of their freedom and bring them into his servitude and suppress them. If he succeeds (from which God preserve us!), not only the common Fatherland and the liberties of the German nation, but also the entire venerable Confederacy and its constituent powers, would share in the wreck.

At Bern, liberty was particularist but no longer communal, the liberty of lords from the arbitrary rule of their king, liberty without equality, and a liberty that gentlemen – in Machiavelli's sense – could enjoy.

Such changes left that old communal particularist Kniebis stranded on the beach of a dying political world. His dreams harked too far back, not to the days of the urban front or the Swabian War, but to the age of the guild revolts and to the glory days of the old Lower Union, when Strasbourg's red-and-white and Colmar's meteor had floated alongside the Bernese bear, Lucerne's blue-and-white, and the great bull of Uri on the fields of Grandson, Murten, and Nancy. Their ancestors had fought for local autonomy and for something else, something that could not be brought back, the right of people "to be their own lords." It no longer made much sense for anyone, oligarchs or subjects, to want to turn Swiss.

Reprise: Nuremberg under the eagle's wings

Herzog Heinrich...
... sich alls heut
mit der ganzen stat Nürnberg freut
ob Carolo dem mechting kaiser,
dem glückhafting sieghaften raiser
und hofft, got werd noch durch in würken
aussdilgen den blutdürsting Türken,
dardurch das römisch reich sich mehr
und auch sein kaiserliche ehr,

gedechtnus wirdig auferwachs.
Das wünschet zu Nürnberg Hans Sachs.[98]

"It is the intention of the princes," Kniebis once wrote, "to bring and to force the cities to such a point, that each city would surrender itself to the nearest prince in exchange for protection, which would be like escaping the wolf only to fall prey to the lion's claws."[99] This fit no other large city so well as it did Nuremberg, the Franconian metropolis, whose government searched on all sides for new allies during the years after 1525. The advance of Lutheran religion, though it estranged Nuremberg from old urban friends, Strasbourg and Ulm, brought a highly welcome respite from the old tensions between the city and Margrave George of Brandenburg-Ansbach (d. 1543), Casimir's brother and heir. The friendship between their top civil servants, Lazarus Spengler and Chancellor Georg Vogler, and a common Lutheranism brought the two old foes, in what may have been one of the Reformation's oddest political achievements, to conduct a common visitation of their lands' churches in 1528 and to issue a common ecclesiastical constitution in 1533, the year before Spengler's death.[100] This long Hohenzollern honeymoon permitted Nuremberg to boycott the Smalkaldic League in 1531 and to maintain the shreds of loyalty to the emperor, for the ideological cement of the Hohenzollern tie was the steadfast denial that any subordinate power might resist the emperor with force, which Nuremberg upheld long after Luther prudently let it fall at the end of 1530.[101] Nuremberg at the end of the 1520s thus pulled away from its old urban allies.[102] Here Spengler played a double game. On the one hand, he labored to keep Nuremberg clear of the "Zwinglian" cities, Stras-

---

[98] "Duke Heinrich ... rejoices today with all the town of Nuremberg about the mighty Emperor Charles, a pilgrim happy and victorious. He hopes that God has in mind to crush through Charles the bloodthirsty Turk, so that the Roman Empire and also the imperial dignity will be honored evermore. So hopes Hans Sachs of Nuremberg." Liliencron, *Volkslieder*, 4:123, no. 459, lines 146–58.

[99] Kniebis to Meyer, Strasbourg, Aug. 13, 1542, in StA Basel, Kirchen-Akten A 8, fol. 39ʳ: "Und selbs bedencken, das ir, der fursten, meynung nit anders dann die stett do hyn zū bringen und tringen, das sy sich jeglicher under den nechsten fursten begeben, die sie dann nach irer hoffnung beschyrmen, das dann were dem wolff entgon und einen lowe zu clagen fallen."

[100] E. Franz, *Nürnberg*, 97–9; Grimm, *Lazarus Spengler*, 109–48; Baron, "Religion and Politics," 614–19; G. Schmidt, "Haltung," 201–14.

[101] Wolgast, *Wittenberger Theologie*, 95–200.

[102] Nuremberg even for a time abandoned the Urban Diet. E. Franz, *Nürnberg*, 107.

bourg and Ulm, while, on the other, he gave their leaders soft words, as much a Nuremberg specialty as *Lebkuchen*, the famous honey-cakes. In June 1529, at the very height of the Lutheran campaign against the "sacramentarians," he wrote to Peter Butz:

Sir Mathis Pfarrer, your brother-in-law, I like very much. He is an admirable, pious, modest, and honorable man. He has doubtless returned [from the Diet of Speyer], so please give him my most humble regards – and also to Sir Jacob Sturm, Sir Claus Kniebis and Sir Martin Herlin. Tell them to stand fast for the gospel and be stalwart in the truth, which I don't doubt they will. For the old God lives still. Please consider me as your brother, who thanks you most heartily for the newsletter and the printed ordinance from Basel, which Sir Mathis Pfarrer gave me.[103]

Spengler's lords, with their apparent indecision and endless capacity for delay, steered a shrewd and prudent course between the Catholic cliff of Habsburg counterreformation and the Zwinglian rocks of armed resistance.

How conservative and loyally monarchist an Evangelical town politician could be is illustrated by the career of Christoph Kress, a wealthy knight whose manner was "suited more to an Italian condottiere than a German burgher."[104] Following an education in Italy, England, and the Netherlands, Kress became a knight and had a distinguished military career. He served in the Bavarian War of 1504, campaigned in Italy under Count Wolf of Fürstenberg in 1507, and served on Nuremberg's nine-man military commission (*Kriegsherren*) during the Württemberg campaign in 1519.[105] Kress served Nuremberg right through the Reformation and signed the great protest at Speyer in 1529 in the city's name. His attitude toward the Reformation was positive but not uncritical. Unlike Jacob Sturm, who removed his younger sister from a Strasbourg convent, Kress declared that if one nun's cowl weren't enough for his sister, she could wear three, and he dared anyone to remove them. It was he who confessed in 1525 that the popular agitation had

---

[103] *PCSS*, 1:379, no. 628.
[104] Strauss, *Nuremberg*, 82.
[105] Kamann, "Ratskorrespondenzen," 246; Strauss, *Nuremberg*, 64; Zophy, "Lazarus Spengler," 40. On Kress's religious views, Zophy asserts (42) that his "connection with the Reformation can be clearly established ..." Seebass rightly comments that the matter has not been fully clarified, and he cites Kress's remark about his sister. "Stadt und Kirche in Nürnberg," 77 and n. 45.

driven him and his colleagues much farther than they had wished to go.[106] Of Luther he had a good opinion, for in 1531 he sent "a good, solid little book" by Luther to his long-time Catholic friend, Abbot Gerwig Blarer (d. 1567) of Weingarten. Of the Lutheran clergy of Nuremberg, however, he was not so fond. "Our priests have established a new church ordinance," he wrote to Blarer in 1533, "which I think will please you, for we are once more to confess our sins and seek absolution for them."[107]

Kress was also a loyal Leaguer and monarchist. He served many times as Nuremberg envoy to the League, and he campaigned under George Truchsess von Waldburg in 1523, when the League's army burned out the robbers' nests in Franconia. "Please God that the League Assembly act for peace and unity," he wrote Blarer in May 1529, and not for division, "which I, as an old Leaguer, would regret."[108] The Nurembergers took no comfort from the Swabian League's demise in 1534. They refused aid to Landgrave Philip's 1534 campaign to restore Duke Ulrich in Württemberg, both because "it is said the land shall become Zwinglian," and, as Kress noted, "because it is against His Imperial Majesty and the king."[109] Kress called himself "a good, old monarchist," though he admitted that "at first I was almost glad to see the landgrave's campaign," because

we must regard this matter as a flying pest or plague, which comes into the land and attacks the people. I hope that through our lords, the emperor and the king, whom I have always favored, everything will be put back in good order.

---

[106] Leonhard von Eck to Duke William of Bavaria, Feb. 27, 1525, in Vogt, *Die bayrische Politik*, 399, and also in Pfeiffer, *Quellen*, 352. See also Lazarus Spengler to Clemens Volckamer, March 8, 1525, in ibid., 355, on Kress's attitude. The story of Sturm's sister is told by Rapp, *Réformes*, 520.

[107] Kress to Gerwig Blarer, July 13, 1531, and Feb. 10, 1533, in Blarer, *Briefe und Akten*, 1:168, lines 25–7, and p. 192, lines 18–20, nos. 271, 311.

[108] Kress to Blarer, Nuremberg, May 31, 1529, in ibid., 133, lines 16–20, no. 210. He reported to Blarer on March 12, 1533 (ibid., 194, lines 9–12, no. 316) his colleagues' indecision about the renewal of the League. On Kress's role in the Franconian campaign of 1523, see Zophy, "Christoph Kress," 40–3.

[109] Kress to Blarer, Nuremberg, April 23, 1534, in Blarer, *Briefe und Akten*, 1:220, lines 1–2, 5–6. On the renewal of the League, see Klüpfel, *Urkunden*, 2:348–56; Naujoks, *Obrigkeitsgedanke*, 103–4; and Schlenck, *Reichsstadt Memmingen*, 87, on Memmingen's proposal for a new league of cities. On the Württemberg campaign, see Kress to Blarer, June 16, 1534, in Blarer, *Briefe und Akten*, 1:230, line 5, no. 372, quoted next, and also no. 381 (July 13, 1534). Only Strasbourg among the large cities supported the campaign, for which see my "Princes' Reformation vs. Urban Liberty," esp. 281 n. 92a.

Also, I must tell you frankly that you and others in the South have grasped the business correctly. The princes intend, as ever, to gobble up us cities and you prelates; and they now start trouble with some and make intrigues day after day. Therefore, the best thing would be for you to pay attention to the matter and do something on your, the prelates', side to prevent this. I am afraid that otherwise bad times lie ahead.

Here a Lutheran town politician warned a Catholic abbot to rally his fellow Catholic prelates against Catholic and Lutheran princes. And Kress was by no means the only Nuremberger who saw things in this light. Karius Huldreich, the military secretary (*Kriegsschreiber*), wrote to Blarer in July 1534 that "here in our region everything is quiet, except that some of the princes would like to subjugate the prelates and smaller cities and then, perhaps, the larger cities. This cannot be tolerated." He hoped "that Our Lord God will grant everywhere the best, and especially that we shall soon have a new league."[110]

A third Nuremberg voice comes from Christoph Fürer, who was, unlike Spengler, no scholar and, unlike Kress, no knight, but rather a typical Nuremberg man of affairs, "cautious, shrewdly vigilant, conscientious, bent on putting every penny to good use."[111] Fürer was a big man in the Thuringian copper smelters, dealt also in zinc, and shipped ebony wood to England.[112] Though a member of the circle of patricians around Staupitz in the late 1510s, Fürer seems to have joined only for a time the general drift to Lutheranism. He and his brother Sigmund did support the efforts in February 1525 of their sister, Ursula Tetzel, to remove her twenty-three-year-old daughter, Margaret, from the Nuremberg Poor Clares, "for she [Ursula] has become convinced through the clear gospel and the preachers, that she cannot in good conscience leave her child in there – and she damned the clerical estate and [the] whole [religious] way of life."[113] The brothers told the abbess, Caritas Pirckheimer (1467–1532), to let the mother have the daughter for four weeks, "so she can be instructed in the true faith and hear the gospel, as it is preached in the city."[114] In the very same month, however,

---

[110] Karius Huldreich to Blarer, Nuremberg, July 14, 1534, in Blarer, *Briefe und Akten*, 1:235, lines 14–16, 27–8, no. 382.
[111] Strauss, *Nuremberg*, 82.
[112] Pfeiffer, *Quellen*, 187–9, 193.
[113] C. Pirckheimer, *Denkwürdigkeiten*, 16, lines 15–18.
[114] Ibid., lines 24–5. See also ibid., pp. 14–25, 68, 79–83; Pfeiffer, *Quellen*, 346–8.

Leonhard von Eck reported that Fürer "said to him, Kress, that if he
met me, he should tell me that I and the other [Bavarian] councillors
should advise Your Princely Grace [Duke William] not to let the Lutherans in, and that Your Princely Grace and the estates should be
guarded from [Lutheranism], which bodes no good."[115] Fürer had many
official dealings with rural rebellion in 1525, and the probability that
these experiences decided him for Catholicism is strengthened by the
comment in his journal (*Geheimbuch*) that Luther's condemnation of
good works would make "the common people so godless, that they would
abandon all good discipline and human morals."[116] In 1528 he left the
government for good.

Fürer had commanded the Nuremberg troops in the Württemberg
campaign in 1519.[117] "Toward Nuremberg," he later wrote,

as toward all the other free cities, no one is better disposed than the emperor.
This is so especially because the Austrian blood, which has ever been well
inclined to the towns, is now mixed with Latin blood, which is far more inclined
to urban life than our German princes are. For all German princes and all
nobles are hostile to the great cities and their citizens' wealth. Day and night
they strive to curb and suppress the cities, who can thus rely for aid and
protection only on themselves, and on the emperor.[118]

Like Kress, Fürer was a good monarchist and a good Leaguer.

The red thread through Nuremberg's policies in this era was the
belief in a natural community of interest between the monarchy and the
free cities. The coming of the Reformation altered not the sentiment
but the completeness with which this community could assume and
maintain an institutional form, though the Nurembergers remained the
best of monarchists, so long as the emperor and King Ferdinand left
religion alone. They stayed out of the Smalkaldic League, and, when
the Swabian League expired and Spengler died in 1534, relations with
Margrave George resumed their normal, wretched state.[119]

---

[115] Eck to Duke William of Bavaria, Feb. 27, 1525, in Vogt, *Die bayrische Politik*, 399; also in
Pfeiffer, *Quellen*, 352.
[116] See Reicke, *Geschichte*, 838–9, who quotes from Fürer's (unpublished) "Geheimbuch." For
Fürer's experiences during the Revolution of 1525, see Pfeiffer, *Quellen*, 2, 9, 55, 70, 71, 72,
74–5, 76.
[117] Kamann, "Ratskorrespondenzen," 260–8.
[118] Quoted by F. Roth, *Einführung*, 157.
[119] E. Franz, *Nürnberg*, 127–34.

As the Swabian League tottered to its end, the Lower Swabian and Franconian free cities, Evangelical or not, looked on with mixed feelings and real misgivings. Heilbronn and Schwäbisch Hall belatedly scuttled into the Smalkaldic League, while Nördlingen pulled back into the dissimulation and shiftiness that were "Nördlingen's basic principle."[120] The Nurembergers began to search for a successor to the League, bearing in mind that King Ferdinand now actively sought the cities' support, which boded well, if the religious issue could be excluded.[121] Partly in response to feelers from Ferdinand through Augsburg, the Nurembergers resurrected the idea of a Three Cities' League of Nuremberg, Augsburg, and Ulm, which "will give us some small support, so we won't sit here alone."[122] The Three Cities' League came into being on May 25, 1533. Nine months later, Clemens Sender noted the passing of the Swabian League.

On St. Blaise's Day [February 3, 1534] at the League Diet held here at Augsburg, the venerable Swabian League was dissolved and mutual commitments to one another abolished – all against the will and orders of His Imperial Majesty and the King of the Romans. This happened only because of the disputes concerning the Christian faith, so that the Lutherans and Zwinglians might remain obdurate in their errors, and that Duke Ulrich might reenter his land, which the League had sold to His Imperial Majesty, who had paid them his money for it. Just as the Swabian League had begun honorably, so it came to an evil result and end here.[123]

It was forty-six years old.

Although Ferdinand could not prevent the death of this most solid pillar of his grandfather's South German system, he did found a new peace-keeping alliance, the Nine Years' League, at Lauingen on the Danube on April 11, 1535.[124] Nuremberg and its Franconian clients, Windsheim and Weissenburg, joined, but Augsburg and Ulm would not, and the otherwise entirely Catholic character of the alliance raised deep

---

[120] Rublack, *Nördlingen*, 239–43.
[121] G. Schmidt, *Städtetag*, 164–7.
[122] Burgomaster and Senate of Nuremberg to Clemens Volckamer and Bernhard Baumgartner, May 3, 1533, quoted by E. Franz, *Nürnberg*, 129. On the Three-Cities' League, see ibid., 127–30; F. Roth, *Reformationsgeschichte*, 2:148.
[123] Sender, "Chronik," 366, also quoted by F. Roth, *Reformationsgeschichte*, 2:147.
[124] Endres, "Der Kayserliche neunjährige Bund," 85–103; E. Franz, *Nürnberg*, 134–7; Salomies, *Pläne*, 81–5.

suspicions among the other Protestant powers. When Ulm's refusal to join became known at Nuremberg, the Junior Burgomaster, Sebald Pfinzing, argued "that my lords should not allow this to discourage them, for Ulm is, after all, in Württemberg... Nuremberg, however – and this becomes more obvious the farther away one gets – is only Nuremberg because, as is right and proper, it has at all times supported its lords, the Roman emperors and kings."[125] The Nurembergers would not only serve "the welfare of the Fatherland" through this new league, he said, but also "assure fame and thanks from their own descendants."

Such commitments and vision gave birth in 1537 to a Nuremberg plan for a new political system.[126] Its principles harked back to Maximilian's dead system, but its structure looked forward to Charles's great plan of 1547–8. The anonymous author addressed the monarchy's lack of a sound financial basis. The first problem "is that a Roman emperor has no substantial support or income from the Empire of the German Nation, with which order, peace, and justice might be effectively maintained. Although the matter has been discussed and treated at many Diets and in many ways, yet nothing definitive has been established or decided upon in these matters."[127] No emperor should be expected to finance the government from his domain (*Kammergut*) or his hereditary lands, for the Empire is very wide (*weitleufig*) and is expensive to govern. Especially so in these times, "when many people... show little obedience to or fear of their lord," even though "His Roman Imperial Majesty, as a just, beneficent, and merciful emperor, who from the beginning of his reign has intended to treat the Holy Empire and the German Nation most loyally and graciously, cannot be accused of dereliction of office." His forefathers, Frederick and Maximilian, established the Swabian League "against those who rebelled against His Majesty." To sum things up, "the Swabian League was the proper form of the German Nation. It was feared by many, and in many ways it protected and sustained the public peace and law and order."

---

[125] Quoted by E. Franz, *Nürnberg*, 135.
[126] Printed by Heide, "Nürnberg, 196–8, whence the following quotes. See Endres, "Der Kayserliche neunjährige Bund," 100. The document bears a very strong resemblance to Charles V's alliance scheme after the Smalkaldic War, though Rabe, *Reichsbund*, 136–42, 152–4, does not mention it. For the context, see Press, "Bundespläne," 55–106.
[127] Heide, "Nürnberg," 196, and there, too, the other quotes in this paragraph.

The remedy for the present situation, the memorialist thought, was "to establish a mighty league in the Empire of the German Nation" and to bring into it "some princes and powers," with whose aid the disobedient powers might be coerced. More practical, however – and here is the proposal's original point – would be *two* leagues, each headed by the emperor. One of them should embrace the existing alliance, including Tyrol and Upper Austria, plus the Upper Palatinate, Würzburg, Württemberg, and the Swabian counts, prelates, and knights. "No prince or power in Upper Germany would be powerful enough to oppose this league with force."[128] The second league should embrace the Netherlands (Flanders and Brabant); the electors of Mainz, Trier, Cologne, and the Palatinate; the Saxons (if they wish); the princes of Jülich and Hesse; the bishops of Liège, Speyer, and Worms; and others. The Rhenish counts and the free cities of Cologne, Strasbourg, Frankfurt, Speyer, and Worms are also mentioned. If some powers are opposed, "and if the majority or even just half of the others lend their authority and material aid, the others will soon get their skulls cracked, if they've a mind to cut up rough." Against a really strong opponent, one league can aid the other, "and no one can doubt that if this league is established, no prince, whatever he might intend or have in mind, would be so foolish to start something." The leagues would also provide a proper executive power for the High Court's decisions. Nuremberg's regime forwarded this memorial to Imperial Vice-Chancellor Dr. Matthias Held on March 27, 1537. This was Nuremberg's bid to reestablish a royal peace-keeping system as a direct successor to the old Swabian League. The division into Franconian-Swabian and Rhenish branches reflected the same considerations that had once divided Maximilian's system into Swabian and Rhenish wings.

Through a restoration of the twin sides of the urban front – urban solidarity and loyalty to the Crown – the Nurembergers thus armed themselves against the increasingly bad temper of Margrave George during the mid-1530s. That this was the fruit of calculation and design and not, as their coreligionists in the Smalkaldic League alleged, simple cowardice, is shown by Nuremberg's refusal to join the purely Catholic

---

[128] Ibid., 197: "Dann wäre kein fürst noch Stand im oberen Deutschland so mächtig, der sich wider diesen bund gewaltiglich setzen dürfte." There, too, the remaining quotes in this paragraph.

League of Nuremberg, which Dr. Held organized against the Smalkaldeners in 1538.[129] Nuremberg strongly supported Charles V in the war with France that began in 1536, and it also backed his policy of religious conciliation through colloquies in 1539–42. Through it all, Nuremberg's rulers managed to remain both "adherents of the Christian Confession of Augsburg" and "good monarchists."[130] When Charles came to Nuremberg in February 1541, his first visit to the great Franconian city, the senate did homage and laid on festivities that lasted for three days and cost about eighty-eight hundred florins. During the following years, as relations between princes and cities both in and outside the Smalkaldic League worsened, Nuremberg helped to renew the Three Cities' League (1541) and supported Charles's plan in 1544 to restore the Swabian League in a nonconfessional form.[131] Charles's ever-empty pockets and the seeming hopelessness of the struggle for urban rights in the Diet nonetheless strained even the Nurembergers' loyalty. The failure of their search for a way to neutralize the religious question prevented them from drawing other leading cities, especially Ulm, back into the Habsburg fold,[132] but every revival of Habsburg alliance policy nevertheless found a ready ear at Nuremberg. During the Smalkaldic War of 1546–7, Nuremberg played precisely the role this line dictated: It remained neutral and sold munitions to both sides.

Nuremberg alone held resolutely, except for the years 1524 to 1533, to the leading principle of Emperor Maximilian's South German system: solidarity of the free cities (and other lesser powers) under the wings of the Habsburg eagle. A contemporary bard recognized just how singular was Nuremberg's fidelity, and he sang during the war summer of 1546 (to the tune of "Oh, you miserable Judas"):

> Woe to you, you miserable free cities,
> What a great miscalculation,
> That you have without cause set yourself
> Against the pious emperor,
> Who is the highest authority,

---

[129] E. Franz, *Nürnberg*, 136–7, 142–3.
[130] Ibid., 146–7, an account of Charles's visit to Nuremberg in 1541.
[131] Ibid., 151–61; G. Schmidt, "Haltung," 219–23. On the struggle in the Diet, see G. Schmidt, *Städtetag*, 251–2.
[132] Rommel, *Reichsstadt Ulm*, 3–5.

Out of envy and hate alone!
Truly, you should now wish
That you had been better behaved.
Lord have mercy! The Spaniards are in the land![133]

When the war was over, Charles V broached to the German powers – victorious, defeated, and neutral – his plan for a great twin league, similar to the Nuremberg scheme of 1537.[134] He and his advisors had come to understand how important the Swabian League had once been to the Habsburg power and the government of the Empire. They had also absorbed the lesson of Nuremberg's loyalism. From August 3 through 18, 1548, the governments of Augsburg and Ulm were forcibly altered in favor of the patricians and against the guilds, a transformation in Nuremberg's image.[135] Four years later, it was the turn of more than twenty other South German free cities, whose governments were remade into much more oligarchical "rabbit regimes" [*Hasenräte*], so named after Charles's councillor, Dr. Heinrich Hass.[136]

Although Charles's grand new alliance schemes never came to fruition, Imperial politics gradually returned to normal. In 1552 came a great rebellion of princes against Charles. Augsburg fell to a rebel army, Frankfurt was besieged by another, and Margrave Casimir's son, Albrecht Alcibiades, moved like a raging boar through the Nuremberg territories. What he did not destroy in the first campaign in 1552, he laid in ashes during a second terrible strike in 1553–4. Finally, in June 1554 he was beaten near Schweinfurt and driven into exile. It was 101 years since the end of the Cities' War.

---

[133] Liliencron, *Volkslieder*, 4:369, no. 539, stanza 1.
[134] See Rabe, *Reichsbund*; and Press, "Bundespläne."
[135] F. Roth, *Reformationsgeschichte*, 4:178–240; Naujoks, *Obrigkeitsgedanke*, 118–53; Warmbrunn, *Zwei Konfessionen*, 104–21.
[136] Moeller, *Deutschland*, 158, calls the installation of the Hasenräte "ein Vorgang von unabsehbarer Tragweite für die deutsche Geschichte und wohl die wichtigste bleibende Folge des Schmalkaldischen Krieges überhaupt." In general, we must still rely on Fürstenwerth, *Verfassungsänderungen*. For details, see Eitel, *Reichsstädte*, 74–6; perhaps the most important recent finding is by Naujoks, *Obrigkeitsgedanke*, 118–31, that Charles took loyal Nuremberg's constitution as a model. This agrees with the Augsburg patricians' petition to Charles, quoted by Moeller, *Reichsstadt*, 66 (English: *Imperial Cities*, 102).

7

Conclusion: turning Swiss – a lost dream

On July 16, 1499, King Maximilian led his army out of Constance and offered battle to the Swiss. When they would not come down to attack, he marched his men back into town. Shortly thereafter, a young Swiss girl arrived in Constance with a letter from the enemy, in which they offered the struggle for arbitration, though they warned the king of their confidence of God's support in defending their ancient liberties. As the messenger stood in the courtyard of the king's lodgings, awaiting the reply Maximilian had decided not to send, a few of his bodyguard approached her and asked what was going on within the Swiss lines. "Don't you see," she replied, "they are waiting for you to attack them?" When pressed to describe the confederates' numbers, she laughed, "If I saw things rightly, you could have counted them a while ago before the city's gates, had your eyes not been blinded by thoughts of flight." A soldier, wishing to frighten her, laid his hand on his sword's hilt and threatened to take her head off. "What a brave fellow you are," she said, looking him coolly in the eye, "to threaten to kill so young a girl. But if you are eager to swing your sword, go out to our lines. Surely you'll find someone there as ready to fight as you are. It is a lot easier, of course, to attack an unarmed, innocent girl than a well-armed foe, who can fight with deeds and not just with words." "I heard this with genuine pleasure," reports Willibald Pirckheimer, "and I marvelled at the naturalness and frankness of the girl in making reply." A few days later, as though touched by the Swiss girl's calm courage, Maximilian retreated with his army up the lake to Lindau.[1]

[1] W. Pirckheimer, *Schweizerkrieg*, 110–13 (book II, chap. 6).

Conclusion: turning Swiss – a lost dream

Pirckheimer shared with the king and many others the feeling that this war – the "Swiss War," they called it – was unlike others. "It was the greatest and most destructive war in living memory," the Nuremberger began his history of it, "not only because of the scale of mobilizations and the numbers of troops, but also because of the wildness of the battles and the numbers of defeats."[2] The "wildness" was that added bit of savagery social wars usually display. On one side were the Swiss "peasants," uplanders from Unterwalden and Zug, valley men from the High Rhine and the districts along the Aare. On the other side were the lords – king, great nobles, and knights – the masters of those who might in the future turn Swiss and the descendants or kinsmen of those whose subjects already had. In the Calven Gorge, by Castle Dorneck, in the Hegau, and all along the front, Swiss victories turned the world topsy-turvy, as natural subjects skewered, hacked, and shot down natural lords.

But look again. On one side wave the blue-and-whites of Lucerne and Zurich, Bern's bear on his red field, and the red-and-white of Solothurn. Across the lines flutter Augsburg's fir cone, Ulm's black-and-white – the image of Fribourg's – and a dozen banners uniting local arms with the Imperial double-headed eagle. It is a war of townsmen against townsmen, free city against free city, a vivid illustration of the political and social ambiguity of the self-governing cities, those communities Karl Marx once called "the acme of the Middle Ages."[3]

The political ambiguity of the self-governing urban community has unfolded in all its richness in the South German tale this book has told. Urban liberty meant local autonomy, and so free cities formed as special cases of feudal privilege. Urban liberty also meant what was "common," however, and the urban communes arose as but one fruit of the broader communal movement. As Machiavelli correctly saw, free republican government demanded both local sovereignty and relative equality, and this combination necessarily lived in tension with feudal power. Two things happened in the South German cities' world between the age of their formation and the later fifteenth century. First, the external networks of lordship had become immensely denser and more powerful.

---

[2] Ibid., 15–21 (book I, chap. 1).
[3] Marx, *Kapital*, book I, chap. 24, sect. 1 (ed. Lieber and Kautsky, 4:867).

Turning Swiss

Second, the growth of the market had stimulated the urban rich to end the social devolution of power and bolster their rule over both urban artisans and rural subjects. The rise of oligarchy came from the action of this double movement on the urban upper classes, and it set them on a path of convergence with the early modern state. The home of communal liberty was thus becoming the citadel of oligarchy.

In South Germany around 1450, this convergence was just fairly underway, and the nobles still regarded the cities not as legitimate lords but as valuable subjects who had temporarily escaped lordship. The Cities' War of 1449–53, with which this story began, was the very last in which free cities alone waged war on princes. Then, in the age of new alliances, they streamed into the federations under the Habsburg eagle's wings, in partnership with Austria. Always stronger in Swabia and Franconia than on the Rhine, the system drew nourishment from struggles against common foes: Bavaria in 1492, the Confederacy in 1499, the Palatine Wittelsbachs in 1504, and Württemberg in 1519. The urban oligarchies fought for a third way, neither the liberation of the land *à la suisse* nor submission to the great nobles. The key to success lay in the centralized, early-modern state, the "Austrian way" to a German monarchy, which would have led in the end – Constance's fate proves it – to Austrian hegemony over the free cities.

Maximilian's South German system flourished at least in part because it conducted with notable success the two-front struggle the urban oligarchies demanded, against the princes of the South German opposition and against the Swissification of South Germany. The system's arena of action stretched from the Alps to the Central Highlands, and it must remain an open question whether the Habsburgs might through the Austrian way have come to rule this region as the French kings ruled their lands and the Spanish ones Castile or Aragon. It is worth noting that every successful absolutist state began with imperial expansion of an older monarchy, based on a rich, relatively densely populated core, over its neighbors. Imperialism gave birth to centralized states, which in turn gave birth to nations.[4] It was the first stage of this process, not the second, that was underway in early sixteenth-century South Germany

---

[4] Kiernan, "State and Nation," 35–6.

and that was halted by the convergence of forces described in this book. What failed to happen – like Conan Doyle's dog, which did not bark in the night – was not the creation of a German national state, whether "from below" or by the "middle class," but the birth of a centralized, dynastic or absolutist state, having all the tools of sovereign power and controlling with such tools the bulk of the German-speaking world. The state, in other words, that might have created a German nation out of a large chunk of the German-speaking world's populations. If successful, the policy of the Austrian way would have joined Austria to the rich, densely populated, centrally located region of South Germany. The policy, frustrated by the factors described in this book, then gave way to what might be called the "Saxon way," though it could just as well be called the "Bavarian way," the policy of princely particularism. The chief historical significance of this victorious particularism was to keep the door open for yet another solution, the "Prussian way," in which a completely peripheral power had time to acquire sufficient heartland through conquest to enable it to bid for the role of statebuilder and creator of the German nation. There was nothing inevitable about this creation of a German state through the Prussian way in the nineteenth century rather than through the Austrian way in the sixteenth. It was the outcome of many decisions and loyalties – of Swiss and of Swabians, of burghers and of peasants, of kings and of commoners, of Germans and of Netherlanders, and of Spaniards and of Turks. It was also the outcome of decisions motivated by almost every conceivable interest, animosity, and desire, but least of all by the conscious aim to create a centralized German state.

Certainly the urban oligarchs of the South never intended to create a centralized state, national or otherwise. They wanted a general climate of law and order and the protection of their own liberties – for which, typically, they were not prepared to pay much – and the Crown offered them the least dangerous and emotionally most satisfying partnership. This relationship gained added strength from the Habsburgs' role as best customers for cash and credit and as biggest dispensers of financial and economic privileges. Very few families, however, risked their destinies entirely on the Habsburg card, and very few oligarchs backed the Crown against their own hometowns, once the Reformation movement began pressing them to make a choice. The Fuggers of Augsburg, whose enormous wealth isolated them from the local oligarchy, were the exception that proves the rule.[5]

Many signs suggest that Maximilian's system was ripe for consolidation around 1520, not least among them the various plans for centralization: the king's own proposal for an Austrian monarchy in 1513; his plan for Austrian (and Imperial) centralization in 1518; and Maximilian van Bergen's very similar plan in 1520/1. The urban oligarchies, pressed increasingly by the growth of antimonopoly sentiment and financial pressure from the Imperial Diet, responded with a solidarity, the urban front, which culminated in the Spanish embassy of 1523. Possibly Charles V's early years were "the crucial moment"[6] for German state formation, but the state that might have then been formed would have had a thoroughly southern base. Powerful ties of trade and investment, true, bound the North and especially the mining lands of the East to South Germany via Nuremberg, but popular sensibility nonetheless identified the term *Empire* with the South and West alone. Saxon travelers westward, for example, said that they were going "into the Empire."[7] The South was the heartland of the Empire, where its governing organs had their seats, where its Diet always met, and where its two most powerful federations, the Swiss Confederacy and the Swabian League, kept the peace. It also became the heartland of all the social movements of the Reformation era: the urban Reformation, the Revolution of 1525, and Anabaptism. The partnership of cities and Crown was also southern, and the new monarchy, to which it might have given birth, would have differed radically in size and shape from either the Prusso-German state established in 1871 or the "greater Germany" its critics demanded. It is therefore idle to ascribe to any sixteenth-century German class or movement the task of "creating a unitary national state,"[8] if the task is understood teleologically in either of these nineteenth-century senses. A South German state did emerge during the sixteenth century, and out of it grew a nation – Austria – that endures to this day. Its size and shape, however, were determined by social forces that debouched onto the stage of Imperial politics during this crucial

[5] Mörke, "Die Fugger," 141–61.
[6] Wallerstein, *World-System*, 1:178.
[7] Blaschke, *Sachsen*, 126.
[8] Steinmetz, "Die frühbürgerliche Revolution in Deutschland," 53.

decade of the 1520s, and that may be symbolized by three place names: Worms, Pavia, Mohács.

The politically potent part of the urban Reformation, the response of ordinary folk to the preachers' gospel, expressed a demand for simpler, cheaper, more satisfying, and more biblically justifiable ways of Christian life. The oligarchies could seldom resist their pressure for illegal changes, which gradually estranged the governments from a sovereign who was determined to preserve them in their and his ancestral religion. Yet, where the oligarchy brought the movement under control, as at Nuremberg, the estrangement was neither total nor permanent. The more sensitive a government was to popular pressure, the more it was likely to require like-minded allies, whether Evangelical Swiss cities or Evangelical German princes. Nuremberg's loyalty counted for more than its heterodoxy, and in the end Charles V reshaped dozens of urban governments in Nuremberg's image.

The Reformation's disruptive effects on the urban front coincided with Charles V's pacification of Spain after the revolts and his deep engagement in the struggle for Italy against Francis I, which culminated at Pavia. Germany entered his calculations chiefly as a source of money, it seems, which is why the great firms became the chief beneficiaries of his attentions. The reinvigoration of Imperial government by the Diet of Worms in 1521, however, suggests what Charles might have achieved as a resident German king.

Ferdinand might well have made a better king than Charles. He was better educated, more prudent, and less thriftless than either his grandfather or his brother. Suleiman's attack on Hungary gave him no time, however, and the catastrophe at Mohács thrust the two Jagellonian crowns into Ferdinand's grasp. The Austrian center of gravity now began to shift eastward from Innsbruck, Stuttgart, and Augsburg to Prague and Vienna, presaging the death of Maximilian's South German system and the birth of Austria-Hungary.

The partnership of cities and Crown could not survive such blows, except as an underlying tendency displayed by Nuremberg's persistent loyalism. The monarchism of the oligarchies flowed not from mindless patriotic traditionalism but from the political calculation of the oligarchies that the Crown was their best chance for the establishment of general law and order. The desperate need for law and order grew even more acute with the expansion of trade and investment, which gradually created a common, supralocal political interest among the cities. Purely local action could never relieve the Augsburg cannon-founder of his need for Tyrolean copper, the Nuremberg merchant's worry about his goods in transit from Lyons, the Strasbourg butcher's concern to buy Hessian sheep and Hungarian cattle, or the Ulm fustian weaver's demand for Egyptian cotton. The wideness of the economic world fueled the search for allies to protect travel and commerce. The most immediate damage to this developing partnership of cities and Crown came from the Common Man's interventions, first in the urban Evangelical movements in 1524, then in the Revolution of 1525.

These interventions also revivified the old communal ethos and raised into prominence once more the ideas of commune and federation. Just before the Reformation got fairly underway, Maximilian van Bergen surveyed South Germany. With Württemberg in a strong Habsburg grip and Bavaria encircled, only a weakened Palatinate and a few bishops faced the Austrian power in the South, and a centralized, westward-oriented Austria, with its political head at Innsbruck and its financial heart at Augsburg, might become the basis of a regenerated Imperial monarchy. Failing a strong hand at the royal helm, however, the free cities and whole territories would slide toward the Confederacy, emboldened by a common corporate-communal heritage. Bergen thus penetrated precisely the urban governments' dilemma: The monarchy was partner of choice, but the Confederacy was a strong second best.[9]

The structure and heritage of the Swiss Confederacy, which created its power as a model, also set its limitations. Unlike the other federations of the age – the United Netherlands, the Huguenot leagues of the French Midi, or the Catholic League in France – the Confederacy united self-governing towns not with nobles but with self-governing rural producers. Future research must decide whether the political autonomy of such peoples depended on economic and military conditions peculiar to the uplands – the pastoral economy and the defensibility of mountain valleys. The uplanders proved their fighting capacities in a great series of battles from Morgarten in 1315 to Schladming in 1525, and the need to bring them under firm control prompted their betters elsewhere to ally with the centralizing, bureaucratic state.[10] North of a certain region, however,

---

[9] It remains an open question whether his Netherlandish origins afforded him the crucial insight.
[10] This is the subject of Rebel's fine *Peasant Classes*.

Conclusion: turning Swiss – a lost dream

the liberation of the land slowed to a halt, from the subversion of the Allgäu peasants in 1405 to the insurrections of 1525. This failure was of great moment for the future development of capitalism, because the expropriation of the increasingly defenseless peasants "formed the foundation of the entire process" of primitive capital accumulation.[11]

The urban oligarchies rejected the strategy of turning Swiss not because they foresaw the rise of capitalism, but for humbler political reasons. The Confederacy presented them with a deep political ambiguity, a union of urban oligarchs and peasant producers, all of whom collectively ruled over yet other subjects, which mirrored the tension between the cities' own oligarchical present and communal past. If there is indeed "an unbroken progressive line"[12] between the communal burghers of this age and the bourgeoisies of a later one, it runs through deep shadows of ambiguity and tension, which flowed from securing the liberties of some through the subjection of others. The great merchants and rentiers of the cities, who were lords as well as citizens, could not help but be deeply suspicious of the ideal of turning Swiss in the sense of ordinary folk wanting "to be their own lords." Yet the fabulous military progress of the Swiss, then at the pinnacle of their glory, enhanced the ideal of turning Swiss in the sense of having the confederates as allies. Finally, the bigger South German cities had simply outgrown the Swiss scale of federation in every respect, for the biggest city men were truly international figures, and their Swiss counterparts were not. More and more, the bigger folk in the cities made their livings from the vast web of market relations, which was replacing the Church as the glue of European civilization, and made their peace with the early modern state.

In these days, when historians are tempted to look with nostalgia on the Holy Roman Empire – "the Old Reich," they familiarly call it – and the rootedness of German burghers in their "hometowns" during the seventeenth and eighteenth centuries, it is well to remember that the security of this sclerotic system exacted a great price at the end of the Middle Ages. Those who paid and those who benefited were not identical, but that is usually true in statebuilding. One great share of the price comprised the political ideals and dreams of the Common Man

---

[11] Marx, *Kapital*, book I, chap. 24, sect. 1 (ed. Lieber and Kautsky, 4:868).
[12] Müller-Mertens, "Bürgerlich-städtische Autonomie," 34.

in South Germany, who had once, inspired by Swiss comrades, dreamt of a different way out of the feudal order. "Only the wall separates the burgher from the peasant," the feudal age had taught, and the early modern state reaffirmed this vision by reducing the ordinary townsmen and their rural counterparts to the common name of "subject," the inert subsoil of the absolutist state. And so the lost dream of turning Swiss faded into the dim past, leaving little to remind the common folk that the cow that mooed on the bridge at Ulm should have been heard in the middle of Switzerland.

Appendix A

∽∽

A list of the Urban Diets, 1471–1585

The Urban Diet, an assembly of envoys from the free cities, emerged as an independent institution during the first half of the 1470s and met at irregular intervals until 1671, exactly two hundred years.[1] The following list of Urban Diets from the beginning until 1585 is based on a document now in the Stadtarchiv Augsburg, Repertorien 328, III. Entitled "Funffter Theil der Erbarn Frey vnnd Reichs Stett Registratur, allain der gehaltnen Stettage sachen vnnd jr, der Stett, sonderbarn Hanndlungen halben besagende," it derives from the old common archive of the Urban Diet, which was established at Speyer in the late 1550s and moved to Frankfurt in 1689.[2]

The day, where given, is the opening day of the Urban Diet. Where an asterisk (*) stands after, or instead of, the day, it means that the Urban Diet met while an Imperial Diet was in session in the same place ("neben dem Reichstag").

This list was transcribed by Katherine G. Brady.

Year	Day	Place
1471	Sept. 8	Frankfurt
1472	Jan. 20	Frankfurt

---

[1] G. Schmidt, *Städtetag*, 15.
[2] Ibid., 104. for a description of the Urban Diet and its political significance, see Chapter 4, section titled "The rise of the urban front."

Appendix A

Year	Day	Place
1472	March 15	Frankfurt
1473	June 24	Frankfurt
1473	July 15	Esslingen
1474	Aug. 1	Speyer
1474	Sept. 14	Speyer
1474	Oct. 16	Speyer
1474	Nov. 30	Speyer
1480	Feb. 2	Esslingen
1480	March 12	Speyer
1480	May 21	Speyer
1481	Feb. 2	Esslingen
1481	Sept. 21	Esslingen
1481	Oct. 16	Speyer
1482	June 6	Speyer
1486	July 13	Esslingen
1486	Aug. 1	Esslingen
1486	Sept. 21	Speyer
1486	Nov. 11	Speyer
1486	Dec. 6	Speyer
1487	Feb. 2	Heilbronn
1487	March 18	Heilbronn
1489	Nov. 30	Speyer
1492	May 27	Speyer
1492	Nov. 30	Speyer
1496	June 5	Speyer
1496	July 25	Speyer

List of Urban Diets

Year	Day	Place
1501	Jan. 6	Speyer
1501	May 1	Speyer
1501	June 15	Speyer
1507	Sept. 14	Speyer
1508	Jan. 20	Speyer
1522	July 25	Speyer
1522	Sept. 1	Nuremberg
1523	March 22	Speyer
1523	June 15	Esslingen
1523	Nov. 6	Speyer
1524	Jan. 6	Nuremberg
1524	July 13	Speyer
1524	Dec. 6	Ulm
1525	July 25	Ulm
1525	Sept. 8	Speyer
1528	July 25	Esslingen
1529	Nov. 25	Esslingen
1535	March 7	Esslingen
1538	Dec. 21	Esslingen
1539	March 1	Frankfurt
1541	*	Regensburg
1541	Nov. 11	Speyer
1542	*	Speyer
1542	Aug. 28	Nuremberg
1543	Apr. 24	Nuremberg
1543	July 8	Frankfurt

Appendix A

Year	Day	Place
1544	*	Speyer
1545	*	Worms
1548	*	Augsburg
1551	*	Augsburg
1555	*	Augsburg
1557	*	Regensburg
1559	*	Augsburg
1560	Feb. 24	Speyer
1561	Feb. 24	Esslingen
1562	Feb. 24	Speyer
1566	*	Augsburg
1570	*	Speyer
1571	Feb. 24	Esslingen
1572	Feb. 24	Speyer
1573	Aug. 24	Esslingen
1574	Aug. 24	Speyer
1575	Aug. 24	Speyer
1576	*	Regensburg
1577	Aug. 24	Frankfurt
1578	Aug. 24	Speyer
1579	Aug. 24	Speyer
1580	Aug. 24	Ulm
1581	Aug. 24	Speyer
1585	Dec. 31	Speyer

Appendix B

~~~~~~

The plan for a centralized Austrian government, 1520

The following document, which is supplied here to support the text in the Chapter 4 section titled "Maximilian van Bergen and the Austrian Way," comes from the archive of the Habsburg government at Stuttgart.[1] Looted in 1534, the archive found its way into the papers of Landgrave Philip of Hesse, the conqueror of Württemberg, and some, though not all, of it came back to Stuttgart in 1908.[2]

The document gives neither date nor author. It can nonetheless be dated after the transfer of Württemberg to Charles V on Feb. 20, 1520, and before the opening of the Imperial Diet of Worms on Jan. 27, 1521. Although the authorship must remain open, the document closely resembles Maximilian I's "Innsbrucker Libell" of 1518, plus the incorporation of Württemberg into Austria, which Maximilian van Bergen had urged on Charles since the autumn of 1519. The document may well stem from Bergen or his lieutenants at Stuttgart. This fair copy, however, was prepared in the German section of Charles V's chancellery, for it is in the same hand as Charles's instruction for his commissioners to treat with the estates of Württemberg, dated Worms, Dec. 15, 1520, which is authenticated by Jean Hannart.[3]

The edition follows in general the guidelines developed by the study group, "Arbeitsgemeinschaft ausseruniversitärer historischer For-

---

[1] The source for the document is HStA Stuttgart, A 2, Bd. 396, fols. 70^r–74^r.
[2] HStA Marburg, PA 361–407, contained the looted Habsburg archive from Stuttgart, but PA 395–407 were returned to Stuttgart in 1908, where they were added to series A 2 but with the old numbers.
[3] HStA Stuttgart, A 2, Bd. 396, fols. 6^r–11^r.

schungseinrichtungen."[4] They call for retaining the original's orthography, except for doubled consonants at the ends of syllables and words that do not affect meaning. Capitals are used only for the initial letters of sentences and of proper nouns and titles. The letter "o" with a superscript "e" has been rendered as "ö," but a superscript "o" over "u" has been ignored. The distinction between "u" and "v" and "i" and "j" – as vowels and consonants respectively – has been normalized.

Text

Regierungen

Item, das im hawss Osterreich vier regiment von justici aufgericht werden, als nemlich ains zu der Newenstat[5] in Osterreich fur die funf Niderosterreichischen furstenthumb und land, das ander zu Inssbrugkh fur die oberosterreichischen land, das drit zu Ensissheim fur die vordern Elsässischen land, und das vierdt zu Stutgartten fur das landt zu Wirtemberg. Doch sollen die appellationes von den zwaÿen regimenten zu Ensisshaim und Stutgartten fur das regiment zu Insprug[6] geen, wie dann bissheer von dem regiment zu Ensissheim auch beschehen ist.

Verrer sollen N. treffenlich personen als fur ain obriste regirung des hawss Osterreichs furgenommen, doch denselben der tittel, Stathalter, Regenten und Rete kunigclicher Maiestät hofrats in Tewtschen Landen, gegeben werden, aus der ursach, das des Reichs regirung demselben hofrat anhengig gemacht werden mag. Vermaint dann die konigliche Maiestät, das es not seÿ, das ir Maiestät ain ansehenliche, geschickhte person aus den Niderlanden beÿ sollichem hofrat hab, die mag ir Maiestät darzue verordnen, doch das dieselb person in allen sachen helf heben und legen. [fol. 70ʳ]

Derselb hofrat soll representieren personam principis und res status Germanie und alles einkommen und aussgeben, auch alle finantz in iren handen haben, handlen und verwalten.

Es sollen auch die gemelten stathalter und rete des hofrats, wann sÿ gar oder zum tail an den enden sein, da die genannten vier regiment

---

[4] "Empfehlungen zur Edition frühneuzeitlicher Texte," *Archiv für Reformationsgeschichte* 72(1981):299–315.
[5] Wiener Neustadt.
[6] Corrected from "Ensisshaim," the only correction in the document.

gehalten werden, macht und gwalt haben, in dieselben regiment zugeen, darein sÿ auch zu allen handlungen gelassen, und inen gar nichts verhalten werden soll. Und darzue verrer macht haben, in furfallenden sachen und notdurften aus denselben vier regimenten ain oder mer personen an ort und end, wie es dann die notdurft zu ÿeder zeit erhaischt, zuerfordern, darinnen und auch in allem andern dieselben vier regiment und ir ÿedes, dem gemelten hofrat an koniglicher Maiestät stat gehorsam und gewertig sein, das alles auch denselben regimenten von koniglicher Maiestät bevolhen und in iren gewalten begriffen werden soll.

Die obgemelten stathalter und rete des hofrats sollen auch die brief, so in irer verwaltung gefertigt werden, under koniglicher Maiestät tittel, insigel und katschet aussgeen lassen. Und diser hofrat soll darumb ain katschet haben, damit sollich brief neben den andern, so in den obangezaigten regimenten, auch under koniglicher Maiestät tittel aussgeen, erkant [fol. 70ᵛ] werden mugen. Sollich katschet mag auch underschidlich gemacht werden, damit man wisse, das sollich brief in gemeltem hofrat und nit beÿ koniglicher Maiestät gefertigt werden seÿen.

Derselb hofrat und die obgemelten vier regiment sollen ain ander correspondieren und in furfallenden sachen und notdurften zusamen setzen und gleich also ain regierung sein.

All partheÿen sachen, so an koniglicher Maiestät gelangen wellen, sollen erstlich dem hofrat angezaigt und durch denselben beratslagt und, sover es not ist, erst nachmals mit des hofrats gutbedunckhen an konigliche Maiestät gepracht werden.

All brief uber hauptmanschaften, phlegen, embter und dergleichen sollen beÿ und durch gemelten hofrat in koniglicher Maiestät namen gefertigt, doch hawbtlewt, phleger und gross ambtleut mit koniglicher Maiestät wissen und auf derselben bevelh aufgenommen werden.

Marggraf Casimir von Brandemburg soll, wie der bestelt ist, obrister veldthawbtman des hawss Osterreichs beleiben und sein aufsehen auf den gemelten hofrat haben. [fol. 71ʳ]

Und nachdem im hauss Osterreich vil versezt ist, auch gross und mergkhlich schulden vorhanden sein, die man zuverhuetung krieg, aufrurn und widerwertigkait annemmen, zufriden stellen und versichern muess, und dann die konigliche Maiestät der mergkhlichen und grossen geschefft halben, damit ir konigliche Maiestät on underlass beladen ist, demselben selbst nit ausswarten mag, desshalben ir konigliche Maiestät dem gemelten hofrat auflegen wolt, sich sollicher schulden und alles wesens im hawss Osterreich anzunemmen und sollichs zu underhalten, doch ausserhalb des kriegs. Damit nu die stathalter und rete des hofrats, sover sÿ sollichen last uber sich laden und annemmen, irer notdurft nach widerumb versichert werden, so soll demselben hofrat ain verschreibung von koniglicher Maiestät und derselben Brueder, Ertzhertzog Ferdinanden, aufgericht und gegeben, darinnen inen ir baider gnaden verschreiben und zuestellen, alles einkommen des hauss Osterreichs, auch was der konigliche Maiestät in dem Reich gefallen wirdet, es seÿ ordinarie oder extraordinarie, hilfgelt, confiscation, fellige lehen und gueter, und ander dergleichen, dermassen und in der gestalt, das die gemelten stathalter und rete von sollichen einkommen und gefellen nit entsezt sollen werden, bis sÿ alles des, darumb sÿ hindergang gethan, aufgebracht, zuegesagt oder verschriben hetten, mitsambt costen und schaden, was und wie der darauf gangen were, widerumb aussgericht und bezalt werden. [fol. 71ᵛ]

Doch so sollen dieselben stathalter und rete nichts zu versezen noch zu verpfenden noch auch ausserhalb des so ordinari ist und sein muess, kain provision noch dienst gelt, zuverschreiben haben, es beschehe dann auf koniglicher Maiestät sonderlichen bevelh.

Der gemelt hofrat soll auch macht haben, etlichen eerlichen, treffenlichen personen, die sÿ in furfallenden hendlen und notdurften, erfordern und geprauchen mugen, zimlicher weiss pensionen zugeben, doch nit anders dann auf koniglicher Maiestät wolgefallen, auch ander rete, es seÿ von hawss aus oder sonst. Item doctores und ander officier und diener aufzunemmen, wie dann solhs die notdurft sollicher regirung erfordern wirdet.

Stathalter und rete des gemelten hofrats sollen auch, wann die konigliche Maiestät in hoch Tewtschen landen ist, alweg beÿ irer Maiestät am hof sein. Wann aber ir konigliche Maiestät ausserhalb Tewtscher Nation ist, so soll sollicher hofrat in den erblanden sein, an orten und enden, da es dann zu ÿeder zeit die maist notdurft erfordert. Und sollicher hofrat gar oder zum tail im Reich sein wurde, so solle er sich bevleissen die versamblung der personen, so in des Reichs sachen zu handlen werden, auf malstet und end zubringen, die den osterreichischen erblanden am nähisten gelegen sein. [fol. 72ʳ]

Und wann stathalter und rete des genannten hofrats nit beÿ koniglicher Maiestät am hof sein, sollen sÿ ain oder mer personen von irentwegen beÿ koniglicher Maiestät am hof haben, die die Tewtschen handel an die konigliche Maiestät bringen und beschaid darauf erlangen und in sollichem dem hofrat correspondieren.

Finantz

Es soll ain schatzmaister sein, der gehaissen soll werden Schatzmaister General in Tewtschen Landen.

Derselb schatzmaister soll neben ime haben ainen Einnemmer General, der alles einkommen von dem gantzen hawss Osterreich, auch was im Reich gefelt, einnemme und verraÿte.

Und der Schatzmaister und Einnemmer General sollen solliche ire embter verwalten und handlen nach laut ainer instruction, so desshalben aufgericht und dem schatzmaister uberantwort werden soll.

Item, es soll ain Cammermaister in den Niderosterreichischen landen sein, der alweg sein aufsehen auf die [fol. 72ᵛ] vitzthumb und exempt ambtlewt in denselben landen hab und dem dieselben vitzthumb und exempt ambt lewt ir einkommen und gefelle uberantworten.

In den Oberosterreichischen landen soll auch ein Cammermaister sein, dem alle under ambtlewt derselben land ir einkommen uberantworten.

In dem land zu Wirtemberg soll ain landtschreiber sein, wie dann bissherr der geprauch gewesen ist, oder dem mag ain anderer tittel gegeben, dem soll alles einkommen, so in demselben land gefallet, uberantwort und durch ine verraÿt werden.

Was nu den gemelten zwaÿen cammermaistern und dem landtschreiber im land zu Wirtemberg jerlich an irem emphang uber die ordinarj aussgaben, so auf underhaltung der regimenten, haubtmans sold, burgkhhutten und alles anders jerlich geet, darumben inen dann ordenlich stet aufgericht sollen werden, uberbeleibt, sollen sÿ dem Einnemer General uberantworten, davon sollen der hofrat provisioner von hawss aus und anders underhalten, auch ander schulden bezalt, darzue auch rent und gult, so am beswerlichisten versetzt, sovil es sein mag, erledigt, und also alles wesen des hawss Osterreichs underhalten, und was dar uber beleibt zu andern koniglicher Maiestät notdurften gewendt werden. [fol. 73ʳ]

Raitcammer

Es soll ain General Raitcammer aufgericht werden und zu Inssbrugg sein, doch ir aufsehen auf den gemelten hofrat haben und demselben gehorsam und gewertig sein. Daselbs sollen der Einnemmer General,

Appendix B

die zwen Cammermaister, der landtschreiber im land zu Wirtemberg, und all vitzthumb und exempt ambtlewt in den Niderosterreichischen landen jerlich, oder wie es fur gut angesehen wirdet, ordenlich raittung von irem einnemmen und aussgeben thun. Und was mengel allenthalben in den embtern gefunden, die sollen mit rat und hilf des hofrats abgestelt und verheut werden.

Es sollen auch alle regiment, hawbtlewt und pfleger schuldig sein, allenthalben die ambtlewt beÿ dem cammergut zu handthaben, auch denselben regimenten, hawbtlewten und phlegern sollichs in ir gewalt und pflicht eingepunden werden.

Und so die gemelten regierungen und raitcammer also aufgericht, so mag alsdann beratslagt werden, wellicher massen mit den under ambtlewten in allen landen durch die ober ambtlewt, als cammermaister, vitzthumb, landtschreiber und ander, auch ordenlichen und koniglicher Maiestät zu bestem nutz gerechnet werden mug. [fol. 73^v]

Berurend das Reich

Das Cammergericht im Reich soll vor allen dingen aufgericht werden.

Dann betreffent die regirung im Reich, die mag dem obgemelten hofrat anhengig gemacht werden, doch kan man vor derselben regirung, wie dieselb sein soll, vor dem kunftigen Reichstag kain lauters wissen haben.[7]

Und damit aber das Cammergericht im Reich nit stilstee, so soll daselb durch den obgemelten hofrat von dem Osterreichischen einkommen underhalten, bis im Reich sovil erlangt wirdet, das sollichs underhaltung nachmals von des Reichs gefellen beschehen mag.

Und dem allen nach, so sollen noch wellen die konigliche Maiestät noch ir Brueder, Ertzhertzog Ferdinand, die stathalter und rete des obangezaigten hofrats mit weiter aussgab nit beladen, bis die einkommen uber die obangezaigten aussgaben etwas zu uberschuss und per restat ertragen.

Ob auch ain krieg entsteen wurde, so soll die konigliche Maiestät denselben gnedigclich vertreten und underhalten.

Darzue auch den Fugger umb die hundert zwaÿundzwaintzig tawsent guldin in ander weg bezalen.[8]

---

[7] The Diet of Worms opened on Jan. 27, 1521.
[8] Jakob Fugger advanced this sum to Charles's agents on Aug. 8, 1519, "zu Handlung unserer Elektion." See Pölnitz, *Jakob Fugger*, 2:428; see also 1:439, 2:436.

Und was uber das alles von gewaltsbriefen, verschreibungen und anders aufzurichten not sein wirdet, das soll die konigliche Maiestät genedigclich fertigen.

Doch soll Ertzhertzog Ferdinand den versicherung und schadlosbrief, die finantz berurend, neben der koniglicher Maiestät auch underschreiben und versiglen. [fol. 74^r]

Appendix C

∞∞∞

The merchants' petition to Charles V against banditry, 1521

The following document is supplied to support the text in the Chapter 4 section titled "Cities under attack."[1] It is a petition to Charles V, written for a group of unnamed merchants assembled at Frankfurt am Main shortly after the Imperial Diet of Worms in 1521. The dangers it describes to the persons and goods of merchants traveling to and from the Frankfurt fairs were conditions of long standing, which had at times led to boycotts of the fairs.[2] I have found no record of a response by Charles to this petition, which clearly meant to take advantage of his presence nearby.[3]

The principles of edition are those indicated in the introductory remarks to Appendix B above.

Text

Supplication gemeiner Kauf- und Handelsleuth ahn Kayserliche Maiestät wider die strassenraubereien [1521] Aller durchleuchtigister, grossmechtigister kayser, aller gnedigster herr. Weylent der alt durchleuchtigster, grossmechtigster furst und her, her Maximilian, römischer kayser, euer kayserlicher Maiestät vorfar und anherr, unser aller gnedister herr hochloblicher gedechtnus, hat vorschinenen jars uff etlichen gehalten reichsdagen mit rede, wissen und bewilligung gemeyner stende des heiligen Reichs, dem heiligen Reich zugude und zu beystendiger enthaltung fridens und rechtens eynen gemeynen landtfriden uffgericht und in dem

---

[1] The source for the document is AMS, AA 374b, fols. 5^r–7^v.
[2] See Jahns, *Frankfurt*, 17.
[3] At least there is none in *RTA, jR*, 2.

selben neben andern gar statlich versehen, in massen dan solchs die gulden Bull und die gemeynen des Reichs beschriben recht on das lauter vermogen, das keyner, von was wirden, stants oder wesens der sey, den andern bevegden mit gewalt oder omecht bekriegen, beschedigen. Sonder were zu den andern zu sprechen habe, das er solchs mit ordentlichem rechten thun und suchen soll, alles bey des heiligen Reichs acht, aberacht und andern schweren penen und pussen in dem selben landtfriden begriffen. Ongeachtet des alles, und wiewol der gemeyne hantwerckman, so des heiligen Reichs strassen besucht und pauth, uss billicheit, vertrostung und sicherheiten auch eynen freyhen handel und wandel, haben soll, ist doch bissher nit allein gegen unsern oberkeiten, denen wir on mittel underworfen, sunder auch wider unser personen, leybe, hab und guter solicher landtfridt verprach. Dan nit allein die selben, unserer oberkeiten, sonder auch ander des heiligen Reichs frey und reichsstett sint nun etwan vil [fol. 5ʳ] jare in manchfeltig weyssen bevehdt und angegriffen, solcher gestalt, das wenig derselben erbern stett im heiligen Reich erfunden werden, die von zeiten uffgerichts landfriden bisshero nit sonderlich beschedigung und vergeweltigung erlitten hetten. Das aber bey menigliche eyn solche verachtung und lichtvertigkeiten im heiligen Reiche hat verursacht, das dieselben landtfridtbruchigen handelung und vorgeweltigung gegen uns dermassen ingebrochen und uberhandtgenommen haben, das wir uns auch des bishero gar beschwerlich erhalt und schir zu gantzem verderben gemussigt sein. Dan ongeacht aller vortrostung, sicherheit, geleyde und gegeben zoll sint wir zu mer maln durch die, so sich in irem vorteil onscheinlicher förderung ongemasst, on erlangt alles rechtens auch onbewardt irer eren, gefangen, wegkgefurt, gestockt, geplackt umb mergliche summa gulden uber unser vermogen geschatzt, in andere hende verkauft, unser guter zu wasser und zu lande uffgehalten, angriffen, aufgehawen, verprendt und verderbt, und gantz tirranisch gegen uns gehandelt, solcher gestalt, das auch das meniglich und sonderlich alle gehorsamen des Reichs underthanen von des deutschen namen wegen zuvernemen erschrecklich, auch allen des Reichs oberkeiten bey frembden nation zu sampt irem merglichen erliden schaden, schmipflich, spotlich und [fol. 5ᵛ] vorchtlich. So ist eurer kayserlichen Maiestät sonders zweyfels onverporgen, das dise nachteiligs beschwerungen und gewalthaten nit allein vor euerer kayserlichen Maiestät zukonft in das Reiche sonder auch sither manchfeltiglich geubt, dan in newlichen dagen und dweil euer kayserliche Maiestät neben andern stenden des heiligen Rychs, auch fremder herschaften uff disen richtsdag zu Wormbs gewest. Sint nit weyt von Worms eyn wagen mit gewant zwischen Fuld und Isenach uffgehawen und entwert. Item eyn welscher kaufman ist, wie wir glaublich bericht, gantz nahendt by der stat Wurms durch etlich geraisig angesprengt, ermort und aller seiner barschaft raublich entwert. Des gleichen ist jezent jungst und nemlich am [blank] nechst vorgangen, sint vier wagen mit etwa vil gutern eynes dapfern wirts, so uss eurer kayserlichen Maiestät Niderlanden her uffgefarn nit weyt von [blank], zum theil euerer kayserlichen Maiestät erblich undertanen in Braband und dan eins theils uns und andern zugehorig, durch etwan vil geryssigen biss in 54 starcken, under denen eyner, Philips von Ruderkom genant, auch [blank] gewest, geweltiglich angewendt, die guter uffgehawen und davon den pesten theil der selben guetter uff der furlent wagen pferde, so sie uss den wagen gespant geladen, von danen gefurt und uff zwo meyl wegs von Franckfurt verpeuth. Welches aber nit allein den beschedigten zu mynderung irer narung und [fol. 6ʳ] irem wybern und kindern zu gantzem verderblichen schaden. Sonder auch zu forderst euer kayserliche Maiestät bey meniglich fur eyn gneigten furderer, hanthaber und beschirmer billicher, erberer und gerechter sachen hochberumbt, so vil dester zu hoherer verlautung recht, so vil die selben theter zuvor diser zeit. Und dweil sie euer kayserliche Maiestät zu Worms in des Reichs merglichen obligen wissen, ire pose strafliche dat denselben euerer kayserlichen Maiestät und allen stenden des heiligen Reichs zuverachtung furnemen, glichwol achten wir darfur, das dise und derglichen gewalthaten und verechtlich beschedigungen nit eynen geringen theil durch unser gnedige hern, etlicher rychsoberkeiten vorgelaitung gewachsen, dan dwil dieselben gelaide etwas mit eynen wayden ussnemen und nit frey in massen alle trostung und sicherheiten uss iren natur und aigenschaften billich sein solten gegeben werden, denen und andern hantieren dieselben mer zu nachteil dan eynichen vorgelaitung. Dan ob wie wol zu mer maln unser lybe, hab und guter ausserhalb der gelait wol hetten getrut, sicher durchzubringen, und wir doch in die gelaide gemussigt, und so wir die genomen, denen auch ohn billich vertraut, haben wir ongeachtet solchs gelaits angezeigte beschedigung entpfangen und erlitten. Wie wol nun [fol. 6ᵛ] wir auch unser oberkeiten soliche onleydenlich beschwerungen, die in allen des Rychs underthanen untreglich sein, sich auch von dagen zu dagen yhe mer und mer zu tragen und ernewern geclagt, umb hulff

und handhabung angesucht, umb widerstattung unserer genomenen und
entwerten habe flelich angelangt, haben wir doch wenig hulff befanden
und keins mals bey ordentlichen rechten gar nit blyben mogen. Welchs
aber, wie euer kayserliche Maiestät als eyn loblicher, hochverstendiger
kayser zubewyssen haben zuhoren, erbermlich auch uns und allen andern des Reichs underthanen erschrocklich ist, dan was uns heut be-
gegnet, mag morgen andern, ja vil hoher und merer personen. Dwil
doch euer kayserliche Maiestät selbst erblich underthanen her in gar
nit verschont wirdt belangen, und so wir aber herin nymant wissen
anzurufen dan euer kayserliche Maiestät als eyn haupt des heiligen
Reichs, zu dem wir noch gar allen unsern trost, hulff und vorsehung
stellen, so ist an die selb euer kayserliche Maiestät unser gantz under-
thenig bitt, der selben zu fussen fallen und uns bedranglich hoher notturft schreyend und flehend, euer kayserliche Maiestät geruchen als eyn
gerechter, milter kayser, der gerechtigkeit und erbar handelung liebt
[fol. 7ʳ] und straflich bos ubungen hasst und verfolgt, diese gemein des
heiligen Reichs all ire undertane und zuvor der erbarn stette beschedigung gnediglich zu hertzen furen und darin gnedig und statlich in-
sehens, das doch gegen disen landfridbrechern und thetern solicher
gewaltaten (den posen zu eyner forcht und entsetzen, den fromen aber
zu eynem trost) mit keyserlicher straf gehandelt und im heiligen Reiche
fride und recht dermassen bevestigt und gehandthabt werden, das wir
solcher on uberwintlicher beschedigung ubersten, das heilig Reichs in
bestendiger, fridlicher ordenung erhalten und in uffname gebracht werde,
daran beschecht sonder zweyfels dem almechtigen ein sonder gut gefallen. Es fordern auch euer kayserliche Maiestät darmit eyn werck, das
euerer kayserlichen Maiestät bey meniglich erlich und rumblich werdet,
das wir auch umb euerer kayserlichen Maiestät alles unsers vormogens
in hochster underthenigkeit gehorsamlich zuvordienen willig sein.

Euerer kayserlichen Maiestät und des heiligen Reichs gehorsame underthanen,
die gemeinen hantierer, werber und kaufleut teutscher nation, so zu Franckfurt
vorsamlet. [fol. 7ᵛ]

Bibliography

Manuscript sources

Augsburg, Stadtarchiv. Litteralien-Sammlung

    Oct. 8, 1519
    Aug. 24, 1523
    Aug. 20, 1525
    Oct. 28, 1525
    April 2, 1526
    Dec. 9, 1528

Basel, Staatsarchiv

    Deutschland B 2 I
    Kirchen-Akten A 8
    Politisches L 2,1; M 8,3

Chicago, The Newberry Library

    Ms. 63, Oraciones varies

Esslingen, Stadtarchiv

    Bürgerbuch II 79

Göttingen, Niedersächsische Staats- und Universitätsbibliothek

    Ms. Hist. 154, Chronik der Stadt Strassburg

Marburg, Hessisches Staatsarchiv

    Politisches Archiv des Landgrafen Philipp 389

Bibliography

Strasbourg, Archives Municipales

AA 309	IV 33/7	IV 68/122	RP1540
AA 313	IV 33/9	IV 68/128	
AA 319	IV 33/14		
AA 374b			

Stuttgart, Hauptstaatsarchiv

A 2, Bd. 396

Ulm, Stadtarchiv

A 521
A 529

Printed sources

This list contains all books and articles, published and unpublished, cited in the notes to this book. Because of the method of citation by short title, sources have not been separated from secondary literature. The entries are alphabetized by author, editor, translator, or title.

Abray, Lorna Jane. *The People's Reformation: Magistrates, Clergy, and Commons in Strasbourg, 1520–1598.* Ithaca, N.Y., and London, 1985.

Ammann, Hektor. *Von der Wirtschaftsgeltung des Elsass im Mittelalter.* Lahr (Schwarzwald), 1955. Also in *Alemannisches Jahrbuch* (1955): 95–202.

Amtliche Sammlung der älteren Eidgenössischen Abschiede. Vol. 3, parts 1, 2: *1478–1520*, ed. A. Philipp Segesser. Zurich, 1858; Lucerne, 1869. Vol. 4, parts 1a, 1b:*1521–1532*, ed. Johannes Strickler. Brügg, 1873; Zurich, 1876. Vol. 4, parts 1c, 1d, 1e: *1533–1555*, ed. Karl Deschwanden. Lucerne, 1876–86.

Anderson, Perry. *Lineages of the Absolutist State.* London, 1974.

Passages from Antiquity to Feudalism. London, 1974.

Angermeier, Heinz. "Begriff und Inhalt der Reichsreform." *Zeitschrift der Savigny-Stiftung für Rechtsgeschichte, Germanistische Abteilung* 75 (1958): 181–205.

Königtum und Landfriede im deutschen Spätmittelalter. Munich, 1966.

Annales de Sébastien Brant. Ed. Léon Dacheux. In *Bulletin de la Société pour la Conservation des Monuments historiques d'Alsace,* series 2, vol. 19 (1897–8): 33–260.

Bibliography

Arbenz, Emil, ed. *Vadianische Briefsammlung*. Part 4: *1526–30*. In *Mitteilungen zur vaterländischen Geschichte* 28 (St. Gallen, 1902).

Arnold, Klaus. "Freiheit im Mittelalter," *Historiches Jahrbuch* 104 (1984): 1–21.

Augustijn, Cornelis. " 'Allein das heilig Evangelium.' Het mandaat van het Reichsregiment 6 maart 1523." *Nederlands Archief voor Kerkgeschiedenis*, new series 48 (1967–8): 150–65.

Aulinger, Rosemarie. *Das Bild des Reichstages im 16. Jahrhundert*. Schriften der Historischen Kommission bei der Bayerischen Akademie der Wissenschaften, no. 18. Göttingen, 1980.

Baader, Joseph, ed. *Verhandlungen über Thomas von Absberg und seine Fehden gegen den Schwäbischen Bund 1519 bis 1530*. Bibliothek des Litterarischen Vereins in Stuttgart, no. 114. Tübingen, 1873.

Bader, Karl Siegfried. *Der deutsche Südwesten in seiner territorialstaatlichen Entwicklung*. Stuttgart, 1950.

Studien zur Rechtsgeschichte des mittelalterlichen Dorfes. 3 vols. Weimar, Vienna, Cologne, and Graz, 1957–73.

Baelde, Michael. "Financiële politiek en domaniale evolutie in de Nederlanden onder Karel V en Filips II (1530–1560)." *Tijdschrift voor Geschiedenis* 76 (1963): 14–30. Also trans. by Chaninah Maschler in *Government in Reformation Europe, 1520–1560*, ed. Henry J. Cohn. Glasgow and New York, 1971.

Baron, Hans. *The Crisis of the Early Italian Renaisssance: Civic Humanism and Republican Liberty in an Age of Classicism and Tyranny*. Rev. ed. Princeton, N.J., 1966.

"Franciscan Poverty and Civic Wealth as Factors in the Rise of Humanistic Thought." *Speculum* 13 (1938): 1–37.

"Religion and Politics in the German Imperial Cities during the Reformation." *English Historical Review* 52 (1937): 405–27, 614–33.

Barth, Karl Franz. "Der bairisch-pfälzische Erbfolgekrieg im Fürstenbergischen und in der Ortenau." *Die Ortenau. Mitteilungen des Historischen Vereins für Mittelbaden* 18 (1931): 8–51.

Bauer, Clemens. "Conrad Peutinger und der Durchbruch des neuen ökonomischen Denkens in der Wende zur Neuzeit." In *Augusta 955–1955*, ed. H. Rinn, pp. 219–28. Munich, 1955.

"Conrad Peutingers Gutachten zur Monopolfrage. Eine Untersuchung zur Wandlung der Wirtschaftsanschauungen im Zeitalter der Reformation." *Archiv für Reformationsgeschichte* 45 (1954): 1–43, 145–96.

"Die wirtschaftlichen Machtgrundlagen Karls V." In *Gesammelte Aufsätze zur Kulturgeschichte Spaniens*, vol. 15, ed. Johannes Vincke, pp. 219–29. Münster (Westphalia), 1960.

Bibliography

Bauer, Wilhelm. *Die Anfänge Ferdinands I.* Vienna and Leipzig, 1907.

Bauer, Wilhelm, and Robert Lacroix, eds. *Die Korrespondenz Ferdinands I.* 3 vols. Veröffentlichungen der Kommission für neuere Geschichte Oesterreichs, nos. 29–31. Vienna, 1912–38.

Baumann, Franz Ludwig. *Geschichte des Allgäus.* 3 vols. Kempten, 1883–94. Reprint. Aalen, 1971–3.

"Schwaben und Alamannen, ihre Herkunft und Identität." In *Forschungen zur schwäbischen Geschichte* by Franz Ludwig Baumann, pp. 500–85. Kempten, 1899.

Ed. *Akten zur Geschichte des Deutschen Bauernkrieges aus Oberschwaben.* Freiburg im Breisgau, 1877.

Baumgarten, Hermann. *Geschichte Karls V.* 3 vols. Stuttgart, 1885–92.

Bebb, Phillip Norton. "Christoph Scheurl's Role as Legal Advisor to the Nürnberg City Council, 1512 to 1525." Ph.D. dissertation, Ohio State University, 1971.

Becker, Winfried. " 'Göttliches Wort,' 'göttliches Recht,' 'göttliche Gerechtigkeit.' Politisierung theologischer Begriffe." In *Revolte und Revolution in Europa. Referate und Protokolle des Internationalen Symposiums zur Erinnerung an den Bauernkrieg 1525 (Memmingen, 24.–27. März 1975),* ed. Peter Blickle, pp. 232–63. Munich, 1975.

Bender, Wilhelm. *Zwinglis Reformationsbündnisse. Untersuchungen zur Rechts- und Sozialgeschichte der Burgrechtsverträge eidgenössischer und oberdeutscher Städte zur Ausbreitung und Sicherung der Reformation Huldrych Zwinglis.* Ph.D. dissertation, University of Berlin. Zurich and Stuttgart, 1970.

Benecke, Gerhard. *Maximilian I (1459–1519). An Analytical Biography.* London, 1982.

Bergier, Jean-François. "From the Fifteenth Century in Italy to the Sixteenth Century in Germany: A New Banking Concept?" In *The Dawn of Modern Banking,* ed. Center for Medieval and Renaissance Studies, University of California, Los Angeles, pp. 105–30. New Haven and London, 1979.

Bernhardt, Walter. *Die Zentralbehörden des Herzogtums Württemberg und ihre Beamten 1520–1629.* 2 vols. Veröffentlichungen der Kommission für geschichtliche Landeskunde in Baden-Württemberg, series B, nos. 70–1. Stuttgart, 1973.

Berthold, Brigitte. "Städte und Reichsreform in der ersten Hälfte des 15. Jahrhunderts." In *Städte und Ständestaat. Zur Rolle der Städte bei der Entwicklung der Ständeverfassung in europäischen Staaten vom 13. bis zum 15. Jahrhundert,* ed. Bernhard Töpfer, pp. 59–111. Forschungen zur mittelalterlichen Geschichte, no. 26. Berlin, 1980.

Bierbrauer, Peter. "Bäuerliche Revolte im Alten Reich. Ein Forschungsbe-

Bibliography

richt." In *Aufruhr und Empörung? Studien zum bäuerlichen Widerstand im Alten Reich*, ed. Peter Blickle, pp. 1–69. Munich, 1980.

"Das Göttliche Recht und die naturrechtliche Tradition." In *Bauer, Reich und Reformation. Festschrift für Günther Franz zum 80. Geburtstag am 23. Mai 1982*, ed. Peter Blickle, pp. 210–34. Stuttgart, 1982.

Bilgeri, Benedikt. *Der Bund ob dem See. Vorarlberg im Appenzellerkrieg.* Stuttgart, Berlin, Cologne, and Mainz, 1968.

Bischoff, Georges. *Gouvernées et gouvernants en Haute-Alsace à l'époque autrichienne. Les états des pays antérieurs des origines au milieu du XVIe siècle.* Publications de la Société Savante d'Alsace et des Régions de l'Est, series "Grandes Publications," no. 20. Strasbourg, 1982.

Bitton, Davis. *The French Nobility in Crisis, 1560–1640.* Stanford, 1969.

Black, Anthony. *Council and Commune: The Conciliar Movement and the Council of Basel.* London, 1979.

Blaich, Fritz. *Die Reichsmonopolgesetzgebung im Zeitalter Karls V. Ihre ordnungspolitische Problematik.* Schriften zum Vergleich von Wirtschaftsordnungen, no. 8. Stuttgart, 1967.

"Die Reichsstädte und die Antimonopolpolitik des Reiches im Zeitalter Karls V." *Jahrbuch für Geschichte der oberdeutschen Reichsstädte* 12/13 (1966–7): 202–13.

Die Wirtschaftspolitik des Reichstages im Heiligen Römischen Reich. Ein Beitrag zur Problemsgeschichte wirtschaftlichen Gestaltens. Schriften zum Vergleich von Wirtschaftsordnungen, no. 16. Stuttgart, 1970.

Blarer, Gerwig. *Briefe und Akten*, ed. Heinrich Günter. 2 vols. Württembergische Geschichtsquellen, nos. 16–17. Stuttgart, 1914–21.

Blaschke, Karlheinz. *Sachsen im Zeitalter der Reformation.* Schriften des Vereins für Reformationsgeschichte, no. 185. Gütersloh, 1970.

Blickle, Peter. "Bäuerliche Rebellionen im Fürststift St. Gallen." In *Aufruhr und Empörung? Studien zum bäuerlichen Widerstand im Alten Reich*, ed. Peter Blickle, pp. 215–95. Munich, 1980.

Deutsche Untertanen. Ein Widerspruch. Munich, 1981.

Landschaften im Alten Reich. Die staatliche Funktion des gemeinen Mannes in Oberdeutschland. Munich, 1973.

Die Reformation im Reich. Uni-Taschenbücher, no. 1181. Stuttgart, 1982.

The Revolution of 1525: The German Peasants' War from a New Perspective. Trans. Thomas A. Brady, Jr., and H. C. Erik Midelfort. Baltimore, 1981.

Die Revolution von 1525. Rev. ed. Munich, 1981.

"Social Protest and Reformation Theology." In *Religion, Politics, and Social Protest: Three Studies on Early Modern Germany*, ed. Kaspar von Greyerz, pp. 1–23. Publications of the German Historical Institute London. London, 1984.

Bibliography

"Zur Territorialpolitik der oberschwäbischen Städte." In *Stadt und Umland. Protokoll der X. Arbeitstagung des Arbeitskreises für südwestdeutsche Stadtgeschichtsforschung Calw 1971*, ed. Erich Maschke and Jürgen Sydow, pp. 54–71. Veröffentlichungen der Kommission für geschichtliche Landeskunde in Baden-Württemberg, series B, no. 82. Stuttgart, 1974.

Bloch, Marc. *French Rural History. An Essay on its Basic Characteristics.* Trans. Janet Sondheimer. Berkeley and Los Angeles, 1966.

Bock, Ernst. *Der Schwäbische Bund und seine Verfassungen 1488-1534. Ein Beitrag zur Geschichte der Zeit der Reichsreform.* Rev. ed. Untersuchungen zur deutschen Staats- und Rechtsgeschichte, old series, no. 137. Aalen, 1968.

Bodin, Jean. *Six Books of the Commonwealth.* Trans. M. J. Tooley. Oxford, n.d.

Bofinger, Wilhelm. "Kirche und werdender Territorialstaat. Eine Untersuchung zur Kirchenreform Herzog Ulrichs von Württemberg." *Blätter für württembergische Kirchengeschichte* 65 (1965): 75–149.

"Oberdeutschtum und württembergische Reformation. Die Sozialgestalt der Kirche als Problem der Theologie- und Kirchengeschichte der Reformationszeit." Ph.D. dissertation, Tübingen, 1957.

Bog, Ingomar. "Betrachtungen zur korporativen Politik der Reichsstädte." *Ulm und Oberschwaben* 34 (1955): 87–101.

Bonadeo, Alfred. "The Role of the 'Grandi' in the Political World of Machiavelli." *Studies in the Renaissance* 16 (1969): 9–30.

"The Role of the People in the Works and Times of Machiavelli." *Bibliothèque d'Humanisme et Renaissance* 32 (1970): 351–78.

Boos, Heinrich. *Geschichte der rheinischen Städtekultur von ihren Anfängen bis zur Gegenwart mit besonderer Berücksichtigung der Stadt Worms.* Vol. 4. 2d ed. Berlin, 1901.

Bornert, René. *La réforme protestante du culte à Strasbourg au XVIe siècle (1523– 1598). Approche sociologique et interprétation théologique.* Studies in Medieval and Reformation Thought, no. 28. Leiden, 1981.

Borst, Otto. *Geschichte der Stadt Esslingen am Neckar.* 3d ed. Esslingen, 1978.

Borth, Wilhelm. *Die Luthersache (causa Lutheri) 1517–1524. Die Anfänge der Reformation als Frage von Politik und Recht.* Historische Studien, no. 414. Lübeck and Hamburg, 1970.

Brady, Thomas A., Jr. "Aristocratie et régime politique à Strasbourg à l'époque de la Réforme (1525–1555)." In *Strasbourg au coeur religieux du XVIe siècle,* ed. Georges Livet, Francis Rapp, and Jean Rott, pp. 19–36. Publications de la Société Savante d'Alsace et des Régions de l'Est, series "Grandes Publications," no. 12. Strasbourg, 1977.

"Jacob Sturm of Strasbourg and the Lutherans at the Diet of Augsburg, 1530." *Church History* 32 (1973): 183–202.

"Jacob Sturm of Strasbourg (1489–1553) and the Political Security of Ger-

Bibliography

man Protestantism, 1526–1532." Ph.D. dissertation, University of Chicago, 1968.

"Patricians, Nobles, Merchants: Internal Tensions and Solidarities in South German Urban Ruling Classes at the Close of the Middle Ages." In *Social Groups and Religious Ideas in the Sixteenth Century*, ed. Miriam U. Chrisman and Otto Gründler, pp. 38–45. Studies in Medieval Culture, vol. 13. Kalamazoo, Mich., 1978.

"Phases and Strategies of the Schmalkaldic League. A Perspective after 450 Years." *Archiv für Reformationsgeschichte* 74 (1983): 162–81.

"Princes' Reformation vs. Urban Liberty: Strasbourg and the Restoration in Württemberg, 1534." In *Städtische Gesellschaft und Reformation*, ed. Ingrid Bátori, pp. 265–91. Spätmittelalter und Frühe Neuzeit. Tübinger Beiträge zur Geschichtsforschung, no. 12. Stuttgart, 1980.

Ruling Class, Regime and Reformation at Strasbourg, 1520–1555. Studies in Medieval and Reformation Thought, no. 23. Leiden, 1978.

" 'Sind also zu beiden theilen Christen des Gott erbarm.' Le mémoire de Jacques Sturm sur le culte public à Strasbourg (août 1525)." In *Horizons européens de la Réforme en Alsace. Mélanges offerts à Jean Rott pour son 65e anniversaire*, ed. Marijn de Kroon and Marc Lienhard, pp. 69–79. Publications de la Société Savante d'Alsace et des Régions de l'Est, no. 17. Strasbourg, 1980.

"Social History." In *Reformation Europe: A Guide to Research*, ed. Steven Ozment, pp. 161–81. St. Louis, 1982.

"The Social Place of a German Renaissance Artist: Hans Baldung Grien (1484/85–1545) at Strasbourg." *Central European History* 9 (1975): 295–315.

"The Themes of Social Structure, Social Conflict, and Civic Harmony in Jakob Wimpheling's *Germania*." *Sixteenth Century Journal* 3 (1972): 65–76.

Brandi, Karl. *The Emperor Charles V: The Growth and Destiny of a Man and of a World-Empire*. Trans. C. V. Wedgwood. 1939. Reprint. London, 1965.

Kaiser Karl V. Werden und Schicksal einer Persönlichkeit und eines Weltreiches. Vol. 1. 6th ed. Munich, 1961. Vol. 2. 2d ed. Darmstadt, 1967.

Brandis, Jakob Andrä Freiherr von. *Die Geschichte der Landeshauptleute von Tirol*. Innsbruck, 1850.

Brant, Sebastian. *Das Narrenschiff*. Ed. Friedrich Zarncke. Leipzig, 1854.

Brauer-Gramm, Hildburg. *Der Landvogt Peter von Hagenbach. Die burgundische Herrschaft am Oberrhein 1469-1474*. Göttinger Bausteine zur Geschichtswissenschaft, no. 27. Göttingen, 1957.

Brecht, Martin. "Die gemeinsame Politik der Reichsstädte und die Refor-

Bibliography

mation." *Zeitschrift der Savigny-Stiftung für Rechtsgeschichte, Kanonistische Abteilung* 49 (1977): 180–263.

"Die gescheiterte Reformation in Rottweil." *Blätter für württembergische Kirchengeschichte* 75 (1975): 5–22.

"Ulm und die deutsche Reformation." *Ulm und Oberschwaben* 42/43 (1978): 96–119.

"Das Wormser Edikt in Süddeutschland." In *Der Reichstag zu Worms von 1521,* ed. Fritz Reuter, pp. 475–89. Worms, 1971.

Broadhead, Philip. "Internal Politics and Civic Society in Augsburg during the Era of the Early Reformation, 1518–37." Ph.D. dissertation, University of Kent, 1981.

"Politics and Expediency in the Augsburg Reformation." In *Reformation Principle and Practice. Essays in Honour of Arthur Geoffrey Dickens,* ed. Peter N. Brooks, pp. 55–70. London, 1980.

"Popular Pressure for Reform in Augsburg, 1524–1534." In *The Urban Classes, the Nobility and the Reformation. Studies on the Social History of the Reformation in England and Germany,* ed. Wolfgang J. Mommsen, R. Alter, and R. W. Scribner, pp. 80–7. Publications of the German Historical Institute London, no. 5. Stuttgart, 1979.

Bucer, Martin. *Deutsche Schriften.* Ed. Robert Stupperich et al. Gütersloh and Paris, 1960-

Buchholz, Franz Bernhard von. *Geschichte der Regierung Ferdinands des Ersten.* 9 vols. Vienna, 1831–6. Reprint. Graz, 1968.

Büchi, Albert, ed. *Aktenstücke zur Geschichte des Schwabenkrieges nebst einer Freiburger Chronik über die Ereignisse von 1499.* Quellen zur Schweizer Geschichte, no. 20. Basel, 1901.

Buck, Hermann. *Die Anfänge der Konstanzer Reformationsprozesse. Oesterreich, Eidgenossenschaft und Schmalkaldischer Bund 1510/22–1531.* Schriften zur Kirchen- und Rechtgeschichte, nos. 29–31. Tübingen, 1964.

Bücking, Jürgen. "Das Geschlecht Stürtzel von Buchheim (1491–1790). Ein Versuch zur Sozial- und Wirtschaftsgeschichte des Breisgauer Adels in der frühen Neuzeit." *Blätter für deutsche Landesgeschichte* 118 (1970): 238–78.

Burger, Heinz Otto. *Renaissance, Humanismus, Reformation. Deutsche Literatur im europäischen Kontext.* Frankfurter Beiträge zur Germanistik, no. 7. Bad Homburg v. d. H., Berlin, and Zurich, 1969.

Buszello, Horst. *Der deutsche Bauernkrieg als politische Bewegung, mit besonderer Berücksichtigung der anonymen Flugschrift "An die versamlung gemayner Pawerschafft."* Studien zur europäischen Geschichte, no. 8. Berlin, 1969.

"Die Staatsvorstellung des 'gemeinen Mannes' im deutschen Bauernkrieg."

Bibliography

In *Revolte und Revolution in Europa. Referate und Protokolle des Internationalen Symposiums zur Erinnerung an den Bauernkrieg 1525 (Memmingen, 24.-27. März 1975)*, ed. Peter Blickle, pp. 273–95. Munich, 1975.

Carande, Ramon. *Carlos V y sus banqueros.* 3 vols. Madrid, 1944–67.

Carlen, Louis. *Die Landsgemeinde in der Schweiz. Schule der Demokratie.* Sigmaringen, 1976.

Carsten, Francis Ludwig. *Princes and Parliaments in Germany from the Fifteenth to the Eighteenth Century.* Oxford, 1959.

Castrillo-Benito, Nicolás. "Tradition und Wandel im fürstlichen Hofstaat Ferdinands von Oesterreich 1503–1564." In *Mittel und Wege früher Verfassungspolitik*, ed. Josef Engel, pp. 406–55. Spätmittelalter und Frühe Neuzeit. Tübinger Beiträge zur Geschichtsforschung, no. 9. Stuttgart, 1979.

Chabod, Federico. "Contrasti interni et dibattiti sulla politica generale di Carlo V." In *Karl V. Der Kaiser und seine Zeit*, ed. Peter Rassow and Fritz Schalk, pp. 51–66. Cologne and Graz, 1960.

Chmel, Joseph, ed. *Urkunden, Briefe und Actenstücke zur Geschichte Maximilians I. und seiner Zeit.* Bibliothek des Litterarischen Vereins in Stuttgart, no. 10. Tübingen, 1845.

Chrisman, Miriam Usher. *Lay Culture, Learned Culture: Books and Social Change in Strasbourg, 1480–1599.* New Haven and London, 1982.

Strasbourg and the Reform: A Study in the Process of Change. New Haven and London, 1967.

Christensen, Carl C. *Art and the Reformation in Germany.* Studies in the Reformation, no. 2. Athens, Ohio, and Detroit, 1979.

Clasen, Claus-Peter. *Anabaptism: A Social History, 1525–1618. Switzerland, Austria, Moravia, South and Central Germany.* Ithaca, N.Y., and London, 1972.

Cohn, Henry J. *The Government of the Rhine Palatinate in the Fifteenth Century.* Oxford, 1965.

Czok, Karl. *Vorstädte. Zu ihrer Entstehung, Wirtschaft und Sozialentwicklung in der älteren deutschen Stadtgeschichte.* Sitzungsberichte der Sächsischen Akademie der Wissenschaften in Leipzig, philologisch-historische Klasse, vol. 121, no. 1. Berlin, 1979.

De Roover, Raymond. "Monopoly Theory prior to Adam Smith: A Revision." In *Business, Banking and Economic Thought in Late Medieval and Early Modern Europe. Selected Studies of Raymond de Roover*, ed. Julius Kirschner, pp. 273–305. Chicago and London, 1974.

Deutsche Reichstagsakten, jüngere Reihe. Vol. 1, ed. August Kluckhohn. Gotha, 1893. Reprint. Göttingen, 1962. Vol. 2, ed. Adolf Wrede, Gotha. 1896. Reprint. Göttingen, 1962. Vol. 3, ed. Adolf Wrede. Gotha, 1901. Reprint.

Bibliography

Göttingen, 1963. Vol. 4, ed. Adolf Wrede. Gotha, 1905. Reprint. Göttingen, 1963. Vol. 7, ed. Johannes Kühn. Stuttgart, 1935. Reprint. Göttingen, 1963. Vol. 8, ed. Wolfgang Steglich. Göttingen, 1970–1.

Deutsche Reichstagsakten, mittlere Reihe. Vol. 3, ed. Ernst Bock. Göttingen, 1972–3. Vol. 6, ed. Heinz Gollwitzer. Göttingen, 1979.

Dickens, Arthur Geoffrey. *The German Nation and Martin Luther.* London and New York, 1974.

Dierauer, Johannes. *Geschichte der Schweizerischen Eidgenossenschaft.* 6 vols. 3d ed., rev. Geschichte der europäischen Staaten, no. 26. Gotha, 1920. Reprint. Bern, 1967.

Dobel, Friedrich. *Memmingen im Reformationszeitalter.* 5 vols. Augsburg, 1877–8.

Dollinger, Philippe. "Charles-Quint et les villes d'Empire." In *Charles-Quint, le Rhin et la France,* pp. 183–92. Publications de la Société Savante d'Alsace et des Régions de l'Est, series "Recherches et Documents," no. 16. Strasbourg, 1975.

Duchhardt, Heinz. *Protestantisches Kaisertum und Altes Reich. Die Diskussion über die Konfession des Kaisers in Politik, Publizistik und Staatsrecht.* Veröffentlichungen des Instituts für Europäische Geschichte Mainz, no. 87. Wiesbaden, 1977.

Duggan, Lawrence G. "The Church as an Institution of the Reich." In *The Old Reich: Essays on German Political Institutions, 1495–1806,* ed. James Allen Vann, pp. 149–64. Brussels, 1974.

Dürr, Emil. *Die Politik der Eidgenossen im XV. und XVI. Jahrhundert. Eidgenössische Grossmachtpolitik im Zeitalter der Mailänder Kriege.* Schweizer Kriegsgeschichte, vol. 4. Bern, 1933.

Ehrenberg, Richard. *Das Zeitalter der Fugger. Geldkapital und Creditverkehr im 16. Jahrhundert.* 2 vols. Jena, 1896. Reprint. Hildesheim, 1963.

Eitel, Peter. *Die oberschwäbischen Reichsstädte im Zeitalter der Zunftherrschaft. Untersuchungen zu ihrer politischen und sozialen Struktur unter besonderer Berücksichtigung der Städte Lindau, Memmingen, Ravensburg und Ueberlingen.* Schriften zur südwestdeutschen Landeskunde, 8. Stuttgart, 1970.

Elliott, J. H. *Imperial Spain, 1469–1716.* New York, 1964.

Endres, Rudolf. "Der Kayserliche neunjährige Bund vom Jahr 1535–1544." In *Bauer, Reich und Reformation. Festschrift für Günther Franz zum 80. Geburtstag am 23. Mai 1982,* ed. Peter Blickle, pp. 85–103. Stuttgart, 1982.

"Zünfte und Unterschichten als Elemente der Instabilität in den Städten." In *Revolte und Revolution in Europa. Referate und Protokolle des Internationalen Symposiums zur Erinnerung an den Bauernkrieg 1525 (Memmingen, 24.–27. März 1975),* ed. Peter Blickle, pp. 151–70. Munich, 1975.

Bibliography

Engelhardt, Adolf. *Die Reformation in Nürnberg.* 3 vols. Nürnberg, 1936–9.

Englert-Faye, C. *Vom Mythus zur Idee der Schweiz. Lebensfragen eidgenössischer Existenz geistesgeschichtlich dargestellt.* Zurich, 1940.

Ernst, Max. "Bernhard Besserer, Bürgermeister in Ulm (1471–1542)." *Zeitschrift für württembergische Landesgeschichte* 5 (1941): 88–113.

Evans, R. J. W. *The Making of the Habsburg Monarchy, 1550–1700. An Interpretation.* Oxford, 1979.

Fabian, Ekkehart, ed. *Die Abschiede der Bündnis- und Bekenntnistage protestierender Fürsten und Städte zwischen den Reichstagen zu Speyer und zu Augsburg 1529– 1530.* Schriften zur Kirchen- und Rechtsgeschichte, no. 6. Tübingen, 1960.

Ed. *Die Beschlüsse der oberdeutschen Schmalkaldischen Städtetage.* 3 vols. Schriften zur Kirchen- und Rechtsgeschichte, nos. 21–4. Tübingen, 1959–60.

Die Entstehung des Schmalkaldischen Bundes und seiner Verfassung 1524/29– 1531/35. Brück, Philipp von Hessen und Jakob Sturm. 2d ed. Schriften zur Kirchen- und Rechtsgeschichte, no. 1. Tübingen, 1962.

Febvre, Lucien. *Un destin: Martin Luther.* 1928. Reprint. Paris, 1952.

Feger, Otto. *Geschichte des Bodenseeraumes.* Vol. 3: *Zwischen alten und neuen Ordnungen.* Constance and Lindau, 1963.

"Konstanz am Vorabend der Reformation." In *Der Konstanzer Reformator Ambrosius Blarer 1492–1564. Gedenkschrift zu seinem 400. Todestag,* ed. Bernd Moeller, pp. 39–55. Constance and Stuttgart, 1964.

"Probleme der Kriegsgefangenschaft im Schwabenkrieg." *Zeitschrift für Schweizerische Geschichte* 30 (1950): 595–601.

Feine, Hans Erich. *Die Besetzung der Reichsbistümer vom Westfälischen Frieden bis zur Säkularisation 1648–1802.* Kirchenrechtliche Abhandlungen, nos. 97– 8. Stuttgart, 1921.

"Die Territorialbildung der Habsburger im deutschen Südwesten, vornehmlich im Mittelalter." *Zeitschrift der Savigny-Stiftung für Rechtsgeschichte, Germanistische Abteilung* 67 (1950): 176–308.

Feller, Richard. *Geschichte Berns.* 4 vols. 4th ed., rev. Bern and Frankfurt a. M., 1974.

Feller, Richard, and Edgar Bonjour. *Geschichtsschreibung der Schweiz vom Spätmittelalter zur Neuzeit.* 2 vols. 2d ed. Basel, 1979.

Fellner, Thomas. "Zur Geschichte der österreichischen Centralverwaltung, (1493–1848), Part I." *Mittheilungen des Instituts für österreichische Geschichtsforschung* 8 (1887): 258–301.

Fellner, Thomas, and Heinrich Kretschmayr, eds. *Die österreichische Zentralverwaltung.* Part I: *Von Maximilian I. bis zur Vereinigung der österreichischen und böhmischen Hofkanzlei (1749).* Veröffentlichungen der Kommission für neuere Geschichte Oesterreichs, no. 5. Vienna, 1907.

Bibliography

Feyler, Anna. *Die Beziehungen des Hauses Württemberg zur schweizerischen Eidgenossenschaft in der ersten Hälfte des 16. Jahrhunderts.* Ph.D. dissertation, University of Zurich. Zurich, 1905.

Fichtner, Paula Sutter. *Ferdinand I of Austria: The Politics of Dynasticism in the Age of the Reformation.* East European Monographs, 100. Boulder, Colo., 1982.

Ficker, Johannes. *Bildnisse der Strassburger Reformation.* Quellen und Forschungen zur Kirchen- und Kulturgeschichte von Elsass und Lothringen, no. 4. Strasbourg, 1914.

Förstemann, Carl Eduard, ed. *Neues Urkundenbuch zur Geschichte der evangelischen Kirchen-Reformation.* Hamburg, 1842.

Franz, Eugen. *Nürnberg, Kaiser und Reich. Studien zur reichsstädtischen Aussenpolitik.* Munich, 1930.

Franz, Günther. *Der deutsche Bauernkrieg.* 7th ed. Bad Homburg v. d. H., 1965.

Der deutsche Bauernkrieg. Aktenband. 3d ed. Darmstadt, 1972.

"Der Kampf um das alte Recht in der Schweiz im ausgehenden Mittelalter." *Vierteljahrschrift für Sozial- und Wirtschaftsgeschichte* 26 (1933): 105–45.

"Zur Geschichte des Bundschuhs." *Zeitschrift für die Geschichte des Oberrheins* 86 (1934): 1–23.

Ed. *Quellen zur Geschichte des Bauernkrieges.* Darmstadt, 1963.

Frey, Siegfried. "Das Gericht des Schwäbischen Bundes und seine Richter 1488–1534. Ein Beitrag zur Geschichte der Rechtsinstitutionen des Einungswesens und ihrer Entscheidungsträger." In *Mittel und Wege früher Verfassungspolitik,* ed. Josef Engel, pp. 224–81. Spätmittelalter und Frühe Neuzeit. Tübinger Beiträge zur Geschichtsforschung, no. 9. Stuttgart, 1979.

Friedensburg, Walter. "Der Regensburger Convent von 1524." In *Historische Aufsätze dem Andenken an Georg Waitz gewidmet,* pp. 502–39. Hannover, 1886.

Der Reichstag zu Speier 1526 im Zusammenhang der politischen und kirchlichen Entwicklung Deutschlands im Reformationszeitalter. Historische Untersuchungen, no. 5. Berlin, 1887. Reprint. Nieuwkoop, 1970.

Zur Vorgeschichte des Gotha-Torgauischen Bündnisses der Evangelischen 1525–1526. Marburg, 1884.

Fuchs, François-Joseph. "L'espace économique rhénan et les relations commerciales de Strasbourg avec le sud-ouest de l'Allemagne au XVIe siècle." *Festschrift für Günther Haselier aus Anlass seines 60. Geburtstages am 19. April 1974,* ed. Alfons Schäfer. Oberrheinische Studien, vol. 3. Karlsruhe, 1975.

"Les foires et le rayonnement économique de la ville en Europe (XVIe siècle)." In *Histoire de Strasbourg des origines à nos jours,* ed. Georges Livet and Francis Rapp, vol. 2: *Strasbourg des grandes invasions au XVIe siècle,* pp. 259–361. Strasbourg, 1981.

"Guerre et économie. Charles-Quint et le projet d'une taxe d'Empire de

Bibliography

5%." In *Charles-Quint, le Rhin et la France*, pp. 123–33. Publications de la Société Savante d'Alsace et des Régions de l'Est, series "Recherches et Documents," no. 16. Strasbourg, 1975.

Fuchs, Walther Peter. "Das Zeitalter der Reformation." In *Handbuch der deutschen Geschichte*, ed. B. Gebhardt, 8th ed., vol. 2, pp. 1–104. Stuttgart, 1956.

Fueter, Eduard. *Der Anteil der Eidgenossenschaft an der Wahl Karls V.* Basel, 1899.

Füglister, Hans. *Handwerksregiment. Untersuchungen und Materialien zur sozialen und politischen Struktur der Stadt Basel in der ersten Hälfte des 16. Jahrhunderts.* Basler Beiträge zur Geschichtswissenschaft, no. 143. Basel, 1981.

Fürstenwerth, Ludwig. *Die Verfassungsänderungen in den oberdeutschen Städten zur Zeit Karls V.* Ph.D. dissertation, University of Göttingen. Göttingen, 1893.

Gachard, Louis Prosper, ed. *Lettres inédites de Maximilien, duc d'Autriche, roi des Romains et empereur, sur les affaires des Pays-Bas.* 2 vols. Brussels, Ghent, and Leipzig, 1851–2.

Gagliardi, Ernst. "Mailänder und Franzosen in der Schweiz 1495–1499. Eidgenössische Zustände im Zeitalter des Schwabenkrieges," parts 1, 2. *Jahrbuch für schweizerische Geschichte* 39 (1914): 1–283; 40 (1915): 1–280.

Gasser, Adolf. *Die territoriale Entwicklung der Schweiz. Eidgenossenschaft 1291–1797.* Aarau and Leipzig, 1932.

Geiger, Gottfried. *Die Reichsstadt Ulm vor der Reformation. Städtisches und kirchliches Leben am Ausgang des Mittelalters.* Forschungen zur Geschichte der Stadt Ulm, no. 11. Ulm, 1971.

Geister, Karl. "Ueber die Haltung der Schweiz während des Schmalkaldischen Krieges." *Jahrbuch für schweizerische Geschichte* 22 (1897): 165–249.

Gemperle, J. C. *Belgische und schweizerische Städteverfassungsgeschichte im Mittelalter. Eine vergleichende Studie.* Wetteren, 1943.

Genovese, Eugene D. *Roll, Jordan, Roll: The World the Slaves Made.* New York, 1972.

Gierke, Otto von. *Das deutsche Genossenschaftsrecht.* 4 vols. Berlin, 1868–1913. Reprint. Graz, 1954.

Gilbert, Felix. *The Pope, His Banker and Venice.* Cambridge, Mass., 1980.

Gisi, W. "Der Anteil der Eidgenossen an der europäischen Politik während der Jahre 1517–1521." *Archiv für schweizerische Geschichte* 17 (1871): 63–132.

Gollwitzer, Heinz. "Capitaneus imperatorio nomine. Reichshauptleute in Städten und reichsstädtische Schicksale im Zeitalter Maximilians I." In *Aus Reichstagen des 15. und 16. Jahrhunderts. Festgabe dargebracht der Historischen Kommission bei der Bayerischen Akademie der Wissenschaften zur Feier ihres hundertjährigen Bestehens*, pp. 248–82. Schriften der Historischen Kom-

Bibliography

mission bei der Bayerischen Akademie der Wissenschaften, no. 5. Göttingen, 1958.

Gothein, Eberhard. *Politische und religiöse Volksbewegungen vor der Reformation.* Breslau, 1878.

Grabner, Adolf. *Zur Geschichte des zweiten Nürnberger Reichsregimentes 1521–1528.* Historische Studien, no. 41. Berlin, 1903.

Greiner, Christian. "Die Politik des Schwäbischen Bundes während des Bauernkrieges 1524/1525 bis zum Vertrag von Weingarten." *Zeitschrift des Historischen Vereins für Schwaben* 68 (1974): 7–94.

Greyerz, Kaspar von. "Stadt und Reformation. Stand und Aufgaben der Forschung." *Archiv für Reformationsgeschichte* 76 (1985).

Grimm, Harold J. *Lazarus Spengler, a Lay Leader of the Reformation.* Columbus, 1978.

Grimm, Jacob, and Wilhelm Grimm. *Deutsche Sagen.* 2d ed. 2 vols. Berlin, 1865–6.

Grube, Walter. "Dorfgemeinde und Amtsversammlung in Altwürttemberg." *Zeitschrift für württembergische Landesgeschichte* 15 (1954): 194–219.

Der Stuttgarter Landtag 1457–1957. Von den Landständen zum demokratischen Parlament. Stuttgart, 1957.

Grundmann, Herbert. "Freiheit als religiöses, politisches und persönliches Postulat im Mittelalter." *Historische Zeitschrift* 183 (1957): 23–53.

Gumbel, Albert, ed. "Berichte Dr. Erasmus Topplers, Propsts von St. Sebald zu Nürnberg, vom kaiserlichen Hofe 1507–1512." *Archivalische Zeitschrift,* new series 16 (1909): 257–314; 17 (1910): 125–229.

Gundlach, Franz. *Die hessischen Zentralbehörden von 1247 bis 1604.* 2 vols. Veröffentlichungen der Historischen Kommission für Hessen und Waldeck, no. 16. Marburg, 1931–2.

Haliczer, Stephen. *The Comuneros of Castile: The Forging of a Revolution, 1475–1521.* Madison, Wis., 1981.

Halkin, Léon E., and Georges Dansaert. *Charles de Lannoy, viceroi de Naples, 1482–1527.* Paris and Brussels, 1934.

Hamburger, Hans. *Der Staatsbankrott des Herzogtums Wirtemberg nach Herzog Ulrichs Vertreibung und die Reorganisation des Finanzwesens. Ein Beitrag zur wirtembergishen Finanzgeschichte in den Jahren 1503 bis 1531.* Schwäbisch Hall, 1909.

Hartung, Fritz. *Geschichte des fränkischen Kreises. Darstellung und Akten.* Vol. 1: *Die Geschichte des fränkischen Kreises von 1521–1559.* Veröffentlichungen der Gesellschaft für fränkische Geschichte, second series, no. 1. Leipzig, 1910. Reprint. Aalen, 1973.

Hasenclever, Adolf. "Balthasar Merklin, Propst zu Waldkirch, Reichsvize-

Bibliography

kanzler unter Kaiser Karl V." *Zeitschrift für die Geschichte des Oberrheins* 73 (1919): 485–502; 74 (1920): 36–80.

Hatt, Jacques. *Liste des membres du grand sénat de Strasbourg, des stettmeistres, des conseils des XXI, XIII et des XV du XIIIe siècle à 1789.* Strasbourg, 1963.

Haushofer, Heinz. "Die Ereignisse des Bauernkriegsjahres 1525 im Herzogtum Bayern." In *Bauer, Reich und Reformation. Festschrift für Günther Franz zum 80. Geburtstag am 23. Mai 1982,* ed. Peter Blickle, pp. 268–85. Stuttgart, 1982.

Hauswirth, René. *Landgraf Philipp von Hessen und Zwingli. Voraussetzungen und Geschichte der politischen Beziehungen zwischen Hessen, Strassburg, Konstanz, Ulrich von Württemberg und reformierten Eidgenossen 1526–1531.* Schriften zur Kirchen- und Rechtsgeschichte, no. 35. Tübingen, 1968.

Headley, John M. *The Emperor and His Chancellor: A Study of the Imperial Chancellery under Gattinara.* Cambridge, 1983.

"Gattinara, Erasmus and the Imperial Configurations of Humanism." *Archiv für Reformationsgeschichte* 71 (1980): 64–98.

"Germany, the Empire and *Monarchia* in the Thought and Policy of Gattinara." In *Das römisch-deutsche Reich im politischen System Karls V.,* ed. Heinrich Lutz, pp. 15–33. Munich and Vienna, 1982.

"The Habsburg World Empire and the Revival of Ghibellinism." *Medieval and Renaissance Studies* 7 (1978): 92–127.

Hegi, Friedrich. *Die geächteten Räte des Erzherzogs Sigmund von Oesterreich und ihre Beziehungen zur Schweiz 1487–1499. Beiträge zur Geschichte der Lostrennung der Schweiz vom Deutschen Reiche.* Innsbruck, 1910.

Heide, G. "Nürnberg und die Mission des Vizekanzlers Held." *Mitteilungen des Vereins für Geschichte der Stadt Nürnberg* 8 (1889): 161–200.

Herde, Peter. "Politische Verhaltensweisen der Florentiner Oligarchie 1382–1402." In *Geschichte und Verfassungsgefüge. Frankfurter Festschrift für Walter Schlesinger,* pp. 156–249. Frankfurter Historische Abhandlungen, no. 5. Wiesbaden, 1973.

Herding, Otto. "Pädagogik, Politik und Geschichte bei Jakob Wimpfeling." In *L'Humanisme allemand (1480–1540). XVIIIe Colloque international de Tour,* pp. 113–20. Humanistische Bibliothek, series 1, no. 38. Munich and Paris, 1979.

"Zu einer humanistischen Handschrift, 63 der Newberry Library Chicago." In *Geschichte, Wirtschaft, Gesellschaft. Festschrift Clemens Bauer zum 75. Geburtstag,* ed. Erich Hassinger et al., pp. 153–87. Berlin, 1974.

Hesslinger, Helmo. *Die Anfänge des Schwäbischen Bundes. Ein Beitrag zur Geschichte des Einungswesens und der Reichsreform unter Kaiser Friedrich III.* Forschungen zur Geschichte der Stadt Ulm, no. 9. Ulm, 1970.

Bibliography

Heusler, Andreas. *Schweizerische Verfassungsgeschichte*. Basel, 1920. Reprint. Aalen, 1968.

Heyd, Ludwig Friedrich. *Ulrich, Herzog zu Württemberg. Ein Beitrag zur Geschichte Württembergs und des deutschen Reiches im Zeitalter der Reformation.* 3 vols. Tübingen, 1841–4.

Höffner, Joseph. *Wirtschaftsethik und Monopole im 15. und 16. Jahrhundert.* Jena, 1941. Reprint. Stuttgart, 1969.

Höhlbaum, Konstantin, ed. "Kölner Briefe über den bayrisch-pfälzischen Krieg im Jahre 1504." *Mittheilungen des Stadtarchivs Köln* 4, nos. 10–11 (1887): 1–40.

Hölbling, Walter. "Maximilian I. und sein Verhältnis zu den Reichsstädten." Ph.D. dissertation, Graz, 1970.

Hoyer, Siegfried. *Das Militärwesen im deutschen Bauernkrieg 1524–1526*. Militärhistorische Studien, new series, no. 16. Berlin, 1975.

Ed. *An die Versammlung gemeiner Bauernschaft. Eine revolutionäre Flugschrift aus dem Deutschen Bauernkrieg (1525).* Leipzig, 1975.

Hruschka, Waltraut. "König Maximilian I. und die bayrisch-pfälzischen Erbfolgehandel von 1503–1507." Ph.D. dissertation, Graz, 1961.

Hug, Heinrich. *Villinger Chronik von 1495 bis 1533.* Ed. Christian Röder. Bibliothek des Litterarischen Vereins in Stuttgart, no. 164. Tübingen, 1883.

Huter, Franz. "Kaiser Maximilian und die oberdeutsche Wirtschaftsmacht." In *Jakob Fugger, Kaiser Maximilian und Augsburg 1459–1959*, by Götz Freiherr von Pölnitz et al., pp. 41–58. Augsburg, 1959.

Hutten, Ulrich von. *Ulrichi Hutteni equitis germani opera quae reperiri potuerunt omnia.* Ed. Eduard Böcking. 7 vols. Leipzig, 1859–70.

Isenmann, Eberhard. "Reichsfinanzen und Reichssteuern im 15. Jahrhundert." *Zeitschrift für historische Forschung* 7 (1980): 1–76, 129–218.

"Reichsstadt und Reich an der Wende vom späten Mittelalter zur frühen Neuzeit." In *Mittel und Wege früher Verfassungspolitik*, ed. Josef Engel, pp. 9–223. Spätmittelalter und Frühe Neuzeit. Tübinger Beiträge zur Geschichtsforschung, no. 9. Stuttgart, 1979.

"Zur Frage der Reichsstandschaft der Frei- und Reichsstädte." In *Stadtverfassung, Verfassungsstaat, Pressepolitik. Festschrift für Eberhard Naujoks zum 65. Geburtstag*, ed. Franz Quarthal and Wilfried Setzler, pp. 91–110. Sigmaringen, 1980.

Jahns, Sigrid. *Frankfurt, Reformation und Schmalkaldischer Bund. Die Reformations-, Reichs- und Bündnispolitik der Reichsstadt Frankfurt am Main 1525–1536.* Studien zur Frankfurter Geschichte, no. 9. Frankfurt a. M., 1976.

Janeschitz-Kriegl, Robert. "Geschichte der ewigen Richtung von 1474." *Zeitschrift für die Geschichte des Oberrheins* 105 (1957): 150–224, 409–55.

Bibliography

Janssen, Johannes, ed. *Frankfurts Reichscorrespondenz nebst anderen verwandten Aktenstücken von 1376–1519.* 2 vols in 3 parts. Freiburg im Breisgau, 1863–72.

Jörg, Josef Edmund. *Deutschland in der Revolutions-Periode von 1522–1526.* Freiburg im Breisgau, 1851.

Kamann, J. "Nürnberger Ratskorrespondenzen zur Geschichte des Württemberger Krieges 1519, namentlich Christoph Fürers Denkwürdigkeiten über den zweiten Bundesfeldzug gegen Herzog Ulrich." *Württembergische Vierteljahrshefte für Landesgeschichte,* new series 13 (1904): 233–70.

Kaser, Kurt. *Politische und soziale Bewegungen im deutschen Bürgertum zu Beginn des 16. Jahrhunderts.* Stuttgart, 1899.

Keim, Karl Theodor. *Die Reformation in der Reichsstadt Ulm.* Stuttgart, 1851.

Kellenbenz, Hermann. "Die Beziehungen Nürnbergs zur Iberischen Halbinsel, besonders im 15. und in der ersten Hälfte des 16. Jahrhunderts." In *Beiträge zur Wirtschaftsgeschichte Nürnbergs,* ed. Stadtarchiv Nürnberg, vol. 1, pp. 456–93. Beiträge zur Geschichte und Kultur der Stadt Nürnberg, no. 11. Nuremberg, 1967.

"Die Finanzierung der spanischen Entdeckungen." *Vierteljahrschrift für Sozial- und Wirtschaftsgeschichte* 69 (1982): 153–81.

"Gewerbe und Handel 1500–1648." In *Handbuch der deutschen Wirtschafts- und Sozialgeschichte,* ed. Hermann Aubin and Wolfgang Zorn, vol. 1, pp. 414–64. Stuttgart, 1971.

"Das Römisch-Deutsche Reich im Rahmen der wirtschaft- und finanzpolitischen Erwägungen Karls V. im Spannungsfeld imperialer und dynastischer Interessen." In *Das römisch-deutsche Reich im politischen System Karls V.,* ed. Heinrich Lutz, pp. 35–54. Munich and Vienna, 1982.

"Die Rolle der Verbindungsplätze zwischen Spanien und Augsburg im Unternehmen Anton Fuggers." *Vierteljahrschrift für Sozial- und Wirtschaftsgeschichte* 65 (1978): 1–37.

"Wirtschaftsleben im Zeitalter der Reformation." In *Nürnberg–Geschichte einer europäischen Stadt,* ed. Gerhard Pfeiffer, pp. 176–85. Munich, 1971.

Keyser, Erich, ed. *Deutsches Städtebuch. Handbuch städtischer Geschichte.* 5 vols. Leipzig and Stuttgart, 1939– .

Kiernan, V. G. "State and Nation in Western Europe." *Past and Present,* no. 31 (1965): 20–38.

Kiessling, Rolf. *Bürgerliche Gesellschaft und Kirche in Augsburg im Spätmittelalter. Ein Beitrag zur Strukturanalyse der oberdeutschen Reichsstadt.* Abhandlungen zur Geschichte der Stadt Augsburg, no. 19. Augsburg, 1971.

"Bürgerlicher Besitz auf dem Land – ein Schlüssel zu den Stadt-Land-Beziehungen im Spätmittelalter, aufgezeigt am Beispiel Augsburgs und

Bibliography

anderer ostswäbischer Städte." In *Augsburger Beiträge zur Landesgeschichte Bayerisch-Schwabens*. Vol. 1: *Bayerisch-schwäbische Landesgeschichte an der Universität Augsburg 1975–1977. Vorträge, Aufsätze, Berichte*, ed. Pankraz Fried, pp. 12–50. Sigmaringen, 1979.

"Herrschaft-Markt-Landbesitz. Aspekte der Zentralität und der Stadt-Land-Beziehungen spätmittelalterlicher Städte an ostschwäbischen Beispielen." In *Zentralität als Problem der mittelalterlichen Stadtgeschichtsforschung*, ed. Emil Meynen, pp. 180–218. Städteforschung, series A, no. 8. Cologne and Vienna, 1979.

Kirchgässner, Bernhard. *Das Steuerwesen der Reichsstadt Konstanz 1418–1460.* Konstanzer Geschichts- und Rechtsquellen, vol. 10. Constance, 1960.

"Der Verlag im Spannungsfeld von Stadt und Umland." In *Stadt und Umland. Protokoll der X. Arbeitstagung des Arbeitskreises für südwestdeutsche Stadtgeschichtsforschung*, ed. Erich Maschke and Jürgen Sydow, pp. 72–128. Veröffentlichungen der Kommission für geschichtliche Landeskunde in Baden-Württemberg, series B, no. 82. Stuttgart, 1974.

Kittelberger, Gerhard. "Herzog Ulrichs Angriffspläne auf die Reichsstadt Esslingen." *Jahrbuch für Geschichte der oberdeutschen Reichsstädte* 17 (1971): 116–19.

Kluckhohn, August. "Zur Geschichte der Handelsgesellschaften und Monopole im Zeitalter der Reformation." In *Historiche Aufsätze dem Andenken an Georg Waitz gewidmet*. Hannover, 1886.

Klüpfel, Karl, ed. *Urkunden zur Geschichte des Schwäbischen Bundes (1488-1533).* 2 vols. Bibliothek des Litterarischen Vereins in Stuttgart, nos. 14, 31. Tübingen, 1846–53.

Knebel, Johannes. *Johannis Knebel capellani ecclesiae Basiliensis diarium (1473–1479).* Ed. Wilhelm Vischer. 2 vols. Basler Chroniken, vols. 2–3. Leipzig, 1880–7.

Knecht, R. J. *Francis I.* Cambridge, 1982.

Knepper, Joseph. *Jakob Wimpfeling (1450–1528). Sein Leben und seine Werke.* Freiburg im Breisgau, 1902. Reprint. Nieuwkoop, 1965.

Nationaler Gedanke und Kaiseridee bei den elsässischen Humanisten. Ein Beitrag zur Geschichte des Deutschtums und der politischen Ideen im Reichslande. Freiburg im Breisgau, 1898.

Koenigsberger, H. G. *Estates and Revolutions. Essays in Early Modern European History.* Ithaca, N.Y., and London, 1971.

The Habsburgs and Europe, 1516–1660. Ithaca, N.Y., and London, 1971.

"Patronage and Bribery during the Reign of Charles V." In *Estates and Revolutions. Essays in Early Modern European History*, pp. 166–75. Ithaca, N.Y., and London, 1971.

Bibliography

"The Reformation and Social Revolution." In *Estates and Revolutions. Essays in Early Modern European History*, pp. 211–23. Ithaca, N.Y., and London, 1971.

Kohl, Benjamin G., and Ronald G. Witt, trans. *The Earthly Republic: Italian Humanists on Government and Society.* Philadelphia, 1978.

Köhler, Hans-Joachim, ed. *Flugschriften als Massenmedium der Reformationszeit. Beiträge zum Tübinger Symposion 1980.* Spätmittelalter und Frühe Neuzeit. Tübinger Beiträge zur Geschichtsforschung, no. 13. Stuttgart, 1981.

Köhler, Walther. "Die deutsche Kaiseridee am Anfang des 16. Jahrhunderts." *Historische Zeitschrift* 149 (1934): 35–56.

Kohls, Ernst-Wilhelm. "Humanisten auf dem Reichstag." In *Der Reichstag zu Worms von 1521*, ed. Fritz Reuter, pp. 415–37. Worms, 1971.

Koller, Heinrich. "Die Aufgaben der Städte in der Reformatio Friderici (1442)." *Historisches Jahrbuch* 100 (1980): 198–216.

Das "Königreich" Oesterreich. Kleine Arbeitsreihe des Instituts für Europäische und vergleichende Rechtsgeschichte an der Rechts- und Staatswissenschaftlichen Fakultät der Universität Graz, no. 4. Graz, 1972.

König, Erich. *Peutingerstudien.* Studien und Darstellungen aus dem Gebiet der Geschichte, no. 9, parts 1, 2. Freiburg im Breisgau, 1914.

Koschaker, Paul. *Europa und das römische Recht.* 4th ed. Munich and Berlin, 1966.

Kothe, Irmgard. *Der fürstliche Rat in Württemberg im 15. und 16. Jahrhundert.* Darstellungen aus der württembergischen Geschichte, no. 29. Stuttgart, 1938.

Krabbe, Helmut, and Hans-Christoph Rublack, eds. *Akten zur Esslinger Reformationsgeschichte.* Esslinger Studien, Schriftenreihe, no. 5. Esslingen, 1981.

Krantz, Frederick, and Paul M. Hohenberg, eds. *Failed Transitions to Modern Industrial Society: Renaissance Italy and Seventeenth Century Holland.* Montreal, 1975.

Kraus, Andreas. "Sammlung der Kräfte und Aufschwung (1450–1508)." In *Handbuch der bayerischen Geschichte*, ed. Max Spindler, vol. 2: *Das alte Bayern*, pp. 269–96. Munich, 1966.

Kraus, Viktor von., ed. "Itinerarium Maximiliani I. 1508–1518, mit einleitenden Bemerkungen über das Kanzeleiwesen Maximilians I." *Archiv für österreichische Geschichte* 87 (1899): 229–318.

Zur Geschichte Oesterreichs unter Ferdinand I. Ein Bild ständischer Parteikämpfe. Vienna, 1873.

Krimm, Konrad. *Baden und Habsburg um die Mitte des 15. Jahrhunderts. Fürstlicher Dienst und Reichsgewalt im späten Mittelalter.* Veröffentlichungen der Kommission für geschichtliche Landeskunde in Baden-Württemberg, series B, no. 89. Stuttgart, 1976.

Bibliography

Landwehr, Götz. *Die Verpfändung der Reichsstädte im Mittelalter.* Forschungen zur deutschen Rechtsgeschichte, no. 5. Cologne and Graz, 1967.

Lanz, Karl, ed. *Korrespondenz des Kaisers Karl V.* 3 vols. Leipzig, 1844–6. Reprint. Frankfurt a. M., 1966.

Lau, Franz. "Der Bauernkrieg und das angebliche Ende der lutherischen Reformation als spontaner Volksbewegung." *Luther-Jahrbuch* 26 (1959): 109–34.

Laubach, Ernst. "Karl V., Ferdinand I. und die Nachfolge im Reich." *Mitteilungen des österreichischen Staatsarchivs* 29 (1976): 1–51.

Laube, Adolf. *Studien über den erzgebirgischen Silberbergbau von 1470 bis 1546. Seine Geschichte, seine Produktionsverhältnisse, seine Bedeutung für die gesellschaftlichen Veränderungen und Klassenkämpfe in Sachsen am Beginn der Uebergangsepoche vom Feudalismus zum Kapitalismus.* 2d ed. Forschungen zur mittelalterlichen Geschichte, no. 22. Berlin, 1976.

Laube, Adolf, and Hans Werner Seiffert, eds., *Flugschriften der Bauernkriegszeit.* Berlin, 1975.

Laufs, Adolf. "Reichsstädte und Reichsreform." *Zeitschrift der Savigny-Stiftung für Rechtsgeschichte, Germanistische Abteilung* 84 (1967): 172–201.

Der Schwäbische Kreis. Studien über Einungswesen und Reichsverfassung im deutschen Südwesten zu Beginn der Neuzeit. Untersuchungen zur deutschen Staats- und Rechtsgeschichte, new series, no. 16. Aalen, 1971.

Layer, Adolf. "Die territorialstaatliche Entwicklung [Bayerns] bis um 1800." In *Handbuch der bayerischen Geschichte,* ed. Max Spindler, vol. 3, part 2, pp. 949–1040. Munich, 1971.

Le Glay, André Joseph Ghislain, ed. *Correspondance de l'empereur Maximilien Ier et de Marguerite d'Autriche, sa fille, gouvernant des Pays-Bays, de 1507 à 1519.* 2 vols. Publications de la Société pour l'histoire de France, no. 7. Paris, 1839.

Ed. *Négociations diplomatiques entre la France et l'Autriche durant les trente premières années du XVIe siècle.* 2 vols. Paris, 1845.

Lehmann, Hartmut. "Universales Kaisertum, dynastische Weltmacht oder Imperialismus? Zur Beurteilung der Politik Karls V." In *Beiträge zur neueren Geschichte Oesterreichs,* ed. Heinrich Fichtenau and Erich Zöllner, pp. 71–83. Vienna, Cologne, and Graz, 1974.

Leiser, Wolfgang. "Territorien süddeutscher Reichsstädte." *Zeitschrift für bayerische Landesgeschichte* 38 (1975): 967–81.

Lestocquoy, J. *Aux origines de la bourgeoisie. Les villes de Flandre et d'Italie sous le gouvernement des patriciens (XIe–XVe siècles).* Paris, 1952.

Lhotsky, Alphons. *Das Zeitalter des Hauses Oesterreich. Die ersten Jahre der Regierung Ferdinands I. in Oesterreich (1520-1527).* Veröffentlichungen der Kommission für die Geschichte Oesterreichs, no. 4. Vienna, 1971.

Bibliography

Lienhard, Marc. "La Réforme à Strasbourg," parts 1, 2. In *Histoire de Strasbourg des origines à nos jours*, ed. Georges Livet and Francis Rapp, vol. 2: *Strasbourg des grandes invasions au XVIe siècle*, pp. 363–432, 433–540. Strasbourg, 1981.

Liliencron, Rochus Freiherr von, ed. *Die historischen Volkslieder der Deutschen.* 5 vols. Leipzig, 1865–96.

Locher, Gottfried W. *Die Zwinglische Reformation im Rahmen der europäischen Kirchengeschichte.* Göttingen, 1979.

Luther, Martin. *D. Martin Luthers Werke. Kritische Gesamtausgabe. Tischreden.* 6 vols. Weimar, 1912–21.

Lutz, Heinrich. *Conrad Peutinger. Beiträge zu einer politischen Biographie.* Abhandlungen zur Geschichte der Stadt Augsburg, no. 9. Augsburg, 1958.

"Das konfessionelle Zeitalter," part 1. In *Handbuch der bayerischen Geschichte*, ed. Max Spindler, vol. 2: *Das alte Bayern*, pp. 297–350. Munich, 1966.

Lutz, Robert H. *Wer war der gemeine Mann? Der dritte Stand in der Krise des Spätmittelalters.* Munich, 1978.

Machiavelli, Niccolò. *Arte della guerra e scritti politici minori.* Ed. Sergio Bertelli. Milan, 1961.

The Chief Works and Others. Trans. Allan H. Gilbert. 3 vols. Cambridge, 1958. Reprint. Durham, N.C., 1965.

Macpherson, C. B. *The Political Theory of Possessive Individualism: Hobbes to Locke.* Oxford, 1962.

Marx, Karl. *Das Kapital. Kritik der politischen Oekonomie.* 3 vols. Vols. 4–6 of *Werke, Schriften, Briefe*, ed. Hans-Joachim Lieber and Benedikt Kautsky. Stuttgart, 1962–4.

Maschke, Erich. "Deutsche Städte am Ausgang des Mittelalters." In *Die Stadt am Ausgang des Mittelalters*, ed. Wilhelm Rausch, pp. 1–44. Linz, 1974. Also in *Städte und Menschen*, pp. 56–99. Wiesbaden, 1980.

" 'Obrigkeit' im spätmittelalterlichen Speyer und in anderen Städten." *Archiv für Reformationsgeschichte* 57 (1966): 7–22. Also in *Städte und Menschen*, pp. 121–37. Wiesbaden, 1980.

Städte und Menschen. Beiträge zur Geschichte der Stadt, der Wirtschaft und Gesellschaft 1959–1977. Supplement no. 68 to *Vierteljahrschrift für Sozial- und Wirtschaftsgeschichte.* Wiesbaden, 1980.

"Die Unterschichten der mittelalterlichen Städte Deutschlands." In *Gesellschaftliche Unterschichten in den südwestdeutschen Städten*, ed. Erich Maschke and Jürgen Sydow, pp. 1–74. Veröffentlichungen der Kommission für geschichtliche Landeskunde in Baden-Württemberg, B 41. Stuttgart, 1967. Also in *Städte und Menschen*, pp. 305–78. Wiesbaden, 1980.

"Verfassung und soziale Kräfte in der deutschen Stadt des späten Mittelalters, vornehmlich in Oberdeutschland." *Vierteljahrschrift für Sozial- und*

Bibliography

Wirtschaftsgeschichte 46 (1959): 289–349, 433–76. Also in *Städte und Menschen*, pp. 170–274. Wiesbaden, 1980.

Matzinger, Albert. *Zur Geschichte der niederen Vereinigung.* Ph.D. dissertation, Basel. Zurich-Selnau, 1910.

Mayer, Theodor. *Die Verwaltungsorganisationen Maximilians I. Ihr Ursprung und ihre Bedeutung.* Forschungen zur inneren Geschichte Oesterreichs, no. 14. Innsbruck, 1920. Reprint. Aalen, 1973.

Ed. *Die Anfänge der Landgemeinde und ihr Wesen.* 2 vols. Vorträge und Forschungen, vols. 7–8. Constance, 1964–5.

Menéndez Pidal, Ramon. "Formación del fundamental pensamiento politico de Carlos V." In *Karl V. Der Kaiser und seine Zeit,* ed. Peter Rassow and Fritz Schalk, pp. 144–66. Cologne and Graz, 1960.

Mertens, Dieter. "Maximilian I. und das Elsass." In *Die Humanisten in ihrer politischen und sozialen Umwelt,* ed. Otto Herding and Robert Stupperich, pp. 177–200. Mitteilungen der Kommission für Humanismusforschung, no. 3. Boppard, 1976.

"Reich und Elsass zur Zeit Maximilians I. Untersuchungen zur Ideen- und Landesgeschichte im Südwesten des Reiches am Ausgang des Mittelalters." Habilitationsschrift, Freiburg im Breisgau, 1979.

Metz, Friedrich, ed. *Vorderösterreich. Eine geschichtliche Landeskunde.* 2d ed. Freiburg im Breisgau, 1967.

Meyer, Friedrich. *Die Beziehungen zwischen Basel und den Eidgenossen in der Darstellung der Historiographie des 15. und 16. Jahrhunderts.* Basler Beiträge zur Geschichtswissenschaft, no. 39. Basel, 1951.

Meyer, Manfred. "Die Haltung der Vertreter der Freien und Reichsstädte auf den Reichstagen von 1521 bis 1526." *Jahrbuch für Geschichte des Feudalismus* 7 (1982): 182–235.

Miskimin, Harry A. *The Economy of Later Renaissance Europe, 1460–1600.* Cambridge, 1977.

Moeller, Bernd. *Deutschland im Zeitalter der Reformation.* Vol. 4 of *Deutsche Geschichte,* ed. Joachim Leuschner. Göttingen, 1977.

"L'édit strasbourgeois sur la prédication du 1.12.1523 dans son contexte historique." In *Strasbourg au coeur religieux du XVIe siècle,* ed. Georges Livet, Francis Rapp, and Jean Rott, pp. 51–61. Publications de la Société Savante d'Alsace et des Régions de l'Est, series "Grandes Publications," no. 12. Strasbourg, 1977.

Imperial Cities and the Reformation. Three Essays. Trans. H. C. Erik Midelfort and Mark U. Edwards, Jr. Philadephia, 1975.

Johannes Zwick und die Reformation in Konstanz. Quellen und Forschungen zur Reformationsgeschichte, no. 28. Gütersloh, 1961.

Bibliography

Reichsstadt und Reformation. Schriften des Vereins für Reformationsgeschichte, no. 180. Gütersloh, 1962.

"Stadt und Buch. Bemerkungen zur Struktur der reformatorischen Bewegung in Deutschland." In *The Urban Classes, the Nobility and the Reformation. Studies on the Social History of the Reformation in England and Germany,* ed. Wolfgang J. Mommsen, R. Alter, and R. W. Scribner, pp. 25–39. Publications of the German Historical Institute, London, no. 5. Stuttgart, 1979.

"Zwinglis Disputationen. Studien zu den Anfängen der Kirchenbildung und des Synodalwesens im Protestantismus." *Zeitschrift der Savigny-Stiftung für Rechtsgeschichte, Kanonistische Abteilung* 56 (1970): 275–334; 60 (1974): 213–364.

Ed. *Stadt und Kirche im 16. Jahrhundert.* Schriften des Vereins für Reformationsgeschichte, no. 190. Gütersloh, 1978.

Mörke, Olaf. "Die Fugger im 16. Jahrhundert. Städtische Elite oder Sonderstruktur?" *Archiv für Reformationsgeschichte* 74 (1983): 141–61.

Mogge, Birgitta. "Studien zum Nürnberger Reichstag von 1524." *Mitteilungen des Vereins für Geschichte der Stadt Nürnberg* 62 (1975): 84–101.

Mommsen, Karl. *Eidgenossen, Kaiser und Reich. Studien zur Stellung der Eidgenossenschaft innerhalb des Heiligen Römischen Reiches.* Basler Beiträge zur Geschichtswissenschaft, no. 72. Basel, 1958.

Mone, Franz Joseph, ed. "Briefwechsel über die Kaiserwahl Karls V." *Anzeiger für Kunde der deutschen Vorzeit* 5 (1836): 13–37, 118–36, 283–98, 396–410.

Moraw, Peter. "Reichsstädte, Reich und Königtum im späten Mittelalter." *Zeitschrift für historische Forschung* 6 (1979): 385–424.

"Versuch über die Entstehung des Reichstags." In *Politische Ordnungen und soziale Kräfte im Alten Reich,* ed. Hermann Weber, pp. 1–36. Veröffentlichungen des Instituts für Europäische Geschichte Mainz, Abteilung Universalgeschichte, supplement no. 8. Wiesbaden, 1980.

Müller, Gerhard. *Reformation und Stadt. Zur Rezeption der evangelischen Verkündigung.* Akademie der Wissenschaften und der Literatur [Mainz], Abhandlungen der geistes- und sozialwissenschaftlichen Klasse, 1981, no. 11. Mainz, 1981.

Die römische Kurie und die Reformation 1523–1534. Kirche und Politik während des Pontifikates Clemens' VII. Quellen und Forschungen zur Reformationsgeschichte, no. 38. Gütersloh, 1969.

Müller, Johannes. "Nürnbergs Botschaft nach Spanien zu Kaiser Karl V. im Jahre 1519." *Historische Zeitschrift* 98 (1909): 302–28.

Müller-Mertens, Eckhard. "Bürgerlich-städtische Autonomie in der Feudalgesellschaft – Begriff und geschichtliche Bedeutung." In *Autonomie, Wirt-*

schaft und Kultur der Hansestädte, Hansische Studien, vol. 4, pp. 11–34. Abhandlungen zur Handels- und Sozialgeschichte, no. 23. Weimar, 1984.

Munz, Peter. *Frederick Barbarossa: A Study in Medieval Politics.* Ithaca, N.Y., and London, 1969.

Muralt, Leonhard von. "Renaissance und Reformation." In *Handbuch der Schweizer Geschichte,* 2d ed., vol. 1, pp. 389–570. Zurich, 1980.

Mutianus, Conradus. *Briefwechsel.* Ed. Karl Gillert. Geschichtsquellen der Provinz Sachsen und angrenzender Gebiete, no. 18. Halle, 1890.

Näf, Werner. "Strukturprobleme des Reichs Karl V." In *Karl V. Der Kaiser und seine Zeit,* ed. Peter Rassow and Fritz Schalk, pp. 167–72. Cologne and Graz, 1960.

Naujoks, Eberhard. "Obrigkeit und Zunftverfassung in den südwestdeutschen Reichsstädten." *Zeitschrift für württembergische Landesgeschichte* 33 (1974): 53–93.

Obrigkeitsgedanke, Zunftverfassung und Reformation. Studien zur Verfassungsgeschichte von Ulm, Esslingen und Schwäb. Gmünd. Veröffentlichungen der Kommission für geschichtliche Landeskunde in Baden-Württemberg, series B, no. 3. Stuttgart, 1958.

"Reichsfreiheit und Wirtschaftsrivalität. Eine Studie zur Auseinandersetzung Esslingens mit Württemberg im 16. Jahrhundert." *Zeitschrift für württembergische Landesgeschichte* 16 (1957): 279–302.

Nebinger, Gerhart. "Die Abstimmunglisten von 1530 über die Reformation der Reichsstadt Ulm." *Blätter des Bayerischen Landesvereins für Familienkunde* 14, no. 2 (1980): 1–36.

Neuhaus, Helmut. "Supplikationen als landesgeschichtliche Quellen. Das Beispiel der Landgrafschaft Hessen." *Hessisches Jahrbuch für Landesgeschichte* 28 (1978): 110–90.

Nieuw nederlandsch biografisch Woordenboek. Ed. P. C. Molhuysen and F. K. H. Kossmann. 10 vols. Leiden, 1911–37.

Obenaus, Herbert. *Recht und Verfassung der Gesellschaft mit St. Jörgenschild in Schwaben. Untersuchungen über Adel, Einung, Schiedsgericht und Fehde im 15. Jahrhundert.* Veröffentlichungen des Max-Planck-Instituts für Geschichte, no. 7. Göttingen, 1961.

Oberlé, Roland. "La Pfalz: coeur et symbole de la vieille République de Strasbourg." *Annuaire de la Société des Amis de Vieux-Strasbourg,* 2 (1971): 39–55.

Oberman, Heiko A. "The Gospel of Social Unrest: 450 Years after the so-called 'German Peasants' War' of 1525." *Harvard Theological Review* 69 (1976): 103–29.

Masters of the Reformation: The Emergence of a New Intellectual Climate in Europe. Trans. Dennis Martin. Cambridge, 1981.

Bibliography

"Stadtreformation und Fürstenreformation." In *Humanismus und Reformation als kuturelle Kräfte in der deutschen Geschichte*, ed. Lewis W. Spitz, pp. 80–103. Veröffentlichungen der Historischen Kommission zu Berlin, no. 51. Berlin and New York, 1981.

Werden und Wertung der Reformation. Vom Wegestreit zum Glaubenskampf. Vol. 2 of *Spätscholastik und Reformation*. 2d ed. Tübingen, 1979.

Ozment, Steven. *The Age of Reform, 1250–1550: An Intellectual and Religious History of Late Medieval and Reformation Europe*. New Haven and London, 1980.

The Reformation in the Cities: The Appeal of Protestantism to Sixteenth-Century Germany and Switzerland. New Haven and London, 1975.

Petri, Franz. "Herzog Heinrich der Jüngere von Braunschweig-Wolfenbüttel. Ein niederdeutscher Territorialfürst im Zeitalter Luthers und Karls V." *Archiv für Reformationsgeschichte* 72 (1981): 122–57.

Peutinger, Conrad. *Briefwechsel*. Ed. Erich König. Munich, 1923.

Peyer, Hans Conrad. *Verfassungsgeschichte der alten Schweiz*. Zurich, 1978.

Pfeiffer, Gerhard. "Die Einführung der Reformation in Nürnberg als kirchenrechtliches und bekenntniskundliches Problem." *Blätter für deutsche Landesgeschichte* 89 (1952): 112–33.

Ed. *Quellen zur Nürnberger Reformationsgeschichte. Von der Duldung liturgischer Aenderungen bis zur Ausübung des Kirchenregiments durch den Rat (Juni 1524– Juni 1525)*. Einzelarbeiten aus der Kirchengeschichte Bayerns, no. 55. Nuremberg, 1968.

Pfeilschifter, Georg, ed. *Acta Reformationis Catholicae ecclesiae Germaniae concernentia saec. XVI. Die Reformverhandlungen des deutschen Episkopats von 1520–1570*. 6 vols. Regensburg, 1959–74.

Piccolomini, Enea Silvio. *Germania*. Ed. Adolf Schmidt. Cologne and Graz, 1962.

Pirckheimer, Caritas. *Die "Denkwürdigkeiten" des Caritas Pirckheimer (aus den Jahren 1524–1528)*. Ed. Josef Pfanner. Caritas Pirckheimer–Quellensammlung, vol. 2. Landshut, 1962.

Pirckheimer, Willibald. *Bilibaldi Pirckheimeri Opera politica, historica, philologica et epistolica*. Ed. Melchior Goldast von Haimensfeld. Frankfurt a. M., 1610.

Briefwechsel, ed. Emil Reicke. 2 vols. Munich, 1940–56.

Schweizerkrieg. Ed. Karl Rück. Munich, 1895.

Pirenne, Henri. *Histoire de Belgique*. Vol. 3: *De la mort de Charles le Téméraire à l'arrivée du Duc d'Albe dans les Pays-Bas (1567)*. Brussels, 1907.

Planitz, Hans. *Die deutsche Stadt im Mittelalter von der Römerzeit bis zu den Zunftkämpfen*. 2d ed. Cologne and Graz, 1965.

Planitz, Hans von der. *Des kursächsischen Rathes Hans von der Planitz Berichte aus dem Reichsregiment in Nürnberg 1521–1523*. Ed. Hans Virck. Schriften

Bibliography

der Königlich Sächsischen Kommission für Geschichte, no. 3. Leipzig, 1899.

Polišenský, J. V. *The Thirty Years War*. Trans. Robert Evans. Berkeley and Los Angeles, 1971.

Politische Correspondenz der Stadt Strassburg im Zeitalter der Reformation. Ed. Hans Virck et al. 5 vols. Strasbourg and Heidelberg, 1882–1933.

Pölnitz, Götz Freiherr von. *Jakob Fugger. Kaiser, Kirche und Kapital in der oberdeutschen Rennaissance*. 2 vols. Tübingen, 1949–51.

"Der Kaiser und seine Augsburger Bankiers." In *Bartholomäus Welser und seine Zeit*, ed. City of Augsburg, pp. 29–58. Augsburg, 1962.

Potter, George R. *Zwingli*. Cambridge, 1976.

Press, Volker. "Die Bundespläne Kaiser Karls V. und die Reichsverfassung." In *Das römisch-deutsche Reich im politischen System Karls V.*, ed. Heinrich Lutz, pp. 55–106. Munich and Vienna, 1982.

Calvinismus und Territorialstaat. Regierung und Zentralbehörden der Kurpfalz 1559–1619. Kieler Historische Studien, no. 7. Stuttgart, 1970.

"Die Erblande und das Reich von Albrecht II. bis Karl VI. (1438–1740)." In *Deutschland und Oesterreich*, ed. Robert A. Kann and Friedrich E. Prinz, pp. 44–88. Vienna, 1980.

"Herrschaft, Landschaft und 'Gemeiner Mann' in Oberdeutschland vom 15. bis zum frühen 19. Jahrhundert." *Zeitschrift für die Geschichte des Oberrheins* 123 (1975): 169–214.

"Stadt und territoriale Konfessionsbildung." In *Kirche und gesellschaftlicher Wandel in deutschen und niederländischen Städten der werdenden Neuzeit*, ed. Franz Petri, pp. 251–96. Städteforschung, series A, no. 10. Cologne and Vienna, 1980.

"Ulrich von Hutten, Reichsritter und Humanist 1488–1523." *Nassauische Annalen* 85 (1974): 71–86.

Puchta, Hans. *Die habsburgische Herrschaft in Württemberg 1520–1534*. Ph.D. dissertation, University of Munich. Munich, 1967.

Quarthal, Franz. *Landstände und landständisches Steuerwesen in Schwäbisch-Oesterreich*. Schriften für südwestdeutschen Landeskunde, no. 16. Stuttgart, 1980.

Raab, Heribert. "Die oberdeutschen Hochstifte zwischen Habsburg und Wittelsbach in der frühen Neuzeit." *Blätter für deutsche Landesgeschichte* 109 (1973): 69–101.

Rabe, Horst. "Befunde und Ueberlegungen zur Religionspolitik Karls V. am Vorabend des Augsburger Reichstags 1530." In *Confessio Augustana und Confutatio. Der Augsburger Reichstag 1530 und die Einheit der Kirche. Internationales Symposion der Gesellschaft zur Herausgabe des Corpus Catholicorum in Augsburg vom 3.–7. September 1979*, ed. Erwin Iserloh, pp. 101–120.

271

Bibliography

Reformationsgeschichtliche Studien und Texte, no. 118. Münster (West-phalia), 1980.

Reichsbund und Interim. Die Verfassungs- und Religionspolitik Karls V. und der Reichstag von Augsburg 1547/1548. Cologne and Vienna, 1971.

Raiser, Elisabeth. *Städtische Territorialpolitik im Mittelalter.* Historische Studien, no. 406. Lübeck and Hamburg, 1969.

Rammstedt, Otthein. "Stadtunruhen 1525." In *Der deutsche Bauernkrieg 1524-1526,* ed. Hans-Ulrich Wehler, pp. 239–76. *Geschichte und Gesellschaft,* supplement no. 1. Göttingen, 1975.

Rannacher, Irmgard. "Dr. Konrad Stürtzel von Buchheim im Dienste Kaiser Maximilians I. in den Jahren 1490 bis 1509." Ph.D. dissertation, Graz, 1976.

Rapp, Francis. "Jean Geiler de Kaysersberg (1445–1510), le prédicateur de la Cathédrale de Strasbourg." In *Grandes figures de l'humanisme alsacien. Courants, milieux, destins,* ed. Francis Rapp and Georges Livet, pp. 25–39. Publications de la Société Savante d'Alsace et des Régions de l'Est, series "Grandes Publications," no. 14. Strasbourg, 1978.

"Préréformes et humanisme. Strasbourg et l'Empire (1482–1520)." In *Histoire de Strasbourg des origines à nos jours,* ed. Georges Livet and Francis Rapp, vol. 2: *Strasbourg des grandes invasions au XVIe siècle,* pp. 177–254. Strasbourg, 1981.

Réformes et réformation à Strasbourg. Eglise et société dans le diocèse de Strasbourg (1450–1525). Paris, 1974.

"Les strasbourgeois et les universités rhénanes à la fin du Moyen Age et jusqu'à la Réforme." *Annuaire de la Société des Amis de Vieux-Strasbourg* 4 (1974): 11–22.

Rausch, Heinz, ed. *Die geschichtlichen Grundlagen der modernen Volksvertretung.* 2 vols. Wege der Forschung, nos. 196, 469. Darmstadt, 1974-80.

Rebel, Hermann. *Peasant Classes: The Bureaucratization of Property and Family Relations under Early Habsburg Absolutism, 1511–1626.* Princeton, N.J., 1983.

Reicke, Emil. *Geschichte der Reichsstadt Nürnberg.* Nuremberg, 1896.

"Willibald Pirckheimer und die Reichsstadt Nürnberg im Schwabenkrieg." *Jahrbuch für schweizerische Geschichte* 45 (1920): 133–89.

Reinhard, Wolfgang. "Die kirchenpolitischen Vorstellungen Kaiser Karls V., ihre Grundlagen und ihr Wandel." In *Confessio Augustana und Confutatio. Der Augsburger Reichstag 1530 und die Einheit der Kirche. Internationales Symposion der Gesellschaft zur Herausgabe des Corpus Catholicorum in Augsburg vom 3.–7. September 1979,* ed. Erwin Iserloh, pp. 62–100. Reformationsgeschichtliche Studien und Texte, no. 118. Münster (Westphalia), 1980.

Rem, Wilhelm. "Cronica newer geschichte, 1512–1527." In *Chroniken der*

Bibliography

deutschen Städte, vol. 25, pp. 1–265. Leipzig, 1896. Reprint. Göttingen, 1966.

Richter, Ernst Arwed. *Der Reichstag zu Nürnberg 1524.* Ph.D. dissertation, Leipzig, 1880.

Ridé, Jacques. "L'image du germain dans la pensée et la littérature allemandes de la redécouverté de Tacite à la fin du XVIème siècle (Contribution à l'étude de genèse d'un mythe)." Thesis, Université de Paris IV, 1976. 3 vols. Lille, 1977.

Riezler, Sigmund. *Geschichte Baierns.* 9 vols. Gotha, 1899. Reprint. Aalen, 1964.

Ed. *Fürstenbergisches Urkundenbuch.* 7 vols. Tübingen, 1877–91.

Rörig, Fritz. *The Medieval Town.* Berkeley and Los Angeles, 1969.

Roersch, Alphonse. "Maximilian Transsylvanus, humaniste et secrétaire de Charles-Quint." *Bulletin de la Classe des Lettres de l'Academie Royale de Belgique,* series 5, vol. 14. Brussels, 1928.

Roesler, Robert. *Die Kaiserwahl Karls V.* Vienna, 1868.

Rommel, Franz. *Die Reichsstadt Ulm in der Katastrophe des Schmalkaldischen Bundes.* Stuttgart, 1922.

Rosenfeld, Paul. "The Provincial Governors of the Netherlands from the Minority of Charles V to the Revolt." *Anciens pays et assemblées d'états* 17 (1959): 1–63. Also in *Government in Reformation Europe, 1520-1560,* ed. H. J. Cohn, pp. 257–64. Glasgow and New York, 1971.

Rosenkranz, Albert. *Der Bundschuh. Die Erhebungen des südwestdeutschen Bauernstandes in den Jahren 1493-1517.* 2 vols. Schriften des Wissenschaftlichen Instituts der Elsass-Lothringer im Reich. Heidelberg, 1927.

Roth, Friedrich. *Augsburgs Reformationsgeschichte.* 4 vols. Munich, 1901–11.

Die Einführung der Reformation in Nürnberg 1517–1528. Würzburg, 1885.

Roth von Schreckenstein, Karl Heinrich Freiherr. *Geschichte der ehemaligen freien Reichsritterschaft in Schwaben, Franken und am Rheinstrome.* 2 vols. Freiburg im Breisgau and Tübingen, n.d.

Das Patriziat in den deutschen Städten, besonders Reichsstädten, als Beitrag zur Geschichte der deutschen Städte und des deutschen Adels. Tübingen, 1856. Reprint, Aalen, 1970.

Rother, Siegfried. *Die religiösen und geistigen Grundlagen der Politik Huldrych Zwinglis. Ein Beitrag zum Problem des christlichen Staates.* Erlangen, 1956.

Rott, Jean. "Artisanat et mouvements sociaux à Strasbourg autour de 1525." In *Artisans et ouvriers d'Alsace,* pp. 137–70. Publications de la Société Savante d'Alsace et des Regions de l'Est, no. 9. Strasbourg, 1965.

"La Guerre des Paysans et la Ville de Strasbourg." In *La Guerre des Paysans 1525. Etudes Alsatiques,* ed. Alphonse Wollbrett, pp. 23–32. Saverne, 1975.

"De quelques pamphlétaires nobles: Hutten, Cronberg et Mathias Wurm

Bibliography

de Geudertheim." In *Grandes figures de l'humanisme alsacien. Courants, milieux, destins,* ed. Francis Rapp and Georges Livet, pp. 135–45. Publications de la Société Savante d'Alsace et des Régions de l'Est, series "Grandes Publications," no. 14. Strasbourg, 1978.

"Un recueil de correspondances strasbourgeoises du XVIe siècle à la bibliothèque de Copenhague (ms. Thott 497, 2°)." *Bulletin philologique et historique (jusqu'à 1610),* 1968: 749-818.

"La Réforme à Nuremberg et à Strasbourg. Contacts et contrastes (avec des correspondances inédites)." In *Homage à Dürer. Strasbourg et Nuremberg dans la première moitié du XVIe siècle,* pp. 91–142. Publications de la Société Savante d'Alsace et des Régions de l'Est, series "Recherches et Documents," no. 12. Strasbourg, 1972.

Rowan, Steven. "Imperial Taxes and German Politics in the Fifteenth Century. An Outline." *Central European History* 13 (1980): 203–17.

Rublack, Hans-Christoph. "Die Aussenpolitik der Reichsstadt Konstanz während der Reformationszeit." In *Der Konstanzer Reformator Ambrosius Blarer 1492-1564. Gedenkschrift zu seinem 400. Todestag,* ed. Bernd Moeller, pp. 56–80. Constance and Stuttgart, 1964.

Eine Bürgerliche Reformation. Nördlingen. Quellen und Forschungen zur Reformationsgeschichte, no. 51. Gütersloh, 1982.

Die Einführung der Reformation in Konstanz von den Anfängen bis zum Abschluss 1531. Quellen und Forschungen zur Reformationsgeschichte, no. 40. Gütersloh, 1971.

"Forschungsbericht Stadt und Reformation." In *Stadt und Kirche im 16. Jahrhundert,* ed. Bernd Moeller, pp. 9–26. Schriften des Vereins für Reformationsgeschichte, no. 190. Gütersloh, 1978.

"Political and Social Norms in Urban Communities in the Holy Roman Empire." In *Religion, Politics, and Social Protest: Three Studies on Early Modern Germany,* ed. Kaspar von Greyerz, pp. 24–60. Publications of the German Historical Institute London. London, 1984.

"Politische Situation und reformatorische Politik in der Frühphase der Reformation in Konstanz." In *Kontinuität und Umbruch. Theologie und Frömmigkeit in Flugschriften und Kleinliteratur an der Wende vom 15. zum 16. Jahrhundert,* ed. Josef Nolte, Helga Tompert, and Christoph Windhorst, pp. 316–34. Spätmittelalter und Frühe Neuzeit. Tübinger Beiträge zur Geschichtsforschung, no. 2. Stuttgart, 1980.

"Reformatorische Bewegung und städtische Kirchenpolitik in Esslingen." In *Städtische Gesellschaft und Reformation,* ed. Ingrid Bátori, pp. 191–220. Spätmittelalter und Frühe Neuzeit. Tübinger Beiträge zur Geschichtsforschung, no. 12. Stuttgart, 1980.

Rundstedt, Hans-Gerd von. *Die Regelung des Getreidehandels in den Städten*

Bibliography

Südwestdeutschlands und der deutschen Schweiz im späteren Mittelalter und im Beginn der Neuzeit. Supplement no. 19, *Vierteljahrschrift für Sozial- und Wirtschaftsgeschichte.* Stuttgart, 1930.

Sabean, David Warren. *Landbesitz und Gesellschaft am Vorabend des Bauernkrieges. Eine Studie der sozialen Verhältnisse im südlichen Oberschwaben in den Jahren vor 1525.* Quellen und Forschungen zur Agrargeschichte, no. 26. Stuttgart, 1972.

Sablonier, Roger. *Adel im Wandel. Eine Untersuchung zur sozialen Situation des ostschweizerischen Adels um 1300.* Veröffentlichungen des Max-Planck-Instituts für Geschichte, no. 66. Göttingen, 1979.

Salch, Charles-Laurent. *Dictionnaire des châteaux de l'Alsace médiévale.* Strasbourg, 1978.

Salomies, Marti. *Die Pläne Kaiser Karls V. für eine Reichsreform mit Hilfe eines allgemeinen Bundes.* Annales Academiae Scientiarum Fennicae, series B, vol. 83, part 1. Helsinki, 1953.

Sattler, Christian Friedrich. *Geschichte des Herzogtums Württemberg unter der Regierung der Herzoge.* 13 vols. Ulm, 1769–83.

Schäfer, Alfons. "Der Anspruch der Kurpfalz auf die Herrschaft über den Rhein von Selz i. E. bis Bingen." *Zeitschrift für die Geschichte des Oberrheins* 115 (1967): 265–329.

Schaufelberger, Walter. "Spätmittelalter." In *Handbuch der Schweizer Geschichte,* vol. 1, pp. 239–388. Zurich, 1980.

Scheible, Heinz. "Fürsten auf dem Reichstag." In *Der Reichstag zu Worms von 1521,* ed. Fritz Reuter, pp. 369–98. Worms, 1971.

Schellhase, Kenneth C. *Tacitus in Renaissance Political Thought.* Chicago, 1976.

Scherlen, Auguste. *Histoire de la ville de Turckheim.* Colmar, 1925.

Scheurl, Christoph. "Die Epistel über die Verfassung der Reichsstadt Nürnberg, 1516." In *Chroniken der deutschen Städte,* vol. 11, pp. 781–804. Leipzig, 1872.

Schib, Karl. *Geschichte der Stadt Schaffhausen.* Thayngen-Schaffhausen, 1945. "Zur Geschichte der schweizerischen Nordgrenze." *Zeitschrift für schweizerische Geschichte* 27 (1947): 1–35.

Schiess, Traugott, ed. *Briefwechsel der Brüder Ambrosius und Thomas Blarer.* 3 vols. Freiburg im Breisgau, 1908–12.

Schilling, Heinz. *Konfessionskonflikt und Staatsbildung. Eine Fallstudie über das Verhältnis von religiösem und sozialem Wandel in der Frühneuzeit am Beispiel der Grafschaft Lippe.* Quellen und Forschungen zur Reformationsgeschichte, no. 48. Gütersloh, 1981.

Schlenck, Wolfgang. *Die Reichsstadt Memmingen und die Reformation.* Memminger Geschichtsblätter, 1968. Memmingen, 1969.

Schmauss, Johann Jakob, ed. *Neue und vollständigere Sammlung der Reichs–Abschiede.* 4 vols. Frankfurt a. M., 1747. Reprint. Osnabrück, 1967.

Bibliography

Schmidt, Georg. "Die Haltung des Städtecorpus zur Reformation und die Nürnberger Bündnispolitik." *Archiv für Reformationsegeschichte* 75 (1984): 194–233.

"Reichsstadt und Territorialstaat. Esslingen, Württemberg und das Städtecorpus um die Mitte des 16. Jahrhunderts." *Esslinger Studien* 21 (1982): 71–104.

Der Städtetag in der Reichsverfassung. Eine Studie zur korporativen Politik der Freien und Reichsstädte in der ersten Hälfte des 16. Jahrhunderts. Veröffentlichungen des Instituts für Europäische Geschichte Mainz, 112. Wiesbaden, 1984.

Schmidt, Heinrich. *Die deutschen Städtechroniken als Spiegel des bürgerlichen Selbstverständnisses im Spätmittelalter.* Schriften der Historischen Kommission bei der Bayerischen Akademie der Wissenschaften, no. 3. Göttingen, 1958.

Schmidt, Heinrich R. "Reichsstädte, Reich, Reformation. Korporative Religionspolitik 1521–1529/30." Ph.D. dissertation, Saarbrücken, 1983.

Schmolz, Helmut. "Herrschaft und Dorfgemeinde im Ulmer Gebiet." *Geschichtliche Mitteilungen von Geislingen und Umgebung* 17 (1962): 30–45.

Schott, Peter. *The Works of Peter Schott (1460–1490).* Ed. Murray A. Cowie and Marian L. Cowie. 2 vols. University of North Carolina Studies in Germanic Languages and Literatures, nos. 41, 71. Chapel Hill, 1963–71.

Schreiber, Heinrich, ed. *Urkundenbuch der Stadt Freiburg im Breisgau.* 2 vols. Freiburg im Breisgau, 1828–9.

Schröcker, Alfred. *Die Deutsche Nation. Beobachtungen zur politischen Propaganda des ausgehenden 15. Jahrhunderts.* Historische Studien, no. 426. Lübeck, 1974.

Schubert, Ernst. *König und Reich. Studien zur spätmittelalterlichen deutschen Verfassungsgeschichte.* Veröffentlichungen des Max-Planck-Instituts für Geschichte, no. 63. Göttingen, 1979.

Schubert, Friedrich Hermann. *Die deutschen Reichstage in der Staatslehre der frühen Neuzeit.* Schriften der Historischen Kommission bei der Bayerischen Akademie der Wissenschaften, no. 7. Göttingen, 1966.

Schubert, Hans von. *Lazarus Spengler und die Reformation in Nürnberg.* Ed. Hajo Holborn. Quellen und Forschungen zur Reformationsgeschichte, no. 17. Leipzig, 1934. Reprinted. New York, 1971.

Schulze, Winfried. *Bäuerlicher Widerstand und feudale Herrschaft in der frühen Neuzeit.* Neuzeit im Aufbau, no. 6. Stuttgart, 1980.

"Reichstage und Reichssteuern im späten 16. Jahrhundert." *Zeitschrift für historische Forschung* 2 (1975): 43–58.

Schürstab, Erhard. "Nürnberg's Krieg gegen den Markgrafen Albrecht (Achilles)

Bibliography

von Brandenburg 1449 und 1450." Ed. Max Lexer. In *Chroniken der deutschen Städte*, vol. 2, pp. 95–352. Stuttgart, 1864. Reprinted. Göttingen, 1961.

Scott, Tom. "Die Bauernkriege und Michael Gaismair." *Veröffentlichungen des Tiroler Landesarchivs* 2 (1982): 289-92.

"The Peasants' War: A Historiographical Review." *Historical Journal* 22 (1979): 693–720, 953–74.

"Reformation and Peasants' War in Waldshut and Environs: A Structural Analysis." *Archiv für Reformationsgeschichte* 69 (1978): 82–102; 70 (1979): 140–68.

Scribner, Robert W. *For the Sake of Simple Folk: Popular Propaganda for German Reformation*. Cambridge Studies in Oral and Literate Culture, no. 2. Cambridge, 1981.

"How Many Could Read? Comments on Bernd Moeller's 'Stadt und Buch.'" In *The Urban Social Classes, the Nobility and the Reformation. Studies on the Social History of the Reformation in England and Germany*, ed. Wolfgang J. Mommsen, R. Alter, and R. W. Scribner, pp. 44–5. Publications of German Historical Institute London no. 5. Stuttgart, 1979.

"Practice and Principle in the German Towns: Preachers and People." In *Reformation Principle and Practice. Essays presented to A. G. Dickens*, ed. P. N. Brooks, pp. 97–117. London, 1980.

"The Reformation as a Social Movement." In *The Urban Classes, the Nobility and the Reformation. Studies on the Social History of the Reformation in England and Germany*, ed. Wolfgang J. Mommsen, R. Alter, and R. W. Scribner, pp. 49–79. Publications of German Historical Institute London, no. 5. Stuttgart, 1979.

"Sozialkontrolle und die Möglichkeit einer städtischen Reformation." In *Stadt und Kirche im 16. Jahrhundert*, ed. Bernd Moeller, pp. 57–65. Schriften des Vereins für Reformationsgeschichte, no. 190. Gütersloh, 1978.

"Why was there no Reformation in Cologne?" *Bulletin of Institute of Historical Research* 49 (1976): 217–41.

Sea, Thomas F. "Imperial Cities and the Peasants' War in Germany." *Central European History* 12 (1979): 3–37.

Seckendorff, Eduard Freiherr von, ed. *Reimchronik über Herzog Ulrich von Württemberg und seine nächsten Nachfolger*. Bibliothek des Litterarischen Vereins in Stuttgart, no. 74. Stuttgart, 1863.

Seebass, Gottfried. "Die Reformation in Nürnberg." *Mitteilungen des Vereins für Geschichte der Stadt Nürnberg* 55 (1966/67): 252–69.

"The Reformation in Nürnberg." In *The Social History of the Reformation*, ed. Lawrence P. Buck and Jonathan W. Zophy, pp. 17–40. Columbus, 1972.

Bibliography

"Stadt und Kirche in Nürnberg im Zeitalter der Reformation." In *Stadt und Kirche im 16. Jahrhundert*, ed. Bernd Moeller, pp. 66–86. Schriften des Vereins für Reformationsgeschichte, no. 190. Gütersloh, 1978.

Sender, Clemens. "Die Chronik von Clemens Sender von den ältesten Zeiten der Stadt bis zum Jahre 1536." In *Chroniken der deutschen Städte*, vol. 23, pp. 1–404. Leipzig, 1894. Reprinted. Göttingen, 1966.

Seyboth, Adolph. *Das alte Strassburg vom 13. Jahrhundert bis zum Jahre 1870. Geschichtliche Topographie.* Strasbourg, 1890.

Shaw, Stanford. *Empire of the Gazis: The Rise and Decline of the Ottoman Empire, 1280–1808.* Vol. 2 of *History of the Ottoman Empire and Modern Turkey.* Cambridge, 1976.

Sigrist, Hans. "Reichsreform und Schwabenkrieg. Ein Beitrag zur Geschichte der Entwicklung des Gegensatzes zwischen der Eidgenossenschaft und dem Reich." *Beiträge zur allgemeinen Geschichte* 5 (1947): 114–41.

Skinner, Quentin. *The Foundations of Modern Political Thought.* 2 vols. Cambridge, 1978.

Slicher van Bath, B. H. *Boerenvrijheid. Rede uitgesproken bij de Aanvaarding van het Amt von Hoogleraar in den Sociale en Economische Geschiedenis aan den Rijksuniversiteit te Groningen op 13. November 1948.* Groningen, 1948.

Slootmans, C. J. F. *Jan metten lippen, zijn familie en zijn stad. Een Geschiedenis der Bergen–op–Zoomsche Heeren van Glymes.* Rotterdam and Antwerp, 1945.

Smend, Rudolf. *Das Reichskammergericht.* Part I: *Geschichte und Verfassung.* Quellen und Studien zur Verfassungsgeschichte des Deutschen Reiches, 4, part 3. Weimar, 1911.

Soden, Franz von. *Beiträge zur Geschichte der Reformation und der Sitten jener Zeit mit besonderem Hinblick auf Christoph Scheurl II.* Nürnberg, 1855.

Spitz, Lewis W. "The Course of German Humanism." In *Itinerarium Italicum: The Profile of the Italian Renaissance in the Mirror of Its European Transformations, dedicated to Paul Oskar Kristeller on the Occasion of His 70th Birthday*, ed. Heiko A. Oberman and Thomas A. Brady, Jr., pp. 371–436. Studies in Medieval and Reformation Thought, no. 14. Leiden, 1975.

The Religious Renaissance of the German Humanists. Cambridge, Mass., 1963.

Stälin, Christoph Friedrich von. "Aufenthaltsorte Kaiser Maximilians I. seit seiner Alleinherrschaft 1493 bis zu seinem Tode 1519." *Forschungen zur deutschen Geschichte* 1 (1862): 347–95.

Steiff, Karl, and Gebhard Mehring, eds. *Geschichtliche Lieder und Sprüche Württembergs.* Stuttgart, 1912.

Steinbach, Franz. "Geschichtliche Grundlagen der kommunalen Selbstverwaltung in Deutschland." *Rheinisches Archiv* 20 (1932): 7–114. Also in *Collectanea Franz Steinbach*, ed. Franz Petri and Georg Droege, pp. 487–555. Bonn, 1967.

Bibliography

"Ursprung und Wesen der Landgemeinde nach rheinischen Quellen." In *Die Anfänge der Landgemeinde und ihr Wesen*, ed. Theodor Mayer, vol. 1, pp. 559–94. Constance, 1960. Also in *Collectanea Franz Steinbach*, ed. Franz Petri and Georg Droege, pp. 559–94. Bonn, 1967.

Steinmetz, Max. "Die frühbürgerliche Revolution in Deutschland (1476–1535)." In *Reformation oder frühbürgerliche Revolution?* ed. Rainer Wohlfeil, pp. 42–55. Munich, 1972.

"Theses on the Early Bourgeois Revolution in Germany, 1476–1535." In *The German Peasants' War 1525: New Viewpoints*, trans. Bob Scribner and Gerhard Benecke, pp. 9–18. London, 1979.

Stenzel, Karl. *Die Politik der Stadt Strassburg am Ausgange des Mittelalters in ihren Hauptzügen dargestellt*. Beiträge zur Landes- und Volkskunde von Elsass-Lothringen und den angrenzenden Gebieten, no. 49. Strasbourg, 1915.

Stern, Alfred. "Der Zusammenhang politischer Ideen in der Schweiz und in Oberdeutschland am Ende des XV. und im ersten Drittel des XVI. Jahrhunderts." In *Abhandlungen und Aktenstücke zur Geschichte der Schweiz*, pp. 13–29. Aarau, 1926.

Strauss, Gerald, ed. and trans. *Manifestations of Discontent in Germany on the Eve of the Reformation*. Bloomington, Ind., 1971.

Nuremberg in the Sixteenth Century. New York, 1966.

Strieder, Jakob. *Studien zur Geschichte kapitalistischer Organisationsformen. Monopole, Kartelle und Aktiengesellschaften im Mittelalter und zu Beginn der Neuzeit.* 2d ed. Munich and Leipzig, 1935.

Stromer, Wolfgang von. *Oberdeutsche Hochfinanz 1350–1450*. 3 vols. Supplements nos. 55–7 of the *Vierteljahrschrift für Sozial- und Wirtschaftsgeschichte*. Wiesbaden, 1970.

"Reichtum und Ratswürde. Die wirtschaftliche Führungsschicht der Reichsstadt Nürnberg 1348–1648." In *Führungskräfte der Wirtschaft in Mittelalter und Neuzeit 1350–1850*, ed. Herbert Helbig, vol. 1, pp. 1–50. Deutsche Führungsschichten in der Neuzeit, no. 6. Limburg (Lahn), 1973.

Taylor, A. J. P. *The Course of German History*. London, 1945.

Tobler, Ludwig, ed. *Schweizerische Volkslieder*. 2 vols. Bibliothek älterer Schriftwerke der deutschen Schweiz, nos. 4–5. Frauenfeld, 1882-4.

Tracy, James D. *The Politics of Erasmus: A Pacifist Intellectual and His Political Milieu*. Toronto, 1978.

Ulmann, Heinrich. *Fünf Jahre württembergischer Geschichte unter Herzog Ulrich 1515–1519*. Leipzig, 1867.

Kaiser Maximilian I. 2 vols. Leipzig, 1884–91.

Ulmschneider, Helgard. *Götz von Berlichingen. Ein adeliges Leben der deutschen Renaissance*. Sigmaringen, 1974.

Bibliography

Vasella, Oskar. "Vom Wesen der Eidgenossenschaft im 15. und 16. Jahrhundert." *Historisches Jahrbuch* 71 (1952): 165–83.

Vater, Wolfgang. "Die Beziehungen Rottweils zur schweizerischen Eidgenossenschaft im 16. Jahrhundert." In *450 Jahre Ewiger Bund. Festschrift zum 450. Jahrestag des Abschlusses des Ewigen Bundes zwischen den XIII. Orten der Schweizerischen Eidgenossenschaft und den zugewandten Ort Rottwell*, ed. Stadtarchiv Rottweil. Rottweil, 1969.

Vaughan, Richard. *Charles the Bold, the Last Valois Duke of Burgundy.* London, 1973.

Valois Burgundy. London, 1975.

Vercauteren, Fernand. "Notes sur les opérations financières de Charles-Quint dans les Pays-Bas en 1523." *Revue historique* 171 (1933): 92–105.

Vögeli, Jörg. *Schriften zur Reformation in Konstanz 1519–1538.* Ed. Alfred Vögeli. 2 vols. in 3. Schriften zur Kirchen- und Rechtsgeschichte, nos. 39–40. Tübingen and Basel, 1972-3.

Vogler, Günter. *Nürnberg 1524/25. Studien zur Geschichte der reformatorischen Bewegung in der Reichsstadt.* Berlin, 1982.

"Ein Vorspiel des deutschen Bauernkriegs im Nürnberger Landgebiet 1524." In *Der Bauer im Klassenkampf,* ed. Gerhard Heitz et al., pp. 49–81. Berlin, 1975.

Vogt, Wilhelm. *Die bayrische Politik im Bauernkrieg und der Kanzler Dr. Leonhard von Eck, das Haupt des Schwäbischen Bundes.* Nördlingen, 1883.

Ed. "Die Correspondenz des schwäbischen Bundeshauptmannes Ulrich Arzt von Augsburg aus den Jahren 1524-1527. Ein Beitrag zur Geschichte des Schwäbischen Bundes und des Bauernkrieges." *Zeitschrift des Historischen Vereins für Schwaben und Neuburg* 6 (1878): 281–404; 7 (1879): 233–380; 9 (1892): 1–62; 10 (1883): 1–298.

Voigt, Klaus. *Italienische Berichte aus dem spätmittelalterlichen Deutschland von Francesco Petrarca zu Andrea de' Franceschi (1333–1492).* Kieler Historische Studien, no. 17. Stuttgart, 1973.

Volk, Julius. "Zur Frage der Reichspolitik gegenüber dem Bauernkrieg." In *Staat und Persönlichkeit. Erich Brandenburg zum 60. Geburtstag dargebracht,* pp. 61–90. Leipzig. 1928.

Waas, Glenn Elwood. *The Legendary Character of Kaiser Maximilian.* Ph.D. dissertation, Columbia University. New York, 1941.

Wackernagel, Hans Georg, ed. *Die Matrikel der Universität Basel.* 3 vols. Basel, 1951–62.

Wackernagel, Rudolf. *Geschichte der Stadt Basel.* 3 vols. in 4. Basel, 1907–24. Reprinted. Basel, 1968.

Walder, Ernst. "Reformation und moderner Staat." In *450 Jahre Berner Ref-*

Bibliography

ormation. *Archiv des Historischen Vereins des Kantons Bern* 64/65 (1980/81): 441–583.

"Zu den Bestimmungen des Stanser Verkommnisses von 1481 über verbotene Versammlungen und Zusammenschlüsse in der Eidgenossenschaft." In *Gesellschaft und Gesellschaften. Festschrift zum 65. Geburtstag von Ulrich Im Hof*, pp. 80–94. Bern, 1982.

"Zur Entstehungsgeschichte des Stanser Verkommnisses und des Bundes der VII. Orte mit Freiburg und Solothurn von 1481." *Schweizerische Zeitschrift für Geschichte* 32 (1982): 263–92.

Waley, Daniel P. *The Italian City-Republics*. New York and Toronto, 1969.

Wallerstein, Immanuel. *The Modern World-System*. Vol. 1: *Capitalist Agriculture and the Origins of the European World-Economy in the Sixteenth Century*. New York, 1974.

Walser, Fritz. *Die spanischen Zentralbehörden und der Staatsrat Karls V. Grundlagen und Aufbau bis zum Tode Gattinaras*. Ed. Rainer Wohlfeil. Abhandlungen der Akademie der Wissenschaften in Göttingen, philologisch-historische Klasse, series 3, no. 43. Göttingen, 1959.

Walther, Andreas. *Die Anfänge Karls V*. Leipzig, 1911.

Walther, Heinrich G. "Bernhard Besserer und die Politik der Reichsstadt Ulm während der Reformationszeit." *Ulm und Oberschwaben* 27 (1930): 1–69.

Walton, Robert C. "The Reformation in the Cities: Another Look." In *Occasional Papers of the American Society for Reformation Research*, vol. 1, pp. 137–50. N.p., 1977.

Warmbrunn, Paul. *Zwei Konfessionen in einer Stadt. Das Zusammenleben von Katholiken und Protestanten in den paritätischen Reichsstädten Augsburg, Biberach, Ravensburg und Dinkelsbühl von 1548 bis 1648*. Veröffentlichungen des Instituts für Europäische Geschichte Mainz, no. 111. Wiesbaden, 1983.

Werner, Theodor Gustav. "Die Beteiligung der Nürnberger Welser und der Augsburger Fugger an der Eroberung des Rio de la Plata und der Gründung von Buenos Aires." In *Beiträge zur Wirtschaftsgeschichte Nürnbergs*, ed. Stadtarchiv Nürnberg, vol. 1, pp. 494–592. Beiträge zur Geschichte und Kultur der Stadt Nürnberg, no. 11. 2 vols. Nuremberg, 1967.

Wettges, Wolfram. *Reformation und Progaganda. Studien zur Kommunikation des Aufruhrs in süddeutschen Reichsstädten*. Geschichte und Gesellschaft. Bochumer Historische Studien, no. 17. Stuttgart, 1978.

Weyrauch, Erdmann. *Konfessionelle Krise und soziale Stabilität. Das Interim in Strassburg (1548-1562)*. Spätmittelalter und Frühe Neuzeit. Tübinger Beiträge zur Geshichtsforschung, no. 7. Stuttgart, 1978.

"Ueber soziale Schichtung." In *Städtische Gesellschaft und Reformation*, ed.

Bibliography

Ingrid Bátori, pp. 5–57. Spätmittelalter und Frühe Neuzeit. Tübinger Beitrage zur Geschichtsforschung, no. 12. Stuttgart, 1980.

Wiesflecker, Hermann. *Kaiser Maximilian I.* 4 vols. Munich, 1971–81.

Wille, Jakob. "Die Uebergabe des Herzogthums Württemberg an Karl V." *Forschungen zur deutschen Geschichte* 22 (1881): 521–71.

Willibald Pirkheimer 1470/1970. Dokumente, Studien, Perspektiven. Anlässlich des 500. Geburtsjahres, ed. Willibald-Pirkheimer-Kuratorium. Nuremberg, 1970.

Witte, Heinrich, ed. "Urkundenauszüge zur Geschichte des Schwabenkriegs." *Mitteilungen der Badischen Historischen Kommission* 21 (1899): m66–m144; 22 (1900): m3–m120.

Wohlfeil, Rainer. "Der Speyerer Reichstag von 1526." *Blätter für pfälzische Kirchengeschichte und religiöse Volkskunde* 43 (1976): 5–20.

"Der Wormser Reichstag von 1521 (Gesamtdarstellung)." In *Der Reichstag zu Worms von 1521,* ed. Fritz Reuter, pp. 59–154. Worms, 1971.

Wolgarten, Rainer. "Das erste und zweite Nürnberger Reichsregiment." Dissertation, University of Cologne, 1957.

Wolgast, Eike. *Die Wittenberger Theologie und die Politik der evangelischen Stände. Studien zu Luthers Gutachten in politischen Fragen.* Quellen und Forschungen zur Reformationsgeschichte, no. 47. Gütersloh, 1977.

Wopfner, Hermann, ed. *Quellen zur Geschichte des Bauernkrieges in Deutschtirol.* Innsbruck, 1908.

Wunder, Gerd. *Die Bürger von Hall. Sozialgeschichte einer Reichsstadt 1216–1802.* Sigmaringen, 1980.

"Reichsstädte als Landesherrn." In *Zentralität als Problem der mittelalterlichen Stadtgeschichtsforschung,* ed. Emil Meynen, pp. 79–91. Städteforschung, series A, no. 8. Cologne and Vienna, 1979.

Wuttke, Dieter. "Sebastian Brant und Maximilian I. Eine Studie zu Brants Donnerstein-Flugblatt des Jahres 1492." In *Die Humanisten in ihrer politischen und sozialen Umwelt,* ed. Otto Herding and Robert Stupperich, pp. 141–76. Mitteilungen der Kommission für Humanismusforschung, no. 3. Boppard, 1976.

"Wunderdeutung und Politik. Zu den Auslegungen der sogenannten Wormser-Zwillinge des Jahres 1495." In *Landesgeschichte und Geistesgeschichte. Festschrift für Otto Herding zum 65. Geburtstag,* ed. Kaspar Elm et al., pp. 217–44. Veröffentlichungen der Kommission für geschichtliche Landeskunde in Baden-Württemberg, series B, no. 92. Stuttgart, 1977.

Yates, Frances A. *Astraea: The Imperial Theme in the Sixteenth Century.* London, 1975.

Zeibig, H. J. "Der Ausschuss-Landtag der gesammten österreichischen Erblande zu Innsbruck 1518." *Archiv für österreichische Geschichte* 13 (1854): 201–366.

Ziehen, Eduard. *Mittelrhein und Reich im Zeitalter der Reichsreform 1356–1504.* 2 vols. Frankfurt a. M., 1934–7.

Zimmermann, Gunter. *Die Antwort der Reformatoren auf die Zehntenfrage.* Europäische Hochschulschriften, series 3, no. 164. Frankfurt a. M. and Bern, 1982.

Zink, Burkhart. "Chronik 1368–1468." In *Chroniken der deutschen Städte*, vol. 5, pp. 1–332. Munich, 1866. Reprint. Göttingen, 1965.

Zophy, Jonathon Walter. "Christoph Kress, Nürnberg's Foremost Reformation Diplomat." Ph.D. dissertation, Ohio State University, 1972.

"Lazarus Spengler, Christoph Kress, and Nuremberg's Reformation Diplomacy." *Sixteenth Century Journal* 5 (1974): 35–48.

Zorn, Wolfgang. *Augsburg. Geschichte einer deutschen Stadt.* 2d ed. Augsburg, 1972.

"Die soziale Stellung der Humanisten in Nürnberg und Augsburg." In *Die Humanisten in ihrer politischen und sozialen Umwelt*, ed. Otto Herding and Robert Stupperich, pp. 35–50. Mitteilungen der Kommission für Humanismusforschung, no. 3. Boppard, 1976.

Zwingli, Huldrych. *Huldreich Zwinglis sämtliche Werke.* Ed. Emil Egli et al. Berlin, Leipzig, and Zurich, 1905– .

Index of personal names

The following, frequently occurring names are not indexed: Maximilian I; Charles V.

Index

Index

Index

Index of place names

The following, frequently occurring names are not indexed: Germany, South Germany, Swiss Confederacy, Switzerland.

Index

Index

Index of subjects

Index

Common Man, 32, 38–9, 45, 62, 123, 143, 151–83, 216, 228–9
Common Penny (*Gemeiner Pfennig*), 44, 47, 59, 82, 85
common weal, *see* common good
communal federations, 30–2
communalism, 28–34, 188–9, 206, 211, 228; and religion, 27, 33–4, 182, 186, 203; sacral commune, 154n, 203; vs. feudalism, 31
communal movement, *see* communalism
communes, 29–31, 175
Compact of Stans (1481), 33, 210
comuneros (Castile), 117, 139, 175
Confession of Augsburg, 220
corporate values, *see* free cities, ideals
corporation, sacral, *see* communalism, sacral commune
council, national (Speyer 1524), 168, 170, 172, 178
councillors, Imperial, 139–43, 162, 184
"Cow-Swiss," 58, 62n
cows: on the bridge at Ulm, 39, 105, 205–6, 230; on the Schwanberg, 39

Diet, Imperial, 48, 114, 135, 140, 157, 160, 165, 174, 177, 203, 226; Cities' House, 120, 134, 168–9; cities' position in, 43–4, 46–8, 53–4, 102; Electors' House, 149; Large Committee, 129; Small Committee, 128, 129, 136; Worms (1495), 44, 57; Augsburg (1500), 70; Constance (1507), 83; Cologne (1512), 128; Worms (1521), 113, 120, 128–30, 132, 167, 226; Nuremberg (1522), 128, 134; Nuremberg (1522–3), 126, 128–9, 136, 167, 170; Nuremberg (1524), 128, 143, 145, 147–50, 161, 166–70, 176, 181; Speyer (1526), 195, 198, 201; Speyer (1529), 213
Diet, Urban, *see* Urban Diet

Edict of Burgos (1524), 178–80, 192
Edict of Worms (1521), 143, 153, 166, 168, 170, 173, 177–8, 182, 185

Ehrbarkeit, *see* Württemberg, social structure
election, Imperial: Charles V, 104, 118, 140; Ferdinand I, 144, 175–6
embassy of cities to Spain (1523), 135, 137–49, 172, 226
emperor: and free cities, 24–5, 75, 78–9, 81–2, 84, 87–9, 118–19, 225; finances 78, 81–2, 87–8, 106–7, 118–19, 225, *see also* monarchism
evangelical movement, 152, 155, 157–9, 180, 182, 187–8, 228, *see also* urban Reformation

feudalism, 223, *see also* biblicism vs. feudalism; communalism vs. feudalism
firms, commercial, 14, 48, 81–3, 118–19, 121–30, 136–7, 139n, 142, 145–6, 148–9
forestalling, 122, 126, *see also* monopolies
free cities, 1, 10; and banditry, 14; and bishops, 19–20, 45–6, 70; and countryside, 12–13; and Imperial government, 44–7; and monarchy, 48–9; and princes, 14–15, 44–6, 70, 96–9, 120, 125, 207–9, 212; constitutional changes of (1548–52), 117, 221, 227; economies, 11–12, 17–18; evaluations, 16–22; ideals, 22–34, 121, 154, 203; merchants in Iberia, 119; oligarchies, 13–14, 210–11, 224; political situation, 8–9; ranks, 11, 134–6; regional distribution, 10; Revolution of 1525, 187–93; social classes, 11–12, 19–22, 223; territories, 12–13; *see also* bishops and cities; leagues; princes and cities; revolts, urban; urban front; urban Reformation
free knights, *see* knights
free market, *see* market

Gesellschaft mit St. Georgenshild, 31n
Gewerke, 125
Ghibellinism, 116–17
Governing Council (*Reichsregiment*), 44, 48, 90, 114, 120, 126, 128, 132–3,

CAMBRIDGE STUDIES IN EARLY
MODERN HISTORY

Society and Religious Toleration in Hamburg c. 1580–1785
JOACHIM WHALLEY

Absolutism and Society in Seventeenth-Century France: State Power and Provincial Aristocracy in Languedoc
WILLIAM BEIK